THE CAMBRIDGE COMP.
AFRICAN AMERICAN WOMEN

The Cambridge Companion to African American
period dating back to the eighteenth century. These specially commissioned
essays highlight the artistry, complexity and diversity of a literary tradition that
ranges from Lucy Terry to Toni Morrison. A wide range of topics are addressed,
from the Harlem Renaissance to the Black Arts movement, and from the performing arts to popular fiction. Together, the essays provide an invaluable guide to a
rich, complex tradition of women writers in conversation with each other as they
critique American society and influence American letters. Accessible and vibrant,
with the needs of undergraduate students in mind, this Companion will be of
great interest to anybody who wishes to gain a deeper understanding of this
important and vital area of American literature.

ANGELYN MITCHELL is Associate Professor of English and African American
Studies, Georgetown University.

DANILLE K. TAYLOR is Dean of Humanities, Dillard University.

A complete list of books in the series is at the back of this book

THE CAMBRIDGE COMPANION TO

AFRICAN AMERICAN WOMEN'S LITERATURE

EDITED BY

ANGELYN MITCHELL

Georgetown University, Washington, DC

AND

DANILLE K. TAYLOR

Dillard University, New Orleans

CAMBRIDGE
UNIVERSITY PRESS

CAMBRIDGE UNIVERSITY PRESS
Cambridge, New York, Melbourne, Madrid, Cape Town, Singapore, São Paulo, Delhi

Cambridge University Press
The Edinburgh Building, Cambridge CB2 8RU, UK

Published in the United States of America by Cambridge University Press, New York

www.cambridge.org
Information on this title: www.cambridge.org/9780521675826

First published 2009

Printed in the United Kingdom at the University Press, Cambridge

A catalogue record for this publication is available from the British Library

Library of Congress Cataloguing in Publication data
The Cambridge companion to African American women's literature / edited
by Angelyn Mitchell and Danille Taylor.
p.   cm.
Includes bibliographical references.
ISBN 978-0-521-85888-5
1. American literature – African American authors – History and criticism.   2. American
literature – Women authors – History and criticism.   3. African American women – Intellectual
life.   4. Women and literature – United States – History.   5. African American women in
literature.   I. Mitchell, Angelyn, 1960–   II. Taylor, Danille.   III. Title.
PS153.N5C343   2009
810.9′9287–dc22
2009005864

ISBN 978-0-521-85888-5 hardback
ISBN 978-0-521-67582-6 paperback

To our mothers,
Gertrude Mann Taylor (1915–2005)
and
Evelyn Wiggins Mitchell,
and
to Adam Taylor Guthrie and Carille Mary Nicole Guthrie,
my home-Mom

La vida es un carnival!   – Celia Cruz

CONTENTS

CONTRIBUTORS

OLGA BARRIOS is a professor in the department of English Studies, Universidad de Salamanca, Spain. She is the co-editor of *Contemporary Literature in the African Diaspora* (1997) and *The Family in Africa and the African Diaspora: A Multidisciplinary Approach* (2003).

HERMAN BEAVERS is an associate professor of English at the University of Pennsylvania. He is the author of *Wrestling Angels into Song: The Fictions of Ernest J. Gaines and James Alan McPherson* (1995), as well as over twenty-five articles and book chapters. He guest-edited issues of both *African American Review* and *Narrative*, and he either served or is serving on the editorial boards of *American Literature, Modern Fiction Studies, Modern Literary Studies*, and *African American Review*. His creative works include the chapbook, *A Neighborhood of Feeling* (1986).

JOANNE M. BRAXTON is the Frances L. and Edwin L. Cummings Professor of English and Humanities at the College of William and Mary. She is the author of *Black Women Writing Autobiography* (1989) and the editor of *Wild Women in the Whirlwind: Afra-American Culture and the Contemporary Literary Renaissance* (1990), *The Collected Poetry of Paul Laurence Dunbar* (1993), and *Monuments of the Black Atlantic: Slavery and Memory* (2004).

LAROSE DAVIS, who recently earned a Ph.D. at Emory University, is a lecturer of English at Spelman College.

MADHU DUBEY is a professor of English and African American Studies at the University of Illinois in Chicago. She is the author of *Black Women Novelists and the Nationalist Aesthetic* (1994) and *Signs and Cities: Black Literary Postmodernism* (2003). She is currently working on a book about Octavia Butler.

FRANCES SMITH FOSTER is Charles Howard Candler Professor of English and Women's Studies at Emory University. She has authored, edited, or co-edited ten books and numerous articles, including *Written by Herself: Literary Production by*

African American Women, (1993), 1746–1892, Minnie's Sacrifice, Sowing and Reaping, Trial and Triumph: Three Rediscovered Novels by Frances Ellen Watkins Harper (1994), Norton Critical Edition of *Incidents in the Life of a Slave Girl* (2001), *The Norton Anthology of African American Literature* (1997), and *The Oxford Companion to African American Literature* (1997).

DIANNE JOHNSON is a professor of English at the University of South Carolina. She is editor of *The Collected Works of Langston Hughes,* vol. II: *The Works for Children* (2003) and *The Brownies' Book* (1996). She is the author (under the name Dina Johnson) of *All Around Town* (1998), *Sunday Week* (1999), *Quinnie Blue* (2000), and *Sitting Pretty* (2000).

KEITH D. LEONARD is an associate professor of English at American University, Washington, DC, where he teaches nineteenth- and twentieth-century American and African American literatures. He is the author of *Fettered Genius: The African American Bardic Poet from Slavery to Civil Rights* (2006). He is currently working on a book-length study of ideals of introspection and political consciousness in contemporary African American poetry and in hip hop culture.

CRYSTAL J. LUCKY is an associate professor of English, African American Studies and Women's Studies at Villanova University, where she currently directs the Africana Studies Program. She has published on Toni Morrison and on women of the Harlem Renaissance.

ANGELYN MITCHELL is an associate professor of English and African American Studies at Georgetown University, where she founded the African American Studies Program. She is the author of *The Freedom to Remember: Narrative, Slavery, and Gender in Contemporary Black Women's Fiction* (2002) and the editor of *Within the Circle: An Anthology of African American Literary Criticism from the Harlem Renaissance to the Present* (1994).

MARILYN SANDERS MOBLEY is Vice President for Inclusion, Diversity, and Equal opportunity at Case Western University. She is the author of *Folk Roots and Mythic Wings in Sarah Orne Jewett and Toni Morrison: The Cultural Function of Narrative* (1992). She is currently completing *Spaces for Readers: Toni Morrison's Narrative Poetics and Cultural Politics.*

JOYCELYN MOODY is the Sue Denman Distinguished Chair of Literature at the University of Texas at San Antonio. She is the author of *Sentimental Confessions* (2001) and editor of the *African American Review.*

ROBERT J. PATTERSON is an assistant professor of English at Florida State University. He is currently working on a book entitled, *Are Many Called, But Few Chosen? The Paradox of Closeness in Contemporary Literature, Politics, and Culture.*

DANILLE K. TAYLOR is dean of humanities and professor of English at Dillard University. She is the editor of *Conversations with Toni Morrison* (1994) and has published on African American literature and culture.

ELEANOR W. TRAYLOR is a professor of English and chair of the English department at Howard University. She has published widely on many key figures in African American literary studies, including Margaret Walker, Henry Dumas, and Toni Cade Bambara.

CHERYL A. WALL is Board of Governors Professor of English at Rutgers University, New Brunswick. She is the author of *Worrying the Line: Black Women Writers, Lineage, and Literary Tradition* (2005) and *Women of the Harlem Renaissance* (1995), and the editor of *Changing Our Own Words: Criticism, Theory, and Writing by Black Women* (1989). She has edited two volumes of writing by Zora Neale Hurston, *Novels and Short Stories* (1995) and *Folklore, Memoirs and Other Writings* (1995), as well as two volumes of criticism on Hurston – *"Sweat": Texts and Contexts* (1997) and *Their Eyes Were Watching God: A Casebook* (2000). She is also an editor of *The Norton Anthology of African American Literature* (1997).

DANA A. WILLIAMS is an associate professor of English and director of undergraduate studies in the English department at Howard University. She is the author of *"In the Light of Likeness – Transformed": The Literary Art of Leon Forrest* (2005), and she is the editor of *The Art of August Wilson and Black Aesthetics* (2004) and *Conversations with Leon Forrest* (2007).

ACKNOWLEDGEMENTS

The editors thank Noni Bourne and Myeidra Miles, Georgetown University graduate students, for their help with the bibliographies and the chronology. We also thank the Graduate School of Arts and Sciences at Georgetown University for its research assistance. Many thanks to Ray Ryan, of Cambridge University Press, for his continued support.

CHRONOLOGY

1526	First Africans brought to North America.
1730	Lucy Terry thought to be born.
1746	Terry composes "Bars Fight," the earliest known piece of literature by an African American.
1753–55	Phillis Wheatley thought to be born.
1757	Phillis Wheatley bought by John Wheatley in Boston.
1773	Phillis Wheatley publishes the first book by an African American, *Poems on Various Subjects Religious and Moral*.
1775–83	The American Revolutionary War.
1775	In Philadelphia, the first antislavery society is formed.
1776	The Declaration of Independence is ratified.
1784	Death of Phillis Wheatley.
1787	The Three-fifths Compromise approved by Congress.
1791	Haitian Revolution begins.
1793	The first Fugitive Slave Law is passed by Congress.
1796	Lucy Terry, the first woman to argue before Supreme Court, wins her case.
1797	Sojourner Truth is born in New York.
1800	Gabriel Prosser's revolt against slavery.
1804	Haiti established as the second independent nation in the Americas.

1808   The importation of enslaved Africans to the United States is prohibited.

1821   Death of Lucy Terry.

1822   Harriet Tubman thought to be born. Denmark Vessey's revolt against slavery.

1830   The end of the transatlantic slave trade.

1831   Nat Turner's revolt against slavery. Maria Stewart's "Religion and the Pure Principles of Morality, the Sure Foundation on Which We Must Build" published.

1832   Maria Stewart becomes the first American woman to participate in public political debates, on the lecture circuit in Boston.

1835   Maria Stewart, *Productions of Mrs. Maria W. Stewart.*

1836   *The Life and Religious Experience of Jarena Lee.*

1841   Ann Plato, *Essays: Including Biographies and Miscellaneous Pieces of Prose and Poetry.*

1846   *Memoirs of the Life, Religious Experience, and Ministerial Travels and Labours of Mrs. Zilpha Elaw, an American Female of Colour.*

1849   Harriet Tubman emancipates herself and becomes a conductor on the Underground Railroad.

1850   The first recorded African American woman to receive a college degree, Lucy Session, graduates from Oberlin College. Sometime during this decade Hannah Crafts writes *The Bondwoman's Narrative*, possibly the first novel by an African American woman published in the United States. Sojourner Truth publishes her autobiography, *The Narrative of Sojourner Truth: A Northern Slave*, with the aid of Olive Gilbert.

1851   Sojourner Truth addresses the Ohio Women's Rights Convention with her now famous "And Ain't I a Woman?" speech.

1852   Harriet Beecher Stowe publishes *Uncle Tom's Cabin.*

1853   Frances E. W. Harper publishes *Eliza Harris.*

1854   Frances E. W. Harper, *Poems on Miscellaneous Subjects.*

1855 After being passed down orally for over one hundred years, Lucy Terry's poem, "Bars Fight," is published.

1857 In the Dred Scott decision, the Supreme Court rules against African American citizenship.

1859 John Brown raids Harpers Ferry. Harriet Wilson enters the copyright for her novel, *Our Nig; or, Sketches from the Life of a Free Black, in A Two-Story White House, North. Showing That Slavery's Shadows Fall Even There*, generally believed to be the first novel by an African American published in the United States. Frances E. W. Harper publishes "The Two Offers," the first short story by an African American.

1861–65 The American Civil War.

1861 Harriet Jacobs, *Incidents in the Life of a Slave Girl*.

1862 President Abraham Lincoln issues the Emancipation Proclamation, freeing enslaved African Americans in rebel states.

1864 The Fugitive Slave Laws are revoked.

1865 Black Codes are established, laws designed to restrict the rights of African Americans and to reestablish the social conditions of slavery. General Sherman's Field Order No. 15, allocating forty acres and a mule, sets aside land for newly emancipated African American families in the South. Mary Church Terrell is born. Terrell later works as a civil rights activist, lecturer, and suffragist. President Abraham Lincoln is assassinated. The Freedman's Bureau is established to attend to the needs of newly emancipated blacks. The Thirteenth Amendment is ratified, and enslaved African Americans are freed throughout the United States.

1866 Congress passes the first Civil Rights Act in order to counter the Black Codes.

1867 Frances E. W. Harper, *Sowing and Reaping: A Temperance Story*.

1868 The Fourteenth Amendment grants citizenship and "equal protection" under the law to all citizens, including African Americans. Elizabeth Keckley, *Behind the Scenes; or, Thirty Years a Slave and Four Years in the White House*.

1869 The National Women's Suffrage Association is founded.

1870   African American men's right to vote is protected under the Fifteenth Amendment.

1877   The end of Reconstruction is signaled by the removal of federal troops from the South.

1883   Death of Sojourner Truth.

1890   Amelia Johnson, *Clarence and Corinne or God's Way.*

1891   Lucy Delaney, *From the Darkness Cometh the Light*; Emma Dunham Kelley, *Megda.*

1892   Anna Julia Cooper, *A Voice from the South*; Frances E. W. Harper, *Iola Leroy*; Ida B. Wells, *Southern Horrors: Lynch Law in All Its Phases.*

1895   Mary Church Terrell becomes the first African American woman to sit on the Washington, DC, Board of Education. Alice Moore Dunbar-Nelson, *Violets and Other Tales*; Emma Dunham Kelley, *Four Girls at Cottage City*; Ida Wells-Barnett publishes *A Red Record: Tabulated Statistics and Alleged Causes of Lynching in the United States.*

1896   The National Association of Colored Women is established. The Supreme Court ruling "separate but equal" in the *Plessy v. Ferguson* case supports racial segregation in the United States.

1897   Death of Harriet Jacobs.

1899   Alice Moore Dunbar-Nelson, *The Goodness of St. Rocque and Other Stories.*

1900   Pauline E. Hopkins publishes *Contending Forces: A Romance Illustrative of Negro Life North and South.*

1902   Susie King Taylor, *Reminiscences of My Life in Camp.*

1909   The National Association for the Advancement of Colored People (NAACP) founded.

1910–30   Large numbers of African Americans move from the South to the North in "The Great Migration."

1910   *The Crisis*, the literary magazine of the NAACP, begins publication.

1913   Death of Harriet Tubman, legendary conductor of the Underground Railroad.

1914–18 World War I.

1914   Death of abolitionist Charlotte Forten Grimké.

1916   Angelina Weld Grimké's play *Rachel* is performed in Washington, DC.

1917   Gwendolyn Brooks is born. The Bolshevik Revolution in Russia.

1918   Georgia Douglas Johnson, *The Heart of a Woman and Other Poems*.

1919   High numbers of lynchings and race riots in the US, known as the "Red Summer of 1919."

1920   Women are granted voting rights by the Nineteenth Amendment. The beginning of what is known as the Harlem Renaissance, also known as the New Negro Renaissance.

1922   Georgia Douglas Johnson, *Bronze*.

1924   Jessie Fauset, *There Is Confusion*.

1925–27 *The Crisis* and *Opportunity* hold annual literary contests.

1925   Marita Bonner's essay "On Being Young – a Woman – and Colored" is published in *The Crisis*.

1926   Negro History Week begins. *Fire!*, a literary journal, is published by Langston Hughes, Zora Neale Hurston, and Wallace Thurman.

1927   Marita Bonner, *The Pot Maker*.

1928   Marita Bonner, *The Purple Flower*; Georgia Douglas Johnson, *An Autumn Love Cycle*; Nella Larsen, *Quicksand*.

1929   The Great Depression begins with the US stock market crash on "Black Tuesday." Marita Bonner, *Exit: An Illusion*; Jessie Fauset, *Plum Bun: A Novel without a Moral*; Nella Larsen, *Passing*.

1931   Toni Morrison is born. Nine black boys are accused of raping two white girls in Scottsboro, Alabama.

1932   Shirley Graham's play-turned-opera, *Tom-Tom: An Epic of Music and the Negro*, opens in Cleveland.

1934	Zora Neale Hurston publishes *Jonah's Gourd Vine*.
1935–40	Works Progress Administration (WPA) provides work for artists and writers.
1935	Zora Neale Hurston, *Mules and Men*.
1937	Death of blues singer Bessie Smith. Zora Neale Hurston, *Their Eyes Were Watching God*.
1938	Zora Neale Hurston, *Tell My Horse*.
1939	Zora Neale Hurston, *Moses, Man of the Mountain*.
1940	Mary Church Terrell, *A Colored Woman in a White World*.
1941–45	US involvement in World War II.
1941	President Truman orders the desegregation of the Armed Forces and the federal government.
1942	Zora Neal Hurston, *Dust Tracks on a Road*; Margaret Walker, *For My People*. Margaret Walker is the first African American poet to win a national award, the Yale Younger Poets Award.
1944	Katherine Dunham establishes the Katherine Dunham School of Dance in New York, a major African American cultural institution until its closing a decade later.
1945	Gwendolyn Brooks, *A Street in Bronzeville*.
1946	Ann Petry's *The Street* is published; it later becomes the first novel by a black woman to sell more than a million copies.
1947	Octavia Butler is born. Ann Petry, *County Place*.
1948	Ntozake Shange is born. Dorothy West, *The Living Is Easy*.
1949	Gwendolyn Brooks, *Annie Allen*; Alice Childress, *Florence*; Ann Petry, *The Drugstore Cat*.
1950	Gwendolyn Brooks becomes the first African American to win a Pulitzer Prize. Gloria Naylor is born. Edith Spurlock Sampson (1901–79) becomes the first African American to serve as a delegate to the United Nations. Bebe Moore Campbell is born.
1951	Terry McMillan is born. Rosa Guy (with John O. Killens) forms the Harlem Writers Guild.

1952	Rita Dove is born.
1953	Gwendolyn Brooks, *Maud Martha*; Ann Petry, *The Narrows*.
1954	The *Brown v. Board of Education of Topeka* case overturns the *Plessy* ruling of "separate but equal." Rosa Guy, *Venetian Blinds*.
1955	Emmett Till is abducted and murdered in August. In December Rosa Parks sparks the Montgomery Bus Boycott by refusing to give up her seat on a bus. Alice Childress wins Obie Award for *Trouble in Mind*.
1956	Gwendolyn Brooks, *Bronzeville Boys and Girls*; Billie Holiday, *Lady Sings the Blues*.
1957	Nine African American students are barred from attending school in Little Rock, Arkansas. Southern Christian Leadership Conference (SCLC) founded. The Civil Rights Act of 1957 signed by President Eisenhower provided additional protection for African American voters.
1959	Death of jazz legend Billie Holiday. Lorraine Hansberry's *A Raisin in the Sun* becomes the first play written by an African American woman on Broadway. Paule Marshall, *Brown Girl, Brownstones*; May Miller, *Into the Clearing*.
1960	Student Non-violent Coordinating Committee (SNCC) is founded. Death of Zora Neale Hurston.
1961	Death of Jessie Fauset, writer and literary editor of the *Crisis* (1919–26). Gwendolyn Brooks, *The Bean Eaters*; Paule Marshall, *Soul Clap Hands and Sing*.
1962	Georgia Douglas Johnson, *Share My World*.
1963	The March on Washington. Four little girls killed in Birmingham, Alabama. Medger Evers assassinated in Mississippi. President Kennedy assassinated in Texas.
1964	Martin Luther King, Jr. awarded the Nobel Peace Prize for his work in the civil rights movement. Freedom Summer is launched after three civil rights workers are murdered in Mississippi. Adrienne Kennedy's first play, *Funnyhouse of a Negro*, is produced. Ann Petry, *Tituba of Salem Village*; Kristin Hunter, *God Bless the Child*. Civil Rights Act of 1964 signed by President Lyndon B. Johnson. Death of Nella Larsen.

1965–73   Vietnam War.

1965   Assassination of Malcolm X in New York. Selma to Montgomery March. Race riots occur in Watts, California. Beginning of the Black Arts movement. Voting Rights Act of 1965 passed. Patricia R. Harris becomes first African American woman appointed as US ambassador. Kristin Hunter's play *The Double Edge* is produced.

1966   The Black Panther Party is founded in Oakland, California. "Black Power" slogan gains popularity. Adrienne Kennedy, *A Rat's Mass*; Carlene Polite, *The Flagellants*; Margaret Walker, *Jubilee*. Constance Baker Motley becomes first African American federal judge, appointed by President Lyndon Johnson.

1967   Urban revolts erupt in Detroit, Newark, and Chicago.

1968   Dr. Martin Luther King, Jr. is assassinated in Tennessee. Gwendolyn Brooks becomes poet laureate of Illinois. Shirley Chisholm becomes the first African American woman elected to congress. Senator Robert Kennedy is assassinated in California. The National Black Theatre founded by Barbara Ann Teer. Gwendolyn Brooks, "In the Mecca"; Nikki Giovanni, *Black Feeling, Black Talk*; Mari Evans, *Where Is All the Music?*; Lorraine Hansberry, *To Be Young, Gifted, and Black*; Kristin Hunter, *The Soul Brothers and Sister Lou*; June Jordan, *Who Look at Me*; Audre Lorde, *The First Cities*; Anne Moody, *Coming of Age in Mississippi*; Carolyn Rodgers, *Paper Soul*; Alice Walker, *Once*.

1969   The first Department of Black Studies founded at San Francisco State. Alice Childress, *Wine in the Wilderness*; Lucille Clifton, *Good Times*; Nikki Giovanni, *Black Judgement*; Paule Marshall, *The Chosen Place, the Timeless People*; Arthenia Millican, *Seeds Beneath the Snow: Vignettes from the South*; Carolyn Rodgers, *Songs of a Black Bird* and *2 Love Raps*; Sonia Sanchez, *Homecoming*; Sarah E. Wright, *This Child's Gonna Live*.

1970   Angela Davis makes FBI's "most wanted" list. Maya Angelou, *I Know Why the Caged Bird Sings*; Toni Cade [Bambara] (ed.), *The Black Woman*; Mari Evans, *I Am a Black Woman*; Nikki Giovanni, *Re: Creation*; June Jordan, *His Own Where*; Audre

Lorde, *Cables to Rage*; Toni Morrison, *The Bluest Eye*; Louise Meriwether, *Daddy Was a Number Runner*; Sonia Sanchez, *We a BaddDDD People*; Alice Walker, *The Third Life of Grange Copeland*; Margaret Walker, *Prophets for a New Day*.

1971   Maya Angelou, *Just Give Me a Cool Drink of Water 'fore I Diiie*; Toni Cade Bambara (ed.), *Tales and Stories for Black Folks*; Nikki Giovanni, *Gemini*; Elaine Jackson, *Toe Jam*; June Jordan, *His Own Where*.

1972   Shirley Chisholm becomes the first black woman to run for president. Barbara Jordan becomes the first black woman from the South to serve in the House of Representatives. Toni Cade Bambara, *Gorilla, My Love*; Gwendolyn Brooks, *Report from Part One*; Lucille Clifton, *Good News about the Earth*; Nikki Giovanni, *My House*; Pinkie Gordon Lane, *Wind Thoughts*; Alice Walker, *Five Poems*.

1973   The *Roe v. Wade* case prohibits state restrictions on abortions. Sarah Webster Fabio, *Rainbow Signs*; Audre Lorde, *From a Land Where Other People Live*; Toni Morrison, *Sula*; Alice Walker, *Revolutionary Petunias* and *In Love & Trouble: Stories of Black Women*; Margaret Walker, *October Journey*.

1974   Virginia Hamilton becomes the first African American to win the Newbury Medal. Maya Angelou, *Gather Together in My Name*; Angela Jackson, *Voodoo/Love Magic*; Audre Lorde, *The New York Head Shop* and *Museum*.

1975   Death of Josephine Baker. Alice Walker publishes her tribute to Zora Neale Hurston in *Ms.*, rescuing her from obscurity and reviving interest in her work. Maya Angelou, *Oh Pray My Wings Are Gonna Fit Me Well*; Gayl Jones, *Corregidora*; Carolyn Rodgers, *how i got ovah: New and Selected Poems*; Ntozake Shange, *for colored girls who have considered suicide / when the rainbow is enuf*; Sherley Anne Williams, *Peacock Poems*; Paulette White, *Love Poem to a Black Junkie*.

1976   Barbara Jordan is the first black woman to deliver a keynote address at a national political party convention. Maya Angelou, *Singin' and Swingin' and Gettin' Merry Like Christmas*; Octavia Butler, *Patternmaster*; Gayl Jones, *Eva's Man*; Audre Lorde,

Coal; Mildred Taylor, *Roll of Thunder, Hear My Cry*; Alice Walker, *Meridian*.

1977   Toni Cade Bambara, *The Sea Birds Are Still Alive*; Octavia Butler, *Mind of My Mind*; Joanne Braxton, *Sometimes I Think of Maryland*; Wanda Coleman, *Art in the Court of the Blue Fag*; "The Combahee River Collective Statement"; Rita Dove, *Ten Poems*; Toni Morrison, *Song of Solomon*; Ntozake Shange, *Sassafrass*.

1978   The Supreme Court rules against quotas on college admissions, but approves selected affirmative action programs. Maya Angelou, *And Still I Rise*; Octavia Butler, *Survivor*; Eloise Greenfield, *Honey I Love*; Pinkie Gordon Lane, *The Mystic Female*; Audre Lorde, *The Black Unicorn*; Carolyn Rodgers, *The Heart as Ever Green*; Ntozake Shange, *Nappy Edges*.

1979   Octavia Butler, *Kindred*; Wanda Coleman, *Mad Dog, Black Lady*; Colleen McElroy, *Winters without Snow*; Alice Walker (ed.), *I Love Myself When I Am Laughing: A Zora Neale Hurston Reader*.

1980   Ntozake Shange wins the Obie Award for *Mother Courage*. Toni Cade Bambara, *The Salt Eaters*; Gwendolyn Brooks, *Primer for Blacks*; Octavia Butler, *Wild Seed*; Barbara Christian, *Black Women Novelists*; Rita Dove, *The Only Dark Spot in the Sky* and *The Yellow House on the Corner*; Joyce Hansen, *The Gift-Giver*; Audre Lorde, *The Cancer Journals*; Carolyn Rodgers, *Translation*.

1981   Death of Harlem Renaissance writer Gwendolyn Bennett. Maya Angelou, *The Heart of a Woman*; bell hooks, *Ain't I a Woman: Black Women and Feminism*; Andrea Lee, *Russian Journal*; Cherie Moraga and Gloria Anzaldua (eds.), *This Bridge Called My Back: Writing By Radical Women of Color*; Toni Morrison, *Tar Baby*; Sonia Sanchez, *I've Been a Woman: New and Selected Poems*; Ntozake Shange, *Three Pieces*; Mildred Taylor, *Let the Circle Be Unbroken*; Alice Walker, *You Can't Keep a Good Woman Down*.

1982   Gloria T. Hull, Patricia Bell Scott, and Barbara Smith (eds.), *All the Women Are White, All the Blacks Are Men, but Some of Us Are Brave: Black Women's Studies*; Audre Lorde, *Zami: A New*

Spelling of My Name and *Chosen Poems: Old and New*; Gloria Naylor, *The Women of Brewster Place*; Ntozake Shange, *Sassafrass, Cypress, and Indigo*; Alice Walker, *The Color Purple*. Sherley Anne Williams, *Some Sweet Angel Chile*.

1983   Gloria Naylor wins the American Book Award for *The Women of Brewster Place*. Alice Walker is awarded the Pulitzer Prize for *The Color Purple*. Maya Angelou, *Shaker Why Don't You Sing*; Pearl Cleage, *Hospice*; Wanda Coleman, *Images*; Toi Dericotte, *Natural Birth*; Rita Dove, *Museum*; Marita Golden, *Migrations of the Heart*; Jamaica Kincaid, *At the Bottom of the River*; Paule Marshall, *Praisesong for the Widow* and *Reena and Other Stories*; Barbara Smith (ed.), *Homegirls: A Black Feminist Anthology*; Claudia Tate (ed.), *Black Women Writers at Work*; Alice Walker, *In Search of Our Mothers' Gardens: Womanist Prose*.

1984   The first Black Miss America, Vanessa Williams, is crowned. Octavia Butler, *Clay's Ark*, "Bloodchild"; Michelle Cliff, *Abeng*; J. California Cooper, *A Piece of Mine*; Mari Evans (ed.), *Black Women Writers (1950–1980): A Critical Evaluation*; Trudier Harris, *Exorcising Blackness: Historical and Literary Lynching and Burning Rituals*; bell hooks, *Feminist Theory: From Margin to Center*; Andrea Lee, *Sarah Phillips*; Audre Lorde, *Sister Outsider: Essays and Speeches*; Colleen McElroy, *Queen of the Ebony Islands*; Sonia Sanchez, *Homegirls and Handgrenades*; Ntozake Shange, *See No Evil: Prefaces, Essays, and Accounts, 1976–1983*; Mildred Taylor, *The Friendship*.

1985   Barbara Christian, *Black Feminist Criticism*; Michelle Cliff, *The Land of Look Behind*; Rita Dove, *Fifth Sunday*; Rosa Guy, *My Love, My Love, or The Peasant Girl*; Jamaica Kincaid, *Annie John*; Pinkie Gordon Lane, *I Never Scream*; Gloria Naylor, *Linden Hills*; Ntozake Shange, *Betsey Brown*.

1986   Maya Angelou, *All God's Children Need Traveling Shoes*; J. California Cooper, *Homemade Love*; Audrey Lorde, *Our Dead behind Us*; Sherley Anne Williams, *Dessa Rose*.

1987   Rita Dove wins the Pulitzer Prize for *Thomas and Beulah* (1986). Maya Angelou, *Now Sheba Sings the Song*; Octavia Butler,

Dawn; Hazel Carby, *Reconstructing Black Womanhood: The Emergence of the Afro-American Women Novelist*; Michelle Cliff, *No Telephone to Heaven*; Lucille Clifton, *Good Woman: Poems and a Memoir* and *Next: New Poems*; Wanda Coleman, *Heavy Daughter Blues*; Terry McMillan, *Mama*; Toni Morrison, *Beloved*; Sonia Sanchez, *Under a Soprano Sky*; Ntozake Shange, *Ridin' the Moon in Texas: Word Paintings*.

1988   Toni Morrison wins the Pulitzer Prize for *Beloved*. Octavia Butler, *Adulthood Rites*; Wanda Coleman, *War of Eyes and Other Stories*; Rita Dove, *The Other Side of the House*; Jamaica Kincaid, *A Small Place*; Audre Lorde, *A Burst of Light*; Gloria Naylor, *Mama Day*.

1989   Tina McElroy Ansa, *Baby of the Family*; Joanne M. Braxton, *Black Women Writing Autobiography: A Tradition within a Tradition*; Octavia Butler, *Imago*; Bebe Moore Campbell, *Sweet Summer: Growing Up with and without My Dad*; Toi Derricotte, *Captivity*; Rita Dove, *Grace Notes*; bell hooks, *Talking Back: Thinking Feminist, Thinking Black*; Terry McMillan, *Disappearing Acts*; Alice Walker, *The Temple of My Familiar*; Cheryl A. Wall (ed.), *Changing Our Own Words*.

1990   Maya Angelou, *I Shall Not Be Moved*; Joanne M. Braxton and Andrée Nicola McLaughlin (eds.), *Wild Women in the Whirlwind*; Michelle Cliff, *Bodies of Water*; Wanda Coleman, *African Sleeping Sickness*; bell hooks, *Yearning: Race, Gender, and Cultural Politics*; Jamaica Kincaid, *Lucy*; Colleen McElroy, *What Madness Brought Me Here: Collected Poems, 1968–1988*; Terry McMillan (ed.), *Breaking Ice: An Anthology of Contemporary African American Fiction*.

1991   Anita Hill testifies at the Senate confirmation hearings of then Supreme Court nominee Clarence Thomas. Lucille Clifton, *Quilting: Poems 1987–1990*; J. California Cooper, *Family*; Gayl Jones, *Liberating Voices: Oral Tradition in African American Literature*; Pinkie Gordon Lane, *Girl at the Window*; Paule Marshall, *Daughters*.

1992   The first black woman, Carol Moseley Braun (Democrat–Illinois), is elected to the US Senate. Death of Audre Lorde. Rita Dove, *Through the Ivory Gate*; Mari Evans, *A Dark and Splendid*

Mass; bell hooks, *Black Looks: Race and Representation*; June Jordan, *Technical Difficulties*; Terry McMillan, *Waiting to Exhale*; Toni Morrison, *Playing in the Dark: Whiteness and the Literary Imagination* and *Jazz*; Gloria Naylor, *Bailey's Café*; Alice Walker, *Possessing the Secret of Joy*.

1993   Toni Morrison becomes the first African American to win the Nobel Prize for Literature. Invited by President Clinton, Maya Angelou is the first woman and the first African American to read at a presidential inauguration, reading her poem, "On the Pulse of Morning." Tina McElroy Ansa, *Ugly Ways*; Octavia Butler, *Parable of the Sower*; Bebe Moore Campbell, *Your Blues Ain't like Mine*; Pearl Cleage, *Deals with the Devil and Other Reasons to Riot*; Lucille Clifton, *Book of Light*; Wanda Coleman, *Hard Dance*; Sarah and Elizabeth Delany, *Having Our Say: The Delany Sisters' First 100 Years*.

1994   Rita Dove is the first African American named US poet laureate. First "Furious Flowering Conference," organized by Joanne Gabbin.

1995   Death of Toni Cade Bambara. Linda Beatrice Brown, *Crossing Over Jordan*; Bebe Moore Campbell, *Brothers and Sisters*; J. California Cooper, *In Search of Satisfaction*; Rita Dove, *Mother Love*; Jamaica Kincaid, *The Autobiography of My Mother*; Dorothy West, *The Wedding* and *The Richer, the Poorer*.

1996   Tina McElroy Ansa, *The Hand I Fan With*; Terry McMillan, *How Stella Got Her Groove Back*; Sapphire, *Push*; Alice Walker, *The Same River Twice*.

1997   Death of Ann Petry. Pearl Cleage, *What Looks like Crazy on an Ordinary Day*; Toi Derricotte, *Tender*; Jamaica Kincaid, *My Brother*; Toni Morrison, *Paradise*; Jill Nelson, *Straight, No Chaser: How I Became a Grown-Up Black Woman*.

1998   Deaths of Margaret Walker and Dorothy West. Octavia Butler, *Parable of the Talents*; Bebe Moore Campbell, *Singing in the Comeback Choir*; Colleen McElroy, *Travelling Music*; Gloria Naylor, *The Men of Brewster Place*; Claudia Tate, *Psychoanalysis and Black Novels*; Alice Walker, *By the Light of My Father's Smile*.

1999	Rosa Parks is awarded the Congressional Medal of Honor. Death of Sherley Anne Williams. Sonia Sanchez, *Shake Loose My Skin: New and Selected Poems*; Sister Souljah, *The Coldest Winter Ever*.
2000	The Million Women March. Deaths of Gwendolyn Brooks and Barbara Christian. Alice Walker, *The Way Forward Is with a Broken Heart*.
2001	The World Trade Center in New York City attacked by terrorists. Trudier Harris, *Saints, Sinners, Saviors: Strong Black Women in African American Literature*; Zane, *Addicted*.
2002	Deaths of June Jordan and Claudia Tate. Karla Holloway, *Passed on: African American Mourning Stories*.
2003– present	The Iraq War.
2003	Toni Morrison, *Love*; Zane, *The Heat Seekers*.
2004	Zane, *Nervous*.
2005	Hurricane Katrina floods New Orleans, creating the largest black diaspora since the African slave trade. Death of Rosa Parks. *The Color Purple* opens on Broadway. Bebe Moore Campbell, *72 Hour Hold*; Cheryl Wall, *Worrying the Line*.
2006	Karinne Stephens publishes her memoir, *Confessions of a Video Vixen*. Alice Walker, *We Are the Ones We Have Been Waiting for*. Deaths of Octavia Butler, Bebe Moore Campbell, Coretta Scott King, and Nellie Y. McKay.

ANGELYN MITCHELL AND DANILLE K. TAYLOR

Introduction

> When I think of how essentially alone black women have been – alone because of our bodies, over which we have had so little control; alone because the damage done to our men has prevented their closeness and protection; and alone because we have had no one to tell us stories about ourselves; I realize that black women writers are an important and comforting presence in my life. Only they know my story. It is absolutely necessary that they be permitted to discover and interpret the entire range and spectrum of the experience of black women and not be stymied by preconceived conclusions. Because of these writers, there are more choices for black women to make, and there is a larger space in the universe for us.
>
> – Mary Helen Washington

When Lucy Terry composed the first known poem by an African American in 1746, she inaugurated a vital and vibrant literary tradition – African American women's literature. Throughout history, African American women writers have chronicled and critiqued the American experience as did Lucy Terry in the eighteenth century. Once marginalized, if not ignored, by mainstream America, African American women writers are now central, indeed essential, to American letters and culture. If, as Frances Smith Foster asserts, African American women writers have "used the Word as both a tool and a weapon to correct, to create, and to confirm their visions of life as it was and as it could become," this volume bears witness to "their visions of life" as well as to their artistic goals and achievements.[1] *The Cambridge Companion to African American Women's Literature* offers critical commentaries on almost three centuries of African American women's writing, spanning from the eighteenth century's Lucy Terry to the twenty-first century's Sapphire. Organized primarily around genres and their contexts, this volume foregrounds the artistry, complexity, and diversity of African American women writers. How this literary tradition grew and flourished is of particular interest to all of the contributors to this volume. In these essays, one reads, to use Hortense Spillers's terms, the "cross-currents and discontinuities" within the tradition.[2] In much the same way that African American women writers seem to be in conversation with each other when one reads the recurrent themes, topics, motifs, and concerns in their writings, the critics gathered here are in conversation with each other as they engage the many "cross-currents and discontinuities."

While African American women writers have written since the eighteenth century, this distinct literary tradition and its importance went largely unnoticed and unacknowledged by literary critics until the emergence of African American women literary scholars and African American women writers in the 1970s. The few critical examinations of African American literature before 1975 that included African American women writers, e.g. Richard Wright's 1937 review of Zora Neale Hurston's *Their Eyes Were Watching God* (1937) or Arthur P. Davis's *From the Dark Tower: Afro-American Writers, 1900–1960* (1974), often minimized or ignored the artistic and literary contributions of African American women writers and often ignored feminist issues or concerns. Like Lucy Terry, who was inspired to create by the historical circumstances surrounding her in Massachusetts, African American women writers have been similarly inspired by their historical circumstances, be it colonial America, the Revolutionary War, slavery, the Civil War, Reconstruction, modernity, the Great Depression, World War II, Jim Crow America, or the civil rights movement.

The 1960s, for example, brought great change, not only politically but also educationally, and these changes gave visibility and accessibility to African American literature, in general, and African American women's literature, specifically. Without the political changes of the 1960s, educational reform by way of canon reformation and expansion would not have taken place. With the dismantling of legal segregation and the political and social enfranchisement of African Americans as a result of the civil rights movement, historically white colleges and universities in the United States began diversifying not only their student bodies, but also their curricula. Thus, a number of Black Studies programs were created, providing intellectual spaces for the critical examination of African American life, culture, experiences, and contributions. Among these spaces, literature was one area of increased scholarly interest. Institutionalizing African American literature and literary studies helped to make literature by both African American men and women more accessible and visible to all of American society. Concomitantly, the women's liberation movement, indebted to the progressive politics and reforms of the 1960s as well as to international influences, also changed United States colleges and universities, giving rise to Women's Studies programs. Like Black Studies programs, Women's Studies programs institutionalized the critical engagement with women's experiences and contributions in American society. Accordingly, courses offered by departments of English literary studies began to include literature by women writers. With these advances and expansions in literary studies, new critical tools were needed as the tools of the time, structuralism/formalism and New Criticism, did not allow for critical considerations of gender or race. In the 1970s, a number of literary critics of African American literature employed structuralist approaches, but post-structuralist approaches became more appealing as they afforded a critical space for the discussion of race; gender issues, however, continued to be largely ignored.[3] Feminist literary theory, aided by French feminist theories born of post-structuralism, became a useful tool in literary analyses that sought to understand the role of gender as well as the roles of patriarchy and sexism in American society and culture; race, however, was not an integral part of these particular interrogations. Race and gender, however, intersected in the literary and cultural criticism of early African American women scholars, such as Barbara Christian, Mary Helen Washington, Nellie McKay, and Claudia Tate, who explored the nexus of race, gender, and power in African American lives as depicted by African American women writers.

In the 1970s, works by African American women writers were unavailable, and often they were xeroxed, as it was then known, for classroom use. Both writer Sherley Anne Williams and literary critic Ann duCille have written about reading in the 1970s Zora Neale Hurston's then out-of-print *Their Eyes Were Watching God* in xeroxed form.[4] Materials – literally books in print – were sorely needed to support the study of African American literature in general, and the study of African American women's literature more specifically. A number of anthologies edited by black women in the 1970s helped to establish the study of African American women's writing. Specifically, Toni Cade [Bambara]'s *The Black Woman* (1970), Mary Helen Washington's *Black-Eyed Susans* (1975), and Roseann Bell, Bettye Jean Parker, and Beverly Guy-Sheftall's *Sturdy Black Bridges* (1979) all helped to institutionalize and to advance the study of African American women's writing. Toni Cade's ground-breaking anthology, *The Black Woman*, presented both creative and critical writings by African American women writers; this anthology became a valuable resource in the teaching of African American women writers. Outlining the political urgencies of African American women writers in her introduction, Cade proclaimed, "We are involved in a struggle for liberation: liberation from the exploitive and dehumanizing system of racism, from the manipulative control of a corporate society, liberation from the constrictive norm of mainstream culture, from the synthetic myths that encourage us to fashion ourselves rashly from without (reaction) rather than from within (creation)."[5] In *Black-Eyed Susans*, a compilation of short stories, Washington established the primary thematic concerns of African American women writers and helped to begin the reclamation of many forgotten African American women writers. Washington theorized in the introduction that African American women writers sought to provide a mirror that more accurately reflected the lives of African American women, and in doing so, they created more possibilities for African American women. "Only [African American women writers] know my story. It is absolutely necessary," Washington wrote, "that they be permitted to discover and interpret the entire range and spectrum of the experience of black women and not be stymied by preconceived conclusions. Because of these writers, there are more models of how it is possible for us to live, there are more choices for black women to make, and there is a larger space in the universe for us."[6] Finally, *Sturdy Black Bridges*, an eclectic anthology, sought to establish the interdisciplinary and diasporic nature of the study of black women's writing. One of its editors, Bettye Parker, challenged the critical community: "If Black criticism is to adequately function on a level proportionate to our literary experience, then the Black critic, both male and female, must move beyond the type of fragmented judgments historically practiced by white critics."[7] All of these early texts helped to establish the terms of engagement for both African American literary analyses and for black feminist criticism, highlighting the urgencies, issues, and concerns of African American women writers.

During the 1980s, a significant number of scholarly works and additional anthologies devoted to African American women writers were published. Barbara Christian's *Black Women Novelists: The Development of a Tradition, 1892–1976* (1980) was the first single-authored, critical study of the African American woman's literary tradition. This seminal work explored the cultural and historical contexts of novels by African American women writers. Additionally, Christian's *Black Feminist Criticism: Perspectives on Black Women Writers* (1985) presented critical insights into this then emerging field of study. Both *The Third Woman* (1980), edited by Dexter Fisher, and *This Bridge Called My Back* (1981), edited by Cherríe Moraga and Gloria Anzaldua, signaled the emergence and importance of the expanding body of American women writers of color. The primary aim of *The Third Woman* was to introduce to its readers the growing body of American women writers of color. The goals of African American women writers, Dexter Fisher proffered, included "authenticat[ing] the experience of black women, establish[ing] a context for understanding the traditions of the past, and creat[ing] a sense of place and community, giving the community back to itself by elevating the commonplace to the artistic."[8] Moving beyond Fisher's anthology, *This Bridge Called My Back* posited a new feminism to meet the cultural and social needs in Asian American, Native American, Latino, and African

American communities and helped to lay the foundation for broader definitions of feminism and sexuality. The editors, Moraga and Anzaldua, explained their motivation as well as their goal: "What began as a reaction to the racism of white feminists soon became a positive affirmative of the commitment of women of color to our *own* feminism ... *This Bridge Called My Back* intends to reflect an uncompromised definition of feminism by women of color in the U.S."[9] All of these works made significant contributions in building the foundation of African American feminist criticism.

The overwhelming success of one collection signaled the status of African American women's writing in the academy. *All the Women Are White, All the Blacks Are Men, But Some of Us Are Brave: Black Women's Studies* (1982), edited by Gloria Hull, Patricia Bell Scott, and Barbara Smith, included historical and sociological essays as well as literary analyses, pedagogical essays, and bibliographies to assist the teaching of African American women's literature. One of its essays, Barbara Smith's "Toward a Black Feminist Criticism," became indispensable to discussions of sexuality in African American women's literature. Calling for a more sophisticated feminist critique, Smith wrote, "A Black feminist approach to literature that embodies the realization that the politics of sex as well as the politics of race and class are crucially interlocking factors in the works of Black women writers is an absolute necessity. Until a Black feminist criticism exists we will not even know what these writers mean."[10] bell hooks's *Ain't I a Woman: Black Women and Feminism* (1981), the first single-authored volume of theory, further advanced the field of black feminist criticism, providing an interdisciplinary theoretical perspective to African American women's writings. The voices of critics, however, were not the only voices interpreting the works of African American women writers. African American women writers had much to say about their own creative enterprises. Claudia Tate's *Black Women Writers at Work* (1983) and Mari Evans's *Black Women Writers (1950–1980)* (1984), both collections of interviews and, in Evans's case, critical essays, deepened the study of black women's writing. Tate and Evans both recognized the need to record and to explore the aesthetic views of contemporary African American women writers. These interviews revealed keen insights about the creative processes of African American women writers in their own words. As more scholars of literature engaged African American women's writings, one of the first collections of critical essays published was *Conjuring: Black Women, Fiction, and Literary Tradition* (1985), edited by Marjorie Pryse and Hortense J. Spillers. This collection explored, theorized, contextualized, and contested the idea of tradition in relation to black women's writing. A few years later, two collections of critical essays – Cheryl A. Wall's *Changing Our Own*

Words: Essays on Criticism, Theory, and Writing by Black Women (1989) and Joanne M. Braxton and Andrée Nicola McLaughlin's *Wild Women in the Whirlwind: Afra-American Culture and the Contemporary Literary Renaissance* (1990) – made clear the rigorous scholarly work necessary in critical analyses of African American women's writing.

While ground-breaking anthologies and critical studies of contemporary African American women writers were published in the 1970s and 1980s, it was essential to the development of the literary and critical traditions that eighteenth- and nineteenth-century writings by African American women be recovered, reissued, and critiqued. To this end, *The Schomburg Library of Nineteenth-Century Black Women Writers* (1988–) and its general editor Henry Louis Gates, Jr., as well as *Afro American Women Writers 1746–1933* (1988), edited by Ann Allen Shockley, encouraged interest and provided access to the literary productions of African American women of these earlier periods. In the foreword to his stellar multivolume set, Gates explained the necessity of recovering these earlier texts by black women: all of the black woman writer's literary tradition "must be received, explicated, analyzed, and debated before we can understand more completely the formal shaping of this tradition within a tradition, a coded literary universe through which, regrettably, we are only just beginning to navigate."[11] Shockley's single-volume anthology made accessible to students, scholars, and a general readership representative works from both the eighteenth and nineteenth centuries. Scholars, such as Hazel V. Carby in *Reconstructing Womanhood: The Emergence of the Afro-American Woman Novelist* (1987), Frances Smith Foster in *Written by Herself: Literary Production by African American Women, 1746–1892* (1993), and Carla L. Peterson in *"Doers of the Word": African-American Women Speakers and Writers in the North 1830–1880* (1995), have enhanced and extended the study and understanding of the African American women's literary tradition with their critical studies of this earlier period. Most recently, the recovery of lost texts continues with Henry Louis Gates's publication of Hannah Crafts's *The Bondwoman's Narrative* (2002), perhaps the first novel written by an African American woman in the 1850s. Although the authenticity of Crafts's novel is not yet conclusive, its existence highlights the complicated nature of recovering the writings of African American women and of constructing the African American woman's literary tradition.

The Cambridge Companion to African American Women's Literature chronicles, interprets, and maps the African American woman's literary tradition and its critical tradition. Divided into two parts, the first part – "History, contexts, and criticism" – offers readers an overview of key periods in and significant aspects of the literary tradition of African American women writers. The second part – "Genre, gender, and race" – presents chapters devoted to specific genres in the tradition. Students and scholars who want to study a specific genre may read the more specialized chapter as well as the contextual chapter engaging their particular interest. For the student or scholar interested in a particular historical moment, such as the Black Arts movement, the corresponding contextual chapter, as well as the chapter devoted to the genre of interest, might be useful. In all, the fourteen chapters here provide readers with both coverage of significant moments in the literary tradition as well as the opportunity to examine specific areas of generic interest. This volume is not intended to be a comprehensive literary history of African American women's writing; rather, it is designed to offer guidance in reading and studying African American women's writing.

The essays in this volume reveal the plurality and multiplicity of African American women's writing. For African American women writers, history has served as both text and context, beginning with Lucy Terry and Phillis Wheatley in the eighteenth century. Often ignored, early African American women writers wrote in a variety of genres, including poetry, autobiography, fiction, non-fiction, and journalism. As Foster and Davis explain in "Early African American women's literature," "Were it not for the scraps of manuscript, brief mentions in histories and diaries, a few books and pamphlets saved and later revealed, the absence of texts by African American women could lead the unimaginative and the ungenerous to believe that before the Civil War, African American culture was oral only." Employing a number of genres, early African American women writers set the thematic concerns for many later writers, themes including citizenship, motherhood, religion, sexuality, and enfranchisement. Advancing civic, social, and political equality preoccupies much of the literature by African American women in the nineteenth century. The most canonized of these genres is the emancipatory narrative, or as it is traditionally known, the slave narrative.[12] In her chapter on the slave narrative, Joycelyn Moody explains its cultural, political, social uses: "In addition to interiority and the humanity it evidences, slave narratives offered proof that in spite of the conditions bondage imposed on their lives, slave women nonetheless pursued and led meaningful, worthy lives, and they had the intelligence and skill to translate those lives into powerful rhetoric." This powerful rhetoric was used in other genres of the time and continues throughout the nineteenth century.

The Harlem Renaissance, characterized by the growing diversity of African Americans and their interests, is considered one of the most vibrant of artistic movements in American history. Of its political climate, Cheryl A. Wall writes in her chapter "Women of the Harlem Renaissance," "The vogue for African and African American art seemed to portend greater support for black peoples' political rights. It did not. But it did open a space for writers, who were able to make art of both the expanded opportunities and the persistent constraints." Identity and class were two of the most provocative themes for African American women writers as they presented and represented African American experiences during this defining moment.

Another defining moment in the tradition is the Black Arts movement. The contributions of African American women writers to the Black Arts movement have largely been ignored. Community-based theater, as well as poetry, provided an effective medium for the writers to enact explorations of political issues and interests. In 1968, Larry Neal proclaimed that "Black art is the aesthetic and spiritual sister of the Black Power concept."[13] This metaphor is particularly ironic as many of the men of the Black Arts movement seemed to ignore women's issues and concerns while addressing issues of race and racism, so much so that blackness seemed synonymous with masculinity. Yet, as Eleanor W. Traylor reveals, a number of African American women writers, including Sonia Sanchez, Nikki Giovanni, Sarah Webster Fabio, Barbara Ann Teer, and Mari Evans, greatly contributed to the black aesthetic(s) of the Black Arts movement. Traylor writes: "The founding mothers [of the Black Arts movement], with other vanguard women writers, strengthen the revolutionary ferment of the movement to resonate its themes: a renegotiation of power relations between black and white America, a disturbance of ideological imperatives of identity, and a redirection of the sources for literary production." During this period, African American women writers often conjoined women-centered issues with issues of nation building.

Moving beyond the Black Arts movement, contemporary African American women writers sought to understand the self in relation to society, historically and politically, as well as the interior self, often through personal experiences, like motherhood and marriage. Explorations into the interior self characterize the diverse works by contemporary African American women writers. "Building on the 1960s ideology that promoted cultural and racial self-discovery and self-awareness," Dana Williams writes, "early 1970s literature by black women also stressed the necessity of loving oneself and one's culture." Self-definition continued to preoccupy the literary imaginations of African American women writers throughout the last decades of the twentieth century.

African American literary scholars in the latter part of the twentieth century have played a major role in recovering, shaping, and codifying the canon of African American women writers. Black feminist literary criticism helped to shape how African American women's writing is read and interpreted. Mapping the political, social, and historical foundations of black feminist literary criticism, Robert Patterson predicts, "As black feminist literary theory advances in the twenty-first century, it must continue to grapple with the ways in which the vectors of race, class, gender, and sexuality intersect, and also consider the ways in which other socializing institutions, such as religion, inflect ... identity."

The genre studies of part II reveal not only the recurrent themes and concerns of African American women writers, but also the cultural and political currency of the genres. In the mid and late nineteenth century, a number of genres, including drama, essay, novel and short story, also present, record, and critique African American experiences, particularly post-slavery. Through poetry, African American women writers have fused the imagination with social critique and responsibility. They have also, as Keith Leonard notes, demonstrated "their faith in the power of poetic language to assert their personal truths in defiance of exclusionary privileging of male thought and expression by claiming the power to name themselves against the silencing dynamics of a male-dominated society."

The novel has been vital as a means of self-expression, artistic production, and cultural conservation. In the novels of African American women, the impact of race, class, and gender is portrayed and critiqued within a dynamic and fluid culture. Madhu Dubey observes in her chapter, "The life-saving power of fiction emerges as a recurrent motif in African American women's novels published from the mid nineteenth to the early twenty-first century." Through the novel, readers are invited to journey to impossible destinations and situations, revealing the possibilities within the reader and the text.

The short story, often overshadowed by the novel in critical examinations, is marked by its accessibility. That it was one of the earliest genres is noteworthy; the brevity of the genre encourages readers to read and writers to write because of its immediacy. Magazines, newspapers, and journals have been and continue to be primary publishing outlets for African American women fiction writers, and as such, short fiction enjoys a wide readership. Crystal Lucky posits, "Because of its accessibility, the short story invites innovation, an opportunity to experiment with style and form, voice and language." A number of writers, such as Ann Petry, Zora Neale Hurston, and Alice Walker, excelled at both the short story and the novel.

Non-fiction prose has deep roots in African American women's activism. The essay documents the cultural history of African American women's social and political thought. Marilyn Sanders Mobley opines, "Free from having to embellish their ideas through language and structures particular to other genres, black women chose the essay to employ the power of the word in a more direct unencumbered way for their audiences." African American women essayists have long advanced the ideology of black feminism, using their prose writings to build and to heal community. African American women essayists engaged social justice issues such as lynching, labor, education, women's rights, civil rights, sexuality, and spirituality. Today's blogging on the internet might be considered an extension of this genre for black women writers.

The autobiographies of nineteenth-century African American women writers, both political and spiritual, provide unique perspectives about American culture and identity as well as African American life and culture. Autobiography remains one of the most popular genres, enjoying a wide readership. For example, Maya Angelou's much-read autobiographical series is a defining example of contemporary African American women's autobiography. Although popular, autobiography also serves political purposes. Joanne Braxton explains, "Defying every attempt to enslave or diminish them or their self-expression in any way, black women autobiographers liberate themselves from stereotyped views of black womanhood, and define their own experiences." Additionally, constructing the self through memory for public consumption is complicated for the African American woman writer by preconceived notions of African American subjectivity.

African American women writers in the performing arts have been critical to the development of African American theater. Olga Barrios explains the sociocultural importance of African American drama in her chapter "African American women in the performing arts": "African American women's early plays have cast new light on North American life and culture by offering a new perspective and more integral picture of African Americans." Performance studies now allow for considerations of race in and as performance, but African American women playwrights have long dramatized the performativity of race. Thus, shaping community and consciousness has been crucial to African American theater in its aim to counter distorted images or cultural erasures.

Concerned with image making and remaking, children's and young adult literature by African American women writers exposes its youth readership to images of African Americans and the history of African Americans. Since early in the twentieth century, African American women writers understood that issues of representation and identification are integral to a child's developing self-concept. Highlighting the artistry within children's and young adult literature, Dianne Johnson observes, "While self-esteem is important, and outstanding children's literature can enhance the self-esteem of young readers, building self-esteem should not be the reason that black children read black children's literature. They should read it, as well, to enjoy outstanding art and what it has to offer – illumination, interpretation, inspiration, exploration, education." Once again, the political and the aesthetic are bound together, particularly in the act of reading African American women's literary productions.

Popular fiction, namely romance, black erotica, speculative fiction, mystery, and urban literature, has generated a strong readership in contemporary African American literature. Moving beyond the academy, popular fiction serves a number of clienteles – readerships with various interests and expectations. Book clubs have helped to popularize the genre. Herman Beavers explores the function of popular fiction for its readers, readers who "are adept at holding the world, the text, and their sense of self in a critical tension that allows them to engage what they read in ways that may serve a didactic function in their lives as it also complicates what it means for them to experience pleasure." In other words, the text still serves as a map to the self, particularly for many African American readers.

While each of this volume's two sections – indeed the subject of each chapter – could be the subject of a single-authored, book-length study, all of the chapters in this volume will provide readers with the key concepts in studying the literary tradition of African American women writers. Rather than focusing specifically on major writers, this volume will help readers understand how major figures, such as Toni Morrison or Anna Deavere Smith, contribute to the African American woman writer's literary tradition as well as to the genre in which they write. Given the continuing popularity of African American women writers, this volume will assist its readers in understanding African American women's literature and will engender more critical conversations about African American women's literature.

NOTES

1. Frances Smith Foster, *Written By Herself: Literary Production by African American Women, 1746–1892* (Bloomington: Indiana University Press, 1993), p. 2.
2. Hortense J. Spillers, "Afterword: Cross-Currents, Discontinuities: Black Women's Fiction," *Conjuring: Black Women, Fiction, and Literary Tradition* (Bloomington: Indiana University Press, 1985), pp. 249–60.
3. See, for example, Henry Louis Gates, Jr.'s *Black Literature and Literary Theory* (London: Methuen, 1984), *Figures in Black: Words, Signs, and the Racial Self* (Oxford: Oxford University Press, 1987), and *The Signifying Monkey: A Theory of Afro-American Literary Criticism* (Oxford: Oxford University Press, 1988). See also Houston A. Baker's *Long Black Song: Essays in Black American Literature* (Charlottesville: University of Virginia Press, 1972) and *Singers of Daybreak: Studies in Black American Literature* (Washington, DC: Howard University Press, 1974).
4. See Sherley Anne Williams's Foreword to *Their Eyes Were Watching God* (Urbana: University of Illinois Press, 1978), pp. v–xv and Ann duCille's "The Occult of True Black Womanhood: Critical Demeanor and Black Feminist Studies," *Signs* 19.3 (Spring 1994), 591–629.

5. Toni Cade [Bambara] (ed.), *The Black Woman: An Anthology* (New York: New American Library, 1970; rpt. New York: Washington Square Press, 2005) p. 7.
6. Mary Helen Washington, Introduction, *Black-Eyed Susans: Classic Stories by and About Black Women*, ed. Mary Helen Washington (Garden City: Anchor Books, 1975), p. xxxii.
7. Roseann P. Bell, Bettye J. Parker, and Beverly Guy-Sheftall (eds.), *Sturdy Black Bridges: Visions of Black Women in Literature* (Garden City, NY: Anchor Press, 1979), p. xxviii.
8. Dexter Fisher (ed.), *The Third Woman: Minority Women Writers in the United States* (Boston: Houghton Mifflin, 1980), p. 140.
9. Cherrie Moraga and Gloria Anzaldua (eds.), *This Bridge Called My Back: Writings by Radical Women of Color* (Watertown, MA: Persephone Press, 1981), p. xxiii.
10. Barbara Smith, "Toward a Black Feminist Criticism," *All the Women Are White, All the Blacks Are Men, But Some of Us Are Brave: Black Women's Studies*, ed. Gloria T. Hull, Patricia Bell Scott, and Barbara Smith (New York: Feminist Press, 1982), p. 159.
11. Henry Louis Gates, Jr., Foreword, *The Schomburg Library of Nineteenth-Century Black Women Writers*, gen. ed. Henry Louis Gates, Jr., 40 vols. (New York: Oxford University Press, 1988–94), p. xviii.
12. See Angelyn Mitchell's *The Freedom to Remember: Narrative, Slavery, and Gender in Contemporary Black Women's Fiction* (New Brunswick: Rutgers University Press, 2002), for a discussion of the term emancipatory narrative.
13. Larry Neal, "The Black Arts Movement," *Within the Circle: An Anthology of African American Literary Criticism from the Harlem Renaissance to the Present*, ed. Angelyn Mitchell (Durham, NC: Duke University Press, 1994), p. 184.

PART I
History, contexts, and criticism

I

FRANCES SMITH FOSTER AND LAROSE DAVIS

Early African American women's literature

Difficult miracles

It is very likely that during the long and terrible voyages from Africa to the North American colonies, African women soothed fears and silenced moans of despair with songs and stories. It is not hard to imagine mothers creating lullabies and lovers composing poems. Surely, they recited their personal histories and created prayers to strengthen their faith, hope, and courage. In the New World, women of African descent passed on the stories of their cultures, their ancestors and their gods, of their tribes, families, and themselves. In the process, they also augmented and embellished them, employing new forms and adding additional incidents and details. And yet, in most literary histories, the contributions of these women, like those of men of African descent, are generally unexamined and often unacknowledged. Were it not for the scraps of manuscript, brief mentions in histories and diaries, a few books and pamphlets saved and later revealed, the absence of texts by African American women could lead the unimaginative and the ungenerous to believe that before the Civil War, African American culture was oral only. After all, it was, as June Jordan has written, "not natural."[1] It was "the difficult miracle" that women of African descent living in the rough and non-literary world of colonial North America composed songs and poems, stories, essays, autobiographies, letters, and diaries. Again June Jordan's words are apt: "Repeatedly singing for liberty, ... repeatedly lifting witness to the righteous and the kindly factors" of their day (p. 29). It was something that should not have happened, but did. Almost from the day they first set foot upon North American soil, women of African descent were creating a literature. Before the United States came into being, African American women were publishing literature in a variety of genres and on many topics.

The earliest known work by an identifiable woman of African descent is "Bars Fight," a ballad that chronicles the people and events of a 1746 battle between settlers and Native Americans in the colony that became Deerfield, Massachusetts. In composing this poem, Lucy Terry, the twenty-two-year-old enslaved African author of "Bars Fight," working in the ways of African griots, helped establish the known beginnings of African American literature both as a poet and as a historian. As the only extant account of that conflict, portions of this poem have been included in United States history books. According to Sidney Kaplan and others, Lucy Terry was a gifted orator and storyteller whose home was a place where people gathered to swap stories and sing songs. Her daughter, Duroxa, was also a poet.

The African woman to whom June Jordan was particularly referring, when she coined the phrase "The Difficult Miracle," was Phillis Wheatley. Wheatley was definitely a miracle. She was about eight years old when she was kidnapped from her West African home and purchased as a slave in Boston, Massachusetts. Four years later, she published her first poem in a language she had only recently learned. During a period when women of any class rarely learned to read or to write, this enslaved woman-child studied English and Latin, literature, history, geography, and theology. At a time when women's words were rarely recorded, Wheatley's poems frequently appeared in newspapers throughout the New England colonies. Her poetry covered many topics as illustrated by the titles which include "Imagination," "Isaiah LXIII," "Atheism," and "Liberty and Peace." She employed a variety of popular and classical forms including ode, elegy, epic, ballad, and acrostic. Wheatley often emphasized her African heritage, calling herself a "vent'rous *Afric* [italics hers]," "an Ethiope," and "one of our sable race." Her *Poems on Various Subjects Religious and Moral* (1773) was one of the first books published by a woman in the American colonies. It was the earliest known collection published by a person of African descent. This volume includes poems such as "To the University of Cambridge, in New England," "On Being Brought from Africa to America," "To Maecenas," and "To the Right Honourable William, Earl of Dartmouth," which are frequently anthologized today.

Phillis Wheatley's poetry illustrates her keen interest in classical mythology, theology, philosophy, aesthetics, and current events. In addressing poems and letters to powerful figures, such as the Earl of Dartmouth, General George Washington, and Harvard University students, Wheatley accomplished two things simultaneously. First, she claimed, for herself and for subsequent generations, the authority to converse with or chastise those individuals whose social position would have deterred many less confident people. Secondly, she entered her critiques and insights into the public discourse, thereby engendering a tradition of African American women's literature oriented towards the public sphere.

Winning over suspicious or even hostile readers seems an inextricable, though not intrinsic, part of African American women's literary tradition. It was, after all, a "difficult miracle" to be black and published before the twentieth century. To prove authenticity, affidavits, portraits, and biographical narratives were sometimes employed. For example, the publisher of Phillis Wheatley's book included her portrait, a biographical preface by her owner and a statement "To the Publick" signed by eighteen prominent men who attested to the fact that the poems "were (as we verily believe) written by PHILLIS, a young Negro Girl." Such authenticating devices were regularly appended to publications written by early African American women writers. As a result, we sometimes know more about the difficulties and accomplishments of African American women writers than their writings reveal. The facts they give and the fact that such appendices were necessary give us additional information about the difficult miracles that these early women writers performed and, indeed, the difficult miracles that they are.

Written by herself

In the antebellum period especially, few women of any class or culture had the leisure, literacy, wealth, connections or luck that publication required. Nonetheless, several others accomplished difficult miracles similar to Terry's and Wheatley's. One common way was by employing others to assist in the process of writing and publishing. Some of these helpers were truly amanuenses or secretaries who recorded verbatim the words African American women spoke. Their only decisions were in terms of spelling, punctuation, capitalization, and, perhaps, syntax and synthesis. Others were editors or even co-authors. A few had such conflicting, prior, or extraneous intentions that the words or purposes barely resembled what the African American woman said or wanted to say. The latter practices complicate our recognition of African American women's literature. Some scholars, such as William L. Andrews in *To Tell a Free Story* (1986) and Jean Fagan Yellin and Cynthia Bond in *The Pen Is Ours* (1991), try to differentiate between the autobiographies and biographies. Others do not.

Such distinctions are not always easily made. For example, consider the works of Sojourner Truth. By all common definitions, she was illiterate. However, Sojourner Truth was extraordinarily articulate, and her words were published far and wide in newspapers and magazines. As historian Nell Irwin Painter and others have documented, Truth dictated her thoughts and experiences to Olive Gilbert who published them as *Narrative of Sojourner Truth: A Northern Slave* (1850). In the 1870s, one of her neighbors, Frances Titus, began appending material from Truth's scrapbook, which Truth called "The Book of Life." Since Sojourner Truth sold these books herself, we presume she was satisfied that they told her story her way. On the other hand, published accounts of some speeches are quite dissimilar, proving not everything attributed to Truth was actually what she said or how she said it.

Among the more interesting edited or dictated separately published antebellum memoirs are *Memoir of Mrs. Chloe Spear, a Native of Africa* (1831), *Elleanor's Second Book* (1839), *Louisa Picquet, the Octoroon* (1861), *Memoirs of Old Elizabeth* (1863), and *The Story of Mattie J. Jackson* (1866). *The Underground Railroad*, published in 1871 by African American abolitionist William Still, is an especially rich source of dictated lives of antebellum African American women. Working from interviews he collected, Still records dozens of personal narratives of fugitive slaves such as "Aunt Hannah Moore," Cordelia Lonely, and Euphemia Williams.

Published anonymously in 1861, for several years *Incidents in the Life of a Slave Girl* was believed to have been written by its editor Lydia Marie Child. Persistent and careful research by Jean Fagan Yellin proved Harriet A. Jacobs was indeed the author and that the narrative was indeed autobiographical. Harriet Jacobs was born a slave in Edenton, North Carolina, in 1813. After years of evading the persecutions of a lecherous owner and his suspicious wife, Jacobs hid – in a crawl space above a storeroom in her grandmother's house – for seven years before she finally escaped to the North. Still, *Incidents in the Life of a Slave Girl* presented another conundrum for readers and scholars interested in defining African American women's literature. It was obviously a fugitive slave narrative, a genre primarily concerned with exposing the true evils of slavery in order to persuade people to support abolition. However, Jacobs's narrative was decidedly unlike the majority of slave narratives which were written by males. Her story focused on the threats that slavery posed to women, particularly, and the ways in which slavery made it hard for mothers to maintain cohesive families and to protect their children. For example, Jacobs writes:

> I would rather drudge out my life on a cotton plantation, till the grave opened to give me rest, than to live with an unprincipled master and a jealous mistress. The felon's home in the penitentiary is preferable. He may repent and turn away from the error of his ways, and so find peace; but it is not so with a favorite slave. She is not allowed to have any pride of character. It is deemed a crime for her to be virtuous.[2]

Though Harriet Jacobs is best known now as the author of *Incidents*, she also wrote numerous letters, lectures, and reports, many of which were published in periodicals both before and after the war. Indeed, she was so prolific a writer that the pending publication of her papers fills two volumes. The Jacobs papers demonstrate that Harriet Jacobs, like many antebellum African American women writers, wrote to document and to change many kinds of conditions. She, along with others, expressed both privately and publicly experiences, ideas, and critiques about establishing schools and hospitals, aiding orphans and poor people, and generally fighting racism, sexism, and other forms of oppression.

The reception of Elizabeth Keckley's 1868 memoir, *Behind the Scenes; or, Thirty Years a Slave and Four Years in the White House*, is another example of contested and contesting authorship. Keckley published a book that combined the postbellum slave narrative with the celebrity memoir. When her account of her life in slavery and of her experiences as a free woman appeared, the public did not question – initially – her authorship. However, the public later castigated her for professing to be Mary Todd Lincoln's confidante and for exposing inappropriate intimate details of the former First Lady's affairs. Later, people began to speculate that Keckley had not written the book herself but that a journalist, either James Redpath or Jane Swisshelm, had ghostwritten her account. Today, Keckley's authorship is rarely questioned, though many readers continue to debate her intentions for the book and to speculate about her reasons for including confidential letters to her from Mary Todd Lincoln in the final chapter.

In 1981, scholars recovered a 1859 publication entitled *Our Nig*. Henry Louis Gates, Jr. and others verified its author as Harriet Wilson, an African American woman born in Milford, New Hampshire, in 1825, and labeled it a novel. More recent scholarship has challenged this classification. Enough of Wilson's personal history has been recovered to allow the book to be considered an autobiography. Scholars, such as P. Gabrielle Foreman and Reginald H. Pitts, in their introduction to Harriet Wilson's *Our Nig*, promote Wilson's work as a significant literary innovation, arguing that "*Our Nig* is prototypical of black antebellum writing in its tendency to blend and challenge the narrative forms it incorporates, weaving together factual and fictional conventions."[3] In 2002, another recovery by Henry Louis Gates, Jr., this time a manuscript called *The Bondwoman's Narrative* and signed "By Hannah Crafts, a Fugitive Slave," offered another mystery about authorship and authenticity. Forensic evidence does prove that the book was written in the mid nineteenth century and contextual evidence suggests that Hannah Crafts may have been a woman of African descent. However, at the time of this writing, no one has conclusively identified Hannah Crafts or verified the race or gender of the writer.

Biography was also a particularly attractive genre for black women writers. In recording the lives and experiences of others, especially of men, these women could augment the historical record, celebrate triumph over adversities, and offer exemplars of inspiration and encouragement without being accused of indecorum. As early as 1835, Susan Paul published *Memoir of James Jackson*, a touching story of the life of one of her students who died at age six. Among the biographers of note are Josephine Brown, who published her account of William Wells Brown as *Biography of an American Bondman, by his Daughter* (1856); Frances Rollin, who used the pseudonym "Frank Rollin" for her 1868 *Life and Public Services of Martin R. Delaney*; Charlotte E., Florence T., and Henrietta C. Ray, whose *Sketch of the Life of Rev. Charles B. Ray* appeared in 1887; and Rosetta Douglass Sprague, whose speech on her mother, the first wife of Frederick Douglass, was published in 1900 as "My Mother as I Recall Her." In fact, from the 1890s through the 1920s, biographical accounts by African American women became a genre unto itself. Octavia Victoria Albert, herself a freedwoman, contributed *The House of Bondage: Or, Charlotte Brooks and Other Slaves* in 1892. Other works include Susan Elizabeth Frazier's "Some Afro-American Women of Mark" (1892), Gertrude E. H. Bustill Mossell's *The Work of the Afro-American Woman* (1894), Pauline Hopkins's "Famous Women of the Negro Race" (1901–2), and Hallie Q. Brown's *Homespun Heroines and Other Women of Distinction* (1926).

Getting published

If becoming a writer was difficult for women, getting published took another kind of miracle. Many African American women succeeded by finding the right patron. Others used their own funds. Until the mid nineteenth century, most publication was done by printers "for the author," because the publishing industry was in its early stages. In nineteenth-century America, both literature and journalism were male-dominated professions. As commercial publishing emerged, literacy among the working classes increased, and as gender roles changed, more women became professional writers and journalists. Laws against literacy, racial discrimination, and particular cultural and economic forces hindered but did not stop women of African descent from participating in the emerging profession of literature. Maria Stewart, a freeborn woman of New England, did both.

Stewart convinced abolitionist publisher William Lloyd Garrison to print her essay "Religion and the Pure Principles of Morality, the Sure Foundation on Which We Must Build" (1831) as a pamphlet. The Friends of Freedom and Virtue published a collection of her speeches and meditations in 1835 as *Productions of Mrs. Maria W. Stewart*. In 1879, Stewart used her own funds to publish a revised and enlarged version of *Productions*. This second edition included a brief autobiography. Stewart's writings often explain the roles of religion in the lives of both individuals and the nation and advocate decisive action toward building the African American community from within. She urges African Americans to embrace a higher moral standard, suggesting that reclaiming morality and eschewing vulgarity would result in a stronger, more practical African American nation.

Stewart, Wheatley before her, and others enjoyed the patronage of white people as well as black people. But most often African American women published in the Afro-Protestant press, which was dominated by men. Although male-dominated, the black press was usually hospitable to women writers. The initial issues of *Freedom's Journal*, the earliest known African American newspaper, set the pattern in 1827 with poems by "Ella" and "Amelia," a biography of Phillis Wheatley, and numerous articles about exemplary women. Over the years, women contributed fiction and poetry, essays and commentaries. Several women, such as Cordelia Ray, Nellie F. Mossell, Victoria Earle Matthews, Lucy Wilmot Smith, and Frances Ellen Watkins Harper, gained significant prominence as journalists. A few, eventually, became section editors for the "Ladies' Page" as well as associate editors for periodicals of general interest to the African American communities. Several belonged to professional associations for African American journalists. Only a handful – Harper, Mossell, and Matthews – published articles in Euro-American and European papers.

During the antebellum period, Mary Shadd Cary is the only known female editor. However, her newspaper *Provincial Freeman* was "one of the longest-operating independent black newspapers of the antebellum period, and was instrumental in the community debates over abolition and emigration."[4] Cary remained the exception for many years. Toward the end of the century, women began to own and to edit their own periodicals. Among these were *Ringgold's Afro-American Journal of Fashion* (1891–95) edited by Julia Ringgold Costen (1891–95); *Woman's Era* (1894–97) edited by Josephine St. Pierre; and *Half-Century Magazine* (1916–25) owned and edited by Katherine Williams. In the postbellum period, Ida B. Wells and Pauline Hopkins were among the very few women who actually owned or edited periodicals that were not exclusively for a female readership.

Multi-tasking in multiple modes

Journalism was an especially accessible genre, but even prominent journalists usually did not confine their writing to this medium. In fact, many are better known for their fiction, poetry, essays, or autobiographical writings. Frances Ellen Watkins Harper is a supreme example of such multifaceted writers.

Born free in the slave state of Maryland in 1825, Harper lived to become the nineteenth century's most popular and prolific writer. In 1890, noted journalist I. Garland Penn pronounced her "the journalistic mother" of the Afro-American press. And indeed, Harper's pioneering contributions of articles, letters, poetry, and stories to periodicals such as *The North Star*, *The Christian Recorder*, and the *Anglo-African Magazine* led the way. During Reconstruction, she penned newspaper columns variously titled "Fancy Sketches" and "Fancy Etchings" in which women characters of different generations, locations, and class standings discussed issues ranging from the relevance of poets for the culturally oppressed to the morality of paying less than a living wage and the unionization of female farmers and laborers. Harper's column presaged Langston Hughes's popular Jesse B. Semple series that ran in the *Chicago Defender* during the World War II era.

Today, most readers recognize Harper as the author of frequently anthologized abolitionist poems such as "Bury Me in a Free Land" (1864) and "The Slave Mother" (1854). However, abolition was but one of the causes to which she dedicated her pen. During her nearly seventy years as a professional writer, Harper published novels, short stories, letters, essays, poems, and news columns. She used her literature as a tool and weapon for social and moral reform. As the title of one poem indicates, her mission was "to make the songs for the people." Harper was an inveterate equal rights activist who championed such causes as suffrage, temperance, pacifism, education, morality, women's political organization, and Christian reformation, and equal rights for all. Harper's first book, *Poems on Miscellaneous Subjects* (1854), sold thousands of copies and was revised, enlarged, or republished for decades. As its title indicated, her first book featured poems on several topics, but it also included three prose sketches. She published or revised at least nine additional volumes of poetry during her career.

Harper's activist agenda did not obliterate her artistic concerns. She believed in the healing powers of art, the imaginative properties and the pleasure that well-written works could bring. Her experimentation with literary form was unparalleled among her peers. She was among the first to publish a short story, "The Two Offers," in 1859. Innovative in form, the short story introduced to the American literary canon one of the first professional black female protagonists who was educated, single, and successful. In *Sketches of Southern Life*, Harper produced a series of linked narrative poems that form a history of antebellum and reconstruction African America. In that 1860s volume, Harper created Aunt Chloe, a female character who seems the foremother of Fannie Lou Hamer, who co-founded the Mississippi Freedom Democratic Party during the 1960s. Like Hamer, Aunt Chloe is a wise, down-to-earth older woman who does not allow her lack of formal education nor her working-class status to obstruct her leadership abilities or silence her opposition to inequity or duplicity. *Moses, a Story of the Nile* (1868) is a dramatic epic poem that refocuses the biblical tale to bring out the roles of women during that period and the relevance of Hebrew history for postbellum America. During the postbellum period, Harper also published at least three serialized novels. She was sixty-seven years old and able to rest upon her laurels when she risked her reputation, once again, to try a new genre. The result was the novel that many consider her best work, *Iola Leroy* (1892). With *Iola Leroy*, Harper created one of the first African American historical novels, an epic like Margaret Walker's *Jubilee* (1966) and Alex Haley's *Roots* (1976), that covers virtually the entire history of antebellum and postbellum African America.

Alice Ruth Moore Dunbar-Nelson was a postbellum writer whose literary versatility and social activism were quite similar to those of Harper. She too worked for and wrote about education, suffrage, and equal rights. Like Harper, Dunbar-Nelson gave public performances that combined activism and aesthetics. She edited two volumes of speeches, *Masterpieces of Negro Eloquence* (1914) and *The Dunbar Speaker and Entertainer* (1920), which foster comparisons of antebellum speakers such as Maria Stewart and Frances Harper with those of the postbellum period. Like Harper, Dunbar-Nelson had a long career in journalism as a regular columnist. Unlike Harper, but like Victoria Earle, Pauline Hopkins, and others, Alice Dunbar-Nelson also worked as a reporter and an editor. Like Harper, Dunbar-Nelson's first two publications, *Violets and Other Tales* (1895) and *The Goodness of St. Rocque and Other Stories* (1899), were collections of poetry, essays, and short stories that weave fact and fiction in and around one another to form a world of many kinds of people affected by and affecting many different issues. Dunbar-Nelson, however, concentrated most of her work in southern Louisiana and the urban North. In this catholicity, Dunbar-Nelson anticipates work of the Harlem Renaissance such as Jean Toomer's *Cane* (1923). Like Harper, Dunbar-Nelson expanded the African American literary repertoire to include characters previously invisible. Dunbar-Nelson gives us mulattos who were not tragic, Creoles and other people of mixed heritage, working-class protagonists, sullen and even violent married couples, and women of ambiguous, if not lesbian, sexuality. Her published poetry attracted the attentions of Paul Laurence Dunbar, the first writer to match Harper in popularity and literary productivity. They courted by correspondence, later marrying in 1898. Those letters, Dunbar-Nelson's diaries, and much of her poetry comprise probably the largest and most provocative caches of personal writings by a nineteenth-century African American woman found to date.

Written for herself

Personal letters, journals and diaries by nineteenth-century African American women are the rarest literary form of the antebellum and postbellum periods. Phillis Wheatley, for instance, personally corresponded with luminaries such as Selina Hastings, Countess of Huntington, Samuel Hopkins, and Samson Occom. Her letters reveal much about her religious beliefs and her ideas about writing, social responsibility, Christian duty, friendship, and romance. Probably the most significant letters are those she addressed to her friend, Obour Tanner, an enslaved African woman in a nearby town. These letters show that colonial African Americans, even enslaved ones, composed and read, bought and sold literature. Of note, the private correspondence between African American women of the antebellum or postbellum era is so rare that its absence seems deliberate. The many letters by these women, internationally known and nationally prominent, are not publicly available, if they do exist at all.

Those that are available were generally published in the twentieth century. In 1984, Gloria Hull published *Give Us This Day: The Diary of Alice Dunbar-Nelson* and, in 1988, the Schomburg Library of Nineteenth-Century Black Women Writers printed more of Dunbar-Nelson's private papers as well as the diaries written between 1854 and 1892 by Charlotte Forten. In 1995, Miriam DeCosta-Willis published *The Memphis Diaries of Ida B. Wells*, and in 1998, Charles Lemert and Esme Bahn included some of Anna Julia Cooper's private writings in their collection entitled *The Voice of Anna Julia Cooper*. In virtually every case, these collections are selected, edited or otherwise less candid and complete than we might desire. Still, they offer fascinating details about the dreams and nightmare experiences, the lives and loves, passions and causes of extraordinary women who lived and traveled during the antebellum and postbellum periods.

One reason that the personal narratives and private thoughts of African American women were rarely made public is because nineteenth-century gender conventions required modesty for respectability. Thus African American women writers routinely began with apologies for calling attention to themselves by publishing their thoughts and experiences. Harriet Jacobs, for example, began *Incidents* by avowing, "I have not written my experiences in order to attract attention to myself; on the contrary, it would have been more pleasant to me to have been silent ... But I do earnestly desire to arouse the women of the North to a realizing sense of the conditions of two millions of women ... still in bondage."[5] Elizabeth Keckley probably did not know how vehement the negative reactions to her autobiography would be, but she did understand that "[i]n writing as I have done, I am well aware that I have invited criticism; but before the critic judges harshly, let my explanation be carefully read and weighed."[6]

Writing the word

The autobiographical accounts of Afro-Protestant ministers and missionaries are the notable exception to the rarely published personal papers. These women by virtue of their faith and conversions believed themselves commissioned to preach the word and make it plain. Even they did not escape criticism for going public, but they defended themselves with biblical references. For example, Jarena Lee prefaces her *Religious Experience and Journal* (1849) this way: "And it shall come to pass ... that I will pour out my Spirit upon all flesh; and your sons, [sic] and your *daughters* shall prophesy"[7] (emphasis in original). *The Religious Experience and Journal of Mrs. Jarena Lee* was an enlarged edition of *The Life and Religious Experience of Jarena Lee, a Coloured Lady*, published in 1839 and in 1836 respectively. Jarena Lee chronicles her journey from the moment she first heard the voice of God through her appointment as "the first female preacher of the First African Methodist Episcopal Church."[8] Jarena Lee was not formally educated, but through the authority of her religious conviction, she "felt a great liberty in the gospel" that empowered her to "speak the Word and make it clear" (p. 58).

Lee's writings exemplify the conversion narratives that became a favorite form for African American women. As usual for this genre, Lee's writings range from repeating her private prayers and meditations to secret prayers to public challenges of gender and theological traditions. Jarena Lee uses the presumed incongruity of her call to minister as proof of God's omnipotence. She valiantly argues that through the instrumentality of a "poor colored female" God revealed His amazing powers. Like many other religious and spiritual women writers, Jarena Lee does not allow gender, class, and race prejudices to become insurmountable roadblocks but instead interprets them as trials and declares that her ability to overcome those obstacles is a direct manifestation of God's will. Other spiritual and religious accounts by African American women include Zilpha Elaw's *Memoirs* (1846), Julia Foote's *A Brand Plucked From the Fire* (1879), and Virginia W. Broughton's *Twenty Years' Experience of a Missionary* (1907). Published in 1981, *Gifts of Power: The Writings of Rebecca Cox Jackson* collects unpublished diaries and documents by an African American woman who served as a Shaker eldress from 1856 until 1871 when she died.

Spirituality, religion, and morality are recurring themes in antebellum and postbellum African American women's literature. To write of one's religious conversion or one's evangelistic experiences was to write of oneself as an individual of worth and of significance. Indeed, within literary traditions throughout the world, the conversion narrative occupies a special status in that it allows women to assert a larger degree of authority. Many women writers use their spiritual and moral authority to create spaces within which they can speak on an ostensibly equal footing. To write of these experiences as a black woman was to revolutionize the genre. In America, where white supremacist notions were often predicated on religious teachings, African American women's religious and spiritual narratives challenged theological dissertations and exegetical innovations. African American women writers became Christian soldiers. Their religious narratives were useful weapons on the battlefields for social equality and moral elevation. As Jarena Lee wrote, "I had my talent and to use it I was not ashamed" (p. 76).

Architects of a new world

Much of the current scholarship favors readings of African American literature as a reaction to enslavement, the reality, however, is that the writings of early African American women and their contributions to literature consist of much more. Though arising, initially, from the context of enslavement, the concerns and themes of early African American literature vary widely. They are far more than reactions to, or railings against, the hostile white world. Freedom – in its many and varied forms – is a persistent concern. But this freedom is desired and reflected in issues ranging from familial life and constructions, to religion, spirituality, and morality, from issues of race to those of class and gender, of educational, economic, legal, and social equality both in the United States and abroad. Such thematic preoccupations construct a continuum that connects antebellum and postbellum African American women's literature while creating a bridge to contemporary writings in the tradition.

In displaying a distinctive desire to construct African Americans as a people who valued their familial connections, African American women writers often depicted, sometimes reified, African American women as mothers. Idealization of motherhood and domesticity happened at a time when spheres of influence were strictly delineated by gender. At least in theory, white men occupied the public space and white women exercised dominion over the private space. By embracing motherhood/domesticity, black women writers redefined and enlarged the domestic sphere. For example, the home became the nursery of future leaders taught and inspired by the wife and mother. In "Religion and the Pure Principles of Morality," Maria W. Stewart writes:

> Did the daughters of our land possess a delicacy of manners, combined with gentleness and dignity, did their pure minds hold vice in abhorrence and contempt, did they frown when their ears were polluted with its vile accents, would not their influence become powerful? Would not our brethren fall in love with their virtues? Their souls would become fired with a holy zeal for freedom's cause.[9]

Stewart encourages women to subscribe to the morality that religion teaches them and to govern their actions by those values. In doing this, Stewart reveals her belief that women can become the inspiration for the improvement of the nation.

Similarly, Harriet Jacobs's *Incidents in the Life of a Slave Girl* epitomizes the drive to reclaim family and motherhood for African American women. Jacobs writes in glowing prose about her first child. "When he was a year old, they called him beautiful. The little vine was taking deep root in my existence; though its clinging fondness excited a mixture of love and pain. When I was most sorely oppressed, I loved to watch his smiles; but there was always a dark cloud over my enjoyment."[10] As the vine took root, he incited in Jacobs a passionate protectiveness. The birth of her daughter amplified her protectiveness and increased her determination to resist enslavement of both body and mind. As she planned her escape, Jacobs writes, "My mind was made up. I was resolved that I would foil my master and save my children, or I would perish in the attempt."[11] Jacobs is willing to give her life to protect her children, and she is ever conscious of the ways that her status, as an enslaved woman, jeopardizes her ability to set a good moral example for her children.

In his preface to Ann Plato's *Essays: Including Biographies and Miscellaneous Pieces, in Prose and Poetry* (1840), Reverend J. W. C. Pennington writes: "[Plato] is willing to be judged by the candid, and even to run the hazard of being severely dealt with by the critic, in order to accomplish something of credit for her people...[she] has followed the example of Phillis Wheatly."[12] One of the poems Plato included in this collection is "Advice to Young Ladies." In this poem, she urges young women to be pious and submissive to God's will, but she prefaces this advice with the stanza:

> The greatest word that I can say, —
> I think to please will be,
> To try and get your learning young
> And write it back to me.[13]

According to Plato, a virtuous woman must educate herself and communicate her knowledge to others. Ann Plato, like many antebellum and postbellum women writers, might appear to advocate submissiveness, piety, domesticity, and purity as essential to "true womanhood," but is actually positing subtle but serious reinterpretations that support a wider sphere for righteous womanhood.

Finally, Pauline Hopkins's novel, *Contending Forces* (1900), presents Dora Smith as an epitome of virtuous African American womanhood. Though the novel revolves around the triangle between Sappho, Willie, and John, Dora acts as a moral compass, indicating to the characters and readers alike the way that they should respond to the secrets unveiled by the narrative voice. Dora is physically beautiful, but more importantly, she is industrious, religious, educated, respectful, and – above all – virtuous. Early in the novel, Dora offers a bit of spiritual guidance to Sappho, a boarder with a mysterious secret. Sappho says of Dora, " 'You are a dear little preacher,' ….'and if our race ever amounts to anything in this world, it will be because such women as you are raised to save us.'"[14] Like Maria Stewart and others, Hopkins suggests that virtuous women, such as Dora, hold the salvation of the race in their hands. Occasionally, it happened that the writers' moral authority or some aspect of their characters might be impugned because of circumstances over which they have no control, such as physical violations valorized by institutional racism and sexism. Then, like Harriet Jacobs or Elizabeth Keckley, African American women writers went to great lengths to prove they had made every effort to retain their virtue, and, especially after the unfortunate incident, they worked diligently to repair any harm and to live exemplary lives.

As with its representations of domesticity, the literature of African American women redefines spirituality and morality as spaces within which these women could critique, chastise, or be in dialogue with Eurocentric and patriarchal ideologies. According to Christian beliefs, all human beings were sinners and salvation was free to all believers. Religion was a great equalizer. Religion, thus, put people on the same plane regardless of race or gender. Spirituality and religion conferred an authority upon these authors, which – by virtue of its source – could not be impugned or revoked. The use of religion to create a common ground is notable from the inception of tradition. It is because of her spiritual beliefs that Wheatley is able to critique the white, male students of Harvard University in her poem "To the University of Cambridge in New England" (1773).

As the poem begins, Wheatley acknowledges the abundant privilege that these young men have as members of an elite group attending one of the most well-known institutions of higher learning in the nation. Even as she acknowledges their privilege, Wheatley reminds the young men that there is a higher power that they have seemingly forgotten in their pursuit of education. Wheatley writes:

> Still more, ye sons of science, ye receive
> The blissful news by messengers from heav'n
> How *Jesus*' blood for your redemption flows.[15]

In reminding the students of Jesus, Wheatley frames the critique on religious and moral grounds, thereby claiming, for herself, an authority to perform that critique. She writes:

> Improve your privileges while they stay,
> Ye pupils, and each hour redeem, that bears
> Or good or bad report of you to heav'n.
> Let sin, that baneful evil to the soul,
> By you be shunned, nor once remit your guard.[16]

In spite of her abject social position, Wheatley is able to transcend the obstacles that would generally preclude such a critique as she chides the students about their morals.

Legacies of Reconstruction

Occurring less than one hundred years after the Revolutionary War, the Civil War represents the penultimate act of national identity formation. By abolishing slavery within its borders, America seemed to grapple with and triumph over the single greatest obstacle in the path of formulating a new national identity that stretched the boundaries of democracy as conceived by its founders. African American women's literature reflects this national preoccupation with defining freedom and citizenship and the connections between these ideas of the burgeoning American identity, shaping those definitions in relation to African American identity. Several prominent novels written in the period between 1865 and 1900 revisit the era of slavery for the purpose of coming to terms with the definitions, privileges, and responsibilities of freedom. These authors actively critiqued the idea that freedom was merely emancipation from enslavement. They explained how constructions of race, class, and gender could fetter individuals and groups. They painstakingly articulated the necessity for educational opportunities, freedom of religion and of expression, and for democratic governance that did not impose the power of a privileged few over the natural rights of the many. They created characters that modeled the personal sacrifices and dangers that African Americans faced. And they often showed that those persons did not always survive or succeed despite their best efforts.

Throughout the early tradition of African American women's literature, writers incorporated the rhetoric of revolution, freedom, and citizenship. They appreciated its potential for making their personal arguments for freedom, humane treatment, and equality all the more publicly persuasive. By manipulating the discourses of revolution, African American women could subtly – and sometimes not so subtly – subvert the systems of oppression that had been constructed to tether blacks. One example is Frances E. W. Harper's serialized novel, *Minnie's Sacrifice* (1867–68). The central character of this novel is Minnie, a young mixed-race woman, who had been adopted by a northern white family. Upon discovering the truth of her origins, Minnie is faced with the choice of acknowledging her connection to an oppressed group of people and joining in the battle for equality, or ignoring that newly discovered information and continuing to enjoy the privileges of being "white." Minnie chooses to identify as African American and goes south to aid in Reconstruction efforts. It is a choice that leads ultimately to her death. Here, Harper articulates a relationship between self-identity, self-esteem, community, race, gender, and freedom. Minnie could have chosen to remain in the North, living a relatively comfortable life, but she believed that as long as any people are in bondage, she, too, wore chains.

The concerns of early African American women writers continue to reverberate for contemporary African American women authors. Like the architects of the tradition, authors – from Jessie Faucet to Toni Cade Bambara – continue the tradition of reflecting diversity among African American women. Contemporary authors continue to test the word and redefine genres, building from the innovations of these early authors. Angelyn Mitchell's *The Freedom to Remember: Narrative, Slavery, and Gender in Contemporary Black Women's Fiction* demonstrates just how intertwined the literatures of the past are with the writings of contemporary African America women writers. She writes, "The focus of these narratives by contemporary African American women writers is not, it seems to me, on the experience of enslavement, but, more importantly on the construct we call freedom. In other words, they do more than narrate movement from bondage to freedom. These narratives analyze freedom."[17] Mitchell's words have equal resonance and relevance for the early authors of this tradition as they have for the most recent authors. Like early authors, contemporary authors engage with a variety of subject matters, challenging traditional notions and articulating new ideas. Writing was and is still very much a public and political act for black woman writers. From texts such as Alice Walker's *Meridian* (1976), an activist novel about the period immediately following the civil rights era, to Toni Morrison's *Paradise* (1998), a meditation novel about women claiming both the place and the right to be, and Octavia Butler's *Fledgling* (2005), a vampire novel that not only tests the boundaries between genders and races but also questions the nature of humanity itself, these writings reflect the heritage of Phillis Wheatley, Frances E. W. Harper, Pauline Hopkins, and Alice Ruth Moore Dunbar-Nelson. They are diverse in style and content. They are unified in their determination to speak and, when possible, to write by themselves, of themselves and others. They believe, like Harper, Hopkins, Maria Stewart, Anna Julia Cooper, and countless other early African American women writers, that literature not only illuminates one's soul and shines the light of truth upon lives, but also brings forth "a brighter coming day."

NOTES

1. June Jordan. "The Difficult Miracle of Black Poetry in America or Something like a Sonnet for Phillis Wheatley," *Wild Women in the Whirlwind: Afra-American Culture and the Contemporary Literary Renaissance*, ed. Joanne M. Braxton and Andrée Nicola McLaughlin (New Brunswick, NJ: Rutgers University Press, 1990), pp. 22–34.
2. Harriet Jacobs, *Incidents in the Life of a Slave Girl: Written by Herself*, (1861) ed. Jean Fagan Yellin (Cambridge, MA: Harvard University Press, 1987), p. 28.
3. Gabrielle Foreman and Reginald Pitts, Introduction to Harriet Wilson's *Our Nig; or, Sketches from the Life of a Free Black* (New York: Penguin, 2004), p. xxx.
4. Jane Rhodes, *Mary Ann Shadd Cary: The Black Press and Protest in the Nineteenth Century* (Bloomington: Indiana University Press, 1998), p. xii.
5. Jacobs, *Incidents*, pp. 439–40.
6. Elizabeth Keckley, *Behind the Scenes; or, Thirty Years a Slave and Four Years in the White House* (New York: Penguin, 2005), p. 3.
7. Joel 2:28.
8. Jarena Lee, *Religious Experiences and Journal of Mrs. Jarena Lee: A Preachin' Woman* (Nashville: Amec, 1992).
9. Maria Stewart, "Religion and The Pure Principles of Morality, the Sure Foundation on Which We Must Build," *Words of Fire: An Anthology of African American Feminist Thought*, ed. Beverly Guy-Sheftall (New York: New Press, 1995), p. 31.
10. Jacobs, *Incidents*, p. 510.
11. Ibid., p. 534.
12. Ann Plato, *Essays: Including Biographies and Miscellaneous Pieces, in Prose and Poetry* (New York: Oxford University Press, 1988), p. xviii.
13. Ibid.
14. Pauline Hopkins, *Contending Forces: A Romance Illustrative of Negro Life North and South* (Boston: Colored Cooperative Publishing, 1900), p. 101.
15. Phillis Wheatley, *Memoir and Poems of Phillis Wheatley, a Native African and a Slave* (Boston: Isaac Knapp, 1838).
16. Ibid.
17. Angelyn Mitchell, *The Freedom to Remember: Narrative, Slavery, and Gender in Contemporary Black Women's Fiction* (New Brunswick, NJ: Rutgers University Press, 2002), pp. 3–4.

2

CHERYL A. WALL

Women of the Harlem Renaissance

Joanna Marshall, the protagonist of Jessie Fauset's *There Is Confusion* (1924), one of the first novels of the Harlem Renaissance, insists "that if there's anything that will break down prejudice it will be equality or perhaps even superiority on the part of colored people in the arts."[1] Fauset shared this belief with other leaders of the New Negro movement, Alain Locke, Charles Johnson, and James Weldon Johnson. The time seemed ripe. During the 1920s almost every Broadway season saw the opening of a production featuring black entertainers, beginning in 1921 with *Shuffle Along*, which introduced Josephine Baker to the theatrical world. Traditional African American dances like the Charleston were featured in Broadway musicals and quickly became national fads. European painters and sculptors drew inspiration from African art. Negro spirituals were made a permanent part of the concert repertoire on the initiative of singers Roland Hayes, Paul Robeson, and Marian Anderson. Through the magic of the newly invented radio and through phonograph recordings, black secular music reached white America. The decade marked the heyday of the classic blues singers whose art reached its pinnacle in the work of Bessie Smith, the so-called Empress of the Blues. The most popular music of the decade was jazz, a music created by blacks that white America enjoyed so much the decade was dubbed the Jazz Age. The vogue for African and African American art seemed to portend greater support for black peoples' political rights. It did not. But it did open a space for writers, who were able to make art of both the expanded opportunities and the persistent constraints.[2]

Harlem Renaissance is the term used most often to identify the cultural awakening of which these artists were part. Harlem, located in New York City, the national cultural capital, became the cultural capital of African Americans during the 1920s. But many of the women writers including Marita Bonner, Alice Dunbar-Nelson, Angelina Weld Grimké, Zora Neale Hurston, Georgia Douglas Johnson, and Anne Spencer spent little or no time there. Some writers referred to the "New Negro Renaissance," to express their sense of a redefined racial identity, one that heralded the spiritual emancipation of black Americans. Yet women writers on the whole seemed less certain that the Old Negro, embodied in the stereotypes of Uncle Tom and Aunt Jemima, had died. In any case, during the 1920s, the vogue for Harlem, or the Negro, was palpable. Achievements by black artists in the United States reached unprecedented levels. Even the onset of the Great Depression in 1929 could not extinguish the creative spark. Hurston's masterpiece, *Their Eyes Were Watching God* (1937), partakes of the Renaissance spirit.

For Joanna Marshall however, the modest success she achieves on the vaude-ville stage is a disappointment. As a young girl, she aspired to the greatness exemplified by Harriet Tubman and Sojourner Truth in the stories her father told. But racism makes it impossible for her to achieve her grand ambitions for the stage. After years of striving for theatrical success, she contents herself with marriage to a physician. Her creator kept the faith. Fauset published four novels, along with short stories, poems, reportage, reviews, translations, and essays. Tellingly, two of Fauset's other protagonists are artists: Angela Murray in *Plum Bun* is a painter; Laurentine Strange in *The Chinaberry Tree* is a seamstress; Marise, a character in *Comedy American Style*, is a performer whose transat-lantic career seems inspired by Josephine Baker's. Despite the challenges of racism and sexism, these characters strive to realize their twin dreams of becoming artists and advancing the struggle for racial equality.

No black woman writer was more committed to these goals than Fauset. From 1919 to 1926 she was literary editor of *The Crisis*, the official journal of the National Association for the Advancement of Colored People, and a premier venue for African American writers. Fauset shepherded the careers of Countee Cullen, Langston Hughes and Jean Toomer; she was particularly steadfast in her commitment to women artists. Not only did she promote the work of Georgia Douglas Johnson, Anne Spencer, and Nella Larsen; she commissioned painters Gwendolyn Bennett, Effie Lee Newsome, and Laura Wheeler Waring to design covers for issues of *The Crisis*. Before moving to New York in 1919, Fauset lived and taught in Washington, DC, where she belonged to a circle of literary women including Douglas Johnson, Dunbar-Nelson, Grimké, Mary Burrill, and May Miller. Both Bonner – a school-teacher, aspiring playwright, and short story writer – and Hurston – Howard University student and soon-to-be folklorist and novelist – later joined Douglas Johnson's "S Street" salon, which met weekly to provide conversa-tion and collegial support to writers. These interconnections suggest the existence of an informal network of literary black women.[3] Although their work ranged widely in style and setting, it explored issues of identity as defined by race, gender, class, and sexuality in ways that continue to resonate for twenty-first-century readers.

Published in *The Crisis*, Bonner's essay, "On Being Young – a Woman – and Colored" (1925), summarizes the dilemmas inherent in the social situation faced by many New Negro women. At a time when the opportunities implicit even in the term "*New* Negro" were widely heralded, Bonner wrote with a deep consciousness of the limitations the racial past imposed on her personal future. Preponderant images in Bonner's essay evoke stasis and claustrophobia, not the change and movement celebrated in *The New Negro*, the manifesto of the Harlem Renaissance Locke edited in 1925. Bonner addresses a female reader, presumably as well educated and refined as she, who cannot plan even an excursion from Washington to New York, for to travel alone would offend propriety. Black women are intensely aware of whites' racist perception of them as "only a gross collection of desires, all uncontrolled." The essay concludes with the speaker's comparing herself to a Buddha "motionless on the outside. But on the inside?"[4] Sexist as well as racist stereotypes continued to haunt New Negro women. But the era's heightened race consciousness made issues of sexism more difficult to raise. Historian Paula Giddings asserts that "femininity not feminism was the talk of the twenties."[5] Amid the effort to forge a revised racial identity, a woman who persisted in raising concerns about sexism might see them dismissed as irrelevant or trivial; she might herself be perceived as disloyal to the race. The women of the Harlem Renaissance evoked all of these responses.

In her title Bonner makes it plain, nevertheless, that she wants to claim a racial *and* a gendered identity. Writing from a position of privilege, Bonner, who graduated from Radcliffe College in 1922, leaves no doubt that she knows exactly what she desires: a career and a marriage defined by mutual respect. She understands already that these goals are complicated by her race, gender, and class. "All your life you have heard of the debt you owe 'Your People' because you have managed to have the things they have not largely had" (p. 3). The effort to discharge that debt entraps her in a doubled ghetto – the ghetto of race and the ghetto within the ghetto that is the gilded cage of the middle class. Bonner writes acidly of the endless rounds of parties and cards, and poignantly of the metaphorical bars that prevent escape. The price of escape is the loss of respectability which for the black woman Bonner apostrophizes carries a racial as well as an individual cost.

Taking this measure of her situation, Bonner did not give up. She published her short stories and plays regularly in *The Crisis* and *Opportunity*, the official publication of the Urban League. After she moved to Chicago in 1930, she explored the dislocation southern blacks experienced in northern cities, the consequent disruption in family life, as well as the concomitant social, economic, and cultural conflicts between black migrants and

European immigrants. But the themes and images set forth in this early essay anticipate characteristics of writing by many of Bonner's peers.

Bonner's words surely resonated with her editor. Born in 1882 in Fredericksville, New Jersey (now Lawnside), Fauset grew up in Philadelphia. After her mother's death, her father, a minister, encouraged her to excel. She did. In 1905 she graduated from Cornell University, having been elected to Phi Beta Kappa. She later earned an MA in Romance Languages from the University of Pennsylvania. Despite these sterling credentials, Fauset could only find employment in the segregated schools of Baltimore and Washington, DC. Indeed so limited were the options for professional black women that at M Street High School her colleagues included two of the first three black American women to earn a Ph.D.

In 1912 Fauset began contributing articles to the two-year-old *Crisis*, whose founder and editor, W. E. B. Du Bois, she deeply admired. The newly-minted journal was on its way to becoming the most important publication in black America, and Fauset's contributions were integral to its success. She contributed a range of material from book reviews to poems, short stories, and essays; for several years she wrote a column called "The Looking Glass." In the early 1920s every issue of the magazine carried her by-line.

Fauset was a particularly gifted essayist, who knew how to construct an argument and to turn a phrase. Many of her essays appeal to sentiment without turning sentimental as her fiction often does. Generally, she enlivened her essays with the kind of telling detail that too rarely turns up in her novels. The essays reveal, moreover, her willingness to grapple with new cultural and political concepts. Through these one can chart the process by which a woman conditioned by background and training to accept a very conservative social ethic assimilated a good many progressive ideas. She reported on nationalism and Egypt as well as the convention of the National Association of Colored Women, an activist group of black women reformers. She penned prose portraits of prominent artists such as comedian Bert Williams and painter Henry Ossawa Tanner. In keeping with the Pan African politics of *The Crisis* she also profiled outstanding men of African descent across the world. In "Nostalgia" she reflects on the longing for home, a desire that Fauset describes as universal but thwarted for black Americans who are alienated in the land of their birth.

Fauset refused to stay in her place. Many of her best essays document her travel. "Tracing Shadows" (1915) recounts her sojourn in France on the brink of World War I; an experience that becomes a rite of passage for the author's persona. "The Enigma of the Sorbonne" (1925) explores the temptation of expatriation for a black American who could live in France without being constantly conscious of race; "Yarrow Revisited" (1925), by contrast, describes the end of her infatuation with French life. "Dark Algiers the White" (1925) reports Fauset's trip to North Africa.[6] In an age when the idea of Africa captivated the political and cultural imaginations of African American intellectuals, Fauset was one of a handful, along with Du Bois, Hughes, and McKay, actually to set foot on the continent. In her travel essays Fauset brought the wider world to her readers. Although some of her observations were ethnocentric, she advanced a global vision that affirmed the subtitle of *The Crisis*, "a Record of the Darker Races."

Her fluency in French furthered this vision. Reviewing four books by Haitian writers, she asserted that they opened up for her an "undiscovered country."[7] Highly conscious of the heroic history of the island republic, she advanced its literary present by translating poems by its leading writers. She had been asked to translate René Maran's prize-winning novel *Batouala* (1922), one of the first novels to make Africans central characters. Fauset reviewed it and praised its anticolonialism, as well as its representation of Africa before colonization. But she declined to be its translator because some of the novel's content was sexually explicit; she feared that she would lose her reputation as a respectable Negro woman.

In other respects, Fauset was willing to break free of the proscriptions of her time and place. In 1921 Fauset attended the Second Annual Pan African Congress and shared her impressions with *Crisis* readers; she responded with enthusiasm to an experience rich in history and drama and one in which very few women took part. The Congress had met in three European capitals – London, Brussels, and Paris – after which a delegation was sent to the League of Nations in Geneva. In her account, Fauset attempts to convey the flavor of these cities while reminding her readers that the wealth and the children of Africa had made much of the Old World charm possible. She described the conditions in various parts of Africa and drew broad parallels between the problems of colonialism in Africa and segregation in the United States.

Fauset admired Du Bois for his erudition and political commitment. As an undergraduate she wrote to thank him for *The Souls of Black Folk*. Sociologist, historian, essayist, and novelist, Du Bois had left the academy to establish *The Crisis*, a monthly journal that vowed to "defend the rights of all men irrespective of color or race, for the highest ideals of American democracy." The overarching goal was to realize "the world-old dream of human brotherhood."[8] By 1919, the mix of editorials, articles, fiction, reviews, and photographs attracted nearly 100,000 readers. In 1921 Du Bois and Fauset launched *The Brownies' Book*, a magazine for children, regrettably short-lived, that conveyed the cosmopolitan vision of both its editors. It published short stories and poetry, African folk tales, games, puzzles, and monthly historical features. An activist scholar, Du Bois continued to write books and maintain an extensive speaking schedule. These commitments kept him on the road. Working in his shadow, Fauset received little credit for her contributions to the publications whose mastheads led with his name. However, Fauset was often the editor in fact. Her respect for her boss notwithstanding, she was confident in her own editorial judgments.

As editor, Fauset solicited contributions from virtually every writer of the Harlem Renaissance. She recognized the experimental talents of Hughes and Toomer. When "The Negro Speaks of Rivers," later one of Hughes's signature poems, arrived in the mail, she took it to Du Bois and wondered how it was possible that such a prodigious talent had escaped their notice. When the nineteen-year-old poet moved to New York in 1921 to attend Columbia University, Fauset sought him out and became a loyal mentor. Fauset paid $5.00 to publish Toomer's "Song of the Son," that became the central poem of his path-breaking volume, *Cane* (1923), but cautioned him to strive for greater clarity. Though neither Hughes's innovations with blues and jazz poetry nor Toomer's experiments with imagism and free verse were her preference, she encouraged talent wherever she recognized it.

She promoted the work of Georgia Douglas Johnson (1880–1966) and helped her prepare her first volume, *The Heart of a Woman* (1918), for publication. Using regular meter and rhyme schemes as well as literary diction, Johnson's poems take on universal topics of love and death, but they do so from a decidedly female perspective. Responding to criticism that she did not consider race in her work, she published *Bronze* (1922), which she claimed was all about race. Even here her approach was indirect, and in *An Autumn Love Cycle* (1928) she returned to love lyrics. By contrast, her plays, 'Plumes' and *A Sunday Morning in the South*, treat racial themes explicitly and employ black folk speech. Out of public view, the widowed Johnson adopted an unconventional lifestyle in dress and demeanor. Her home became such a popular meeting place for writers that visitors to Washington added it to their itineraries.

One frequent guest, Alice Dunbar-Nelson (1875–1935) might be considered a forerunner of the Harlem Renaissance having published *Violets and Other Tales*, a volume of poetry, sketches, and short stories in 1895. In 1898 she married Paul Laurence Dunbar, the leading black poet of his generation; they separated in 1902 and she married journalist Robert John Nelson in 1916. Making her home in Wilmington, Delaware, she taught high school, wrote for various journals, was a sought-after public speaker, and eventually established a school for delinquent girls. In 1918 and 1919 she published a play and a story in *The Crisis*. Despite the superficial glamor of her life, she was sometimes almost destitute. Her diary both reveals the long odds against a black woman writer in the early twentieth century and documents the existence of a network of black women cultural workers.

Angelina Weld Grimké (1880–1958) was a regular at Johnson's Saturday night salon. The only child of lawyer, diplomat, and activist Henry Grimké, she was usually the only Negro in the prestigious schools she attended. Like Fauset, she found employment at Washington's M Street High School. She wrote surreptitiously. Few of her poems, some of which expressed same-sex desire, were published. But her play *Rachel*, a powerful antilynching drama, attracted considerable attention when it was produced in 1916 and published in 1921. Rather than focusing on the physical violence of lynching, it explored the psychological impact on the women and children who mourn the victim.

Anne Spencer (1882–1976) did not often leave Lynchburg, Virginia, but as black writers traveled through the segregated South, they often stopped over at the home she shared with her husband and son. She showed visitors her beautiful garden (the source of her local fame), requested support for her political causes (she established a branch of the NAACP), and read her poems. Fauset, along with Du Bois and Weldon Johnson, were eager to put the poems in print. In her art, Spencer often invents a world in which racism and sexism do not exist, or in which some unexpected source of beauty transforms the ugliness of social reality. In the sonnet "Substitution," for example, as the speaker and auditor wrestle with philosophical imponderables, the addressee is lifted clear "Of brick and frame to moonlit garden bloom, – / Absurdly easy now our walking, dear, / Talking, my leaning close to touch your face. / His All-Mind bids us keep this sacred place."[9]

Gwendolyn Bennett (1902–81) expresses a similar need to find refuge from reality in "Fantasy," which begins "I sailed in my dreams to the land of Night," and depicts a dreamscape lit by "moon-veiled light" which reveals "the loveliest things," among them a peacock, "a garden of lavender hues," and most incredibly, a "dusk-eyed queen." The vision of this dark woman inspires the speaker's song. Ruler of the realm, the queen sits in the garden in an "amethyst chair," with her feet in "hyacinth shoes."[10] But, even as she directs her song to the queen, the speaker hides herself behind a bush. The concealed speaker may be read as a metaphor for the poet. Like most of the women poets, Bennett never collected her poems in a book. Born in Giddings, Texas, and raised in Washington, DC, she taught art at Howard University and studied in Paris during the 1920s; she also wrote a literary gossip column, "The Ebony Flute," for *Opportunity*, for which she illustrated covers, as she had for *The Crisis*. After she married a physician, she left Harlem and the literary world. In the late 1930s she returned to New York and became a respected art teacher.

Younger poets, Bostonian Helene Johnson (1906–95) and Philadelphian Mae Cowdery (1909–53), proved more daring in form and theme than their elders. Johnson, who moved to New York with her cousin, novelist Dorothy West, won awards for her early poems. "Sonnet to a Negro in Harlem" represented an urban scene rarely evoked by Harlem Renaissance female poets. Her speaker exulted in the pride and beauty of her subject. "Poem" spoke in the idiom of the black vaudevillians it celebrated. Johnson married and left Harlem in the early 1930s and did not resurface until the 1990s. She continued to write however, and a volume of poems, *This Waiting for Love*, was published posthumously. Cowdery's poems are noteworthy for their explicit treatment of sexuality, a topic that many women poets avoided, perhaps due to their consciousness of negative stereotypes. Winning a *Crisis* award for her poetry as a high school senior, Cowdery took Edna St. Vincent Millay as a model for art and life. In a cover portrait, she was dressed in a man-tailored suit with her closely cropped hair slicked down. In "Longings" her persona yearns to dance, to dream, to listen to the wind, and to talk with God. Other poems represent same-sex desire. Her book, *We Lift Our Voices and Other Poems*, appeared in 1936, after which Cowdery disappeared from public view. She eventually committed suicide.

This pattern of short-lived success followed by years of anonymity suggests how difficult it was for a black woman in the early twentieth century to sustain a career as a writer. For many women, the competing demands of marriage and career, along with the requirement that their art advance the cause of racial equality, created an untenable situation. Even as they struggled against the odds, many were highly conscious of the obstacles they faced. Fauset's *Plum Bun* (1929) dramatizes this struggle. Its protagonist is an aspiring artist, and as the novel charts her development, it shows how keenly cultural politics are determined by the politics of race, class, and gender.

No one encourages Angela Murray's artistic aspirations: her father has wanted both his daughters to pursue the security of the teaching profession. Even her sister Jinny – the novel's most idealized character – finds Angela's resistance to the paternal injunction inexplicable. Only their mother, who is otherwise depicted as a childlike, foolish woman, briefly dreams of artistic careers for her daughters. She quickly defers to her husband's superior wisdom. Angela's peers are no more understanding. Although they indulge her eccentricities in deference to her beauty, their philistine attitudes toward art are manifested in their racial politics. One character is urged to become a dentist rather than another "half-baked poet" so as to benefit the race.

Angela is forced to withdraw from art school in Philadelphia, when her white classmates discover she is black. When she moves to New York to pursue her studies, she passes for white. She justifies the decision easily:

"'Why should I shut myself off from all the things I want most, – clever people, people who do things, Art' – her voice spelt it with a capital, – 'travel and a lot of things which are in the world for everybody but which only white people, as far as I can see, get their hands on. I mean scholarships and special funds, patronage.'"[11] Repeatedly, Angela, who believed that artists were both sophisticated and tolerant, is disillusioned. Rachel Powell, the one visibly black student in her class, is gifted and highly disciplined, yet alienated by and from her peers. In a plot sequence derived from an actual incident involving sculptor Augusta Savage, Rachel wins a competition for a fellowship abroad; when the donors learn that she is black, they revoke the award and explain that they are interested "not in Ethnology but in Art" (p. 359).

Passing into the white world of bohemian Manhattan forces Angela to understand the impact of sexism on women's lives. She observes the constricted ambitions of the young white women with whom she studies. She observes as well the compromises that define their personal lives. In one of the novel's most compelling passages, "She remembered an expression 'free, white and twenty one,' – this was what it meant then, this sense of owning the world, this realization that other things being equal, all things were possible … She knew that men had a better time of it than women, colored men than colored women, white men than white women" (p. 88). Although Angela's analysis is apt, she exaggerates the degree of her own freedom and independence. As the plot unfolds, the novel corrects Angela's misunderstanding.

Angela is seduced and abandoned by Roger Fielding, a rich blond aristocrat, whose racist attitudes toward blacks and sexist attitudes toward women coincide perfectly. Fauset modernizes the oldest plot in the tradition of the novel in English not only by adding the aspect of race, but by giving her protagonist artistic ambitions. In her exploration of these ambitions, Fauset fills in her own aesthetic, even as she suggests parallels between the situation of the artist kept by her patron and the mistress kept by her paramour. That aesthetic rests on an inclusive definition of American identity. As an artist, Angela is best known for her depictions of urban Americans, or "Fourteenth Street Types," in the novel's shorthand. She observes her subjects most often as they stand before a music store, where a player-piano operates in the window. Both the subjects and the music represent the ethnic diversity of Manhattan. But the singularly American music is jazz. As an artist Angela seeks to capture the noble and heroic in the lives of ordinary people. Her most fully realized piece represents the face of a black woman domestic worker, who worked for her family.

The novel ends in Angela's marriage rather than her fulfillment as an artist and its resolution of class issues is incomplete. But *Plum Bun* is a key statement of the challenges faced by women in the Harlem Renaissance. Like Bonner's essay, *Plum Bun* argues for a revised racial *and* gender identity for black Americans. In a social hierarchy that decreed that men should have power over women, whites over blacks, and rich over poor, it was courageous, if foolhardy for a poor black woman to aspire to be an artist. Only one who combined Angela's boldness and her sister Jinny's commitment to a goal greater than herself could hope for even a small measure of success. Jessie Fauset herself possessed this rare combination. She found publishers for her four novels: after *Plum Bun, The Chinaberry Tree* appeared in 1931 and *Comedy: American Style* in 1933, by which time Fauset had returned to the classroom.

Though not an artist herself, Helga Crane, the protagonist of Nella Larsen's *Quicksand*, has a refined aesthetic sense. She surrounds herself with exquisite things – a Chinese carpet, a brass bowl filled with nasturtiums, a silk-covered stool – which no one else at Naxos, a fictionalized counterpart of Tuskegee, where she teaches, can appreciate. Her love of books, sophisticated conversation, and fashion further set her apart. Her sense of "difference," which she attributes in part to her interracial parentage also derives from her quest for beauty. Thwarted in that quest, she herself becomes a beautiful object for her colleagues, her lovers, her Danish relatives, and the larger European community to which they belong. Helga collaborates in her objectification, not only because she enjoys the attention but because she is trapped in the quicksand of racist and sexist self-definitions.

Nella Larsen (1891–1964) interrogated such definitions in *Quicksand* (1928) and *Passing* (1929). Witty and cosmopolitan, she was already a fixture on the Harlem scene; her name, like Fauset's, turned up in the community's social pages. Born in Chicago and educated at Fisk University, Larsen was secretive about her past, though she acknowledged having a white mother and a black father. Her marriage provided a social pedigree. Her husband, Elmer Imes, was a physicist; his brother pastored an elite Harlem congregation. Though trained as a nurse, Larsen worked at the 135th Street Library, a literary nexus in the 1920s. To her friend Carl Van Vechten, she confided her desire to "catch that flying glimpse of the panorama" of her time, which she did by becoming a writer.[12] Her first effort, "Scandinavian Games," appeared in *The Brownies' Book*; she published two short stories under a pseudonym. *Quicksand* announced the arrival of one of the most accomplished novelists of the Harlem Renaissance.

The novel represents Helga's dissatisfaction with any of the options available to her as a middle-class black woman. She chafes against the constrictions of ladyhood: the stifling conformity of the bourgeoisie, vapidity of the social whirl, and sexual repression. Insecure about her background, she cannot easily claim or refuse her class status. On her quest to forge a fulfilling self-definition, she leaves Naxos for Chicago where she is too well educated for the available jobs. Arriving in Harlem she believes she has found a community of affluent, progressive, and like-minded New Negroes; she thinks she has come home.

That feeling is short-lived, because Harlem is "too cramped, too uncertain, too cruel."[13] Racial definitions are as confining as those of gender. Floundering in a maze of contradictions, these New Negroes are unable to confront themselves and their situation honestly. The peculiar demands of the Jazz Age further complicated matters. As more and more white New Yorkers, like Americans generally, were drawn to black culture – or at least what they believed to be black culture – the New Negroes felt compelled to increase their own identification with their traditions. Often as ignorant of these traditions as anyone else however, many embraced the popular imitations instead. Larsen uses a nightclub scene, an almost obligatory feature in Harlem novels, to examine the packaging of manufactured blackness. After the "extraordinary music" dies, Helga regains her composure: "She wasn't, she told herself, a jungle creature" (p. 59). None of the club's patrons were, of course. This image was nonetheless foisted on blacks as Harlem barrooms were refurbished to resemble African jungles; as bands, even the best ones like that of Duke Ellington, advertised the latest in "jungle music." It all made Harlem a more exotic tourist attraction. In Larsen's interpretation, the ersatz culture marketed to blacks as their own was clearly insufficient. It borrowed enough of the authentic traditions to retain some power, but it existed dysfunctionally in a vacuum. *Quicksand* satirizes the spectacle of these urbane, middle-class New Yorkers attempting to find their cultural roots in the basement of a Harlem speakeasy. For Helga, the artifice was repelling.

Despite the fact that Denmark promises "no Negroes, no problems, no prejudice," it in fact intensifies the pressure on Helga to define herself as exotic and "Other." Her relatives dress her in batik dresses, leopard-skin coats, feathers, furs, and glittering jewelry. She enjoys the clothes, the physical freedom, and the fact that her dark skin so despised in America makes her the source of endless fascination to the Danes. When she realizes that she has become the object of sexual fantasies, she feels rage and powerlessness. Like Josephine Baker, who became a sensation to European audiences for whom she personified the exotic, Helga attracts the attention of artists. Axel Olsen paints a portrait of Helga the subject does not recognize. Whether Baker recognized herself as drawn or sculpted by Paul Colin, Henri Laurens, Alexander Calder, and Picasso is not known. However, unlike Helga, Baker was able to mock the role of exotic primitive even as she played it. Helga remains a silent spectator. Eventually, haunted by the image of herself refracted in the European cultural mirror, she flees. Clinging to a few of the books and beautiful things which surrounded her in the opening scene, the protagonist ends up mired in the quicksand of racism, sexism, and poverty in the US South.

Larsen's second novel *Passing*, which followed quickly on the first, explored similar concerns, particularly the options available to affluent African American women. Most of its characters pass for white – even if only occasionally – and their survival depends on looking like the white matrons they pretend to be. Like its nineteenth-century precursors, William Wells Brown's *Clotel*, Charles Chesnutt's *The House Behind the Cedars*, and Frances Ellen Watkins Harper's *Iola Leroy, or the Shadows Uplifted*, *Passing* interrogates the meaning of race. Rather than an essential entity, it can be performed as "black" women put on and take off "whiteness." It uses two protagonists, Irene Redfield and Clare Kendry, to enact this drama and to represent the risks these performances entail.

Irene, the physician's wife from whose perspective the novel is told, perceives Clare's life as a series of performances. She relishes the rumors of the glamorous life that Clare allegedly leads after crossing into the white world. Fearful of losing her own place, she envies Clare's ability to evade the obsession with propriety that Bonner describes, but she would never dare to risk her social status. She perceives her friend as an aesthetic object: exquisite and golden. According to some critics, Irene desires Clare sexually.[14] An unreliable narrator, Irene does not acknowledge such desires; neither does she recognize that her own habit of passing as white for social convenience disqualifies her from judging Clare. Moreover, while Clare's survival depends literally on her ability to keep up appearances – were her racist husband to discover she is not white he would divorce her or worse – it is the same for the other female characters. Each relies on a husband for material possessions, security, and identity. Each reflects and is a reflection of her husband's class status. Clare's is merely an extreme version of a situation they all share. For Larsen's characters beauty is defined by whiteness and the accouterments of bourgeois life. They chafe against the limitations these impose, but lack the courage and means to challenge them. As the central metaphors of "quicksand" and "passing" indicate, these characters cannot overcome the constraints of race, gender, and class.

In a landmark essay, "Characteristics of Negro Expression" (1934), Hurston argued that "we each have our own standards of art, and thus we are all interested parties and so unfit to pass judgment upon the art concepts of others." She outlined principles of the black folk aesthetic. First and foremost was the primacy of drama. "Every phase of Negro life is highly dramatised," she wrote. "There is an impromptu ceremony always ready for every hour of life."[15] As an ethnographer, her task was to record those ceremonies; as a novelist, she would recreate them not to provide "local color," but to appropriate the ritualized improvisation that was at the core of the folk aesthetic. Secondly, Hurston named and defined the "will to adorn" that could appear to the eyes of outsiders as excess. She was happy to concede that "decorating a decoration" was the point. Behind this will to the beautiful was a "feeling" that "there can never be enough of beauty, let alone too much" (p. 834). Unlike most of her contemporaries, she defined and adopted an aesthetic that was predicated on the beauty she identified in black culture.

Born and raised in the South and attuned to its folkways, Hurston (1891–1960) was heir to the legacy inherent in the spirituals and blues, folk tales and sermons. Her experience of growing up in the all-black town of Eatonville, Florida, and her education, especially her training in anthropology at Barnard under the direction of Franz Boas, deepened her appreciation for an understanding of the culture of rural blacks. In four novels, two volumes of folklore, a memoir, scores of essays and short stories, and several plays, she represented their lives, theorized their culture, transcribed their language, and thus inspired, created a literary language of her own.

At a time when most social scientists and political leaders believed strongly in the inferiority of African people, Hurston's assertion of the linguistic richness of black culture was heretical and courageous. Conventional wisdom held that black people did not speak standard English because they could not. Some scholars attributed the failure to physiological differences between the races; others just believed in the intellectual differences. Hurston gave no quarter to such pseudo-science. Wielding a welter of examples from her fieldnotes, she asserted that African Americans had contributed to the development of the English language through the use of (1) metaphor and simile; (2) the double descriptive; and (3) verbal nouns. More important than the specific linguistic practices was the attitude toward language that they represent. Hurston saw in the "will to adorn" an experimental attitude toward language, a willingness among her informants to make things up and to make things new.

From 1927 to 1932 Hurston traveled throughout Florida, Alabama, and Louisiana. She published her findings in *Mules and Men* (1935), which in addition to the seventy folk tales it recounts, documents the everyday experiences of black Americans in the rural South. The tales do not exist apart from the lives of the people. Consequently, the book shows when and how, by and for whom tales are told. In addition to the Brer' Rabbit tales that previous collectors had highlighted, Hurston, who was the first African American to publish a volume of African American folklore, introduced the cycle of

John-and-Master tales in which the slave John frequently outwits his master. *Mules* presents storytelling in a context of work and play; an appendix contains "Negro songs with music." As if to confirm the observation that "there is an impromptu ceremony always ready for every hour of life," *Mules* reports cultural practices including card games and courtship rituals, lying sessions and religious rites – including rites of conjure or hoodoo, a pre-Christian belief system derived from African traditions that gave women spiritual authority. *Mules* is literature as well as ethnography. The protagonist, Zora, is a much more diffident character than her namesake; the most assertive character, Big Sweet, is a larger-than-life figure, who becomes Zora's guardian and guide.

Reflecting on her fieldwork, Hurston averred, "I picked up glints and gleams out of what I had and stored it way to turn to my own use."[16] The results are apparent in her first novel, *Jonah's Gourd Vine* (1934). Loosely based on the lives of her parents, it tells the story of Lucy and John Pearson's courtship and marriage, John's swift rise to prominence as a Baptist minister, his equally swift fall as a result of his marital infidelities, Lucy's strength and perseverance, and the family's ultimate dissolution. The "will to adorn" is evident on every page. "Ah means tuh prop you up on eve'y leanin' side" is a declaration of love.[17] "Ah got divorce in mah heels" puts action into words (p. 55). Ritualized improvisation is a principle at work in each interaction. John, who is a poet/prophet, preaches about a Judgment Day, "when de two trains of Time shall meet on de trestle / And wreck de burning axles of de unformed ether / And de mountains shall skip like lambs" (p. 181). At John's funeral, the eulogist evokes a Christian heaven but the drums and chants that respond to his sermon suggest an African spirituality. The performance alludes to a spiritual connection between Africa and African Americans, transmitted through music and memory. Black writers throughout the twentieth century would explore this connection. Yet too often the novel's profusion of metaphor and simile overshadows the plot. As Robert Hemenway asserts, *Jonah's Gourd Vine* is best understood as "a series of linguistic moments."[18]

Critics agree that *Their Eyes Were Watching God* is Hurston's masterpiece. From its opening scene, *Their Eyes* establishes its concern with the properties of words. "Burning statements" and "killing tools" resolve themselves into "a mood come alive. Words walking without masters; words walking together like harmony in a song."[19] The setting is the store porch, the liminal space Hurston often draws in her writing. Neither wholly public nor private, it fosters free expression for blacks whose labor is exploited during the day. For women however, it is not a safe space. The protagonist Janie Crawford is the object of the sitters' leering ridicule. *Their Eyes* emphasizes throughout the obstacles a woman faces in the struggle to gain a voice in a culture that places a premium on speaking.

Janie's quest for identity depends on her ability to speak herself into being. But she is thwarted by the presence of powerful speakers whose voices drown hers out. Her grandmother Nanny is an accomplished storyteller, skilled autobiographer, and inspired preacher, whose metaphors fuse the biblical and the domestic in arresting ways. "Ah wanted to preach a great sermon about colored women sittin' on high, but they wasn't no pulpit for me. Freedom found me wid a baby daughter in mah arms, so Ah said Ah'd take a broom and a cook-pot and throw up a highway through de wilderness for her" (p. 15). Nanny's experience as a slave limits her vision; the only freedom she can imagine is premised on the privileged life of her owners. Nevertheless her eloquence – and emotional blackmail – overwhelm Janie, who agrees to marry a man she does not love.

Janie's second husband, Joe Starks, helps her escape, but his ambition to be a "big voice" portends further unhappiness (p. 43). Even before he has consolidated his power as landlord, storekeeper, postmaster, and mayor of Eatonville, he claims the platform his growing status ensures. Joe becomes a great speechmaker. Though the townspeople admire his accomplishments, they find him overbearing. As one observes, "he loves obedience out of everybody under de sound of his voice" (p. 46). Everybody includes Janie. Joe's template for success is borrowed from the dominant society that oppresses him and his community. He uses his wife, as he does his big white house and accouterments of wealth, to mark the difference between himself and others. Janie tries to resist domination by both Nanny and Joe by forcing them to take her dreams seriously – particularly the vision of love and marriage that encapsulates her gift of metaphor as well as her idealism. But she fails. She is too diffident to challenge her grandmother, and her dependence on her husband is reinforced by his physical violence. Eventually she does "talk back" to Joe and reclaims a measure of her self-respect. But only after Joe dies is Janie free to devise a life of her own choosing.

Her partner in this new life is Tea Cake, a blues troubadour several years younger than she, who exemplifies the principles Hurston set forth in "Characteristics." Everything he does is acted out. Tea Cake makes a performance out of leaving a room. He plays an imaginary guitar after he pawns his real one and begs Janie's forgiveness by singing her a song. His speech is dipped-in-blues. Playful and erotic, their relationship is also egalitarian: they both work in the fields and do household chores. Ultimately, Janie must kill Tea Cake in order to save her own life. By the novel's end she overcomes the self-hatred that is the residue of racism and loosens the constraints of sexism. She assumes authority in and for her own life.

Hurston's project was to create a literary language informed by the perspective as well as the poetry of rural black southerners. While most critics have agreed that her ear was attuned to the poetry, they have debated whether Hurston represented the perspective accurately. Her black male contemporaries thought not. They faulted her books for an alleged lack of racial militancy. Alain Locke, for example, wrote that *Their Eyes* was an "oversimplification" of southern black life and wondered when Hurston would "come to grips with motive fiction and social document fiction." Richard Wright offered a more hostile response. He wrote in *New Masses* that the novel lacked a theme "that lends itself to serious interpretation." He located it instead in the tradition of minstrelsy, a tradition that "Miss Hurston *voluntarily* continues ... Her characters eat and laugh and cry and work and kill; they swing like a pendulum eternally in that safe and narrow orbit in which America likes to see the Negro live: between laughter and tears."[20]

Defining the novel in essence as one of feeling rather than of ideas was, from Wright's masculinist perspective, another way of saying that *Their Eyes* is a woman's story. The feminists who initially reclaimed Hurston's novel clearly responded to its politics, a politics of gender to which Wright was oblivious. Subsequent critics have found in the novel a wealth of commentary on the politics of race, ethnicity, and culture.[21] Hurston was determined not to create characters according to type – minstrel or otherwise. Her decision to concentrate on intraracial community rather than interracial conflict was similarly deliberate. She was more interested in probing "that which the soul lives by" than in documenting the oppression and exploitation that defined the material existence of most African Americans in the 1930s. Even her most ardent admirers have wished that she had acknowledged more explicitly the then unyielding power of the forces of oppression. And yet, Hurston represented the reality that the most insidious aspect of racism is the extent to which its victims internalize the attitudes of their oppressors. Nanny, Joe Starks, and eventually even Tea Cake begin to take their measure from the society that holds them in contempt. The deepest wounds of oppression, whether of racism, sexism, or class, are those that scar the soul.

NOTES

1. Jessie Fauset, *There Is Confusion* (1924; Boston: Northeastern University Press, 1989), p. 97.
2. Signal histories of the Harlem Renaissance include Nathan Huggins, *Harlem Renaissance* (New York: Oxford University Press, 1971) and David Levering Lewis, *When Harlem Was in Vogue* (New York: Knopf, 1981). For literary and

cultural interpretations, see Houston Baker, *Modernism and the Harlem Renaissance* (Chicago: University of Chicago Press, 1987); Ann Douglas, *Terrible Honesty* (New York: Farrar, Straus, and Giroux, 1995); and George Hutchinson, *The Harlem Renaissance in Black and White* (Cambridge, MA: Harvard University Press, 1995).

3. For biographical information, see Lorraine Roses and Ruth E. Randolph, *Harlem Renaissance and Beyond* (Boston: G. K. Hall, 1990). For extended analyses, see Gloria Hull, *Color, Sex, and Poetry: Three Women Writers of the Harlem Renaissance* (Bloomington: Indiana University Press, 1987) and Cheryl A. Wall, *Women of the Harlem Renaissance* (Bloomington: Indiana University Press, 1995).

4. "On Being Young – a Woman – and Colored," *Frye Street & Environs: The Collected Works of Marita Bonner* (Boston: Beacon Press, 1987), p. 5. Subsequent references to this edition will be cited parenthetically in the text.

5. *When and Where I Enter* (New York: William Morrow, 1984), p. 183.

6. "Tracing Shadows," *The Crisis* (Sept. 1915), pp. 247–51; "Yarrow Revisited," *The Crisis* (Jan. 1925), pp. 107–9; "Dark Algiers the White," *The Crisis* (April 1925), pp. 16–20 and (May 1925), pp. 16–22.

7. "Pastures New," *The Crisis* (Sept. 1920), p. 224.

8. *The Crisis* (Nov. 1910), p. 10. See David L. Lewis, *W. E. B. Du Bois: Biography of a Race, 1868–1919* (New York: Henry Holt, 1993), chapters 15, 17.

9. Anne Spencer, "Substitution," *Time's Unfading Garden: Anne Spencer's Life and Poetry*, ed. J. Lee Greene (Baton Rouge: Louisiana State University Press, 1977), p. 176.

10. Gwendolyn Bennett, "Fantasy," *Shadowed Dreams: Women's Poetry of the Harlem Renaissance*, ed. Maureen Honey (New Brunswick, NJ: Rutgers University Press, 1989), p. 159.

11. Jessie Fauset, *Plum Bun* (1928; Boston: Beacon Press, 1990), p. 78. Subsequent references to this edition will be cited parenthetically in the text.

12. Quoted in Wall, *Women of the Harlem Renaissance*, p. 93. See Thadious Davis, *Nella Larsen: Novelist of the Harlem Renaissance* (Baton Rouge: Louisiana State University Press, 1994).

13. *"Quicksand" and "Passing"*, ed. Deborah McDowell (1928 and 1929; New Brunswick, NJ: Rutgers University Press, 1986), p. 96. Subsequent references will be cited parenthetically in the text.

14. Deborah McDowell, Introduction to *"Quicksand" and "Passing"*, pp. xxvi–xxxi.

15. In Cheryl A. Wall (ed.), *Zora Neale Hurston: Folklore, Memoirs, and Other Writings* (New York: Library of America, 1995), p. 830. Subsequent references will be cited parenthetically in the text.

16. *Dust Tracks on a Road* (1942; New York: HarperCollins, 1991), p. 51.

17. *Jonah's Gourd Vine* (1934; New York: HarperCollins, 1990), p. 79. Subsequent references will be cited parenthetically in the text.

18. Robert Hemenway, *Zora Neale Hurston: A Literary Biography* (Urbana: University of Iuinois Press, 1977), p. 192.

19. *Their Eyes Were Watching God* (1937; New York: HarperCollins, 1990), p. 2.

20. Locke, "Literature By and About the Negro," *Opportunity*, 1 June 1938; Richard Wright, "Between Laughter and Tears," *New Masses*, 5 October 1937, pp. 22, 25.

21. For a range of critical perspectives, see Michael Awkward (ed.), *New Essays on "Their Eyes Were Watching God"* (New York: Cambridge University Press, 1990), Henry Louis Gates and K. Anthony Appiah (eds.), *Zora Neale Hurston, Critical Perspectives Past and Present* (New York: Amistad/Penguin, 1993), and Cheryl A. Wall (ed.), *Zora Neale Hurston's "Their Eyes Were Watching God" A Casebook* (New York: Oxford University Press, 2000).

3

ELEANOR W. TRAYLOR

Women writers of the Black Arts movement

> Let uh revolution come.
> Couldn't be no action like what
> I dun already seen.
> – Carolyn M. Rodgers (1969)

The reimagination of America, the overarching project of the 1960s and 1970s Black Arts movement (BAM), remains its continuing legacy. This project emphasized the discovery that "there is no American literature; there are American literatures ... [by] those who have their roots in the most ancient civilizations – African, Asian, Mexican [,]... Native American... [and] the literature of the European settlement regime ..."[1] This study examines the work of black women writers in poetry, drama, fiction, autobiography, and theoretical essays as it highlights the deep implication and outcomes of that discovery. In *Black Fire*, the signal anthology of the period, Amiri Baraka and Larry Neal introduce "the founding fathers and mothers of our nation."[2] The founding mothers, with other vanguard women writers, strengthen the revolutionary ferment of the movement to resonate its themes: a renegotiation of power relations between black and white America, a disturbance of ideological imperatives of identity, and a re-direction of the sources for literary production. They also interject another theme: a renegotiation of the power relations between black men and women – itself a revolutionary advent.

Reimaginations pervade in the poetry, drama, fiction, autobiography, and theoretical essays of black women writers accentuating and being accentuated by the Black Arts movement. As Carolyn Gerald – black aesthetic theorist – argues, "Image making is part of the human experience ... We are speaking here of the image created by the magic of words."[3] Ending a theoretical essay with a poem encoding its central theme, Gerald exclaims:

> Dress the muse in black...
> No!
> Kill her!

> Now
> We'll find our own saint
> (or another name for her)
> No need for hell's fire now
> The fire's weak
> And burned out
> The Universe is black again.   (p. 356)

Gerald's 1969 essay, "The Black Writer and His Role," may be read as a response to the question addressed in Nikki Giovanni's "Reflections on April 4, 1968" – a prose poem which nudges Gerald's pronoun (the male-centered "his"). The question resonates over the era:

> What can I, a poor Black Woman, do to destroy america? This is the question, with appropriate variation, being asked in every Black heart. There is one answer. I can kill. There is one compromise – I can protect those who kill. There is one cop-out – I can encourage others to kill. There are no other ways.
>
>   The assassination of Martin Luther King is an act of war.[4]

A purpose blazes:

> ...We seek the freedom of free men
> And the construction of a world
> Where Martin Luther King could have lived
> and preached non-violence.[5]

An ultimatum is declared:

> We must prepare
> For Operation Total Victory
> Step One
> Shave and a haircut free
> For Miss America.[6]

Women's "voice prints,"[7] reverberating the time, trace two concepts necessary to the reimagination of America: black power and black art. "One is concerned with the relationship between art and politics; the other with the art of politics."[8]

Inspired by the liberatory goals of both concepts, as Gwendolyn Brooks reminds us, women writers of the BAM entered every literary genre and constructed a language that took poetry to the taverns, streets, bars, housing projects, libraries, prisons, parks, newly founded theaters, and time-honored churches; language that redirected the conventional expectations of the stage; that interrupted the familiar story told in autobiography; that introduced new discourses, reconstructed the generic expectations of fiction; and that set the premises of theoretically invested essays. Like any artist inspired by the spirit of the era, the work of women writers engaged the enterprise of "reversing the power relation between black and white America."[9] That reversal involved "killing" the premises that have supported a racist concept of two Americas, one white and one black. The decapitation of that concept is the urgency of Carolyn Gerald's image as she affirms Larry Neal's account of "the real impulse in back of the [Black Power/]Black Arts Movement, which is the will toward self-determination and nationhood, a radical reordering of the nature and function of art."[10] In that sense, Gwendolyn Brooks's salute to Chicago-based Black Arts poet, theorist and institution builder Don L. Lee (later Haki Madhubuti) is cogent:

> Don Lee wants
> not a various America
> Don Lee wants
> a new Nation
> under nothing ...
> wants
> new art and anthem; will
> want a new music screaming in the sun.[11]

Understood as a "Declaration of Independence" in America to revolutionize thought in the public sphere, direction in philosophical inquiry, and practice in artistic production, the Black Arts movement may be read from a postmillennial view as a revision of the terms of self-identification and of social, economic, and political existence. This Declaration coheres in a moment when two words were reborn to conjure ever-continuing discourses. If, as Haki Madhubuti has put it, "into the sixties a word was born," the word was *Black*; that word had been born by 1903 in a self-referential encyclical entitled *The Souls of Black Folk*, by a father of non-traditional thought, W. E. B. Du Bois. If into the seventies a word was born, that word was *Woman*; it had been parented around 1851 by a mother of non-traditional thought in a question as resonant now as then – "Ain't I a woman?" – raised by the self-named Sojourner Truth. Through both words, *Black* and *Woman*, "an emphasis is paroled," as phrased by a spirit guide and mentee of the movement, Gwendolyn Brooks, in her poem "The Wall."[12] The emphasis, *Black Feeling, Black Talk* (1968), the title of the first collection of poems by Nikki Giovanni, became the subject of world-scapes of thought inspiring yet evolving conversations. And by 1970 when the words embrace – as in *The Black Woman: An Anthology*, by Toni Cade [Bambara] – alternative ways of reading and writing the world which anticipate terms now labeled *postmo-dern*, *post-structuralist*, *postcolonial* offer emphatic critiques in the works of women writers of the Black Arts movement and their antecedents. A declaration of self-determined, liberational aspirations expressed in theory, poetry, fiction, dramatic arts, music, dance, painting, sculpture, and textiles, the Black Arts movement – heir of an always already non-traditional legacy in thought and production – responded to a call issued in 1942 by spirit guide Margaret Walker Alexander. Her now famous poem "For My People" sings, "Let the martial songs be written, let the dirges disappear."[13]

Like the Declaration of 1776, the Declaration issued by the Black Arts movement of the 1960s enunciated a deep desire, as phrased by Gwendolyn Brooks, "to assume a sovereignty ourselves."[14] And as re-sounded by Nikki Giovanni in "Love Poem (for Real)":

> … it's a question of power
> which we must wield
> if it is not
> to be wielded
> against
> us.[15]

The "we" of the poem in 1967 responds, as many poems of the period do, to the 1964 "SOS" call – "calling black people / calling all black people, man woman, child / wherever you are"[16] – of brother poet Amiri Baraka (LeRoi Jones), theorist, dramatist, novelist, institution builder, namer, and heralded founder of the Black Arts movement, along with poet-theorists Larry Neal, Askia Mohammed Touré, and others. It also anticipates the wake-up alarm of the sonorous voice of Nina Simone in her 1972 release *Emergency Ward!*. "Recorded live in concert at various locations including Fort Dix," the choral arrangement of *Emergency Ward!* is exemplar of one aspiration of the BAM: an erasure of distance between performer and audience. The album opens with the rousing chant of a participatory audience intoning "We want Nina," segues to the *Al-le-luia* of the Bethany Baptist Church Mass Choir, from which the wailing voice of Nina Simone soars singing, "Lord, I wanna see you" for "today is a killer."[17]

Choral assent to solo voices – like that distinctive of the black church – summoning a sovereign black subject to agency in life and in art marks the contemporary turn in the performative and literary arts. This choral assent sounding a "We the People" characterizes the genius of BAM musicians and poets, just as it figures the response of a critical consensus necessary to the ratification of a will to self-determined government. Music – the transcommunal, transcontinental communicant of the transgressive black voice summoning multitudes of respondents – now predominantly influences and is influenced by the liberatory spirit of the spoken word. Nikki Giovanni reports it in "Revolutionary Music":

> While the mighty mighty impressions have told the
> world
> for once and for all
> "We're a Winner"
> even our names – le roi has said – are together
> impressions
> temptations
> supremes
> delfonics
> miracles
> intruders (i mean intruders?)
> not beatles and animals and white bad things like
> young rascals and shit
> we be digging all
> our revolutionary music consciously or un
> cause sam cooke said "a change is gonna come."[18]

Poetry

When poetry entered the public spaces heretofore the domain of the music and from theaters newly founded by black artists and entrepreneurs, a paradigm shift occurred. Sonia Sanchez recalls that

> at The Black Arts Repertory Theatre, I heard, on a Sunday afternoon, Abbey Lincoln, Sister Aminata Lincoln ask the question, "Who will revere the Black woman?" I still see her, coming in with the most beautiful natural [afro] and discussing this out loud there at that place. I still see people lining up outside on the block there in Harlem in front of that brownstone, waiting to get inside in order to come and see some of Baraka's plays or to come and hear some of us read our poetry.[19]

The public arts – spoken word poetry and drama – fulfilled another aspiration of the BAM: to evoke a consciousness of something called the *self* and, from that site, to create an identity called *one people*. Only that identity would forge awareness that … "whenever any form of Government becomes destructive, … it is the Right of the People to alter or abolish it, and to institute new Government, laying its foundation on such principles and organizing its powers in such form, as to them shall seem most likely to effect their Safety and Happiness …"[20] Confident of the mission to call into being a self-reflexive consciousness rooted in an oral and written heritage of liberational thought and cultural production, BAM poets proclaimed a "community of memory,"[21] as heard in Nikki Giovanni's "My Poem":

> if i never write
> another poem
> or short story
> ....
> or do a meaningful
> black thing
> it won't stop
> the revolution
> the revolution
> is in the streets
> and ... if i never do
> anything
> it will go on.[22]

Not only did the revolution go on, its revolutionary impulses fulfilled an urgent requisite necessary to the achievement of any literature.

The popularity of poetry and its huge achievement during the era are forecast by black poet and pioneering cultural critic Sterling A. Brown, who introduced the study of black folklore into the academy during the 1940s at Howard University. As early as 1930, in his essay "Our Literary Audience," Brown emphasizes one inescapable determinant of artistic achievement: "I refer to the Negro artist's audience within his own group ... [T]hose who might be or should be a fit audience for the Negro artists are ... by and large, fundamentally out of sympathy with his aim and his general development ..."[23] Like Whitman, Brown (re-)pronounces the determinant: "*without great audiences we cannot have a great literature*" (p. 78, italics added). In addition to developing an audience, Black Arts poetry and drama, "[e]mphasizing the oral and performative traditions of African Americans, particularly such Vernacular Practice as 'rapping,' 'signifying,' 'sounding,' and 'running it down,' ... created a public cultural space for the later emergence of 'hip hop' and 'spoken word' poetry."[24] As Angela Jackson, Black Arts poet of Chicago's Organization of Black American Culture (OBAC), points out: "popular culture and its touchstones are where day-to-day memory is posited and reposited. As a poet, I live in popular and 'high' culture and all that lives above and between ... I subvert popular culture and pose moral and ethical questions that arise out of my conflict with popular culture's stereotypes and communal symbols and myths."[25]

The posing of moral and ethical questions pervading the poetry of vanguard Black women writers emerging in the 1960s – such as Nikki Giovanni, Sonia Sanchez, Carolyn Rodgers, June Jordan, Alice Walker, Sherley Anne

Williams, Sarah Webster Fabio, Audre Lorde, Elouise Loftin, Jayne Cortez, Jewel Latimore (Johari Amini), Barbara Simmons, Julia Fields, Carol Freeman, Rikki Lights, and Jackson herself – enjoins the practice of senior poets writing before and with them: Gwendolyn Brooks, Margaret Walker, Maya Angelou, Mari Evans, Margaret Danner, Margaret Burroughs, Pinkie Gordon Lane, and Naomi Long Madgett. Through subverting imposed identity and exposing what James Baldwin in *Notes of a Native Son* (1955) has called *theologies* which deny one life[26] and what Jean-Francoise Lyotard, following later in *The Postmodern Condition* (1979), called *les grands recits* (loosely translated, the master narratives), the poetry of the period also led to "self-generating standards and unflinching critical evaluation."[27] Establishing what Houston Baker, following philosopher Albert Hofstadter, calls "a reference public"[28] and what Stephen Henderson in *Understanding the New Black Poetry* had called a "Soul Field,"[29] the poetry of black women writers intersected that of men to assume the common literary project of the BAM, even as it "adjudicate[d] competing claims."[30] From OBAC poet Carolyn Rodgers, we hear:

> I've had tangled feelings lately
> About everything
> About writing poetry, and other forms
> . . . .
> How do I put my self on pages
> The way I want to be or am and be
> Not like any one else in this
> Black world but me.[31]

Working through this same dilemma, addressing a popular reference public during the 1960s, poetry itself discovered its own identity as *black*. Moreover, in doing so, it awakened a complementary revolutionary project for social examination and literary experimentation: a renegotiation of the power relationship between men and women.

Like the anguished cry for "Black Power" uttered in 1966 by civil rights worker and president of the Student Non-Violent Coordinating Committee (SNCC), Stokely Carmichael (later Kwame Toure), the mournful cry of Nina Simone sobbing, "The King! The King of Love is dead!" at the Westbury Music Fair in a concert which became the LP entitled *Nuff Said* (1968), is a marker of the turn which Cheryl Clark calls "the loss of lyric space" in black women's poetry.[32] For Clark, that loss expressed in a line from Gwendolyn Brooks's pivotal poem "In the Mecca" (1968) – "we part from all we knew of love" – is also indicated by Brooks's abandonment of the sonnet form. Like the freedom songs of the civil rights movement as recorded by Bernice

Johnson Reagon and Sweet Honey in the Rock, the poetry of black women writers of the period builds upon the oral traditional genius of the African American folk, the incomparable lyricism of the spirituals, sorrow songs and gospels (some arranged and composed by Thomas A. Dorsey and his sister Bernice Dorsey Johnson). In 1968, the year of "In the Mecca," Audre Lorde's *First Cities*, Nikki Giovanni's *Black Feeling, Black Thought*, Carolyn Rodgers's *Paper Soul*, and Alice Walker's *Once* lead the recovery of the dynamic lyrical voice of African poetic practices.

What histories report and what the poetry of the BAM reflects as disillusionment in the mid 1960s contextualize the turn from an "ebb tide of hope" to a "flood tide" of revolutionary black consciousness.[33] As Houston Baker explains, "After the arrests, bombings, and assassinations that comprised the white South's reaction to nonviolent, direct-action protests by hundreds of thousands of Civil Rights workers, ... it was difficult for even the most committed optimist to feel that integration was an impending American social reality."[34]

The time had come, as Alice Walker phrases it, for "Rebellious. Living. / Against the Elemental Crush."[35] And, as sung by Maya Angelou, marking one of the most violent acts of the 1960s:

> Ministers make Novena with the
> Charred bones of four
> Very small
> Very black
> Very young children...[36]

Ironically, the "loss of lyric space" may be measured in part by the effulgence of two epic poems: Margaret Walker's *Prophets for a New Day* (completed in 1968 but published in 1970) and Gwendolyn Brooks's "In the Mecca." Both embrace the full encounter of African American poetry with Euro-American (western) traditional forms. Opening with the voice of a child singing, "We're hoping to go to jail," *Prophets for a New Day* proceeds through twenty-two poems composing a panegyric – including pastoral, monody, biblical antitype, and a plenitude of elegiac stanza – to immortalize the heroes of the civil rights movement. The eighth-century prophet Amos becomes Martin Luther King (assassinated in 1968); Andy Goodman, Michael Schwerner, and James Chaney (young white and black civil rights workers, murdered) become "Three leaves / Floating in the melted snow / Flooding the Spring." Malcolm (inspirational voice of the BAM, assassinated in 1965) becomes a "dying swan," singing most beautifully at his death.[37]

By comparison, "In the Mecca," rising from an epigraph – "Then comes a time when what has been can never be again" – opens with the voice of an oracle commanding, "Sit where the light corrupts your face. / Mies Van der Rohe retires from grace. / And the fair fables fall."[38] The epic of the "Mecca," in 813 lines, travels through all the spaces of western prosodic traditions as it unwinds the mystery of a missing girl. Cheryl Clark reads the poem beautifully in *"After Mecca": Women Poets and the Black Arts Movement* (2005) to disclose how "the fair fables" fell under the pen of the BAM. In a fourteen-line disturbance of the traditional sonnet, Mari Evans provides the clue to the mystery in her poem "I Am a Black Woman": "I / am a black woman… / defying place / and time / and circumstance / assailed / impervious / indestructible / Look / on me and be / renewed."[39] Indeed, new sources for poetic energy appear in diction, syntax, structure; in a compression of verse forms such as Japanese *haiku* and *tanka*, and *sonku* (created by Sonia Sanchez); in an introduction of black geographical regions, neighborhoods, sites of contemplation and community action; in the rites of young girls becoming black women; in subjective agency; in praise poems, African style, in spoken-word performance poetry; and in inscapes of the heart. This embrace of non-western traditional poetic sources highlights the poetry of BAM women poets, and startling images, such as "revolutionary petunias" (Alice Walker), a "blue / black magical woman" (Sanchez), and a "black unicorn" (Audre Lorde) redirect traditional expectations. From roughly 1967 to 1978, homage to her warrior-women – from Fannie Lou Hamer and Ella Baker and Rosa Parks back to Harriet Tubman – and her writerly women – from Phillis Wheatley forward – and tributes to her civil rights and Black Arts heroes ascend in black women's poetry. And the invention of forms to inscribe her and him – chanting, wailing, "improvisating," drawing upon black speech and black music – what Stephen Henderson calls "The Forms of Things Unknown"[40] – accounts for the technical suasion of black women poets of the BAM. The sense conveyed in this "Afro femme"[41] poetic outpouring may be best represented in the consciousness singing through the title words of Sonia Sanchez's first and second collections of poetry: *Homecoming* (1969) and *We a BaddDDD People* (1970).

Drama/performance arts

As heard from the stage of the New Lafayette Theatre (and others), BAM cultural producers – in this case playwrights – assumed a role and announced an identity in literature henceforth defined as *contemporary*. For the stage and for independent film, the contemporary "involves the enormous task of reconstructing cultural memory, of revitalizing usable traditions of cultural practices, and of resisting the wholesale and unacknowledged appropriation of cultural items – such as music, language style, posture – by the industry that then attempts to suppress the roots of it..."[42] That task created a paradigmatic reordering of the shape and communicative systems of the stage, a reordering characterized by emphatic shifts from the conventional uses of the proscenium arch required by the well-made play to a "thrown open stage … a breaking through any fixed time [to] keep the hook-up of past and present fluid,"[43] from "textual reliance to extratextual improvisational acts responsive to the call of the spirit,"[44] from "*mimesis*, or representation of an action, to *methexis*, or communal 'helping out' of the action by all assembled, … a process that could be described alternatively as a shift from *drama* – the spectacle observed – to *ritual* – the event which dissolves traditional divisions between actor and spectator, between self and other,"[45] from "recollecting the disremembered past to recentering and revalidating the self … to centralizing the voice, experience, and culture of women."[46] The title character of Sonia Sanchez's *Sister Son/Ji* (1969) voices that project: "today i shall bring back yesterday as it can never be today. as it shd be tomorrow."[47]

Women playwrights anticipate much of the purpose and practice of theater developing in the 1960s and beyond. As a voice of Harlem's American Negro Theatre (ANT), established in 1940, Alice Childress created a consciousness-raising drama grounded in the mission of the ANT: to "avoid conventional Broadway-born clichés; to say something significant and meaningful to the people … putting to artful use the fluency and rhythm that lie in the Negro's special gifts."[48] In Childress's *Trouble in Mind* (1955), Millicent realizes the lie of the roles into which she has been cast and rebels. The lie of the roles and the agonizing struggle to peel away the masks that obfuscate a black consciousness – the desire for wholeness – surrounds the theater of Adrienne Kennedy, specifically in *Funnyhouse of a Negro* (1964) and the *The Owl Answers* (1965). What hopefully *could not be* brought back was the fate of the ANT: its success was its demise. When its well-honed, committed main repertory company – " 'Harlem's Company' – took its *Anna Lucasta* to Broadway, there to experience a great hit, the company never came back."[49] What *could be* brought back was the memory of brutality suffered by a people, seen when James Baldwin's powerful protest drama, *Blues for Mister Charlie* (1964), memorialized fourteen-year-old Emmett Till, lynched in Mississippi in 1955. What *never can be again* is the protest genre epitomized by Baldwin's *Blues*; that genre now metamorphosed as the theater of revolt – the reordering of the Black Arts movement. What *could be* brought back was the genius of Lorraine Hansberry in centralizing the black family as a source for powerful dramatic discourse. What *could not* be brought back was the integrationist dream of the Younger family in her *A Raisin in the Sun* (1959).

For the theater, *Blues* and *Raisin* apotheosize the aspirations of the nonviolent civil rights movement and forecast the arrival of a revolutionary stage re-dressed in the forms of other genres. One of these, the *agit/prop* (agitation and propaganda) system of communications of the BAM, is exemplified in three plays of Sonia Sanchez: *Sister Son/Ji* (1969), *The Bronx Is Next* (1968), and *Uh Uh, But How Do It Free Us?* (1974). These plays directly address black urban communities, issuing challenges to "clean-up your act" and "reach out and touch" in the enterprise of consciousness-raising. Another genre, the *gospel musical*, drawing from the call-and-response modalities of the black church, is the mode of dramaturges Vinette Caroll and Micki Grant in such productions as *Don't Bother Me, I Can't Cope* (1972) and *Your Arms Too Short to Box with God* (1975). These musicals embrace the community, call it to pride and exultation in its own creative productions: music, dance, word-magic.

For Amiri Baraka, foremost theorist of the Black Arts movement, "the revolutionary theatre, even if it is Western, must be anti-Western."[50] Such a theatre, like *the folk play* previously explored by Negro dramaturges, now becomes reimagined to fulfill Black Arts aspirations. The folk play was congruent to the goals of the Black Arts movement as it stepped away "from the straight line, build-to-crisis at the end of the scene, Western formula which is complementary to the capitalist mode: Time is money; ergo jump it ... and get back to the office."[51] The pioneers of the folk play, though not necessarily sharing the political objectives of the revolutionary theatre, are, unarguably, Zora Neale Hurston – one of the most salient rediscoveries of the BAM – and Langston Hughes, exemplar poet and theorist of the New Negro movement or Harlem Renaissance of the 1920s. Anticipating this evolution in the development of Negro/black theater, Zora Neale Hurston foreshadowed Baraka's paradigm of BAM theater as early as 1934, when she advised: "To those who want to institute the Negro Theatre, let me say it is already established... The real Negro Theatre is in the jooks and the cabarets. Self-conscious individuals may turn away the eye and say, let us search elsewhere for our dramatic art. Let'em search, they certainly won't find it."[52] *Mule Bone* (1930), the collaboration of Hurston and Hughes, resulted in "a treasury of folklore, filled with proverbs, riddles, dance, song, story-telling, call-response, children's games, and a language rich in imagery and polyrhythms."[53] By 1964, James Baldwin had contemporized the folk play, adapting it to problematize parochial roles in African American (and wider) life and art practices. His *The Amen Corner* (1964) situates Sister Margaret in the pastoral role additionally occupied by men. Building on *Mule Bone* and Baldwin's *The Amen Corner*, experimental responses to the uses of the folk drama during the BAM continued in the productions of Val Gray Ward, director of the Kuumba Theatre and the ETA Creative Arts Foundation under the foundership of Abena Joan Brown in Chicago; it resonates in the smart-talk-teaching one-woman performances of Sarah Webster Fabio, in the rites of a young girl's passage to become an artist in J. E. Franklin's *Black Girl* (1971), and in various discourse-making dramas of the period by women playwrights as diverse as Jean Wheeler Smith, Lucy M. Walker, P. J. Gibson, Regina O'Neal, Beah Richards, Sharon Stockard Martin, Abbey Lincoln, Elaine Jackson, Carol Freeman, and Ann Flagg.

And yet, what fired the imagination of dramaturges – among them Barbara Ann Teer, founder of the National Black Theatre and the Temple of Liberation in 1968; Glenda Dickerson, professor and director; Ntozake Shange, poet, linguist, and novelist – was the idea of a "consciousness-raising [theatre...] characterized as either *rituals* or revivals, not plays"[54] (italics added). The National Black Theatre pioneered "the creation of a black theory of acting and liberating" (p. 87). For Barbara Ann Teer, "when one is sincerely interested in dealing with the roots of blackness and of black life-style, it is impossible to deal with those roots without dealing with Africa" (p. 86). As a liberatory mode and as a performance style, ritual infused BAM experimental theater. "Dance and drums preceded the word ... magic/ religion came before 'criticism,' and words (*Nommo*) were the trappings of not one but thousands of spirits. Centuries before the 'literary capitals' of London, Paris, and New York, Ife in Nigeria was the home of the Necromancers, heavier than Solomon, conjurers of dread and joy."[55] These words of Ishmael Reed, prefacing his 1970 anthology *19 Necromancers*, illuminate Carolyn Gerald's observation: "when a self-definition has pre-ceded spontaneously, the literature will reflect not only group consciousness, shared points of view, common ancestry, common destiny and aspirations, but it reflects these in spiritual oneness with whatever natural/or supernatural powers preside over and guide that destiny."[56] If black theater, like black poetry, "served no other purpose, it would prove invaluable for the steps it had already taken to legitimize for the illegitimate all phases and facets of their lives."[57] In other words, rather than accepting an imposed identity, Black Arts dramatists engaged the task of reconstructing cultural memory and revitalizing usable traditions of cultural practice in the enterprise of inspiring group consciousness and a pride of identity.

Drum, dance, and mask as identifying features of African and diasporic performance had long informed the creative imaginations of choreographers such as Katherine Dunham and Pearl Primus, who had found inspiration in the Caribbean and Africa during the 1930s and 1940s and whose influence has informed subsequent African American dance companies and theaters. In fact, such companies as the National Dance Theatre Company of Jamaica under the direction of Rex Nettleford, the Ghana Dance Ensemble under the direction of Albert Opoku and Grace Nuamah, and Haitian troupes inspired by Lavinia Williams shared reciprocity with the Alvin Ailey Company and those of Rod Rogers, Eleo Pomare, Diane McIntyre, and many other Black Arts artists. The dance motifs of these troupes infused Black Arts Ritual Theatre. Much earlier, as historian James Hatch reports, the African influence on "[e]very tide of liberation for Black America has thrown up waves of renewed interest in folk customs of African origin."[58] Yet in the theater of the early twentieth century, "the single greatest tribute to Africa was organized and written by W. E. B. Du Bois," whose *The Star of Ethiopia* (1913), a pageant, was set in an Egyptian Art temple with painting, sculpture, and other works by colored people.[59] In the Black Arts era, the rising tide of independent African states, intensification of the struggle against *apartheid* in South Africa following the Sharpeville Massacre, opposition to America's racial politics even after the sweep of the civil rights movement, as in Nikki Giovanni's performance poem, and American intervention in liberational efforts from the Congo to Vietnam impacted an aesthetic movement seeking to link "artistic expression more directly to the collective political activity that would hasten social change."[60]

The response of women dramaturges to a performance style, an ensemble rather than a star system, which, in the words of Teer, would "create an alternative system of values to the western concept [and create] a black theory of acting and liberation,"[61] is reflective of the objective of BAM ritual theater. Speaking of the chauvinism of the English language, Ntozake Shange resounds a Black Arts practice: "our métier is improvisation ... a learned response, a highly complicated intellectual, spiritual, and aesthetic response to the loss of control of our lives and our languages."[62] Her 1975 choreopoem, "for colored girls who have considered suicide/when the rainbow is enough" – a stunning example of the renegotiation of power relations between men and women – breaks through patriarchal colonizing attitudes and actions, just as Audre Lorde's 1978 collection of poems, *The Black Unicorn*, exposes homophobic notions of identity. Moreover, the choreopoem exemplifies most splendidly what Amiri Baraka, speaking of ritual theater, defined as *Bopera*: "poetry, heightened rhythmic speech but not outside the events of everyday life ... motion, games, ritual, form, and content at once. Lights, Music, Dance, Sets, Speech ... so that the social 'use' of the experience we are creating gets registered on several levels."[63]

In an account of his arrival, "Uptown Harlem", leading to the establishment and naming of the Black Arts Repertory Theatre, Amiri Baraka (then LeRoi Jones) remembers that "when we came up out of the subway, March 1965, cold and clear, Harlem all around us staring us down, we felt like pioneers of the new order." The arrival, he recounts, "can only be summed up by the feeling jumping out of Césaire's *Return to My Native Land* or Fanon's *The Wretched of the Earth* or Cabral's *Return to the Source*."[64] By recalling

Aimé Césaire, Martinician poet, dramatist, and essayist, Baraka invokes one of the three herald poets of the Negritude movement in France during the 1930s, which had been inspired by the Harlem Renaissance. Césaire, later mayor of Fort-de-France; Léon Damas of French Guyana; and Léopold Sédar Senghor, later President of Senegal, had, as students in Paris, infused black consciousness as subject and as stylistic prosody in French poetry. By recalling Frantz Fanon, Algerian psychiatrist and philosopher hailed as a founding theorist of postcolonial studies, Baraka is pointing to his alignment with Fanon's caveat that "[de]colonization is the veritable creation of newmen ...; the 'thing' which has been colonized becomes man during the same process by which it frees itself."[65] Likewise, by recalling the poet and essayist Amilcar Cabral, he is modeling the fierce freedom fighter's participation in the struggle for the liberation of Guinea-Bissau. In sum, he is signifying the international consciousness and reach of his generation. Baraka's account inspires Kalamu Ya Salaam (formerly Val Ferdinand) in his valuable entry in *The Oxford Companion to African American Literature* – delineating events and organizations antecedent of the Black Arts movement, its outgrowth across the country, key participants, editors, journals, books, theories, and practices – to consider the "arrival" of Jones in Harlem as "the symbolic birth of the Black Arts Movement."[66] Interestingly, Larry Neal recalls that "in the spring of 1964, Le Roi Jones, Charles Patterson, William Patterson, Clarence Reed, Johnny Moore, and a number of other artists opened the Black Arts Repertory Theatre School."[67] Dates differ, but symbols become resonant references. Baraka's account depicts an ascent from an underground place – the habitat of Richard Wright's *The Man Who Lived Underground* (1942–45), Ralph Ellison's *Invisible Man* (1952), and his own *Dutchman* (1964). If ascent, as expressed by Amiri Baraka and his male contemporaries, identifies one mood of the Black Arts movement, then "turning" by Lucille Clifton and her female contemporaries (as we shall see) identifies another. Both symbiotically express the spirit of the time.

Fiction and autobiography

Having eschewed the aesthetics of life outside or on the underside of history, "The middle-class native intellectual ... having dug, finally, how white he has become, now, classically, comes back to his countrymen charged up with the desire to be black, uphold black, etc ... [as] a fanatic patriot."[68] The return, emphatically, signals a turn in the production of fiction by black authors of the Black Arts ascent. We may comprehend this turn as a paradigm shift from modernism's double consciousness to contemporary intertextualities (like jazz) which write with and against tradition; from Euro-humanistic positivism to a questioning of canonized *isms*; from the establishment of more *isms* to a critique of all *isms*; from naturalism and realism to re-vision; from protest to assertion. What Kalamu Ya Salaam calls the symbolic birth of the Black Arts movement may also be understood in terms of Philip Brian Harper's incisive analysis of the emergent "politically aware, socially conscious, black nationalist subject... The designation *black*, from the middle 1960s through the early 1970s, represented an emergent identification among nationalist activists and intellectuals and not a generic nomenclature by which any person of African descent might be referenced."[69]

The black subject, so long a-birthing in black communities of the USA, receives prominent narratological rendering, especially in the fiction of black women writers of the BAM. Much of the labor of that birth had been borne by writer-activist organizations which coincided with the opening of Baraka's Black Arts Theatre School in 1965 shortly after the assassination of Malcolm X. Many women writers developing in the 1960s began their apprenticeships in these organizations. The little-known Brenda Walcott was a member of the Umbra group spearheaded by Askia Muhammad Touré, who founded *Umbra Magazine* in 1963 on Manhattan's Lower East Side; that group included Ishmael Reed, who was to become a renowned contemporary novelist, and Tom Dent, who, with Kalamu Ya Salaam, founded BLKARTSOUTH. *Umbra* had grown out of *On Guard for Freedom*, founded by Calvin Hicks. Its members included Harold Cruse, author of the widely referenced *The Crisis of the Negro Intellectual*; LeRoi Jones (to become Amiri Baraka); Rosa Guy, prolific and yet under-read writer of discourse-raising young adult novels; and Sarah Wright, under-read novelist of large impact. Led by John Oliver Killens, novelist, it was the Harlem Writer's Guild, focusing on the production of prose and fiction and including Egyptologist and story writer John Henrik Clarke, that numbered among its members Maya Angelou, who was to re-constitute the subject and widen the breadth of three centuries of African American autobiography; Alice Childress, playwright; Paule Marshall and Sarah Wright, novelists; and Jean Carey Bond, essayist. Elijah Muhammed's Chicago-based and New York-branched Nation of Islam, ideologically important in its impact on the Black Arts movement, principally through Minister Malcolm, had, for a time, attracted the membership of vanguard BAM poet Sonia Sanchez. Sanchez was also active in the founding of Black Studies in the academy when she was professor at San Francisco State University (1965–69).

By 1967 when he taught at San Francisco State University, LeRoi Jones became attracted to Karenga's philosophy of *KAWAIDA* and his inauguration of *KWANZA*. He also met founding members of the Black Panther Party, Bobby Seale and Eldridge Cleaver, and later Henry Newton and George Jackson. From their association with the Black Panther Party, autobiographers Angela Davis (never a member), Assata Shakur (affiliated briefly with the Harlem branch of the Black Panther Party), and Elaine Brown (becoming minister of information of the Los Angeles Chapter in 1971) provide histories of liberational struggle in the United States during the first decade of the BAM. Each of these women is the subject of Margo V. Perkins's *Autobiography as Activism* (2000). Though the Mississippi-born Anne Moody was not an affiliate of any of these groups, her autobiography *Coming of Age in Mississippi* (1968), which may be read as a critique of the civil rights movement, foreshadowed a similar critique in Alice Walker's *Meridian* (1976).

Like other chronicles, this study faces the challenge of dating the Black Arts movement. Appropriately, most histories begin with its naming. Yet the word *movement* signifies a flow as from what Henry Dumas imaged as a canal to the sea. Indeed, the naming of the Black Arts movement, like the crest of a huge wave, crowns the tributaries and currents of thought, creative production, and activism leading to its swell and auguring its tidal turns. For example, before the 1964/65 naming, Gwendolyn Brooks's poetic novella *Maud Martha* (1953) had begun the journey inward through the agency of a young girl's consciousness. Such a journey into what Larry Neal calls "the private field of language," turning from "the public field"[70] stressed at first by Black Arts writers, would eventually distinguish the fiction of black women writers influencing and being influenced by the Black Arts movement. The dearest wish of the novella's title character, Maud Martha Brown, is "to be cherished."[71] In one chapter, entitled "love and gorilla" – a dream sequence – Maud Martha encounters a gentle, caged gorilla; when passers-by stop and stare, the supine creature rises and shakes its cage. As if to commemorate this coming of age novella with its demystification of marriage motif, Toni Cade Bambara entitles her first collection of stories *Gorilla, My Love* (1972) – a collection which empowers the voices of children. By 1962, Paule Marshall's "Reena," a story first published in *Harper Magazine*'s special supplement entitled "The American Female" and later in Toni Cade [Bambara]'s *The Black Woman: An Anthology* (1970), had forecast the question of identity central to Black Arts discourses. In posing the question of "what it means to be a Black woman in America – a definition formulated by others to serve out their fantasies"[72] – the critical observation of the "Reena" story had preceded women's consciousness groups springing up in the 1970s, just as it had preceded Kate Millet's touted *Sexual Politics* (1969).

A movement embellished by rediscoveries, one of the BAM's most resounding was the rediscovery of anthropologist, dramatist, theorist, and novelist Zora Neale Hurston. Hurston's 1920s/30s community-based fiction – transmitting the oral storytelling voices of its inhabitants, asserting the sovereignty and pervasiveness of its progenitive cultural richness, establishing its worldview through its unique private field of language, portraying its self-empowered women, and critiquing community and wider American impositions on identity that dwarf the possibilities self-actualization – has impacted the production of fiction by African American women ever since, from Sarah E. Wright's *This Child's Gonna Live* (1969) to Toni Morrison's *Love* (2003), from Alice Walker's *In Love and Trouble* (1967) to Gloria Naylor's *Mama Day* (1988), and from Sherley Anne Williams's "Tell Martha not to Mourn" (1970) to Terry McMillan's *Waiting to Exhale* (1992). Progenitive also has been Margaret Walker's *Jubilee* (1966), a novel which would begin, as Toni Morrison later pointed out regarding her own fiction, "a journey to a site to see what remains were left behind and to reconstruct the world that these remains imply."[73] *Jubilee* revisits the life of a slave woman; it therefore forecasts such historical and revisionary novels as Octavia Butler's *Kindred* (1979), Toni Morrison's *Beloved* (1987), and Sherley Anne Williams's *Dessa Rose* (1986). In the year before the floodgate of writing by black women, Sarah E. Wright's novel *This Child's Gonna Live* unveiled a black family saga, not that of the urban family in Lorraine Hansberry's play *A Raisin in the Sun* but that of a family enduring impoverishment on the Eastern Shore of Maryland during the 1930s. "This woman-centered story informed by the dual influence of Black Power and Women's Rights"[74] may be fruitfully read comparatively with Alice Walker's *The Third Life of Grange Copeland* (1970). *This Child's Gonna Live* earned notice by *The New York Times* (June 1969) as the most important book of 1969, and Sarah E. Wright received the Zora Neale Hurston award for Literary Excellence in 1988.

In 1970, when *The Black Woman: An Anthology* brought to publication twenty-eight activist writers – among them Nikki Giovanni, Audre Lorde, Paule Marshall, Alice Walker, and Sherley Anne Williams – language, mining the reimagination of America, the over-arching project of the 1960s Black Arts movement, assumed a turn. As Toni Cade [Bambara] expressed it in her Preface: "what characterizes the current movement of the 60's is a turning away from the larger society and a turning toward each other ... [W]hat typifies the current spirit is an embrace, an embrace of the community and a hard-headed attempt to get basic with each other."[75] This turning meant that language engaged the speech register of the people of its direct address – its reference public – and found renewal in its "Soul Field." The year 1970 saw the publication of Mari Evans's *I Am a Black Woman*, Sonia Sanchez's *We a BaddDDD People*, Louise Meriwether's *Daddy Was a Number Runner*, Pauli Murray's *Dark Testament*, Audre Lorde's *The First Cities*, Nikki Giovanni's *Re:Creation*, Maya Angelou's *I Know Why the Caged Bird Sings*, Alice Walker's *The Third Life of Grange Copeland*, and Toni

Morrison's *The Bluest Eye*. Through Pecola, *The Bluest Eye*'s black female child, othered in her home and in her community, an unprecedented black subjectivity was born into literature. This turning had already initiated the discourse that would soon emerge as visible black feminist/woman-centered reclamation, as evidenced by the Combahee River Collective's "A Black Feminist Statement" (April 1977).

Legacy

There is a prevalent view that by 1975, the Black Arts movement had been destroyed by disagreement among its most respected theorists; by the death of its progenitive editor Hoyt W. Fuller, who published in *Negro Digest/Black World* nearly all of its representative voices, as had Dudley Randall at Broadside Press, Naomi Long Madgett at Lotus Press, Haki Madhubuti at Third World Press, Amiri Baraka at Jihad, and Joe Goncalves in *The Journal of Black Poetry*; by the disruption of black political organizations by repressive government measures such as COINTELPRO; and by the replacement of Black Studies activist leadership by academicians. However, another view ascends. That view predominates and reveals the BAM as a many-sided, multi-voiced, social, and self-critical project whose errors, limitations, and failures are as crucial to the process of self-liberation as are its achievements. Like any literary, cultural, and social movement, the Black Arts movement cannot be comprehended as a time-bound event. It grew out of a lineage of activist, intellectual, and creative activity which fomented its aspirations, discourses, and primary objectives. Peaking in the 1960s and 1970s, the BAM earned the attention of wide audiences of its reference public, hugely increasing communities of reading and writing. It earned what the resplendent voice of Aretha Franklin sang as RESPECT from its globally responsive community. Its call has evoked literary communities silent before the latter part of the twentieth century. The revolutionary spirit of the Black Arts movement is the genesis of curriculum revisionary studies in the academy, out of which, for example, evolved Black Women's Studies. That revolutionary spirit continues to ask ethical questions and to demand ethical answers in the political and social arenas of policy-making. Perhaps the most distinctive characteristic of the BAM is its transformative nature, no more compellingly rendered than through Lucille Clifton's poem "turning":

> turning into my own
> turning on in
> to my own self
> at last
> turning out of the

> white cage, turning out of the
> lady cage
> turning at last
> on a stem like a black fruit
> in my own season
> at last.[76]

The Black Arts movement continues to turn.

NOTES

1. Toni Cade Bambara, *Deep Sightings and Rescue Missions: Fiction, Essays, and Conversations* (New York: Pantheon Books, 1996), p. 140.
2. Larry Neal (ed.), *Black Fire: An Anthology of Afro-American Writing* (New York: William Morrow, 1968), p. xvii.
3. Carolyn F. Gerald, "The Black Writer and His Role" (1969), *The Black Aesthetic*, ed. Addison Gayle, Jr. (Garden City, NY: Doubleday, 1971), pp. 349–51.
4. Nikki Giovanni, *Black Feeling, Black Talk, Black Judgment* (New York: William Morrow, 1970), pp. 54–5.
5. Giovanni, "The Funeral of Martin Luther King, Jr.," *Black Feeling*, p. 56.
6. June Jordan, *Things That I Do in the Dark: Selected Poetry* (Boston: Beacon Press, 1977), p. 93.
7. June Jordan (ed.), *Soulscript* (New York: Harlem Moon, 2004), pp. xvi–xvii.
8. Larry Neal, "The Black Arts Movement" (1968), *Within the Circle: An Anthology of African American Literary Criticism from the Harlem Renaissance to the Present*, ed. Angelyn Mitchell (Durham, NC: Duke University Press, 1994), 184.
9. Cheryl Clarke, *"After Mecca": Women Poets and the Black Arts Movement* (New Brunswick, NJ: Rutgers University Press, 2005), p. 40.
10. Neal, "The Black Arts Movement," p. 184.
11. Gwendolyn Brooks, "In the Mecca" (1968), *Blacks* (Chicago: David Co., 1987), pp. 423–24.
12. Ibid., pp. 444–45.
13. Margaret Walker, *This Is My Century: New and Collected Poems* (Athens: University of Georgia Press, 1989), pp. 6–7.
14. Brooks, *Blacks*, p. 72.
15. Giovanni, *Black Feeling*, p. 34.
16. Amiri Baraka, *The LeRoi Jones/Amiri Baraka Reader*, ed. William J. Harris and Amiri Baraka (New York: Thunder's Mouth Press, 1991), p. 218.
17. Nina Simone, *Emergency Ward!* (RCA Victor ALSP 4757, 1972), sound recording.
18. Giovanni, *Black Feeling*, pp. 75–76.
19. Jennifer Jordan, "Making the Connections: An Interview with Sonia Sanchez," *BMa: The Sonia Sanchez Literary Review* 8.1 (Fall 2002), 17.
20. Declaration of Independence, 1776.
21. Robert N. Bellah, *Habits of the Heart: Individualism and Commitment in American Life* (New York: Harper & Row, 1986), p. 153.
22. Giovanni, *Black Feeling*, pp. 95–97.

23. Sterling A. Brown, "Our Literary Audience" (1930), *Within the Circle*, ed. Mitchell, p. 69.

24. Harryette Mullen, "The Black Arts Movement: Poetry and Drama from the 1960s to the 1970s," *African American Writers*, ed. Valerie Smith, 2nd edition, vol. 1 (New York: Scribner's, 2001), p. 51.

25. Angela Jackson, "What Is American About American Poetry?" www.poetrysociety.org/jackson.html.

26. James Baldwin, *Notes of a Native Son* (New York: Dial, 1963), p. 23.

27. Clayton Riley, "On Black Theatre," *The Black Aesthetic*, ed. Gayle, p. 311.

28. Houston A. Baker, "Generational Shifts and the Recent Criticism of Afro-American Literature," *Within the Circle*, ed. Mitchell, pp. 291–96.

29. Stephen Henderson, *Understanding the New Black Poetry: Black Speech and Black Music as Poetic References* (New York: William Morrow, 1973), p. 41.

30. Mae G. Henderson, "Speaking in Tongues: Dialogics, Dialectics and the Black Women's Literary Tradition," *Changing Our Own Words: Essays on Criticism, Theory, and Writing by Black Women*, ed. Cheryl A. Wall (New Brunswick, NJ: Rutgers University Press, 1991), p. 23.

31. Carolyn Rodgers, "Breakthrough," *Songs of a Black Bird* (Chicago: Third World Press, 1969), pp. 31–33.

32. Clark, *"After Mecca"*, pp. 22–46.

33. Eugenia Collier, "Fields Watered with Blood: Myth and Ritual in the Poetry of Margaret Walker," *Fields Watered with Blood: Critical Essays on Margaret Walker*, ed. Maryemma Graham (Athens: University of Georgia Press, 2001), p. 99.

34. Baker, "Generational Shifts," p. 286.

35. Alice Walker, *Revolutionary Petunias and Other Poems* (New York: Harcourt Brace Jovanovich, 1973), p. 70.

36. Maya Angelou, *Just Give Me a Cool Drink of Water 'Fore I Diiie* (New York: Random House, 1971), p. 29.

37. Margaret Walker, *Prophets for a New Day* (Detroit: Broadside Press, 1970).

38. Brooks, "In the Mecca," *Blacks*, p. 407.

39. Mari Evans, *I Am a Black Woman* (New York: William Morrow, 1970), p. 95.

40. Henderson, "Overview," *Understanding*, pp. 1–69.

41. Bambara, *Deep Sightings*, p. 97.

42. Ibid., pp. 141–42.

43. Toni Cade [Bambara] (ed.), *The Black Woman: An Anthology* (1970; rpt. New York: Washington Square Press, 2005), p. 306.

44. Eleanor Traylor, "Two Afro-American Contributions to Dramatic Form," *The Theatre of Black Americans: A Collection of Critical Essays*, ed. Errol Hill vol. 1 (New York: Prentice Hall, 1980), p. 59.

45. Kimberly W. Benston, "The Aesthetic of Modern Black Drama: From Mimesis to Methesis," *The Theatre of Black Americans*, ed. Hill, vol. 1, p. 62.

46. Bambara, *Deep Sightings*, p. 99.

47. Sonia Sanchez, *Sister Son/Ji. New Plays from the Black Theatre: An Anthology*, ed. Ed Bullins (New York: Bantam Books, 1969), pp. 98–107.

48. Ethel Pitts Walker, "The American Negro Theatre," *The Theatre of Black Americans*, ed. Hill, vol. II, pp. 49–62.

49. Ibid., pp. 57–62.

50. Amiri Baraka, "The Revolutionary Theatre," *Home: Social Essays* (New York: Apollo, 1966), p. 211.

51. James Hatch, "Some African Influences on the Afro-American Theatre," *The Theatre of Black Americans*, ed. Hill, vol. I, p. 27.

52. Zora Neale Hurston, "Characteristics of Negro Expression" (1934), *Within the Circle*, ed. Mitchell, pp. 79–94.

53. Hatch, "Some African Influences," p. 26.

54. Jessica Harris, "The National Black Theatre: The Sun People of 125th Street," *The Theatre of Black Americans*, ed. Hill, vol. II, p. 87.

55. Ishmael Reed, "Preface to *19 Necromancers from Now*," rpt. in *The Black Aesthetic*, ed. Gayle, pp. 381–82.

56. Gerald, "The Black Writer and His Role," p. 353.

57. Riley, "On Black Theatre," p. 297.

58. Hatch, "Some African Influences," p. 13.

59. Ibid., p. 13.

60. Mullen, "The Black Arts Movement," p. 51.

61. Lundeana M. Thomas, "Barbara Ann Teer: From Holistic Training to Liberating Rituals," *Black Theatre: Ritual Performance in the African Diaspora*, ed. Paul Carter Harrison, Victor Leo Walker II, and Gus Edwards (Philadelphia: Temple University Press, 2002), p. 350.

62. Ntozake Shange, "Porque Tu No M'entrende? Whatcha Mean You Can't Understand Me?" *Black Theatre*, p. 397.

63. Amiri Baraka, "Bopera Theory," *Black Theatre*, pp. 378–81.

64. Baraka, *Reader*, p. 367.

65. Frantz Fanon, *The Wretched of the Earth* (1961), trans. Constance Farrington (New York: Grove Press, 1963), pp. 36–37.

66. Kalamu Ya Salaam, "Historical Overviews of the Black Arts Movement," *The Oxford Companion to African American Literature* (New York: Oxford University Press, 1997), p. 70.

67. Larry Neal, *Visions of a Liberated Future: Black Arts Movement Writings*, ed. Michael Schwartz (New York: Thunder's Mouth Press, 1989), p. 67.

68. Baraka, *Reader*, p. 367.

69. Philip Brian Harper, *Is It Nation Time? Contemporary Essays on Black Power and Black Nationalism*, ed. Eddie S. Glaude, Jr. (Chicago: University of Chicago Press, 2002), p. 183.

70. Larry Neal, "The Writer as Activist–1960 and After," *The Black American Reference Book*, ed. Mabel M. Smythe (Englewood Cliffs, NJ: Prentice Hall, 1976), pp. 767–90.

71. Brooks, *Blacks*, p. 144.

72. Cade [Bambara], *The Black Woman*, p. 20.

73. Toni Morrison, "The Site of Memory," *Inventing the Truth: The Art and Craft of Memoir*, ed. William Zinsser (Boston: Houghton Mifflin, 1987), p. 192.

74. Jennifer Campbell, "It's a Time in the Land: Gendering Black Power and Sarah E. Wright's Place in the Tradition of Black Women's Writing," *African American Review* 31.2 (Summer 1997), 211–22.

75. Cade [Bambara], *The Black Woman*, p. 7.

76. Lucille Clifton, *Good Woman: Poems and a Memoir, 1969–1980* (Brockport, NY: BOA Editions, 1987), p. 143.

4

DANA A. WILLIAMS

Contemporary African American
women writers

Contemporary African American women writers are perhaps best characterized as diverse. From Toni Morrison's first novel, *The Bluest Eye* (1970) to
Rita Dove's award-winning collection of poems, *Thomas and Beulah* (1986),
to Suzan-Lori Parks's experimental drama, *Topdog/Underdog* (2001), full
circle, back to Morrison's eighth novel, *Love* (2003), contemporary African
American literature by African American women writers offers full expressions of the complexity of contemporary African American life, particularly
as this life relates to the black woman. Setting the tone for the literature to
come and its corresponding social critique was Toni Cade [Bambara]'s all-
important, simply yet magically titled *The Black Woman: An Anthology*
(1970). As she concedes that the work she wanted to do in the anthology
was "overly ambitious" from the beginning, a "lifetime's work," she is clear
about what the text does achieve: "This then is a beginning – a collection of
poems, stories, essays, formal, informal, reminiscent, that seem best to reflect
the preoccupations of the contemporary Black woman in this country."[1] As
Eleanor W. Traylor notes in her introduction to the 2005 reprinting of the
text, *The Black Woman* "explores first the interiority of an in-the-head,
in-the-heart, in-the-gut region of a discovery called the *self*. It tests the desires,
the longings, the aspirations of this discovered self with and against its
possibilities for respect, growth, fulfillment, and accomplishment."[2] As accurately as Traylor describes the anthology specifically here, her statements also
describe, more generally, the literature of contemporary African American
women writers – literature which explores the *self*, its desires, its longing, its
aspirations, and its possibilities, particularly in the post-civil rights United
States. And while this exploration of the self was not then so much a new
phenomenon in the tradition of African American women's writing, by 1970,
black women writers, as they extended the beauty and breadth of the Black
Arts movement, blossomed in their aggressive pursuit of their inquires into
black womanhood. Offering varied responses to these inquiries were both
writers who were well established in the tradition – among them, for instance,

Gwendolyn Brooks, Nikki Giovanni, Adrienne Kennedy, Audre Lorde, Paule Marshall, Sonia Sanchez, and Margaret Walker – and writers who made their literary and dramatic debuts in the emerging period – Maya Angelou, Toni Cade Bambara, Toni Morrison, Ntozake Shange, and Alice Walker among many others. These then-emergent writers have been at the front of depicting and historicizing contemporary African American life. More importantly, post-1970s African American women writers explore the black feminine self, a self heretofore unexamined.

As Barbara Christian intimates in "Trajectories of Self-Definition: Placing Contemporary Afro-American Women's Fiction," contemporary African American women's writing evolved (and continues to evolve) in phases.[3] Building on the 1960s ideology that promoted cultural and racial self-discovery and self-awareness as well as the celebration of blackness, early 1970s literature by black women also stressed the necessity of loving oneself and one's culture. Mari Evans's oft-anthologized, quoted, and recited poem, "I Am a Black Woman" (from the collection of poems of the same title), Nikki Giovanni's poem "Nikki-Rosa," and Sonia Sanchez's revolutionary collection *We a BaddDDD People* (1970), for example, celebrated the black woman, her versatility, her strength, and her culture.

Yet, even in this celebration of blackness and its corresponding "black is beautiful" rhetoric which characterized the 1960s, contemporary black women writers also began to critique black communities for their perpetuation of western beliefs and ideals which stunted the development of black people in general and black women in particular. Notably, this critique distanced black women writers from the Black Arts literature of their male counterparts, if only minimally. Morrison's *The Bluest Eye* is perhaps the best example of this critical celebratory dichotomy. In the sense that the community adopts two dangerous western concepts – physical beauty and romantic love – without any adaptation of these notions to accommodate blackness, the novel highlights the dangers of all-out assimilation and integration. And even as the black community has the wherewithal to sustain itself in the novel, this same community's conscious and unconscious willingness to perpetuate the racist idea that white is better destroys the novel's central character Pecola Breedlove. Unlike Pecola, who wants blue eyes, Claudia, the young character from whose voice we primarily hear the narrative, seems to understand the trappings of uncritically adopting western ideas about beauty. Claudia concludes that she has limited (if any) access to whiteness and that she is deficient in this constructed racial binary, so she despises, more than anything, the "thing" that makes white better. That Claudia, Pecola's peer, presumably likes who she is as a young black girl suggests that Pecola's desire for blue eyes has to do with much more than anything as simple as her family's and the community's failure to deem her beautiful. The complexity of the novel and of its corresponding critical commentary, then, becomes characteristic of the sophisticated analysis in which contemporary African American women writers ground their literature.

Like the community in *The Bluest Eye*, the community in Alice Walker's *The Third Life of Grange Copeland* (1970) imposes limitations on its women, even as it sustains the community at large. Christian contends, in fact, that one of the characteristics of early 1970s fiction by black women is its suggestion that the community is "a major threat to the survival and empowerment of women."[4] Like Claudia who, in *The Bluest Eye*, creates her own self-definition as she sees the limitations of accepting others' definition of her, Ruth, in *The Third Life of Grange Copeland*, is able to construct an identity for herself strong enough to influence her community, if only minimally, because she has witnessed and overcome "the destruction of women in the wake of [the community's] prevailing attitudes" (p. 241).

This ambiguity about the community and woman's development within it continues in Maya Angelou's *I Know Why the Caged Bird Sings* (1970), where the young Marguerite (Maya) refuses to speak for an extended period of time after she is raped by a member of the community, her mother's lover, in fact. Yet, it is also presumably the males in her familial community who protect her from future encounters by murdering her rapist. In spite of the rape, however, Maya is, for the most part, able to define herself both through the strategy of silence and through and within the community. Throughout most of the autobiography, she recognizes the customs and traditions of the community and the culture as forces that allow people to live through their difficulties. From informal gatherings in her grandmother's general store to summer picnics, black folk congregate both to celebrate and to lament – the point is that they do it together. And while she frequently leaves different communities, unable to find her place in them, ultimately, she leaves one community to (re)define herself in another.

Like a number of black women writers, Angelou does not limit her writing to a particular genre. As progenitor of contemporary black "life writing," Angelou has not only published five autobiographies but also eight books of poetry. As an initiator of a subgenre, she anticipates Ntozake Shange, who has published successfully in multiple genres as well and who also experiments with form. Shange's dramatic choreopoem *for colored girls who have considered suicide / when the rainbow is enuf* (1976) combines the dramatic form with poetry and dance and continues the tradition of black women writers questioning how well black women can define themselves within the context of the community. Each of the seven women in *for colored girls* – Lady in Red, Orange, Yellow, Green, Purple, Blue, and Brown – has suffered some great loss at the hands of a man, and what each comes to realize is that women cannot find love outside of themselves without loving themselves and each other first. In keeping with the choreopoem's feminist rhetoric, each of the women eventually discovers a sense of her god-*self* and "loves her fiercely." This theme of self-love and self-definition runs throughout many of Shange's major works, among which are three novels, *Sassafrass, Cypress, and Indigo* (1982), *Liliane* (1984), and *Betsey Brown* (1985); several volumes of poetry, including *Nappy Edges* (1978); a host of plays, including *Three Pieces: Spell #7; A Photograph: Lovers-in-Motion; Boogie Woogie Landscapes* (1981); and a collection of essays *See No Evil: Prefaces, Essays and Accounts, 1976–1983* (1984). And in each of these texts, we see Shange's artful escape of boundaries and her exploration and rewriting of form, two features that are among her greatest contributions to black women's writing.

By the mid 1970s, literature by black women makes a "visionary leap" and moves into its second phase where "the woman is not thrust outside her community. To one degree or another, she chooses to stand outside it, to define herself as in revolt against it."[5] Christian cites Morrison's *Sula* (1973), Walker's *Meridian* (1976), and Paule Marshall's *The Chosen Place, the Timeless People* (1969) as texts which support this notion. Sula is sexually uninhibited, chooses not to be a mother, and sleeps with her best friend's husband, all with no remorse. Her actions clearly defy the idea of community, and the community's response is to ostracize her. Not quite as radical as Sula, Meridian and Merle (*The Chosen Place*) act out their rebellion by insisting upon their place within a patriarchal space, even as they often find themselves outside of it. In addition to Shange's *colored girls*, Gayl Jones's *Eva's Man* (1975), Gloria Naylor's *The Women of Brewster Place* (1982), and Walker's *The Color Purple* (1982), among others, can be added to this list of somewhat radical texts whose female protagonists rebel against patriarchy and racism.

Yet, not all readers identify these women as radical enough or as successful in their quests to make themselves subject. bell hooks, for example, contends that in much of the fiction by contemporary black women writers – she writes specifically about Walker's *Color Purple* and *Third Life*, Morrison's *Sula*, and Bambara's *The Salt Eaters* (1980) – "the struggle by black female characters for subjectivity, though forged in radical resistance to the *status quo* ... usually takes the form of black women breaking free from boundaries imposed by others, only to practice their newfound 'freedom' by setting limits and boundaries for themselves."[6] By the end of *Color Purple*, hooks notes, Celie is back in a domestic and familial situation; Grange Copeland ultimately fights against whites by himself in *Third Life*, though he has schooled Ruth to be a fighter too; unable to live as a self-actualized woman even in a novel, Sula dies at the end of Morrison's text; and Velma spends a great deal of time in

Salt Eaters trying to decide whether or not she really wants to be well, which hooks associates with her uncertainty about being revolutionary. For many readers, however, these protagonists' attempts at rebellion or their acts of resistance are, in and of themselves, points of celebration. That Sula dies relatively young at the end of the novel speaks more about society than it does about any notions of her rebellion as failure. And while the first question Velma must answer in *Salt Eaters* is, "Are you sure, sweetheart, you want to be well," ultimately, she chooses wellness.[7]

In many ways, this query in *Salt Eaters* initiates a third phase in contemporary African American women's literature – the journey to healing through inquiry. While the longing for selfhood is one which has been consistently investigated in black women's literary tradition, by the latter part of the 1970s, a corresponding desire for mental and spiritual healing had become a central trope in contemporary African American women's literature. In addition to using the ancestral matriarchal past to help heal the contemporary woman, as the fabled healer Minnie Ransom does for Velma Henry in *Salt Eaters*, one of the key ways writers have approached the trope is by using historical narratives to question both history and its relationship to the present. Thus, a number of writers situate their protagonists in slavery. In Gayl Jones's *Corregidora* (1976), the novel's protagonist, Ursa Corregidora, struggles with the burden of the past as it impacts her present. After she falls down the stairs during a fight with her husband, Ursa is rendered infertile and thus unable to meet her matriarchal family's mandate to "make generations."[8] Her foremothers insist that she remember their oppressive pasts – they are raped and made prostitutes by their slave-holding father/lover – but what they fail to realize is that their past, and their unwillingness to allow Ursa to move beyond it, imposes limitations on Ursa, who, after the fall, stands in need of both physical and emotional healing. By invoking history and the legacy of slavery, *Corregidora* suggests not only that connections must be made between the past and the contemporary moment but that only those usable elements of the past must be retained if present and future wellness is to be ensured.

Like *Corregidora*, Octavia Butler's *Kindred* (1979), Sherley Anne Williams's *Dessa Rose* (1986), and Morrison's *Beloved* (1987) are novels that invoke the slave past and interrogate its role in the construction of the female *self*. In each novel, the relationship between the past and the present is highlighted. Butler's protagonist in *Kindred* is, in fact, periodically transported back to the antebellum South. Butler's two main characters – Dana Franklin, a black woman who must protect her white racist ancestor to ensure her presence in the future, and her husband Kevin, a white man who comes to understand the cruelty of the slave past after he too is transported back to slavery – experience time-travel to show the relevance of the past to the present. By the novel's end, Dana returns to the present injured physically – she loses her left arm – but emotionally and spiritually healed because she better understands the relationship between the past and the present.

Expanding the recurring enterprise of investigating the legacy of slavery in the contemporary moment, *Dessa Rose* moves beyond simply invoking slavery at different points in its narrative and, instead, experiments with the form of a fictional slave narrative. In part one of the novel, a white male writer, Adam Nehemiah, attempts to tell Dessa's story. With so many contradicting versions of her story existing, and Dessa only replying to Nehemiah indirectly, Williams highlights the ambiguity of history and questions its written versions when someone other than the subject tells the story. Part two of the novel highlights the tension between Dessa and Ruth, a white woman Dessa must trust if she is to survive. When Ruth is almost raped by a white man, Dessa comes to realize the similarities between black women and white women as regards their shared vulnerabilities. And they both come to realize that they need each other, if only temporarily, if they are going to survive in the present and thrive in the future. By part three, Dessa, finally safe and free, asserts her own voice in an attempt both to defy Nehemiah and the others who attempt to tell her story and to define her *self*. By telling her own story, she ensures that she controls her self-definition and her legacy of revolt.

Louise Meriwether, who is perhaps best known for her first novel, *Daddy Was a Number Runner* (1970), invokes this theme of slave revolt some years later in *Fragments of the Ark* (1994), also an historical novel in the tradition of *Dessa Rose* and *Beloved*. Meriwether, however, uses a male protagonist to investigate the past. The novel is based on the life of Robert Smalls, a military hero whom Meriwether had written about some years earlier in *The Freedom Ship of Robert Smalls* (1971); only this time she fictionalizes Smalls's story and creates the character Peter Mango, a gunboat pilot who steals a confederate military vessel and turns it over to the Union. The women in the novel, Mango's wife, Rain, and his mother, Lily, find ways to sustain themselves while Mango fights in the Union Navy. Ultimately, he retires having served with distinction, but he and his family face the uncertain future of the Reconstruction years.

Like *Corregidora* and *Kindred*, Morrison's *Beloved* moves back and forth between slavery and later moments, though *Beloved* never engages the contemporary moment. Instead, the novel's present is some ten years immediately following slavery, but the legacy of slavery haunts both "124," the personified house on Bluestone Road, and its inhabitants. Sethe, the novel's protagonist, kills her daughter rather than allow her to be enslaved. And while she never indicates that she regrets this act, it denies her the ability to define herself outside of the experience. When Beloved returns and overtakes Sethe's life, Sethe must experience an emotional healing in the present before she is destroyed physically by Beloved and the past. With the help of the women of the community, ironically the same women who neglect to warn her family of the white men's arrival some years earlier, Sethe exorcises Beloved's ghost and, finally, in the end with Paul D's help, comes to realize that she, not Beloved, is her own "best thing."[9]

While contemporary African American women writers continue to use the legacy of slavery to interrogate the past and its tellers and to investigate black womanhood and ways of ensuring her healing throughout the 1990s – J. California Cooper in *Family* (1991), Michelle Cliff in *Free Enterprise* (1993), and Lorene Cary in *The Price of a Child* (1995), for instance – a number of 1980s texts explore strategies for healing without engaging slavery directly, focusing instead on more contemporary maternal figures (many of whom are imbued with ancestral spirits) as healers. Gloria Naylor's *The Women of Brewster Place* and *Mama Day* (1988), Walker's *The Color Purple*, and Marshall's *Praisesong for the Widow* (1983) are exemplary texts in this regard. Notably, in each of these texts, the laying on of hands is central to the woman's healing. In *The Women of Brewster Place*, Mattie metaphorically bathes and rocks Ciel back to wellness after Ciel's baby dies; and in *Mama Day*, Mama Day heals many of the island's inhabitants with her hands but most notably Bernice, who had been infertile, and her niece Ophelia, who has been poisoned by another character's jealously. In *Color Purple*, Celie, though unable to experience healing fully herself until many years later, bathes Shug and heals her physically, giving rise to Celie's own emotional healing; and in *Praisesong*, Rosalie bathes, oils, then kneads Avey's flesh until she is ultimately reconnected to her cultural community. Rosalie acts in the tradition of her father, whom Marshall uses to reconstruct Elegbara, the African god from whom the healer gets authority. By the novel's end, Avey, like Merle Kinbona in Marshall's *The Chosen Place, the Timeless People* and Ursa Mackenzie in her *Daughters* (1991), comes to see the importance of African diasporic traditions in the western world.

Aggressively reconnecting with the black diaspora, in fact, might well be considered a fourth phase in contemporary African American women's writing. Excepting Morrison in *Tar Baby* (1981), however, which is set primarily in the Caribbean, it is largely African/Caribbean American women writers who interrogate issues specific to the black diaspora to highlight the tension created by an insider/outsider position, which they represent both through their subject position as immigrants who have adopted the United States as their home and through their position as minorities in a majority culture that often fails to make easy their self-definition. Marshall's *Brown Girl,*

Brownstones (1959) is a paradigmatic text in this regard. A number of writers who, like Marshall, are Caribbean-born American immigrants and who follow in her tradition – among them Michelle Cliff, Edwidge Danticat, and Jamaica Kincaid – make inquiries into diasporic women's experiences in America similar to the inquiries about belonging Marshall makes in *Brown Girl*.

Like Selina Boyce in *Brown Girl*, Clare Savage, the autobiographical character of two of Michelle Cliff's novels, *Abeng* (1984) and *No Telephone to Heaven* (1987), spends a significant amount of time in her narratives interrogating her personal identity, particularly as it relates to her Caribbean heritage. Using a polyphonic narrative form to express the complexity of its characters' heritage, *Abeng* investigates the grammar of language forms, in this case Jamaican Creole, to reveal the submerged histories that have been erased through colonization. In *No Telephone to Heaven*, Clare's character returns, but Cliff also creates and uses a number of characters to investigate Jamaica's legacy of colonization, oppression, and revolt. As Clare moves back and forth between America, England, and Jamaica, her own middle passage of sorts, she seeks to define and liberate herself and those with whom she comes in contact.

In a manner similar to Cliff's use of characters to investigate the island of Jamaica, Edwidge Danticat creates characters who struggle to live successfully in Haiti and in the United States. *Krik?Krak!* (1991), the collection of short stories which marks Danticat's fictional debut, is inspired by the Haitian practice of storytelling where someone calls out "Krik?", and the response "Krak!" would initiate storytelling. Her first novel, *Breath, Eyes, Memory* (1994), invokes Haiti as well and is structured to reflect the struggle of language and self-expression for postcolonial peoples. In *The Farming of Bones* (1998), the characters seek to retell history as they tell stories about the 1937 Haitian massacre. Her latest novel, *The Dew Breakers* (2004), continues this investigation of Haitian life, as a young woman is forced to come to terms with the "truth" about her father. Ultimately, the novel which, at first, reads like a series of short stories, details the interconnected stories of people whose lives have been affected by the father, a "dew breaker," the term used to describe thugs who tortured and killed rebels under the Duvalier regime in Haiti. In addition to investigating Haiti's history, Danticat also engages a global feminist agenda, themes of migration, and mother–daughter relationships as tropes to interrogate ways that women can empower themselves and each other throughout her fiction.

Like Danticat's fictional delineation of Haiti, Jamaica Kincaid depicts the impact of colonialism on the people of her native island, Antigua, in most of her fiction and especially in the non-fictional *A Small Place* (1988). However, the theme most readily associated with this writer and which is foregrounded in much of her work is the tenuous mother–daughter relationship that recurs in Caribbean women's writing. As Caroline Rody suggests in *The Daughter's Return: African-American and Caribbean Women's Fictions of History*, the mother figure in Caribbean women's writing is an ambivalent one due largely to Caribbeans' identification first with Europe as mother figure during colonization, then with Africa during the age of Negritude, and finally with the islands themselves beginning with the postcolonial years. Hence, the fact that Kincaid repeatedly explores the love–hate relationship between mother and daughter in her fiction comes as no surprise. But this tension is not central to her writing as a means to investigate simply the mother–daughter metaphor of colonizer/colonized. Rather, it acts as a foil for her investigation into the growing consciousness of young girls, especially in *At the Bottom of the River* (1983), a series of vignettes; in *Annie John* (1983) and *Lucy* (1990), both semi-autobiographical novels; and in her latest novel, *Autobiography of My Mother* (1994), where the mother figure (the young protagonist's birth mother is dead) is represented by a self-hating surrogate who keeps the young girl from ever learning how to love or to be loved.

Perhaps because they were American born to Caribbean parents who migrated to the United States, June Jordan and Audre Lorde, who are also considered African/Caribbean American women authors, write not only with less ambivalence about mother figures but also with more hopefulness about their diasporic heritages. A poet, essayist, spoken-word artist, playwright, children's book writer, and novelist, Jordan is concerned foremost with language and voice, particularly as both can be used to highlight the theme of black subjectivity and to show connections between black peoples of the diaspora. A prolific writer, she has published more than ten books of poetry and children's/young adult literature, produced two plays, and produced two recordings. Perhaps best known for her poetry, Jordan's first collection of poems, *Some Changes*, appeared in 1971, while what is considered her major collection of poems, *Things that I Do in the Dark*, appeared in 1977 under Toni Morrison's editorship at Random House. Like her poetry and children's books, Jordan's collection of essays, letters, and speeches, *Civil Wars* (1981), highlights the use of language and the power of "the word" to effect change in the world.

As Bambara suggested in her review of *Civil Wars*, Jordan's complete body of work makes a significant contribution to feminist literary and social criticism. Similarly, Audre Lorde, who frequently describes herself as a "black lesbian feminist warrior poet," offers her writing as a guide for her vision of a better world. From *Cables to Rage* (1970) to *Zami: A New Spelling of My Name* (1982), Lorde has used her literature to give voice to what was once a largely unrepresented group in the African American literary tradition – African American lesbians. Like Ann Shockley's *The Black and White of It* (1980), for instance, which leaves the reader with a certain amount of hopefulness about black lesbian love even in the midst of unwarranted social oppression, Lorde's work reminds the reader of the importance of love, even in the midst of struggle and pain. Before dying of cancer in 1992, Lorde published ten books of poetry and four of prose, all of which helped create a space for lesbian literature by African American women writers, among them Cheryl Clarke, Sharon Bridgforth, Jewelle Gomez, Cherry Muhanji, Pat Parker, Sapphire, and April Sinclair.

Lorde's openness about her lesbianism undoubtedly helped facilitate what Christian notes as one "radical change in the fiction of the 1980s" – the "overt exploration of lesbian relationships among black women and how these relationships are viewed by black communities."[10] From Walker's *Color Purple* to Naylor's *Women of Brewster Place* to Shange's *Sassafrass* to Lorde's *Zami*, lesbian relationships are depicted, first, more openly and then differently, reflecting the complexity of these relationships and the varying ways to which communities respond to them. And while a sometimes homophobic African American community is far from a perfect place for African American women to explore their sexuality aggressively, the candor of lesbian writers and the insistence of black feminist literary criticism and queer theory that writers deal uncompromisingly with female sexuality generally and with lesbianism specifically have begun to create a space where lesbianism can fit more comfortably in the African American literary tradition.

Throughout the 1980s and extending to today, romantic relationships in general, not just lesbian relationships, figure prominently in literature by African American women writers. In many ways, this focus on love relationships, coupled with a focus on African American upward mobility, marks the latest phase in contemporary African American women's writing, one which has been dominated by popular culture and one which is oft critiqued. Before publishing her novel *1959* (1992), Thulani Davis, an already established playwright, for instance, laments in a *Village Voice Literary Supplement* article "Don't Worry, Be Buppie" that recent (1990) African American women writers seem more concerned with selling their texts in the mainstream than with producing works which move beyond the small, the simple, and the selfish (an act which moves the tradition backward not forward) and which uphold and build on the tradition of African American women writers as trailblazers, as community advocates, and as activists.[11] Entering the critique with a different lament are black male authors, who claim, first, that too much of the popular culture writing by African American women draws its power from male bashing and, second, that the overwhelming attention publishing houses have now begun to give these writers simply reverses the gender discrimination women writers spent years combating. An inevitable conversation around this issue of "pop culture writing as 'literature'" has already begun to sound off in the halls of academia, forcing critics either to defend or to expand traditional ideas of canon formation.

Should the likes of Terry McMillan, Sapphire, Bebe Moore Campbell, and Sister Souljah, for instance, be taught alongside Morrison, Walker, Bambara, and Naylor? And what is to be made of writers like Tina McElroy Ansa, A. J. Verdelle, J. California Cooper, and Pearl Cleage, who rest in that liminal space between "popular" and "literary"? If, as E. Shelley Reid writes as a seemingly convincing response to Davis's thoughtful commentary, "a generation of writers [Morrison and Walker's] focused intently on helping their black women characters learn to define themselves positively instead of just reacting against others' stereotypes, and gave them the power to speak their own names and stories,"[12] then might these "popular" writers be simply actualizing what their literary foremothers initiated, or must their responses mimic the artistic value that birthed them? And, finally, who judges them as artistic or not?

In many ways, such queries are flawed from the start. The assumption of readers, critics, and academics alike is that, once upon a time, "good" literature was easy to find, while in reality "good" literature has always been scarce. And in recent years, it has been extremely hard to sell, as publishing houses have become more commercial and, correspondingly, more concerned with profit than with artistry. With the exception of Morrison, who has an inexplicable cross-over appeal to both popular and literary audiences, authors who are taught in academic settings and read by "intellectuals" have seldom experienced tremendous or sustained commercial success. Focusing too much on what has been called a "crisis in aesthetics" perhaps does a disservice to lesser-known writers who are publishing artistically sound literature. Tayari Jones's debut novel, *Leaving Atlanta* (2002), balances art, politics, and accessibility to fictionalize beautifully the experiences of children who lived through the Atlanta child murders. Z. Z. Packer and Dana Johnson's short stories *Drinking Coffee Elsewhere* (2003) and *Break Any Woman Down* (2001), respectively, balance art, humor, and accessibility to tell the stories of a new generation of women and their communities. Olympia Vernon's first two novels, *Eden* (2003) and *Logic* (2004), are indeed challenging but, like a Morrison novel, artistically and aesthetically rewarding. These emerging writers must be read, talked about, and written about critically, for it is through these writers that the tradition of black women writers who challenge what stories are told, the ways these stories are told, and for whom they are told will continue. Writing that makes us think; writing that challenges us to be better; writing that "saves" us, as Toni Cade Bambara frequently suggested, must continue to be written, published, and read.

Among these writers, we are likely to find, in the coming years, authors who continue in yet another tradition of African American writers – making significant contributions not only to American literature but to the world at large. As Stephen E. Henderson suggests in his introduction to Mari Evans's crucial text *Black Women Writers (1950–1980): A Critical Evaluation* (1984), the impact of the contemporary black woman's "revolution within the Revolution" can be felt in "virtually all aspects of contemporary life, in the everyday world around us and in the special worlds of arts and culture. It is particularly dramatic in literature, to which it has brought dimensions of feeling and analysis that were hitherto missing."[13] To these contributions, one might add experimentation with form. In poetry, one need only consider, for example, Sonia Sanchez. What she does with the Japanese haiku leaves an unmistakably black and female imprint on this traditional composition. By characterization, if not by definition, the haiku focuses on the present moment, thus rejecting introspection, and on the external nature (that which can be experienced by senses – sight, sound, smell, taste, and touch), thus rejecting metaphor and simile. Yet, throughout "Haikus/Tankas and Other Love Syllables," the fifth section of *I've Been a Woman* (1978), Sanchez's haikus combine function (describing an experience as it is perceived at that moment) with ethos (introspection which is culturally, ideologically, and gender specific), and she uses similes and metaphors to enlarge the form. The haiku dedicated to Gwendolyn Brooks, for instance, becomes both an experience perceived in the moment and one loaded with a distinctly cultural sensibility, so much so that it is as much tribute/praise song as it is haiku.

One might also consider, more recently, the poet laureate Rita Dove, whose significance rests not so much in how she adapts form as it does in how she employs a distinctly black and female sensibility to leave cultural markers on traditional forms. Through her use of epic and lyric forms, Dove manages the art of storytelling without succumbing simply to writing prose and offering it as poetry. Most of her collections, like *Thomas and Beulah* (1986) for example, utilize the grouping of the poems to tell the story. While each poem can be read separately, to experience the poem and the collection fully, the poems must be read in sequence and in their entirety. By invoking traditional forms with folk sources, she is able to convey folk ideas and folk ways without using folk speech. Her affinity with polyphony (the use of multiple voices) too reflects the African American tendency to allow multiple voices to coexist at once, forcing readers to question the validity of any history that is written as monologue. Such is the case in *Thomas and Beulah* where we hear variations of the same story, once from Thomas and once from Beulah, so that both sides of the story are told. In all her works, Dove's most significant contribution to American letters, however, perhaps rests in her use of myth to highlight how magical real lives are, both past lives and contemporary lives. Through her manipulation of myth, it is no longer a far away thing that lives only in the imagination. Real people achieve mythical status, and their real experiences are mythologized as she imposes onto traditional myths experiences of race, gender, and class discriminations. Ultimately, she revises two forms – western myth and Africana fable/folk tale, combining the two to create a form of her own in the likeness of that which she has transformed.

In drama, one need only consider the avant-garde theater of Suzan-Lori Parks to see the impact contemporary African American women writers are having on American literature and culture. Parks's maneuvering of space and time in her postmodern plays has expanded what had become typical of mainstream Broadway theater – the use of realistic characters and time-confined situations. As projects of revision, Parks's plays give voice to absence and question and revise presence. The space between history and the con-temporary moment is erased, and history is rewritten, this time to include voices, African Americans' in particular, which history has traditionally ignored. But Parks's dramas are not without their imperfections. At times, her characters reinscribe the very stereotypes they are designed, on a larger scale, to critique. In *Topdog*, Lincoln and Booth are hustling con artists who support the stereotype of black male violence and black-on-black crime. And in *In the Blood* (2000), where Parks draws upon Bertolt Brecht's Mother Courage and Nathaniel Hawthorne's Hester Prynne to give voice to these besieged literary heroines, her black female character, Hester La Negrita, is homeless and has five children by different fathers, thus reinscribing the loose black woman and the black welfare woman stereotypes. Unfortunately, this reinscription weakens, if not counteracts, the character's corresponding cri-tique about patriarchy and the hypocrisy of the men with whom she sleeps. Even so, like that of Adrienne Kennedy and Ntozake Shange, the foremothers with whom she claims to have aligned herself in her early years, Parks's impact on contemporary American theater cannot be denied.

In fiction, the significance of contemporary African American women writers is invaluable. Few can argue against the contributions of these women's works to the African American novel. Rejecting the definitive and declarative stance of the traditional American novel, the African American novel by the contemporary woman is one of inquiry. Leaving a Morrison or Bambara text, one has a clear sense of what *is* impossible. So, one leaves with more ques-tions. The purpose of the journey or the quest, according to contemporary African American women writers, is to probe, to scrutinize that which has made the journey or the quest necessary. The quest is seldom completed, and the result is often an impermanent wellness which may require further and future investigation.

In science fiction, contemporary African American women writers like Nalo Hopkinson, Sheree R. Thomas, Virginia Hamilton, Tananarive Due, and Octavia Butler have not only advanced the genre; they have changed the face of it. Before them, science fiction, traditionally a white male adolescent genre, was limited mainly to ideas about futuristic advances in technology often couched in interplanetary plots. But these writers write women into full beings, debunking limiting stereotypes of women. They also often use the genre to deal with the current rather than the future society on this, not another, planet. Expressing the freedom so characteristic of experimental African American women writers working outside of traditional forms, Butler, early in her career, claimed not to write in a particular genre. *Kindred*, she professes, was not written as science fiction. It had no science in it, only time travel. And it was originally released as fiction, not *science* fiction. Yet, the novel eventually forced critics to expand the limits of science fiction. It dealt with fantasy, not as people traditionally thought of fantasy (with magic and sorcery) but fantasy nonetheless. Eventually, Butler's and her contemporaries' science fiction gained cross-over appeal with both mainstream and science-fiction audiences; and, more recently, it is largely these writers who have encouraged critics to take the genre seriously as an aesthetically rich literary form.

In the *Bildungsroman*, the chief contribution of contemporary African American women writers involves function. As Geta LeSeur has noted, because the African American writer's experience of exile is within her own country, "her motive for writing the *Bildungsroman* is not to rediscover a 'lost domain' or recapture an 'experience,' but to expose conditions which robbed her of a memorable and happy childhood."[14] Thus, *Bildungsroman* fiction by contemporary African American women writers adopts a platform of protest even as it seeks to inform. From Brooks's *Maud Martha* (1953) to Morrison's *Bluest Eye* to Kincaid's *Annie John*, black women writing the *Bildungsroman* force the world to consider how race influences one's coming of age in particular and one's life in general. Amending the genre's tradition of being white and male and its corresponding tendency to ignore race and gender, the black woman's *Bildungsroman* presents the realities of being black and female in a society in which she is doubly marginalized, all the while investigating the ways in which the protagonist's coming of age might best negotiate and accept her marginalized cultural past rather than adopt the culture of an other.

To the traditional autobiography, contemporary African American writers add variety. From Angelou's innovations in her autobiography series – she moves from *Bildungsroman* to "life writing" to travel writing effortlessly – to Lorde's "biomythography" to one type of political autobiography in Angela Davis to yet another in Anita Hill or Lani Guinier, to more recently, the personal essay as autobiography as recounted in Trudier Harris's *Summer Snow* (2003) or Deborah McDowell's *Leaving Pipe Shop: Memories of Kin* (1998), contemporary African American women writers are expanding the rubric of autobiography as form. Craig Werner suggests, in "On the Ends of Afro-American 'Modernist' Autobiography," that the genealogy of the genre can be divided into three stages: an exploratory stage in which writers shifted attention from *writing* to *life* and *self*, a second stage which relied almost exclusively on conventional voice, and a recent stage where *writing* is again a central concern of the genre.[15] What we find with contemporary African American women writers, however, is a blending of these stages at times and a denial of them when necessary. Anita Hill's *Speaking Truth to Power* (1998), for instance, resists the simple narration of life tendency which has again become characteristic of autobiography and, instead, operates out of resistance to someone else's definition of her African American female *self*. She writes almost exclusively from a platform of protest in an attempt, first, to defend and, ultimately, to define herself.

Clearly, even as contemporary African American women authors write to distinguish themselves, they also inevitably enhance the grand tradition of American letters. And they do so by telling their multifaceted stories. Ntozake Shange's lady in brown issues the call: "somebody/anybody/sing a black girl's song/bring her out/to know herself."[16] What we find in contemporary African American women writers are many "black girls" singing their own songs, and they sing them bravely, boldly, and remarkably.

NOTES

1. Toni Cade [Bambara] (ed.), *The Black Woman: An Anthology* (New York: New American Library, 1970; rpt. New York: Washington Square Press, 2005), p. 6.
2. Eleanor W. Traylor, "Re Calling the Black Woman," *The Black Woman*, ed. Cade xi.
3. Barbara Christian, *Black Feminist Criticism* (New York: Pergamon, 1985).
4. Barbara Christian, "Trajectories of Self-Definition: Placing Contemporary Afro-American Women's Fiction," *Conjuring: Black Women, Fiction, and Literary Tradition*, ed. Marjorie Pryse and Hortense Spillers (Bloomington: Indiana University Press, 1985), p. 240; rpt. in Christian, *Black Feminist Criticism*, pp. 171–86.
5. Christian, "Trajectories," p. 241.
6. bell hooks, "Revolutionary Black Women: Making Ourselves Subject," *A Howard Reader: An Intellectual and Cultural Quilt of the African-American Experience*, ed. Paul E. Logan (New York: Houghton Mifflin, 1997), p. 56.

7. Toni Cade Bambara, *The Salt Eaters* (New York: Random House, 1980).
8. Gayl Jones, *Corregidora* (New York: Random House, 1976).
9. Toni Morrison, *Beloved* (New York: Knopf, 1987), p. 273.
10. Christian, "Trajectories," p. 246.
11. Thulani Davis, "Don't Worry, Be Buppie: Black Novelists Head for the Mainstream," *Village Voice Literary Supplement* (May 1990), 26–29.
12. E. Shelley Reid, "Beyond Morrison and Walker: Looking Good and Looking Forward in Contemporary Black Women's Stories," *African American Review* 34 (Summer 2000), 313–28.
13. Stephen E. Henderson, Introduction *Black Women Writers (1950–1980): A Critical Evaluation*, ed. Mari Evans (Garden City, NY: Anchor, 1984), p. xxiv.
14. Geta LeSeur, "One Mother, Two Daughters: The Afro-American and the Afro-Caribbean Female *Bildungsroman*," *Black Scholar* 17 (March/April 1986), 27.
15. Craig Werner, "On the Ends of Afro-American 'Modernist' Autobiography," *Black American Literature Forum* 24 (Summer 1990), 203–20.
16. Ntozake Shange, *for colored girls who have considered suicide / when the rainbow is enuf: A choreopoem* (New York: Macmillan, 1976), p. 4.

5

ROBERT J. PATTERSON

African American feminist theories and literary criticism

So when [Nel and Sula] met, first in those chocolate halls and next through the ropes of the swing, they felt the ease and comfort of old friends. Because each had discovered years before that they were neither white nor male, and that all freedom and triumph was forbidden to them, they had set about creating something else to be. Their meeting was fortunate, for it let them use each other to grow on.

– Toni Morrison, *Sula*

Let's face it. I am a marked woman, but not everybody knows my name. "Peaches" and "Brown Sugar," "Sapphire" and "Earth Mother," "Aunty," "Granny," God's "Holy Fool," a "Miss Ebony First," or "Black Woman at the Podium": I describe a locus of confounded identities, a meeting ground of investments and privations in the national treasury of rhetorical wealth. My country needs me, and if I were not here, I would have to be invented.

– Hortense Spillers, "Mama's Baby, Papa's Maybe: An American Grammar Book"

In the penultimate paragraph of Harriet Jacobs's *Incidents in the Life of a Slave Girl, Written by Herself* (1861), Jacobs confides, "reader, my story ends with freedom; not in the usual way, with marriage."[1] Cherishing the freedom that she has secured for both herself and her children, Jacobs nevertheless laments the fact that "the dream of [her] life is not yet realized," for she does "not sit with [her] children in a home of [her] own" (p. 664). Jacobs's narrative differs from both the autobiographical narratives of formerly enslaved African American men and the sentimental novels of Anglo-American and European women. Whereas Frederick Douglass's *Narrative of the Life of Frederick Douglass, Written by Himself* (1845) ends with him marrying and securing a home, Jane Austen's *Pride and Prejudice* (1813) culminates in an idealized bourgeois marriage in which happiness and prosperity are gained. Even Susan Warner's *The Wide, Wide World* (1850), despite the protagonist's financial and emotional hardships, closes with the protagonist's marriage, which, as the text implies, will undoubtedly improve her life. Jacobs, who possesses some contentment, but neither a home nor prosperity, had hoped that freedom would have provided her with, at minimum, economic independence. Yet, she realizes that what made her such a viable commodity in the slave economy, i.e. her status as a black female, with the potential to produce children who would then "belong" to her owner, are the very identities that make her unable to purchase a home in the "free" North. Slavery has stripped her of the economic wherewithal to actualize "the dream of her life," and although she is no longer enslaved, the possibility that she might someday own a house seems unlikely. As a text that establishes "the constructed discourse that gives rise to the contemporary Black woman's text," Jacobs's narrative, as Angelyn Mitchell explains, "sets forth the terms of discussion for so many narratives that follow in the literary tradition of Black women by providing ample opportunity to examine the feminist themes of female sexuality, motherhood, individualism, and community."[2] While African American feminist writing has existed for centuries, the field of African American feminist scholarship is relatively new. However, such a field would be impossible without the groundbreaking work of authors such as Jacobs, as they theorize black female subjectivity through their work.

Jacobs's narrative foregrounds the ways in which her gender compounds the experience of racial disenfranchisement she experiences at the hands of her licentious and lascivious owner, Dr. Flint. Her insistence throughout the text that it is her dual status – as both woman and African American – that gives Dr. Flint the license to make sexual advances toward her positions her as a literary foremother, an ancestor who "provides a certain kind of wisdom"[3] into what it means to be black and female in what bell hooks describes as a "white supremacist, capitalist, patriarchal society."[4] Jacobs's text, like black feminist political and literary theory, grapples with one primary question – and that is – how do the categories of gender and sexuality, along with class and other subject positions, inform our understanding of what it means to be an African American? In fact, black feminist literary criticism, like black feminist political theory, analyzes how different systems of oppression interlock and function to disenfranchise black women, while proposing solutions to eradicate oppression for everyone. Black feminist theory, as a political enterprise, embodies analogous goals, and has used black women's writing, including fiction, poetry, autobiography, memoir, and manifestos as loci from which to theorize its goals and responsibilities.

I begin this discussion of black feminist literary criticism with an analysis of *Incidents* to demonstrate the fact that well before the 1960s civil rights, Black Power, and women's liberation movements, which undoubtedly provided the momentum and point of departure for the development of black feminist political and literary theory as *formal* modes of inquiry/praxis, African American women's writing exemplified the textual and thematic concerns that ultimately defined black feminist literary criticism. Like Nel and Sula of Morrison's *Sula*, whose epigraphic inscription suggests that because they are not white (male or female) or male (white or black) they lack the privileges afforded to those subject positions, Jacobs also understood identity and oppression as interlocking and overlapping. As a racially marked woman, Jacobs can assume that her male counterparts, who certainly are at least racially terrorized, are not subjected to the same sexual demands to which she is expected to respond, and willfully resists. In an environment in which both law and cultural practices placed Jacobs outside of normative definitions of womanhood (white) and blackness (male), Jacobs asserts her will and recognizes its might. In so doing, Jacobs secures freedom, inscribes herself into the historical narrative, and argues for the abolition of chattel slavery.

If Jacobs's text provides the blueprint that outlines (not circumscribes) the themes that preoccupy some of black feminist literary criticism, then the 1960s provided the resources, both material and ideological, that allowed for the reproduction and dissemination of that blueprint and others like it. In fact, the black feminist movement paved the way for black women's writing to be recovered and later institutionalized in the academy, as well as the emergence of black feminist literary theory. Barbara Smith conceptualized the black feminist movement and black feminist literary criticism as mutually constituting and redefining each other: "Logically developed, black feminist criticism would owe its existence to a black feminist movement while at the same time contributing ideas that women in the movement could use."[5] Of course, not all black women's writings are feminist, nor is there a linear move from Harriet Jacobs, to Zora Neale Hurston, to Margaret Walker, to Toni Morrison, to Alice Walker. I am, however, suggesting that Jacobs's text foreshadows the thematic and formal concerns that persist throughout African American women's writing, and that, in the words of Hortense Spillers, "speak[s] to a particular historical order as a counter-tradition, a counter-myth."[6] Historical context gives any observed similarity its particular meaning. Historicity, then, figures centrally in the discussion of black feminist literary criticism, which is inextricably linked to the political, economic, and social factors that propelled the larger political movement from which it emerged. In tracing the development of black feminist literary criticism, highlighting the key essays, books, and conversations that helped to define and expand the field, this chapter considers the relationship black feminist literary criticism has to black feminist political theory, how black feminist literary theory has redefined its foci and responsibilities over the past thirty years, and finally what tasks continue to lie ahead for black feminist political and literary theory.[7] Although the chapter intends to be comprehensive, it is by no means exhaustive, which bears witness to how the field has flourished during the past three decades.

In terms of its political goals, black feminist theory aims to obtain gender equality for black women, as well as to inscribe black women and their cultural contributions into the historical narrative. In so doing, it aims to expose sexism alongside racism within and outside the black community, and to eliminate all forms of oppression *for everyone*. As Beverly Guy-Sheftall explains, black feminism's goals are to "provide clarity about the impact and interface of racism, sexism, heterosexism, and classism on the lives of African American women" and to create "a world in which race, class, gender, and class hierarchies are no longer viable."[8] As formulated here, oppression cannot be understood or eliminated if it is not conceptualized as overlapping and interlocking. Thinking about oppression in this way not only elucidates the ways in which different forms of oppressions operate analogously, but also undermines the notion, to borrow from Audre Lorde, that hierarchies of oppressions exist. Put another way, black feminism, for example, challenged the notion that black men, who, as a result of racism, could not enact patriarchy exactly like white men, were more oppressed than black women – that racial oppression was more disempowering than gender oppression was. Unlike the civil rights and Black Power movements, which privileged black men's empowerment over black women (and often contributed to their oppression), and the white women's liberation movement, which attempted to gain rights for white middle-class women, black feminism used black women and their experiences of disenfranchisement as the basis for constructing a model by which to eradicate oppression. If, as black feminists contended, oppression positioned black women at the lowest rung on the social ladder, then eradicating their oppression would necessarily ameliorate oppression for everyone.

This intersectional approach to understanding oppression, which concepts such as multiple jeopardy, triple jeopardy, and intersectionality emphasized, became the ur-defining analytical framework through which black feminism understood and tackled black women's oppression. While Kimberlé Crenshaw coined the term intersectionality in her study, "Mapping the Margins: Intersectionality, Politics, and Violence against Women of Color" (1995),[9] which suggested that legal theory must consider the intersections of race, class, gender, and sexuality in order to understand how laws, which purport to be equitable, do not treat black women fairly, the intersectional concepts figured prominently early in the black feminist movement. In 1970, for example, Frances Beale posited the notion of double jeopardy in "Double Jeopardy: To Be Black and Female," arguing that black women's statuses as both black and female made them doubly vulnerable and oppressed.[10] In 1988, Deborah King advanced this argument further in "Multiple Jeopardy, Multiple Consciousness," clarifying that multiple forms of oppression, i.e.

racial, class, gender, and sexuality, are not additive.[11] Rather, as her phrase "multiple jeopardy" suggests, when many forms of disenfranchisement coalesce, the result is exponential disempowerment. As King explains, "The modifier 'multiple' refers not to several, simultaneous oppressions but to the multiplicative relationships among them as well. In other words, the equivalent formulation is racism multiplied by sexism, multiplied by classism" (p. 297). These notions of multiple and intersecting forms of oppression become the analytical lenses through which black feminist literary criticism also examined black women's writing.

Black feminism's desire to be inclusive of all black women was not always actualized, however, in that it failed to consider the experiences of black lesbians, whose literary (mis)representations served as Barbara Smith's point of departure to outline criteria for a more inclusive black feminist literary criticism. Although black lesbians had been ardent activists in the black feminist movement, black feminist theorizations failed to include them.[12] In its now famous declaration, "A Black Feminist Statement," the Combahee River Collective urged black feminists to acknowledge black lesbians' participation in the movement and to interrogate their own heterosexism:

> The most general statement of our politics at the present time would be that we are actively committed to struggling against racial, sexual, heterosexual, and class oppression and see as our particular task the development of integrated analysis and practice based upon the fact that the major systems of oppression are interlocking. The synthesis of these oppressions creates the conditions of our lives. As black women we see feminism as the logical political movement to combat the manifold and simultaneous oppressions that all women of color face.[13]

The Combahee River Collective's attention to lesbianism extended the notion of double jeopardy further, well before King's essay, perhaps making King's notion of triple jeopardy "quadruple" jeopardy. Not only did it suggest that lesbian identity was another disenfranchised subject position, it challenged heterosexual black women to acknowledge the heterosexual privilege that they possessed in the midst of their other oppressions. The publication of this statement in the same year (1977) that Barbara Smith published "Toward A Black Feminist Criticism" inserted black lesbians into the historical narrative, forcing black feminist literary and political theory to actualize its emancipatory goal for, and inclusive of, all black women and not just heterosexual ones.

Before the publication of Smith's essay, the tenets of black feminist literary criticism, notwithstanding the fact that it had not adopted this formal name, nurtured the unearthing and publishing of black women's writing, which served as a primary basis for the development of black feminist literary criticism as an academic subject. During the 1970s, in what now has been termed the Black Women's Renaissance, African American women's writing flourished, "explor[ing] family violence, sexual oppression and abuse, and the corrosive effects of racism, and poverty."[14] Inaugurated by Toni Cade [Bambara]'s publication of *The Black Woman: An Anthology* (1970), African American women's writing increased not only the volume of its critiques of racism, sexism, classism, and homophobia in American and African American communities, but also the number of works published throughout the 1970s. Cade [Bambara]'s collection, as the words of Farah Jasmine Griffin explain, "is one of the first major texts to lay out the terrain of black women's thought that emerged from the civil rights, Black Power, and women's liberation movements. *The Black Woman* was published in 1970, in the same era that produced Toni Morrison's *The Bluest Eye* (1970) and Alice Walker's *The Third Life of Grange Copeland* (1970)."[15] Foregrounding sexual and gender rights as just as central to African Americans' full enfranchisement as racial rights were, these texts challenged the notion that black women should help black men gain their masculinity, while participating in their own sexual and gender disenfranchisements. Bambara's collection, in particular, critiqued the masculinist norms that typified the Black Nationalist movement and contributed to women's oppression. Outlining the ideas that subsequent black feminist texts would expound upon, including the notion that a black male patriarchy would inevitably lead to black women's disempowerment, Bambara's anthology featured pieces by black women, including Audre Lorde, Alice Walker, Paule Marshall, and Nikki Giovanni, all of whom figure prominently in the black feminist literary and liberation movements.

The issue of advocating for black men to have their "rights," while ignoring black women's gender rights, became one of the defining conversations around which the black feminist political movement constructed its agenda because such conversations implicitly and explicitly also addressed motherhood, sexuality, community, family, and economic empowerment. In "An Argument for Black Women's Liberation as a Revolutionary Force," Mary Ann Weathers argues that the notion of giving black men their manhood not only contributes to the oppression of women, but also infantilizes black men:

> It is really disgusting to hear black women talk about giving black men their manhood – or allowing them to get it. This is degrading to other black women and thoroughly insulting to black men (or at least it should be). How can someone "give" one something as personal as one's adulthood? That's precisely like asking the beast for your freedom. We also chew the fat about standing behind our men. This forces me to question: Are we women or leaning posts or props? It sounds as

if we are saying if we come out from behind him, he'll fall down. To me, these are clearly maternal statements and should be closely examined.[16]

Weathers's critique elucidates her understanding that "standing behind" black men, or subordinating gender equality for racial equality, undoubtedly would result in black women's oppression by placing them in gender roles that ultimately strip them of their economic and sexual agency. Several other black feminists, for example, interpreted Black Nationalists' desire for black women to give birth to and care for (male) babies (warriors) for the revolution as a way to consign black women to the role of mother and force their economic dependence. Gayl Jones's novel *Corregidora* (1975) critiques this notion, and Madhu Dubey's critical study *Black Women Writers and the Nationalist Aesthetic* (1994)[17] considers how black women's literary texts, including *Corregidora*, produced during the 1970s challenged the aesthetic and ideological demands that the Black Nationalist movement and its attending counterpart, the Black Arts movement, made for black women's texts. For example, as Jones does in *Corregidora*, Toni Morrison in *The Bluest Eye* (1970), and Alice Walker in *The Third Life of Grange Copeland* (1970), black women writers' exposure of the sexual and familial violence that existed in both their literature and lives not only defied the movement's imperative to portray only "positive" images of black families and relationships, but also exposed the movement's conceptualization of liberation as empowering only black men.

Prior to the proliferation of texts in the 1970s, African American women's writing undoubtedly engaged the themes that Cheryl Wall identifies – family violence, sexual abuse and oppression, and the effects of racism – which is why black feminist political and literary theorists have claimed black feminist foremothers who pre-date the 1970s movement. Sojourner Truth's speech "And Ain't I a Woman" (1851), Frances Ellen Watkins Harper's poem "The Slave Mother" (1854), Harriet Wilson's novel *Our Nig; or, Sketches from the Life of a Free Black, in a Two-Story White House, North* (1859), Anna Julia Cooper's collected essays *A Voice from the South* (1892), Nella Larsen's novel *Passing* (1929), Zora Neale Hurston's novel *Their Eyes Were Watching God* (1937), Ann Petry's novel *The Street* (1952), Gwendolyn Brooks's novel *Maud Martha* (1953), and Lorraine Hansberry's play *A Raisin in the Sun* (1959) are but a few representative texts across genres that black feminist criticism would ultimately identify as embodying the thematic concerns around which it would construct a tradition and theoretical framework. In fact, black feminist movements paved the way for black feminist literary criticism to be institutionalized within the academy, thereby constructing a canon and tradition of black women's writing that forever altered the notions of literary tradition and canonicity in the academy.

When activist and writer Alice Walker "rediscovered" Zora Neale Hurston's *Their Eyes Were Watching God*, both the text and the author herself had remained, to borrow a phrase from Toni Morrison's *Beloved* (1987), "disremembered and unaccounted for."[18] Walker's discovery, while impacting the academy, was first published in *Ms. Magazine*, a woman's magazine and not an academic journal. Throughout the 1970s, this "recovery" and "exposure" work figured centrally in the institutionalization of black women's writing in the academy and black communities. While this chapter focuses particularly on literary developments, it should be noted that the black feminist practice of discovering and disseminating black women's writings, histories, and other forms of cultural production extended into other disciplines, especially history. This point notwithstanding, when Barbara Smith published her theoretical essay, black women's writing had gained more visibility than it previously had. As Smith's essay demonstrated, one of the early goals of black feminist literary theory was to establish a tradition that could also be "theorized."

In her defining essay, "Toward a Black Feminist Criticism" (1977), Barbara Smith criticizes black feminist literary critics for failing to engage sexual politics, or, more precisely, black lesbianism, in their analyses of black women's writing, and foregrounds the relationship that the black feminist movement has to black feminist literary criticism. Situating North American feminism as the catalyst that brought attention to white women's literature and the experiences and values inscribed therein, Smith argued that black feminist criticism, if it were to gain the same momentum, could make similar strides. Without a "body of political theory whose assumptions could be used in the study of black women's art," black women's literature would remain either ignored, dismissed, or under-analyzed. To that end, Smith argued that "a black feminist approach to literature that embodies the realization that the politics of sex as well as the politics of race and class are crucially interlocking factors in the works of these black women writers is an absolute necessity."[19]

For Smith, white feminist and black male critics' failures to engage seriously black women's writing underscored the urgency and necessity for a model for black feminist criticism. Accordingly, Smith proposed three principles that should guide the black feminist critic, a critic she implied must be a black woman: (1) "work from the assumption that black women writers constitute an identifiable tradition"; (2) "look for precedents and insights in interpretation within the works of other black women," and "be aware of the political implications of her work and assert the connections between it and the political situation of all black women"; and (3) "overturn previous assumptions about it and expose for the first time its actual dimensions."[20] Smith aimed to construct a methodology for interrogating black women's writing that used black women's *own* writing to consider the ways in which they have conceptualized their lives and experiences, and to develop the relationships that exist among these texts. Emphasizing her third claim, which offers new interpretations of a text, Smith analyzed Toni Morrison's *Sula* as a lesbian novel. By lesbian novel, Smith meant that it critiqued the institution of marriage and focused on the relationship between women. While critics disagreed, including Morrison herself, whether or not *Sula* should be termed a lesbian novel, a disagreement and resistance that buttress Smith's notion that "lesbian" literature is marginalized, no discussion of black feminist literary criticism can ignore the prominence of Smith's defining essay. While this essay defined the specific criteria for a black feminist analysis, it, along with her publication of *Home Girls: A Black Feminist Anthology* (1983) and *The Truth That Never Hurts: Writings on Race, Gender, and Freedom* (2000), also demonstrated her commitment to foregrounding lesbian sexuality and identity as central to black feminist political and literary theory's formulations.

In "New Directions for Black Feminist Criticism" (1980), Deborah McDowell, like Smith, illuminated the shortcomings of white feminist and black male literary criticism, arguing that "not only have Black women writers been 'disenfranchised' from critical works by white women scholars on the 'female tradition,' but they have also been frequently excised from those on the Afro-American literary tradition by Black scholars, most of whom are males."[21] Doubly assaulted, black female scholars, according to McDowell, find themselves "resurrecting forgotten Black women writers and revising misinformed critical opinions about them."[22] Although McDowell valued the literary historiography that emerges in texts such as Mary Helen Washington's "The Black Woman's Search for Identity: Zora Neale Hurston's Work" (1972), Alice Walker's "In Search of Zora Neale Hurston" (1975), and Roseann Bell's and Beverly Guy-Sheftall's *Sturdy Bridges: Visions of Black Women in Literature* (1979), for example, she maintained that black feminist literary criticism has remained under theorized, arguing that "no substantial body of black feminist criticism – either in theory or practice – exists."[23] For McDowell, Smith's essay is an exemplar par excellence of her critique.

Although McDowell believed that Smith's desire for literary criticism to have practical applications to the feminist movement is too idealistic, her more general concern with Smith's first two formulations was that they do not specify how a certain "precedent" or "insight" is particular to, or functions within, black women's writing. When Smith maintained, for example, that Zora Neale Hurston, Margaret Walker, Toni Morrison, and Alice Walker employ a "specifically black female language to express their own and their characters' thoughts," McDowell would like her to explicate what this black female language is. McDowell's consternation, about this particular matter, stems from the fact that she does not believe that there is an essential black female language that is universal. McDowell maintains that black women who work in the academy likely will not employ the same "language" as one who has not completed high school. Moreover, she questions the degree to which the relationship between black feminist political theory and literary theory can inform each other, while seemingly ignoring the fact that much of the theorization about black feminist theory emerged from reading black women's creative writing. In short, McDowell critiqued Smith for making what she considers an essentialized, ahistorical, universal argument.

Accordingly, McDowell argued for a contextually based black feminist criticism, one that "exposes the conditions under which literature is produced, published, and reviewed."[24] Such a shift would free black feminist criticism from its politically based ideologies which McDowell argued undermines its ability to perform *rigorous* textual analysis. In *The Changing Same: Black Women, Literature, Criticism, and Theory* (1995), McDowell rescinds this initial critique of Smith, admitting, "I was fairly harsh in my judgment. I faulted [Smith] for allowing ideology to inform critical analysis, but now I know there is no criticism without ideology."[25] McDowell's initial critique of Smith, while ardent, marked a time at which the academy, which had only begun to institutionalize the study of black women's writing and black feminist criticism, considered "identity politics" based criticism as less rigorous than theory or outright without merit.[26]

The 1980s produced several texts that further established black women's literature as an integral part of black women's studies, but also that established black women's literature as a tradition dating back to the eighteenth century. Gloria T. Hull, Patricia Bell Scott, and Barbara Smith (eds.), *All the Women are White, All the Blacks Are Men, But Some of Us Are Brave: Black Women's Studies* (1982) not only further institutionalized black women's studies in the academy, but also engaged the theoretical and pragmatic concerns that Smith's and McDowell's texts raised. This text played a central role in establishing black women's studies and black feminist literary criticism partly because of its editors, who decidedly constructed it as a pedagogical tool. Moreover, it aimed to examine "the general political situation of Afro-American women and the bearing this has had upon black women's studies" and "the relationship of black women's studies to Black feminist politics and the black feminist movement."[27] The final sections of the anthology, which include literary criticism, syllabi, bibliographies, and "how to teach" essays, foregrounded the notion that black feminist political and literary theories, while not the same, informed each other.

Claudia Tate's *Black Women Writers at Work* (1983), Mari Evans's *Black Women Writers (1950–1980): A Critical Evaluation* (1984), and Marjorie Pryse's and Hortense Spillers's *Conjuring: Black Women, Fiction, and the Literary Tradition* (1985) further helped to institutionalize and analyze black women's writing. Pryse and Spillers's collection at once posited a literary tradition that spanned the nineteenth and twentieth centuries, while at the same time questioning the very notion of "tradition." Moreover, it helped to establish the critical analyses of black women's texts. Mary Helen Washington's essay, "'The Darkened Eye Restored': Notes Toward a Literary History of a Black Women" (1987), charted the development of a literary history that focused on black women's "thoughts, words, feelings, and deeds,"[28] arguing for the need to continue such recovery work, while Hazel Carby's *Reconstructing Womanhood: The Emergence of the Afro-American Woman Novelist* (1987) and Hortense Spillers's essay "Mama's Baby, Papa's Maybe: An American Grammar Book" (1987) expanded the developing boundaries of black feminist criticism. Whereas Carby's text revised and clarified ideas about tradition and womanhood, Spillers's essay entered black subjects into psychoanalytic theoretical discussions from which they still remained overwhelmingly ignored.

Reconstructing Womanhood: The Emergence of the Afro-American Woman Novelist examined the ways in which black women's literary and political activism appropriated conventional notions of womanhood in nineteenth-century America, and thereby produced an alternative black womanhood. Carby focused on these differing notions of black womanhood and white womanhood, which Jacobs's text demonstrates, to elucidate the fact that there did not exist a common sisterhood among black and white women, as white feminist literary historiography might have suggested. Sojourner Truth's now famous speech, "Ain't I a Woman?" (1851) and the black woman's more general omission from the nineteenth-century white women's feminist movement remind us that a common womanhood did not exist – that race and class also (over)determined the definition of womanhood. In her analysis of nineteenth-century African American women's writing and political activism, Carby challenges the notion that the 1970s was the first African American women's writing renaissance:

> An examination of the literary contributions of Frances Harper and Pauline Hopkins and the political writings of Anna Julia Cooper and Ida B. Wells will reconstruct our view of this period. Writing in the midst of a new "black women's renaissance" the contemporary discovery and recognition of black

women by the corporate world of academia, publishing, and Hollywood – marked by the celebrity of Alice Walker and Toni Morrison – I try to establish the existence of an earlier and perhaps more politically resonant renaissance so we may rethink the cultural politics of black women.[29]

Carby does not establish an earlier existence of black women writers and activists to forge a literary or political activist tradition that extends between the nineteenth and twentieth centuries. In fact, Carby critiques Smith and other black feminists who, in the desire to create a tradition, essentialize black women's identities and ahistoricize their experiences. One consequence of such practices is the elision of class differences, to name but one, that exist between black women. Carby's work highlights these unstated differences, and considers the ways in which class and race inflect the meaning of sexuality at a particular historical moment. In so doing, it becomes an exemplar of what it is that she maintains black feminist criticism should be – "regarded critically as a problem, not a solution, as a sign that should be interrogated, a locus of contradiction."[30] As a locus of contradiction, black feminist criticism had to consider how it would continue to establish the notion of a literary tradition, while not suggesting that the tradition developed linearly. In other words, Hortense Spillers's notion of a tradition shaped by discontinuities expressed in *Conjuring*, which provided a descriptive and not prescriptive way of thinking about the literary tradition, foreshadowed this ongoing conversation. Another question that black feminist literary criticism addressed involved the subject and the subject position; put another way, to what subjects/objects could black feminist criticism be applied? Were the only doers of black feminist criticism, black women, as Barbara Smith had suggested? Were black women's texts the only ones that were subject to a black feminist analysis? Hortense Spillers, Sherley Anne Williams, Michael Awkward, and Valerie Smith each offered critical responses to these questions that continue to shape the field of black feminist literary criticism.

Hortense Spillers's analysis of Toni Morrison's *Sula* (1973) established her place as a black feminist literary critic who recognized black women's literature as a site of ideological resistance and pragmatic revolution:

> If we identify Sula as a kind of countermythology, we are saying that she is no longer bound by a rigid pattern of predictions, predilections, and anticipations. Even though she is a character in the novel, her strategic place as *potential being* might argue that *subversion* itself – law breaking – is an aspect of liberation that women must confront from its various angles, in its different guises. Sula's outlawry may not be the best kind, but that she has the will toward rebellion itself is the stunning idea.[31]

Foregrounding Sula as a character whose refusal to be circumscribed by society's expectations exemplifies the potential that black feminist analyses can have for African Americans' political climate, Spillers extends this argument further in her 1987 essay, "Mama's Baby, Papa's Maybe: An American Grammar Book." Shifting her focus from black women's literary texts to black women's communities more generally, this essay considered the ways in which chattel slavery specifically marked black women's (and black men's) bodies in a slave economy that conflated the body with monetary and ontological values.[32]

Slavery's devaluation of black women's bodies and sexuality, as Spillers clarifies, is the process by which black subjects became "reduced." Overturning the notion that black bodies were inherently "inferior" or debased, Spillers demonstrated how cultural inscriptions, and, in the instance of slavery, literal bodily inscriptions, by making humans transferable capital, attempted to strip blacks of their value. This process, Spillers argued, set in motion a catalogue of events that resulted in Africans being physically displaced, and their gender and familial structures being pushed into a crisis:

> motherhood incarcerated by the laws and practices of ownership, a dual patrimony that could not, either way, speak its name, woman undifferentiated by type and severity, women as "men," men as "women," or the loosening the cinctures of gender, the pregnant body of the bonded woman "split" into social economy between the belly and the unborn and the penally constituted backside.[33]

Spillers's attention to how black women experienced slavery not only disrupted notions that black men had more oppressive experiences with slavery than did black women, but also aimed to foreground how any discussion of black womanhood, or manhood for that matter, and black family structure would have to consider both the physical and psychic ruptures that the institution inaugurated. It is this attention to the psychic in this essay that foreshadows Spillers's later analysis of psychoanalysis and race theory in the African American literary tradition. Yet, Spillers's analysis of slavery, black women, and black families undoubtedly influenced African American literary studies, where Claudia Tate, Ann duCille, Sharon Holland, and a host of other literary critics remain indebted to her formulations.

Claudia Tate's *Domestic Allegories of Political Desire: The Black Heroine's Text at the Turn of the Twentieth Century* (1992) inaugurated the conversation concerning the tropes of marriage and the domestic sphere in black women's narratives after slavery. Tate argues that the trope of marriage complicates the notion of enfranchisement and citizenship for black women.[34] Building on Tate's study, Ann duCille's *The Coupling Convention: Sex, Text, and Tradition in Black Women's Fiction* (1993) extended the conversation by examining the ways in which race, class, gender, and sexuality inflect the meaning of marriage, an institution which American chattel slavery altered for African Americans. Marking a period in American history when African Americans could not legally marry, the term coupling illuminates the fact that enslaved African Americans maintained relationships that would have been classified as marriage, if the participants themselves were not considered property. DuCille's study considers how the coupling tradition redefines the European marriage plot, as well as how African American writers, like Jacobs, appropriated its structure "for their own emancipatory purposes."[35] In her analysis of texts from slavery through the Harlem Renaissance, duCille asserts that the black women's texts "construct and are constructed by a black feminine ego and a black feminist consciousness; and, ultimately, how these novels reclaim and resexualize the black female body."[36] DuCille's study engages how the novels reify and subvert the aesthetic, social, and political demands that occasioned their production and reception. Her analysis of the final scene from *Incidents in the Life of a Slave Girl Written by Herself* that begins this chapter, for instance, maintains that Jacobs "acknowledged both her awareness of the marriage tradition in literature and her own subversion of that tradition."[37] Moreover, she posits, "Jacobs identified two issues with which black women writers were to be preoccupied throughout her century and ours: the pervasiveness of patriarchal power and the struggle of black women to reclaim political freedom and female authority."[38]

DuCille's invocation of Jacobs not only claims her as a literary foremother who participates in the development of black women's literary tradition, but also as one who alters the terms by which "tradition" is defined. DuCille's focus on black women's consciousnesses and egos situates her project within a psychoanalytic framework that Hortense Spillers outlines in her 1996 essay, "'All the Things You Could Be by Now if Sigmund Freud's Wife Was Your Mother': Psychoanalysis and Race."[39] If, as Griffin contends, "Spillers sees the psychoanalytic as a way of getting to a more complex black subjectivity, not simply that which is created by oppression, domination, violence, and economic exploitation, but subjectivity that is created by agency,"[40] then black feminist criticism's investigations of how black women, to borrow from Angelyn Mitchell, "exert agency within circumscribed environments,"[41] conceptualize the ways in which black women writers have written themselves into (literary) history and altered it in so doing.

Informed by the white feminist movement's exclusion of black women from its organizations and discourses in the 1970s, Alice Walker coined the term womanist, which she at once used to differentiate and analogize black women's feminism to white women's. Asserting that feminist is to lavender as womanist is to purple, Walker, on the one hand, suggested that womanism is a form of feminism that foregrounds black women as the subject of their discourse. On the other hand, Walker wanted to underscore the fact that, unlike feminism, which had been accused of being divisive along gender lines, it was "committed to the survival and wholeness of [an] entire people, men and women."[42] It is this focus on both men and women that Sherley Williams addresses in her essay, "Some Implications of Womanist Theory," where she argues that a womanist black literary criticism would call for a thorough examination of black men's literature in addition to black women's. A womanist analysis of black men's literature, according to Williams, would allow critics to examine not only what black men have written about black women, but also what they have written about themselves:

> Womanist inquiry, on the other hand, assumes that it can talk both effectively and productively about men. This is a necessary assumption because the negative, stereotyped images of black women are only part of the problem of phallocentric writings by black males. In order to understand that problem more fully, we must turn to what black men have written about themselves.[43]

Williams's contention overturned Smith's earlier notion that black women's writing was the only possible subject of black feminist criticism. In so doing, Williams suggested that black women's and men's literature developed and existed coextensively, and believed that the application of womanist theory to male texts would end "the separatist tendency in Afro-American criticism."[44] Williams's analysis admonishes black feminist literary criticism to avoid the pitfalls of replicating the same exclusionary practices that it rightfully accused white feminist and black male literary critics of. Michael Awkward's *Negotiating Difference: Race, Gender, and the Politics of Positionality* (1995), in which his second chapter, "A Black Male's Place in Black Feminist Criticism," critically addresses the potential gains and dangers of black men engaging in black feminist analyses, generally forces critics to consider how their own identities inform the politics and practice of literary analysis.[45] Published five years after black feminist sociologist Patricia Hill Collins had argued that black women have a privileged standpoint from which to theorize and analyze black women's experiences, Awkward's book elucidated the fact that all acts of interpretation are rooted in a position, or a standpoint, and, I would add, questioned the notion that one particular group was necessarily in a better position to analyze its cultural production than an outsider.

Valerie Smith's *Not Just Race, Not Just Gender: Black Feminist Readings* (1998) foregrounded black feminist criticism as a strategy that could be used to analyze not only literature, but also other forms of cultural media, including film, art, and music. For Smith, black feminist criticism functioned as a strategy of reading that analyzes the "intersection of constructions of race, gender, class, and sexuality."[46] According to Smith, a white woman or a black man committed to this type of analysis could render a black feminist analysis of a cultural text. Conversely, Smith maintained that a black woman's status as a black woman does not make her inherently (essentially) more qualified to engage in a black feminist analysis than someone who is neither black nor female. While not discounting altogether the role that experience has in informing the critics' analysis, Smith remains sensitive to black feminists' desire that black feminism not be colonized or co-opted by non-black women. This point notwithstanding, Smith emphasized the fact that one must be trained to engage in black feminist analysis, and that the more people involved in implementing its goals, the more likely it is that its goals will be actualized. Smith, like Williams and Awkward, conceptualizes black feminist criticism as a project that could be undertaken by individuals who were committed to engaging critically black women's writings, lives, and histories.

At the conclusion of the twentieth century, black feminist literary criticism and black feminist political theory undoubtedly worked coextensively to excavate black women's literary and cultural texts that had not been published, were out of print, or otherwise absent. In so doing, both projects established the fact that black women's writing, from its inception, consciously considered what it meant for African American women to be "raced," "sexed," "gendered," to name three subject positions, in American society. Both literary texts and activist writings anticipated the notion of intersectionality, which has become the analytical framework through which black feminist political theory analyzed black women's lives and black feminist literary criticism examined black women's writing. These endeavors have resulted in an increased awareness of black women, their cultural contributions, experiences with oppression, and efforts to achieve enfranchisement. In terms of literary criticism, specifically, the movements have established a canon of black women's writing that forever altered the notions of literary tradition and canonicity in the academy, and have disseminated black women's writing to American communities outside the academy. Making black women's writing more visible, black feminist literary criticism elucidates black women's history of writing, inscribing them into historical narratives and resisting their marginalization. As figured here, reading and writing are forms of activism and resistance. It is this particular conceptualization of writing's potential that conjoins the black feminist literary movement with the political one. The confluence of black feminist criticism and the black feminist political movement is evidenced in the development of African American studies, women's studies, gender studies, and queer studies, which use its goals and methodologies as their respective basis for organization. As black feminist literary theory advances in the twenty-first century, it must continue to grapple with the ways in which the vectors of race, class, gender, and sexuality intersect, and also consider the ways in which other socializing institutions, such as religion, for example, inflect representations of the traditional categories of identity. While critiques of religion and Christianity persist throughout African American women's writing, and the advent of Womanist theology has provided us with a heuristic to interrogate such critiques, more attention might be paid to how other religious traditions, e.g. Islam, might challenge existing formulations about religion, gender, and race. Both black feminist political theory and literary criticism possess many directions and possibilities for the future. That they might one day eradicate cultural and structural oppression for everyone makes that future look brighter.

NOTES

1. Harriet Jacobs, *Incidents in the Life of a Slave Girl, Written by Herself*, ed. Henry Louis Gates, Jr. *The Classic Slave Narratives* (New York: Signet Classic, 2002), p. 664.
2. Angelyn Mitchell, *The Freedom to Remember: Narrative, Slavery, and Gender in Contemporary Black Women's Fiction* (New Brunswicky, NJ: Rutgers University Press, 2002), pp. 22–23.
3. Toni Morrison, "Rootedness: The Ancestor as Foundation," *Literature in the Modern World*, ed. Dennis Walder (New York: Oxford University Press, 1990), p. 330.
4. bell hooks, *Outlaw Culture: Resisting Representations* (New York, Routledge, 1994), p. 282.
5. Barbara Smith, "Toward a Black Feminist Criticism," *Within the Circle: An Anthology of African American Criticism from the Harlem Renaissance to the Present*, ed. Angelyn Mitchell (Durham, NC: Duke University Press, 1994), p. 417.
6. Hortense Spillers, "Afterword: Cross-Currents, Discontinuities: Black Women's Fiction," *Conjuring: Black Women, Fiction, and Literary Tradition*, ed. Marjorie Pryse and Hortense Spillers (Bloomington: Indiana University Press, 1985), p. 252.
7. See Farah Jasmine Griffin, "That the Mothers May Soar and the Daughters May Know Their Names: A Retrospective of Black Feminist Literary Criticism," *Signs* 32.2 (2007), 483–507, for an excellent examination that considers diasporic approaches to black feminist literary criticism in the twenty-first century.
8. Beverly Guy-Sheftall (ed.), *Words of Fire: An Anthology of African-American Feminist Thought* (New York: New Press, 1995), p. xviii.
9. Kimberlé Crenshaw, "Mapping the Margins: Intersectionality, Politics, and Violence against Women of Color," *Stanford Law Review* 43.6 (July 1995), 1241–99.
10. Frances Beale, "Double Jeopardy: To Be Black and Female," *Words of Fire*, ed. Guy-Sheftall, pp. 146–55.

11. Deborah King, "Multiple Jeopardy, Multiple Consciousness: The Context of Black Feminist Ideology," *Words of Fire*, ed. Guy-Sheftall, pp. 294–318.

12. For a discussion on black lesbian contributions to the feminist movement, see Cheryl Clarke, "The Failure to Transform: Homophobia in the Black Community," *Home Girls: A Black Feminist Anthology*, ed. Barbara Smith (New York: Women of Color Press, 1983), pp. 190–201; and "Lesbianism: An Act of Resistance," *Words of Fire*, ed. Guy-Sheftall, pp. 242–252.

13. Combahee River Collective, "A Black Feminist Statement," *Words of Fire*, ed. Guy-Sheftall, p. 232.

14. Cheryl Wall quoted in Marianne Hirsch, "Knowing Their Names: Toni Morrison's *Song of Solomon*," *New Essays on Song of Solomon: The American Novel*, ed. Valerie Smith (New York: Cambridge University Press, 1995), p. 73.

15. Farah Jasmine Griffin, "Conflict and Chorus: Reconsidering Toni Cade's *The Black Woman: An Anthology*," *Is It Nation Time? Contemporary Essays on Black Power and Black Nationalism*, ed. Eddie Glaude (Chicago: University of Chicago Press, 2002), p. 117.

16. Mary Weathers, "An Argument for Black Women's Liberation as a Revolutionary Force," *Words of Fire*, ed. Guy-Sheftall, p. 158.

17. Madhu Dubey, *Black Women Writers and the Nationalist Aesthetic* (Bloomington: Indiana University Press, 1994).

18. Toni Morrison, *Beloved* (New York: Penguin, 1987), p. 276.

19. Smith, "Toward a Black Feminist Criticism," p. 412.

20. Ibid., pp. 416–17.

21. Deborah McDowell, "New Directions for Black Feminist Criticism," *Within the Circle, Renaissance to the Present*, ed. Mitchell, p. 429.

22. Ibid., p. 430.

23. Ibid., p. 430.

24. Ibid., p. 434.

25. Deborah McDowell, *The Changing Same: Black Women's Literature, Criticism, and Theory* (Bloomington: Indiana University Press, 1995), p. 23.

26. For a discussion of the vexed relationship that black feminist literary criticism has had in the academy, see Griffin, "That the Mothers May Soar."

27. Gloria T. Hull, Patricia Bell Scott, and Barbara Smith (eds.), *All the Women Are White, All the Blacks Are Men, But Some Of Us Are Brave: Black Women's Studies* (New York: Feminist Press, 1982), p. xvii.

28. Mary Helen Washington, " 'The Darkened Eye Restored': Notes Toward a Literary History of Black Women," *Within the Circle*, ed. Mitchell, pp. 442–53.

29. Hazel Carby, *Reconstructing Womanhood: The Emergence of the Afro-American Woman Novelist* (New York: Oxford University Press, 1987), p. 7.

30. Ibid., p. 15.

31. Hortense Spillers, "A Hateful Passion, A Lost Love: Three Women's Fictions," *Black, White, and in Color: Essays on American Literature and Culture*, ed. Hortense Spillers (Chicago: University of Chicago Press, 2003), p. 118.

32. Hortense Spillers, "Mama's Baby, Papa's Maybe: An American Grammar Book," *Black, White, and in Color*, pp. 203–29.

33. Ibid., p. 19.

34. Claudia Tate, *Domestic Allegories of Political Desire: The Black Heroine's Text at the Turn of the Twentieth Century* (New York: Oxford University Press, 1992).

35. Ann duCille, *The Coupling Convention: Sex, Text, and Tradition in Black Women's Fiction* (New York: Oxford University Press, 1993), p. 3.
36. Ibid., p. 4.
37. Ibid., p. 5.
38. Ibid., p. 5.
39. Hortense Spillers, "'All the Things You Could Be by Now if Sigmund Freud's Wife Was Your Mother': Psychoanalysis and Race," *Critical Inquiry* 22.4 (Summer 1996).
40. Griffin, "That the Mothers May Soar."
41. Mitchell, *Freedom to Remember*.
42. Alice Walker, *In Search of Our Mother's Garden: Womanist Prose* (New York: Harcourt, 1983), p. xi.
43. Sherley Anne Williams, "Some Implications of Womanist Theory," *Within the Circle*, ed Mitchell, p. 517.
44. Ibid., p. 520.
45. Michael Awkward, *Negotiating Difference: Race, Gender, and the Politics of Positionality* (Chicago: University of Chicago Press, 1995).
46. Valerie Smith, *Not Just Race, Not Just Gender: Black Feminist Readings* (New York: Routledge, 1998), p. xiii.

PART II

Genre, gender, and race

6

JOYCELYN MOODY

African American women and the United States slave narrative

Introduction

The origins, development, generic conventions, and major themes of the slave narrative are fundamental to understanding the genre of the slave narrative, a literary genre first seriously studied by Marion Wilson Starling in the 1946 dissertation that became her vast book titled *The Slave Narrative*.[1] Dictated, shaped, and, in one unique case, written by enslaved and formerly enslaved African American women before the ratification of the Thirteenth Amendment to the United States Constitution and the Reconstruction era that followed, the slave narrative – its complex artistry and aesthetics – continues to inform the literary forms subsequently developed by African American women writers. Studies in the slave narrative have examined the critical and imaginative shifts the genre has made over time. Just as the conventional, often confessional slave narratives of the eighteenth century assume a different form and undertake issues different from those in later autobiographies by African Americans, the antebellum slave narrative differs from its postbellum counterpart in terms of its relationship to national ideals. Furthermore, post-Emancipation narratives differ from post-Reconstruction era narratives, which share relatively few traits with the twentieth-century narratives collected from elderly ex-slaves as part of the Federal Writers Project and the Workers Progress Act in the 1930s and 1940s. The antislavery autobiographies published as books, pamphlets, and serial articles during the early nineteenth century arguably have the most in common with the postmodern neoslave narratives of the late twentieth century and afterward.

On the early nineteenth-century abolitionist platform, (usually male) slaves' bodies served as powerful corporeal condemnation of the "peculiar institution." The exhibition of the scarred body of the putatively voiceless slave provided a visual testimony against the brutalities of chattel slavery.

Thus, to the extent that slaves literally wore bondage on the body, their narratives demonstrate that they could also intellectualize and narrativize – which is to say, organize and articulate – their life experiences no less than could white autobiographers, whose corporeality as a rule also embodied their divergent social and political privileges. In other words, the literary genre of the slave narrative offered an alternative to the story of bondage whipped onto the backs of slaves.[2]

Traditionally, antebellum and other pre-emancipation narratives of slavery, written or dictated by both male and female former, free(d), fugitive, or bound slaves, are characterized by the following conventions: para- and extra-textual apparati such as prefatory and postscript testimonials (predominantly written by whites) to verify both the existence of the slave whose life is recounted and the authenticity of the slave narrative attributed to him or her; scenes of physical and psychological torture and deprivation; depictions of grueling labor; the sale and separation of slave families and further assaults on their integrity; descriptions of both the narrator's own and other slaves' sufferings; yearnings for literacy; and meditations on the ways that, as Mary Prince asserts, "slavery hardens white people's hearts towards the blacks."[3] Slave narratives also typically detail attempts to escape the site of enslavement for short periods of time, as when the narrator of the *Memoir of Old Elizabeth* at age eleven walks twenty miles from one farm to see her parents and siblings, who resided on another, or to escape for longer periods, if not escape altogether.[4] Overall, anxiety and despair punctuate the representation of slavery and the degradation of the fugitive or manumitted (ex-)slave.

Although they tell stories of unfathomable pain, injustice, and atrocity, ex-slave and enslaved women's narratives also tell stories of exceptional triumph over both the obstructions of adversity and the inadequacies of language. Enslaved and formerly enslaved women were compelled to expand beyond the most effective strategies of reconstructing slavery deployed by men, to devise a unique set of literary conventions for the telling of their lives in bondage, primarily because the rhetorical tropes and formulae available to other blacks – which is to say, to men – and to other women – which is to say, predominantly to white women – were either unavailable to them or did not allow them to articulate sufficiently the complex conditions of their lives.[5] More remarkable yet is the innovation of slave women who faced and overcame the physical, sociopolitical, and linguistic challenges that typically obstructed the transformation of their lives into print literature. Thus, the very reality of US women's slave narratives attests to black women's sophisticated manipulations of English language usage as storytellers, autobiographers, and producers of cultural texts.

No less than their male counterparts, women who narrated slavery faced charges of inauthenticity and incredibility as the genre emerged and developed. From the early 1800s through abolition, slaveholding whites persistently challenged the authority of slave narratives in part by rejecting their truthfulness. From this castigation of the accuracy and credibility of slave narratives grew the myth that Africans are naturally unreliable as truth-tellers and even incapable of not prevaricating. In addition, proponents of slavery declared that, since widespread illiteracy among blacks meant that slave narratives were written more often by (northern) whites than by bound or fugitive blacks, these whites and other abolitionists were not in fact representing the words or stories of actual enslaved persons, but instead creating fictions in order to threaten and thwart southern slaveholding states' political and economic power.[6] Moreover, the discursive and practical difficulties that slave women had to confront in order to develop accessible and creditable accounts of their lives become illuminated under the consideration that the majority of (white) Americans, even those who opposed slavery, did not necessarily accept women of African descent as reliable narrators, either literally or figuratively speaking. Although many Anglo-American readers from the late eighteenth century through the Civil War exoticized blackness and black people as sources of fascination, titillation, and entertainment, as Eric Lott and other literary scholars have shown, they nonetheless regarded with suspicion black testimony of virtually any type.[7] In other words, because black women and their amanuenses and African American women authors knew that auto/biographies by or about blacks were more likely than not to be read with distrust and disbelief – in their authenticity and authority, in their verity and veracity – they had to construct serious, earnest texts that would engage curious Other readers and, furthermore, to construct those Others as trusting rather than resisting readers. If black women writers and slavewomen's amanuenses could not achieve that textual goal, then their pre-abolition slave narratives would fail their collective mission of antislavery reform. Because slave narrators knew that most whites and other non-black readers would be skeptical of their accounts of slavery, their narratives are imbued with self-conscious rhetorical strategies, imbued with self-consciousness *about* their rhetorical strategies, as well as imbued with tempered assertions of details that those who had not experienced slavery could find both difficult to read and difficult to accept. Given that virtually all extant pre-abolition slave narratives by women were dictated rather than self-authored, this "self"-awareness obviously emanates both from the enslaved or ex-slave woman and through her amanuensis.[8]

Origins of the genre

Slavery occasioned an originary moment in that it inspired, or rather, provoked in enslaved persons the expression and production of their survival of bondage, their resistance to it, and the cultures they produced and sustained within it. The earliest narratives of bondage that slavery instigated were, perhaps more than the abolitionist treatises that followed them, attempts to re-member the African self, to articulate an African character outside Africa, to transcend or otherwise come to terms with diasporic displacement, to name and thereby to govern the (reconstruction of) conditions of black life beyond the African continent. Often, those narratives also analyze the Europeans with whom those blacks came in contact. In the nineteenth century, the goals and conventions of early slave narratives were generated by the sociopolitical needs of enslaved people, often as defined not only by slaves themselves but also by former slaves committed to the struggle to end slavery within the US. After abolition, there were significant shifts in the aims and conventions, for inasmuch as the earlier narratives had functioned as vessels for an abolitionist message, post-emancipation autobiographies could pursue a vastly different set of social, political, and economic needs specified by the newly freed African Americans and their allies.

The earliest extant account of a woman's experiences of violent capture in Africa, involuntary transport through the Atlantic Middle Passage, then arduous captivity in the New World American colonies is not a traditional slave autobiography but instead a 1782 petition to the state of Massachusetts for reparations for her compulsory, unpaid labor. Specifically, one elderly and infirm Belinda, "an African Slave," sought damages to be paid to herself and her aging daughter by the estate of Isaac Royall of Medford. Joanne Braxton's *Black Women Writing Autobiography* provides the full title of this pregeneric third-person narrative, which is included in the 1787 inaugural issue of the serial *American Museum and Repository of Ancient and Modern Fugitive Pieces*, as "The Cruelty of Men Whose Faces Were Like the Moon: The Petition of an African Slave to the Legislature of Massachusetts."[9] John Ernest notes that Belinda's petition "joins with the story of the American Revolution to form an argument for her portion of the wealth of an enslaver who was 'compelled' by the Revolution" to end his days "where lawless dominion sits enthroned."[10] The strategy that she and her attorney(s) deployed went beyond portraying one woman's subjective account and personal perceptions – though that portrayal in and of itself marks a significant achievement – to situating that one woman within a web of systems that included whites and other free people, other people invested in securing national and individual freedoms. By appealing to the Massachusetts

Legislature for compensation for Belinda's labors, the white lawyers demonstrated their own conviction in her right to remuneration, and at the same time they accurately imagined a post-Revolution legislature comprised of whites who would be amenable to the petition, perhaps especially because of the triumph of national freedom and individual rights only a few years before they filed the petition on Belinda's behalf.

Invoking a traditional definition of *narrative* in his Introduction to *Classic African American Women's Narratives*, William L. Andrews cites Sojourner Truth's autobiography as the first description published in the US of "the outrages of slavery from a female slave's point of view."[11] The *Narrative of Sojourner Truth* first appeared in 1850, although Truth had been dictating her life story to her amanuensis Olive Gilbert since 1846, a mere year after Frederick Douglass published his famous *Narrative of the Life of Frederick Douglass, an American Slave*. Notably, then, black women born in the US (as opposed to those like Belinda who endured the Middle Passage) began making contributions to the tradition of classic antebellum slave narratives almost from its inception.

Goals of the genre

Belinda's petition encodes a slave woman's experience for reparations for her unpaid labor. The fundamental goals of the slave women's narratives that followed Belinda's appeal similarly constitute an alternative documentation of bondage. They sought to control, to shape, and where advantageous to alter and transform the ways that free people thought about the institution and those suffering under it, in part such that they would feel motivated to agitate for its cessation. In addition, slavewomen's narratives, particularly of the antebellum era, strove to arrest whites' production of racist stereotypes of black women as primitive barbarians, beasts of burden, slave breeders, indulgent mammies, sex-hungry Jezebels, tragic mulattas, and so on. Directly and indirectly, they called as well for an end to myths about black people that were no more than products of an Anglo-American cultural imagination integral to a project of white supremacy – whether through the enslavement of Africans and their American descendants or through the sentimental condescension of white benevolence. Ironically, just as its proponents predicated slavery on blacks' putative natural dependence and moral weakness, white abolitionists depicted enslaved women as helpless, ignorant victims dependent on well-meaning whites for significant existence. Furthermore, enslaved and ex-slave women's narratives published through collaboration with literate amanuenses could interrupt, and contest, accounts of slaves' experiences as recorded by persons who had not known bondage; they could correct erroneous details of second-hand (or fabricated) reports of slavery. Emphasizing the primacy of eye-witness *cum* I-witness to the dehumanizing effects of slavery, they argue effectively that the most creditable accounts of slavery are generated by those who have witnessed slavery firsthand. The compelling subjectivity of African American women that emerges in most slave women's narratives invalidates the assessments of the women as morally weak and as constitutionally needy, even where their agency has perhaps been compromised by an amanuensis's mediation.

The slave narrative was a form that empowered blacks to challenge white-authored myths of African inhumanity and stereotypes of black character and capabilities. Like the conventional and traditional autobiography, a slave narrative reconstructs the life of the subject. In the case of slave women, such an endeavor is both remarkable and audacious, for it challenges the belief that enslaved people of African descent have no life worth living, no life that they "own." Some eighteenth- and nineteenth-century whites argued that the life of a slave was synonymous with that slave's owner's life, for theoretically, slaves were by definition either naturally devoid or legally dispossessed of a life apart from their masters' – or both.

The slave narrative genre, moreover, challenges the myth of Africans' basic lack of interiority – a myth that buttressed the institution of slavery. The myth asserted that since blacks are beasts of burden, then their enslavement is neither criminal nor immoral. Thus, the slave narrative genre gave blacks the opportunity to reveal and express their interiority and consciousness. That opportunity seized, the slave narrative subverts the bases on which the institution of slavery was founded. In addition to interiority and the humanity it evidences, slave narratives offered proof that in spite of the conditions bondage imposed on their lives, slave women nonetheless pursued and led meaningful, worthy lives, and they had the intelligence and skill to translate those lives into powerful rhetoric. And where they are unable to circumvent slavery's forced illiteracy, they could collaborate with amenable amanuenses to transform their lives into informative and creditable texts. Just as the cultural work of the traditional autobiography includes establishing as valuable the life of its subject, a slave narrative similarly, simultaneously performs and documents the intrinsic value of the life of its subject.

Central to the specific and distinctive goals of slave women's narratives is the exposé of the atrocities of slavery, particularly with respect to family ties – from being sold away from one's immediate family at a young age, as happened to Elizabeth, to having one's children sold away from one, as happened to Sojourner Truth. As Nellie McKay asserts, "For [enslaved] women, there is always a strong female bond that exists with forebears, and this invests them with the power to resist, survive, and transcend their own oppression."[12] Slave women's narratives' painful truths about enslaved motherhood manifest this bond and the devotion and power it yielded. Paradoxically, however, these narratives also strive to veil and to mask the full effects of slavery's horrors. Harriet Jacobs's *Incidents in the Life of a Slave Girl, Written by Herself*, for example, opens with the sentence, "Reader, be assured this narrative is no fiction," but the preface also reveals that the author has "concealed the names of places, and given persons fictitious names" (p. 5). Indeed, Jacobs writes, "No pen can give an adequate description of the all-pervading corruption produced by slavery" (p. 79). Like the amanuenses of other slave women's narratives, Jacobs further condemns slavery as a system so vicious it could not but corrupt the basic instincts for morality and virtue of those bound under it. Jacobs stands apart, however, in that she also argues, subversively, that blacks naturally possess a greater sense of virtue and morality than whites, as demonstrated by the fact that whites held blacks in bondage with apparent impunity and blacks generally hated the institution.

Above all, however, slavery was a complex economic system built on human labor. Therefore, in addition to the goals of documenting and lambasting slavery's legal, psychological, communal, spiritual, and ethical damages to black people, slave women's narratives collectively specify the harshness and severity of slave women's diverse forms of labor, chiefly fieldwork (to raise livestock, to produce tobacco, food, clothing, and other consumable goods), domestic service, childcare and child rearing, sexual work (from concubinage to breeding), and textile manufacture (from spinning to sewing). Perhaps the most grisly account of the staggering cruelty of slave women's working conditions is provided by Mary Prince in describing slaves' labor in the salt mines at Turk's Island, West Indies. For their myriad labors, slave women received virtually no remuneration and rare and random compensation, perhaps in the form of cast-off clothing from slaveholders. That they sometimes managed to manipulate slavery into a system that afforded them any material reward at all for their arduous work indicates black women's deep capacity for intellectual endeavors. Funded in large measure by a combination of true grit and abolitionist patronage, their slave narratives achieve a similar end: they illustrate the ingenuity of ex-slave and enslaved women to transform reconstructions of their lives, especially their survival of slavery, into material resources that would enable them to go on surviving their subjugation as blacks and as women. In the case of Louisa Picquet, for example, the manumitted narrator maintains the specific and ironic objective of applying funds from the sale of the mediated story of her own enslavement across the South to the purchase of her mother still bound in Texas.

Notable representatives of the genre

If the term *slave woman's narrative* signifies an account of the life and bondage of a woman of African descent, then the canon of extant pre-abolition narratives written or dictated by women of African descent consists almost entirely of the 1782 petition of Belinda to the State of Massachusetts (cited above); the legal documents of Elizabeth Freeman, "who sued for her freedom in 1781 and won, basing her case on a new constitution of Massachusetts"; *Memoir of Mrs. Chloe Spear, a Native of Africa [written] by a Lady of Boston* [Rebecca Warren Brown?] (1832); *The History of Mary Prince, a West Indian Slave*, narrated in London to Susanna Strickland (Moodie) and published by Thomas Pringle in 1831; *Narrative of Sojourner Truth: A Bondswoman of Olden Time*, published by Olive Gilbert in 1850 (revised by Frances Titus in 1878 for a second edition that contained Truth's *Book of Life*); the trial documents and court proceedings, historicized in the late twentieth century by Melton McLaurin, of a Callaway County, Missouri, woman named Celia, who murdered her owner Robert Newsom in 1855; the extraordinary partnership of Ellen Craft and her husband, who reconstructed their lives as fugitives in *Running a Thousand Miles for Freedom: The Escape of William and Ellen Craft from Slavery* (1860); Harriet Jacobs, the only woman in this canon who authored her own narrative, as Jean Fagan Yellin has indisputably validated; *Louisa Picquet, The Octoroon: A Tale of Southern Slave Life*, written by Rev. Hiram A. Mattison and published in 1861; and *Memoir of Old Elizabeth, a Colored Woman* (1863).[13] In addition, Braxton further cites: "*Memoir of Jane Blake* (1834), *Narrative of Joanna, an Emancipated Slave of Surinam* (1838), *Aunt Sally; or the Cross the Way to Freedom* (1858), [and] *Narrative of the Life of Jane Brown* (1860)."[14] *The Story of Mattie J. Jackson*, by Dr. L. S. Thompson, is arguably an *antebellum* slave woman's narrative inasmuch as it was dictated and published in 1866, just months after the surrender at Appomattox and the ratification of the Thirteenth Amendment. Two significant postbellum narratives also appeared in the wake of the war: Sarah H. Bradford's secular *Scenes in the Life of Harriet Tubman* (1869), predating its revised successor *Harriet Tubman, Moses of Her People* of 1886, and Elizabeth Keckley's 1868 account of her life among the Lincolns and fraught friendship with the widowed Mary Todd Lincoln in *Behind the Scenes; or, Thirty Years a Slave and Four Years in the White House*. Back in the eighteenth century, many of the poems of Phillis Wheatley as well as the seven surviving letters she wrote to Arbour Tanner, her black woman friend living in Newport, Rhode Island, also narrate and protest slavery, and substantiate the claim by Darlene Clark Hine and Kathleen Thompson that "unlike her owners, [Wheatley] was a fiery apostle of freedom."[15] Frances Whipple Greene's (auto)biography of another woman of African descent, the black and Native American entrepreneur Elleanor Eldridge, freeborn in Rhode Island in 1785, also exhibits conventions of the early slave narrative, demonstrating both that racialized discrimination in the nominally free northern states restricted blacks' civil rights to a grave extent and that a black woman's rhetorical collaboration with a white amanuensis, even one with whom she shared female gender, necessarily implied a knotty and complex cross-racial, cross-cultural relationship.

Distinguishing rhetorical and thematic features

Dictated or written by enslaved and ex-slave women themselves, women's slave narratives dramatically underscore the sense of self that the women possessed, despite all the ways that the slaveocracy strove to divest them of it. The slave woman's narrative as historical and cultural document attests to black women's collective conviction that their lives and life stories were worthy of telling. Sometimes that telling was an anguishing experience, as seems to have been the case for Louisa Picquet, who apparently evaded her amanuensis's prurient inquiries so skillfully that Mattison seems almost by her design to reveal his own lasciviousness more than her sexualized sufferings. Such scholars as Saidya Hartman and Hershini Bhana Young explore the tropes of the mask and the veil, as well as the gaps and omissions, in slaves' narratives to confirm that the reconstruction of a life in bondage often traumatized slave narrators.[16] But those narratives also abundantly declare that though slavery was a site of trauma, the opportunity to proclaim to a reading public slaves' own conviction about the value of their lives and their experiences as human beings was one too important to forgo. To the extent that virtually everything in eighteenth- and nineteenth-century America militated against the articulation of lives in bondage and, foremost, against a high estimation of those lives, then every extant slave narrative, particularly each woman's, confirms the commitment of those positioned to do so to tell slavery and in so doing, to tell slaves' self-actualization. Thus, slave narratives themselves and the conditions under which they were produced indicate that the production of a slave narrative was a major feat and its subsequent publication the result of an agonistic struggle. Enslaved women's struggle for self-determination, as Frances Smith Foster asserts about Jacobs's in particular, "was a battle fought less on the physical level than on intellectual, emotional, and spiritual planes."[17]

The slave narrative genre enabled the inscription of a distinct black female self: the slave narrative by enslaved and ex-slave women differs from its counterpart by enslaved or ex-slave men in that it emphasizes gender differ-ences in the experiences and treatment of men and women slaves. In *Incidents*, Jacobs poignantly proclaims that "Slavery is terrible for men; but it is far more terrible for women" (p. 119). One key rhetorical feature of the slave narrative from a woman's perspective is precisely the articulation of these terrible gen-dered differences, primarily the biological experience of reproduction. Consequently, women's narratives often articulate how the biological factors of reproduction (viz., childbirth and motherhood) and heterosexual sex acts (viz., rape, breeding, and concubinage) distinguished women's experiences of bondage from men's. For example, pregnancy impeded a woman's chances of successful acts of short-term truancy, especially slipping beyond her owners' range of vision. Pregnancy made women conspicuous: hypervisible, pregnant women were more easily detected when "out of place." Pregnancy could mean, on the one hand, that women were less likely, for better or worse, to be hired out by their owners as laborers to others who desired to purchase their labor for a limited time. On the other hand, according to Jonathan D. Martin, author of *Divided Mastery*, some women seem to have become pregnant deliberately in an effort to control for whom they worked (or did not work) and whether they could remain with their families and loved ones rather than to be loaned or traded away from them, for example.[18] Similarly, female biology and patriar-chal socialization determined that a woman could not escape slavery as easily as a man could. As Mattie Jackson tells in her *Story*, her mother, Ellen Turner Jackson Brown Adams, "lost" more than one husband by encouraging each to pursue his freedom even though his escape required leaving her and their children behind. Ellen herself tried clandestinely to leave more than one slave owner but failed because she was literally weighed down by the physical burden of her children. Ironically, Ellen's immobility illustrates the perversion of the 1662 Virginia legislation that assigned to children the condition of bond or free in accordance with their mother's status. It is further ironic that, in 1664, Maryland officials enacted a statute that had cast the bound-for-life fate of children born of enslaved fathers with those fathers. A heinous combination of the pursuits of white supremacy and legalized rape of chattel slaves led to the ultimate adoption of the 1662 Virginia law throughout the slaveocracy.[19] However, as Foster has cogently demonstrated, for Jacobs and other enslaved women, while flight may not be the first option they had to resist slavery, neither was it their only option.[20] Rather than leave her children behind in a "pit of vipers," Jacobs reports, she hid for seven years in a garret in her (freed) grandmother's house in North Carolina from which she could daily see her children and other relatives – and also keep watchful eye upon "the venomous old reprobate," her owner, Dr. James Norcom, pseudonymously identified in *Incidents* as Dr. Flint (p. 117).

Braxton, McKay, and Joycelyn Moody, among other (black feminist) scholars, have discussed the slave narrative as a site of celebration of slave-women's heroes, particularly their own mothers, as Mattie Jackson's *Story* filially honors Ellen Adams by detailing the latter's maternal dedication. Perhaps the primary virtue that slave women champion in other black women is the determination to triumph over slavery, largely by drawing on a stupefying depth of internal fortitude and identifying and marshalling other resources for survival – human and circumstantial. As Andrews observes in his Introduction to *Six Women's Slave Narratives*, for example, Thomas Pringle, a principal in the British Anti-Slavery Society, labels Mary Prince as a woman with an arrogant, tempestuous personality, but at the same time Pringle demonstrates that Prince's alleged behavioral and character "defects" undoubtedly more than once saved her from slaveholders' cruelty and viola-tion.[21] At other times, slave women narrators subversively exalt qualities that early white Americans as a rule considered socially taboo, inappropriate. Sometimes black women overcame slavery through large-scale acts of tru-ancy, as in the case of Harriet Tubman's renowned travels on the Underground Railroad, or smaller escapes, as when, feeling "so lonely and sad I thought I should die, if I did not see my mother," young Elizabeth defies her master's express orders in order to spend a few days with her mother on a distant farm (*Memoir*, pp. 3–4).

The slave woman's narrative functioned, then, as a space in which to document African American women's moral, mental, intellectual, and psy-chological strength, their capacity to endure the horrors of slavery as well as to develop and maintain a strong and abiding sense of self-respect and self-determination. By representing the various ways that black women coped with slavery and their extraordinary survival skills, they also upended the patriarchal condescension to white women enshrined in the view that women as a class are biologically inferior to men. At the same time, enslaved and ex-slave women narrators insisted that, as Africans, they were not subhuman but human *and* female. Their ability to cope with the brutal aspects of slavery had been used to validate the false claim that females of African descent are subhuman and therefore not to be afforded the same (proscribed) civil and human rights as white women. Thus, black women collaborated with their amanuenses – white and black, male and female – to use their life stories to assert black women's humanity and also to expose the ways they were subjugated on the basis of both race and gender. Their first-person declara-tions, their repeated use of the autobiographical "I" debunked myths that decreed them inhuman and inferior.

Moreover, slavewomen's narratives argued in multifarious ways for indi-vidual and communal freedoms. Some of these texts inscribe freedom as an unhindered pursuit of a personal relationship with the Christian God. Freedom manifests itself as a capacity for love for and from the Christian God. To be free, they posit, is to be spiritually and mentally available and receptive to religious salvation. The publication in 1850 of the autobiography of Sojourner Truth marks the blending of black women's dictated slave narratives with the tradition of black women's spiritual narrative that had begun with the autobiographical *Productions of Mrs. Maria W. Stewart*, first published in 1835, a tradition sustained by such African American spiritual autobiographies as the *Memoirs of the Life, Religious Experience, and Ministerial Travels and Labours of Mrs. Zilpha Elaw* (1846) and the *Religious Experience and Journal of Mrs. Jarena Lee* (1849). Like Lee's *Journal* and Elaw's *Memoirs*, Stewart's *Productions* and Truth's *Narrative* constitute hybrid texts in that they map onto one another conventions of at least two different literary forms. For their part, Lee and Elaw respectively narrate experiences as freeborn northern itinerant ministers whose work takes each among slaves in the US South. Each woman's powerful spiritual autobiography assumes a hybridized aspect in that its narrator opposes slavery both as an institutional violation of secular, sociopolitical civil and human rights and as an offense against the teachings of the Christian Gospel. Another slave woman's hybrid text joins this rich tradition: discussed above, the *Memoir of Old Elizabeth, a Colored Woman*, was dictated to an anonymous amanuensis, then published by the American Tract Society in 1863. It also integrates the Christian conversion autobiography with the slave woman's narrative.

Another mediated slave woman's narrative, Mattison's *Louisa Picquet*, perhaps incautiously defines freedom as the capacity to avoid being "helped" into harm by an ostensibly well-intentioned abolitionist.[22] If Mattison does indeed endeavor to get Picquet to divulge more particulars of the physical and sexual abuses she suffered, and Picquet chafes under his questioning, as that narrative insinuates, then freedom for the former slave woman would lie in her ability to redirect his lewd attention, to deflect his piercing questions, and still maintain his commitment to publishing her narrative so that she can raise funds to buy her mother's freedom.

Slavewomen's narratives also form a hybrid genre to the extent that they blend conventions of early American sentimental novels and domestic fictions for (white) women with the conventional male fugitive slave narrative of rugged masculinity and individual heroic self-actualization. To dramatize slave women's gross susceptibility to sexual aggression by slave traders and slave owners and to protest the sexual violence that she and other enslaved women suffered, Jacobs ironically seized the Christianized morality tale's emphasis on virgins in distress and virtue under siege. Foster summarizes the codified sentimental aspects of Jacobs's slave narrative when she states, "*Incidents* reads like a story of pursuit and evasion, one full of heroes and villains ... and of desperate maidens trying to preserve their virtue, of mothers trying to protect their children and of the hardworking poor trying to survive the greed and exploitation of the powerful and wealthy."[23] Jacobs subverted that melodramatic story, however, by inscribing in *Incidents* the very impropriety and inadequacy of the conventions available to her as a woman writer – what served both traditional and innovative literary texts by white women like her editor Lydia Maria Child proved only ill-fitting and confining for the documentation of Jacobs's *resistance* to perverse, state-sanctioned sexual molestation.

Foster's observation about Jacobs's deployment of the True (white) Woman's discursive practices points toward an important reversal in slave women's mediated narratives: their amanuenses generally perceived – and, ironically, also illustrated – that in the universe of (white women's) sentimental rhetorics, bondage and blackness rendered slave women intrinsically sentimental and thus objects to be written and spoken about but not speaking subjects empowered to tell their own stories. As bell hooks has argued, the publication of their life stories empowered enslaved African Americans "to move from object to subject, from silence into speech," and this move effected an important and transformative revolutionary literature.[24]

Slave narratives explicitly pursued freedom in that they endorsed abolition and other civil rights projects, especially women's rights. Their exposure of the violation of slaves' fundamental human rights, as articulated by those who could offer an eyewitness account of the atrocities, performed the cultural work of attempting to inspire free (white) people to fight against human bondage as well as toward challenging white supremacy manifest as sentimentalized "charity."[25] Jacobs announces at the beginning of *Incidents in the Life of a Slave Girl* that she wants her book to rally the free (white) women of the North to work on behalf of their enslaved sisters in the South. She calls for a righting of the wrongs perpetrated against enslaved women. Five years after *Incidents* appeared, Mattie Jackson and her amanuensis L. S. Thompson would go even farther than Jacobs; in unison they insist, as Andrews notes, that slavery (had) meant the economic exploitation of black people as well as their political, social, and psychological disfranchisement.[26] Indeed, Jackson's tacit, astute appeal for material and educational remuneration for her labors and losses echoes Belinda's petition for reparations, made to the Massachusetts legislature in 1782.

Recurring themes and tropes

A wide range of themes and tropes permeate the slavewomen's narratives that appeared over the century before abolition was legislated. The primary concerns of ex-slave and enslaved women aggregated around the black female body, chiefly because African women had entered the New World as putatively mindless physical laborers. Generally, as Michael Bennett and Vanessa Dickerson state, the work that enslaved women performed was twofold: there were both "the physical labor demanded by the plantation economy" and the reproductive labor that replenished slaveholders' stock.[27] Enslaved motherhood confirmed slave women's own condition as chattel commodities, a heinous condition that they passed on to their offspring as well. As physical laborers and mothers, Bennett and Dickerson note, the enslaved black female body was simultaneously masculinized and feminized by the dominant culture; in short, her body was disparaged as grotesque.[28] This destabilizing representation is borne out by the spectacles made of the bodies of Sojourner Truth and Harriet Tubman, for just two examples – in narrative treatments of these illustrious women by both their respective ostensibly well-intentioned amanuenses and the popular media of their era.

African American women launched multiple forms of resistance to these abuses against their collective personhood and womanhood, not all of them literary. To thwart slavers' sexual dominance over their bodies and the proliferation of slave progeny, they resisted reproduction by covertly practicing African forms of contraception and abortion, and, albeit rarely, some enslaved women desperately took their children literally in hand via infanticide. They resisted the denial of their rights to sustained romantic relationships with lovers and partners of their own choosing and to marriage by engaging the assistance of literate others to help maintain bonds despite being separated by long distances. For example, Elizabeth Keckley reprints in her postbellum autobiography letters from her father to her mother after he had been sold away from his family. (Keckley's inclusion of these and other letters also functions as a subtle critique of the slaveocracy's compulsory illiteracy of slaves that ensued from southern laws against black education.) The sharpest, most vigorous condemnation of the exploitation of enslaved women's corporeality is Jacobs's self-authored *Incidents in the Life of a Slave Girl* with its emphasis on the sexual violation of black women. *Incidents* subverts the codification of women's delicacy and decorum, the patriarchal and capitalist institution of marriage, and, in Barbara Welter's scholarly shorthand, the Cult of True Womanhood in eighteenth- and nineteenth-century sentimental novels for women. In courageously confessing to a (white) female readership taught to feel superior to an enslaved woman, to a "mulatta," and to an unmarried sexually active woman who asserts her right to choose a lover and, more taboo yet, to bear him two children, Jacobs reveals the extent to which slavery demanded that enslaved women reverse conventional moral and social codes if they were to enact any sense of agency and subjectivity whatsoever. Their amanuenses notwithstanding, dictated narratives like those by Truth and Picquet, and extant autobiographical legal documents like those of Belinda and Celia – all enslaved mothers of children produced from rape – corroborate *Incidents*'s implicit, astute conceptualization of resistance as the power required to subvert one's more powerful adversaries.

According to Bennett and Dickerson, "the most remarkable emblem of the black body's instability perhaps resided in the figure of the mulatta."[29] The patheticized, or "tragic," version of the figure of the mulatta gained special currency in literature and popular culture with the publication of William Wells Brown's 1853 novel *Clotel; or, the President's Daughter*, the oldest extant novel by an African American.[30] A few years later in 1859 it was refigured by a mixed-race woman writer in the novelized depiction of the ostensibly free Frado, the heroine of Harriet E. Wilson's *Our Nig: Sketches from the Life of a Free Black, in a White House, North, Showing that Slavery's Shadows Fall Even There* (which may well have been the first novel written and published by an African American woman). To be sure, Wilson subtitled her novel specifically to call attention to slave and black codes that severely hindered the freedom of African Americans living in the nominally free US North. As in *Incidents*, for which Jacobs borrows heavily from the sentimental and domestic novels of her day, in the fictions by Brown, Wilson, and virtually all other black writers of the era, the mulatta type is used to embody and critique a nexus of race, blood, sex, gender, wealth, caste, and subjection that reified and endowed with power such forces as white masculinity, cultural whiteness, sexual dominance, and notions of miscegenation. In sum, they demonstrate and castigate the dominant society's demonization of the black female body that grew out of Euro-American sadism and negrophobia. Indeed, the capriciousness of the ways of white folk, to invoke a phrase from Langston Hughes, and intricate black resistance to those peculiar ways form a significant theme in texts written and dictated by ex-slave and enslaved women.

One additional recurring theme in the narratives of ex-slave and enslaved women is also another cultural form of resistance to slavery: the assertion of the black woman's voice in interpersonal contexts, or in the vernacular, back-talk: verbal warfare, speaking up, speech acts of retort and retaliation against oppressors, talking back to challenge authority figures. Braxton identifies this form of slave women's resistance as "sass," and describes it as "a mode of verbal discourse ... and a weapon of self-defense."[31] Significantly, Braxton suggests the longevity of the tradition when she traces the etymology of *sass* to a West African word "associated with the female aspect of the trickster."[32] In another black feminist scholarly investigation of early black women's modes of resistance, Harryette Mullen explores slavewomen's "runaway tongue" as a self-preserving strategy.[33] Profoundly, albeit provocatively, Mullen declares this resistant speech impudent, then traces the derivation of that characterization to the *pupenda*, an organ of female biology.

Influences of slave women's narratives on other writings by African American women

While slavery and the genre of the slave narrative influenced virtually every aspect of the earliest literary traditions developed by and about black women, the spiritual autobiography titled *Life and Narrative of Nancy Prince* (published in multiple editions between 1850 and 1860) is notable for its abbreviated reconstruction of the life of the freeborn author's enslaved mother. Specifically, Prince's *Life and Narrative*, published in the same year that Harriet Beecher Stowe's *Uncle Tom's Cabin* first began appearing serially in the *National Era*, gives an account of her mother as a woman driven mad by the horrors of slavery in the pre-emancipation North, including desertion by several husbands who escaped to freedom and the incapacity to care adequately for her many children. Joining the spiritual autobiography tradition of Zilpha Elaw and Jarena Lee, Prince produces a hybrid narrative that condemns slavery within a superficially free Christian nation.[34]

In the decades following the Thirteenth Amendment and the Reconstruction era, the rhetorical conventions and social concerns of pre-abolition slave women's narratives influenced later black women's literary output as well, perhaps most profoundly such works as Frances E. W. Harper's novel *Iola Leroy; or Shadows Uplifted* (1892), Pauline Hopkins's novel *Contending Forces* (1901), and *Crusade for Justice: The Autobiography of Ida B. Wells* (posthumously published in 1970 by Wells-Barnett's daughter Alfreda Duster) and *The Memphis Diary of Ida B. Wells*, edited in 1995 by Miriam DeCosta-Willis. Three highly acclaimed twentieth-century innovative novels that borrow heavily from slave women's narratives are Zora Neale Hurston's *Their Eyes Were Watching God* (1937), Toni Morrison's *Song of Solomon* (1977), and Gloria Naylor's *Mama Day* (1988). Among the late twentieth-century writings by African American women poets that invoke and appropriate conventions of earlier slave women's narratives are Lucille Clifton's autobiographical *Generations: A Memoir* (1976), Rita Dove's *Thomas and Beulah* (1986) and *Mother Love* (1995), and Elizabeth Alexander's *The Venus Hottentot* (1990). In 1991, cinematographer Julie Dash received significant serious attention for *Daughters of the Dust*, her feature film exploring the originary moment of continental modern migration among descendants of slaves in the South Carolina and Georgia coastal islands. Dash published a novel under the same title in 1997.

Perhaps most importantly, a series of novels produced by African American women writers in the second half of the twentieth century, some of them autobiographical and all defined by a number of scholars as neoslave narratives, revisit and revise the major conventions, tropes, and themes of the earliest slavewomen's narratives.[35] The authors of these neoslave narratives self-consciously acknowledge their debt to the enslaved and ex-slave black women who came before them. They include Margaret Walker (*Jubilee*, 1966), Maya Angelou (*I Know Why the Caged Bird Sings*, 1970), Gayl Jones (*Corregidora*, 1975), Octavia Butler (*Kindred*, 1979), Paule Marshall (*Praisesong for the Widow*, 1983), Toni Morrison (*Beloved*, 1987), Sherley Anne Williams (*Dessa Rose*, 1987), Barbara Chase-Riboud (*Sally Hemings*, 1979), Alice Randall (*The Wind Done Gone*, 2001), and Nancy Rawles (*My Jim*, 2004).

From the beginning of the slave trade throughout the African diaspora, enslaved black women – including the earliest historians of slavery, the abducted themselves – have recognized the capacity of recounting narratives of bondage to broadcast black sufferings, to agitate for abolition among the hegemonic and powerful, to testify and witness, perhaps to heal. Thus, telling stories of capture, bondage, and survival – individual and collective – has always been a political act for enslaved black women and their descendants. Both by joining with their male counterparts to expose the slaveocracy's crimes and by passing on stories of slavewomen's experiences situated where blackness, female gender, motherwit, and chattel caste meet and mingle, African American women have since the seventeenth century participated in the literary reconstruction of their daily lives, extraordinary and mundane. Just as the character and conventions of slavewomen's narratives have evolved, the scholarly record and analysis of those narratives continues to take new forms. Recent studies of the history of US slavery and African American enslaved women's lives have been influenced by academic trends of cultural studies, women's studies, and scrutiny of the social construction of identity categories, broadening what we know and how we can know about US slavery.[36] Such studies have wisely taken their cues from the abundant and profound literature produced by enslaved women and the women who have proudly descended from them.

NOTES

1. Marion Wilson Starling, *The Slave Narrative: Its Place in American History* (Washington, DC: Howard University Press, 1988).
2. John Ernest, *Liberation Historiography: African American Writers and the Challenge of History, 1794–1861* (Durham, NC: University of North Carolina Press, 2004), p. 165.

3. Moira Ferguson (ed.), *The History of Mary Prince, a West Indian Slave, Related by Herself* (1831; Ann Arbor: University of Michigan Press, 1997), p. 4.

4. In William L. Andrews (ed.), *Six Women's Slave Narratives* (New York: Oxford University Press, 1989), pp. 3–4.

5. See Valerie Smith (ed.), Introduction, *Incidents in the Life of a Slave Girl, by Harriet Jacobs* (New York: Oxford University Press, 1988), p. xxviii.

6. See Ann Fabian's discussion of John Greenleaf Whittier and James Williams in "Hannah Crafts, Novelist; or, How a Silent Observer Became a 'Dabster at Invention,'" *In Search of Hannah Crafts: Critical Essays on The Bondwoman's Narrative*, ed. Henry Louis Gates and Hollis Robbins (New York: BasicCivitas, 2004), pp. 44–48.

7. Eric Lott, *Love and Theft: Blackface Minstrelsy and the American Working Class* (New York: Oxford University Press, 1993).

8. Jennifer Fleischner, *Mastering Slavery: Memory, Family, and Identity in Women's Slave Narratives* (New York: New York University Press, 1996), p. 9.

9. Joanne M. Braxton, *Black Women Writing Autobiography: A Tradition within a Tradition* (Philadelphia: Temple University Press, 1989), p. 211.

10. Ernest *Liberation Historiography*, p. 164.

11. William L. Andrews (ed.), Introduction, *Classic African American Women's Narratives* (New York: Oxford University Press, 2003), p. xiv.

12. Nellie Y. McKay, "The Souls of Black Women Folk in the Writings of W. E. B. Du Bois," *Reading Black, Reading Feminist: A Critical Anthology*, ed. Henry Louis Gates, Jr. (New York: Meridian, 1990), p. 232.

13. For discussion of Spear, see Darlene Clark Hine and Kathleen Thompson (eds.), *A Shining Thread of Hope: The History of Black Women in America* (New York: Broadway, 1998), p. 4. For more accounts of enslaved women's life experiences, see the slave narratives and slavery-related documents that are available through the University of North Carolina-Chapel Hill *Documenting the American South* database, online at http://docsouth.unc.edu/.

14. Braxton, *Black Women Writing*, p. 22.

15. Hine and Thompson (eds.), *A Shining Thread of Hope*, p. 25.

16. Saidya Hartman, *Scenes of Subjection: Terror, Slavery, and Self-Making in Nineteenth-Century America* (New York: Oxford University Press, 1997); Hershini Bhana Young, *Haunting Capital: Memory, Text, and the Black Diasporic Body* (Lebanon, NH: University Press of New England, 2006).

17. Frances Smith Foster, *Written by Herself: Literary Production by African American Women, 1746–1892* (Bloomington: University of Indiana Press, 1993), p. 103.

18. Jonathan D. Martin, *Divided Mastery: Slave Hiring in the American South* (Cambridge, MA: Harvard University Press, 2003), pp. 55–56.

19. Sally Ann H. Ferguson, "Christian Violence and the Slave Narrative," *American Literature* 68.2 (1996), 297–320.

20. Foster, *Written by Herself*, p. 95.

21. Andrews (ed.), Introduction, *Six Women's Slave Narratives*, p. xxxviii. This volume contains the antebellum dictated narratives by Mary Prince and "Old Elizabeth" as well as *The Story of Mattie J. Jackson* (dictated and published in 1866), Lucy A. Delaney's self-authored *From the Darkness Cometh the Light or Struggles for Freedom*, published circa 1891, Kate Drumgoold's self-authored *A*

Slave Girl's Story (1898), and Annie L. Burton's *Memories of Childhood's Slavery Days* (1909).

22. Cf. P. Gabrielle Foreman, "Who's Your Mama? 'White' Mulatta Genealogies, Early Photography, and Anti-Passing Narratives of Slavery and Freedom," *American Literary History*, 14.3 (2002), 505–39. See also DoVeanna S. Fulton, *Speaking Power: Black Feminist Orality in Women's Narratives of Slavery* (Albany: SUNY Press, 2006).

23. Foster, *Written by Herself*, p. 103.

24. bell hooks, "Writing the Subject: Reading the Color Purple," *Reading Black, Reading Feminist: A Critical Anthology*, ed. Henry Louis Gates, Jr. (New York: Meridian, 1990), pp. 464–66.

25. For a fuller discussion of these two phenomena, see Ernest, *Liberation Historiography* and also Hartman, *Scenes of Subjection*.

26. Andrews (ed.), *Six Women's Narratives*, p. xxxv.

27. Michael Bennett and Vanessa D. Dickerson (eds.), *Recovering the Black Female Body: Self-Representations by African American Women* (New Brunswick, NJ: Rutgers University Press, 2001), pp. x–xi.

28. Ibid., p. xi.

29. Ibid., p. xi.

30. *The Bondwoman's Narrative* (1857?) is a novel apparently written by a woman named Hannah Crafts. In 2002, it was recovered and published for the first time by Henry Louis Gates, Jr. That Crafts was an African American woman has not been indisputably authenticated.

31. Braxton, *Black Women Writing*, p. 10.

32. Ibid., p. 31.

33. Harryette Mullen, "Runaway Tongue: Resistant Orality in *Uncle Tom's Cabin, Our Nig, Incidents in the Life of a Slave Girl*, and *Beloved*," *The Culture of Sentiment*, ed. Shirley Samuels (New York: Oxford University Press, 1992), pp. 244–64.

34. For more discussion of this tradition, see Joycelyn Moody, *Sentimental Confessions: Spiritual Narratives of Nineteenth-Century African American Women* (Athens: University of Georgia Press, 2000.)

35. For a fuller discussion of this genre, see Ashraf H. A. Rushdy, "The Neo-Slave Narrative," *The Cambridge Companion to the African American Novel*, ed. Maryemma Graham (Cambridge: Cambridge University Press, 2004), pp. 87–105.

36. Edward E. Baptist and Stephanie M. H. Camp (eds.), Introduction, *A History of the History of Slavery in the Americas. New Studies in the History of American Slavery* (Athens: University of Georgia Press, 2006), pp. 1–18.

7

JOANNE M. BRAXTON

Autobiography and African American women's literature

Black women's autobiographical writing in the Americas has been shaped by a unique literary inheritance, by challenges faced, and by day-to-day experience. The inheritance is a rich one rooted not only in written literary models, but also in the African American oral tradition of spiritual narrative and bearing witness, in traditions of protest, in work song and blues, in Anglo-European aesthetic and linguistic models, and in rich and subtle variations of diverse and creolized origin. In *Black Women Writing Autobiography* (1989), I argued that black women autobiographers constitute a tradition within a tradition, operating within the dominant, familiar, and essentially masculinist modes of autobiography.[1] Simultaneously, however, these same black women writers reshape and redefine their inherited formulae.

Defying every attempt to enslave or diminish them or their self-expression in any way, black women autobiographers liberate themselves from stereo-typed views of black womanhood, and define their own experiences. In the parlance of Audre Lorde, black women writers attempt to dismantle the master's cardboard house of false superiority, threatening not only the notion of "whiteness" but also patriarchy and with it the very idea that man is closer to God than woman.[2] They construct instead a uniquely black and female autobiographical self, leaving a literary legacy and providing guidance, encouragement, and direction both for readers and for future literary trends. This chapter does not propose to cover every instance of black women's autobiographical writing, but rather to pursue the relationship between letters and liberation in representative examples of black women's writing as they develop in response to the challenges faced by successive generations.

The scarcity of written contributions by black women to the autobiographical genre in eighteenth-century America reflects their displacement and marginalization within the dominant society. While Ben Franklin sat comfortably at his desk writing *The Autobiography*, black women toiled in the fields and labored in the heat of colonial kitchens; few women of any race had more than minimal literacy. Black men were similarly challenged, though they were more prolific (or at least more frequently published) than black women in the early years. While there is no eighteenth-century autobiographical work by a black woman to rival the eighteenth-century narratives of Quobna Ottobah Cugoano or Olaudah Equiano, surviving autobiographical fragments confirm black women's conscious effort to document life experiences and invoke positive change.

In the beginning, the memory of Africa and the Middle Passage was represented in the "as told to" stories of Yamba, born on the Gold Coast turned slave coast of West Africa, and of Belinda, a woman of probable Nigerian origin. Neither Belinda nor Yamba was able, in the terms established by critic William Andrews, "to tell a free story," as both were enslaved and neither was able to read or write. Belinda's *The Cruelty of Men Whose Faces Were Like the Moon* (1787) appears in the form of a petition to the state legislature of New York for reparations from the estate of her late master. Although she was dependent on someone else to give form and shape to her story, Belinda's petition conveys her memories of family and Africa, the shock of enslavement, the Middle Passage, and her attempts to grasp a new language and render it to service.[3]

Yamba, whose story was presented in first-person song form by a sympathetic listener (probably the English feminist, evangelist and antislavery writer, Hannah More), recounted experiences similar to those of Belinda. A bond servant who presumably learned English as an adult, she too relied on a sympathetic listener:

> From the bush at even tide
> Rush'd the fierce man-stealing Crew;
> Seiz'd the Children by my side,
> Seiz'd the wretched Yamba too.[4]

The usual questions persist: did Yamba really exist and is this her own story or the creation of a passionately antislavery ghostwriter? How much is a true and a faithful representation? Were there embellishments and/or exaggerations? What might have been altered or left out for the sake of an intended audience? Without being able to verify Yamba's existence, even the most basic of these questions cannot be answered, yet the first-person claim for truth value, even if fictive, remains haunting and pregnant with possibility.

Diverse African cultures were rich in oral literature, and, therefore, the inability to write did not mean that a bondswoman might not be able to express herself autobiographically in another form. Given the prevalence of poetic language and song in African culture, one imagines many Yambas and Belindas, seventeenth- and eighteenth-century Billie Hollidays and Nina

Simones, singing their lives in their very own languages, unnoticed or dismissed as happy slaves, and, finally, erased.

Phillis Wheatley, a native of Senegambia often portrayed in the Americas and England as an apologist for slavery, wrote these anguished and angry words:

> I, young in life, by seeming cruel fate,
> Was snatch'd from Afric's fancy'd happy seat:
> What pangs excruciating must molest,
> What sorrows labour in my parent's breast?
> Steel'd was that soul, and by no misery mov'd,
> That from a father seized the babe belov'd.[5]

Freed, Wheatley was still not free; she did indeed make concessions to her imagined "white" reader on many occasions. Here, however, she subverts the traditional sonnet form to protest her kidnapping and enslavement. Operating both within and without dominant literary modes, Wheatley critiques the proffered patriarchal model by reminding the reader of her outraged and bereaved African father.

If I were writing a book on black women's autobiography today, I would still begin by looking at the works of fugitive and former slave women, because however one looks at a tradition of black women writing autobiography, the slave narrative, or, if you prefer, the narrative of emancipation, is primary. William Andrews observes that "[t]he slave narrative evolved between 1830 and 1860 as a way of letting slaves themselves have a voice in their cause as both eyewitnesses to the horrors of slavery and I-witnesses to their own feelings as human beings caught up in such a monstrous system."[6] This is an important distinction, for of the many who were "eyewitnesses," only a few would seize the self-liberatory impulse and fasten it to literary "I-witnessing" in autobiography.

Harriet Jacobs's *Incidents in the Life of a Slave Girl: Written by Herself* (1861), once devalued and now canonized with greater and lesser degrees of satisfaction, has been fully authenticated and reclaimed, thanks to the works of Jean Yellin, William Andrews, Frances Smith Foster, Hazel Carby, and others. In my earlier work, I posit the heroine Linda Brent (Jacobs) and her grandmother as primary examples of the outraged mother archetype and Linda Brent's verbal use of "sass" as a weapon of self-defense used against her would-be rapist master. Meanwhile, entire volumes are now devoted to analysis and scrutiny of Jacobs's narrative and its placement within the slave narrative genre and traditions of autobiography and women's writing. I refer the reader to Yvonne Johnson's *The Voices of African American Women* (1998), Angelyn Mitchell's *The Freedom to Remember* (2002), and *Harriet Jacobs* and *"Incidents in the Life of a Slave Girl": New Critical Essays* (1996), the volume edited by Rafia Zafar and Deborah H. Garfield. There is, in addition, a plethora of other books and articles which treat Jacobs's autobiographical work, which remains at the center of any discussion of black women's participation in the slave narrative genre. And the importance of the slave narrative, or the narrative of emancipation, to the larger tradition of African American letters has long been acknowledged.

Central to the early autobiographical writings by black women, as several scholars have argued, is a definition of black womanhood posed against conventional white notions of "true womanhood," with their myriad pretensions. Unlike masculinist autobiographies where the author or protagonist is most frequently himself, the black and female slave narrator often sites or situates her mother or another celebrated black and female figure as the heroine of the text. Angelyn Mitchell argues that "[i]n African American culture, feminist individuality has little in common with the Anglo-American concept of rugged individualism. For mainstream Anglo-America, individuals refer to the efforts by which the isolated individual advances. In African American female culture, the individual's efforts are part of and supported by the community."[7] From a similar perspective, William Andrews notes "the slave mother or some comparable black and maternal figure, more than the female narrator herself, plays the hero's role in most black women's autobiographies."[8]

In *Incidents*, Linda Brent successfully subverts the enslaver's language and letters and uses them as a means to her own liberation: "When Flint finds the beautiful slave girl teaching herself to write, he attempts to pervert her quest for literacy into a seduction."[9] Flint even forces Linda's brother William to take her a sexually explicit note, degrading both brother and sister. However, Linda turns the tables. After she has secreted herself in her grandmother's home, she deceives Flint into thinking that she has escaped to the North by having a friend mail her letters from New York and Boston; these are her *letters of liberation*. Her ultimate triumph, though, is her *backtalking* narrative, *Incidents in the Life of a Slave Girl*. In many cases, autobiographies become the black woman's letters of liberation, addressed first to herself, then to the community that surrounds and supports her, and, finally, to the hostile outside world.

Like Harriet Brent Jacobs, Susie King Taylor and Elizabeth Keckley are outraged mothers seeking brighter futures for their children; they also critique patriarchy, freedom, and the hypocritical but accepted notions of legitimacy and ideal womanhood. In *Behind the Scenes; or, Thirty Years a Slave and Four Years in the White House* (1868), Keckley, a mixed race woman, asks the question, "Why should my son be held in slavery?" Keckley believed that all enslaved persons were entitled to freedom, but the fact that both her son's father and her own were white, is clearly part of the irony that she probes. In *Reminiscences of My Life in Camp With the U.S. 33rd Colored Troops (1902)*, Susie King Taylor details her experiences as a Union nurse behind the Confederate lines in South Carolina. After the war, she makes a dangerous trip deep into Louisiana to go to her son, who was urgently in need of medical care. Taylor concludes her narrative on a plaintive and ironic note: "It seemed very hard, when his father fought to protect the Union and our flag, and yet this boy was denied a berth to carry him home to die, because he was a Negro."[10] Even her husband's military service in the Civil War fails to legitimize his son's citizenship rights.

Other notable slave (and ex-slave) narratives by black women include: *The History of Mary Prince* (1831), *Memoir of Old Elizabeth, a Colored Woman* (1863), *The Story of Mattie J. Jackson* (1866), *From the Darkness Cometh the Light or Struggles for Freedom* (c.1891), Kate Drumgoold's *A Slave Girl's Story* (1898), and Annie L. Burton's *Memories of Childhood's Slavery Days* (1909). Conveniently published as *Six Women's Slave Narratives* (1988) and with an introduction by William Andrews, these autobiographies continue in their celebration of the enslaved black women who mothered and mentored others. Andrews observes, "[A]s early as Prince's story, female slave narrators portrayed the enslaved black woman as a person of near-indomitable dedication to the highest principles of human dignity and individual freedom."[11]

Even though these post-emancipation accounts do not focus on a quest for physical freedom, they reflect earlier works in the tradition:

> Writing narratives of slavery offered women like Drumgoold and Burton, who had had little direct experience of bondage, the opportunity to celebrate their mothers as examples of genuine female heroism ... the most dramatic scenes in the autobiographies of Jackson, Delaney and Burton are those that depict the herculean (and usually successful) efforts of slave mothers to keep their families together in slavery and to reunite them after emancipation.[12]

This pattern of praising the maternal heroine repeats itself in the twentieth-century autobiographies of Maya Angelou, Audre Lorde, and others.

Narratives of vision and power constitute an important "type" among early spiritual autobiographies by black American women. These narratives combine a quest for personal power with the assertion of a literary self; the authors seek "power with God' and experience dreams, premonitions, and visions. Such works include *Productions of Mrs. Maria Stewart* (1835); *The Life and Religious Experience and Journal of Mrs. Jarena Lee; Giving an Account of Her Call to Preach the Gospel* (1936); *Memoirs of the Life, Religious Experience and Travels of Mrs. Zilpha Elaw* (1846); *A Brand*

Plucked From the Fire: An Autobiographical Sketch of Mrs. Julia A. J. Foote (1879); *Elizabeth, A Colored Minister of the Gospel Born in Slavery* (1889); *Twenty Year's Experience of A Missionary* (1907); and *Gifts of Power: The Writings of Rebecca Cox Jackson, Black Visionary, Shaker Eldress* (1981). The four works by Stewart, Lee, Foote, and Broughton appear together in *Spiritual Narratives* (1988) with an exquisite introduction by Sue E. Houchins;[13] there is also the earlier and still very valuable *Sisters in the Spirit: Three Black Women's Autobiographies* (1986), edited by William Andrews.

Looking closely at nineteenth-century autobiographies by African American women, the student and the scholar must also acknowledge travel accounts, memoirs and texts that defy or straddle genres – works like Nellie Arnold Plummer's *Out of the Depths or The Triumph of the* Cross, Plummer's unique spiritual memoir and family history. Plummer, a school teacher and church leader, had few "leisure hours to devote to contemplation and study," but her *Out of the Depths* (1927) is an intriguing volume that is rarely written about – a blend of history, memoir, and reminiscence. Plummer claimed to be inspired by the "Voice of God." Her volume contains spiritual visions, revelations and biblical imagery which guide the author and her family and at the same time give form to the text. Telling the collected stories of her family in their movement from slavery to freedom was so important to Plummer that she mortgaged the family farm to self-publish the book.

Other nineteenth-century hybrids include *A Narrative of the Life and Travels of Mrs. Nancy Prince* (1850) and *An Autobiography: The Story of the Lord's Dealings With Mrs. Amanda Smith* (1893), both the work of free black women. Prince's evangelical travel narrative records her experiences in Russia and her work as a missionary in Jamaica. Like both the author of the slave narrative and the more traditional spiritual autobiographer, Prince relies on divine deliverance. In defining her autobiographical identity, Prince wrote about her clash with church officials about her appropriate role as a *female* missionary and also about her direct contributions to the education and uplift of the black race, especially women. Because her younger sister had become a prostitute, Prince's "gospel temperance" preaching often targeted younger women. Amanda Berry Smith's *Autobiography* is another work that defies or straddles genre. A gifted "Holiness" preacher, Smith incorporates a spiritual journey motif within her missionary travel narrative, which follows her to Liberia, India, England, Ireland, Scotland, and Wales. Meanwhile, "as told to" autobiographical accounts by Harriet Tubman and Sojourner Truth, while they do not qualify as "free stories," nonetheless have a place in the tradition as they "'radicalize' the form of spiritual autobiography and recreate it as a tool for temporal liberation."[14]

Inevitably, many, and perhaps most, autobiographers, journal keepers and authors of personal narratives die without seeing their works published. A few examples of important autobiographical writings published posthumously are worth mentioning here: *The Journal of Charlotte Forten* (1953, 1988), transcribed from Forten's five 1854–92 diaries by Anna Julia Cooper and subsequently edited first by Ray Allen Billington and then Brenda Stevenson; *Crusade for Justice: The Autobiography of Ida B. Wells* (1970), written for publication by Wells herself between 1928 and 1934, and edited and published by her daughter, Alfreda M. Duster; and Rebecca Cox Jackson's *Gifts of Power* (1971), a collection of autobiographical documents written by the Shaker eldress between 1833 and 1864, retrieved from Shaker archives and edited by Jean Humez. Of these three, only Wells prepared her autobiography for publication; working on her kitchen table from notes and papers, Wells died leaving her work in mid-sentence. Forten, who served behind Confederate lines as a teacher of black "contrabands" during the Civil War, published excerpts of her wartime diary in *The Atlantic Monthly*, but left the bulk of her journal behind as a series of handwritten diaries. Bringing each of these autobiographies to light required an extraordinary effort on the part of the individual editors, in essence an intergenerational collaboration between the living and the dead.

Ida B. Wells intended her life story, eventually published as *Crusade for Justice: The Autobiography of Ida B. Wells*, a title supplied by the University of Chicago Press, "not only as her own but also as the story of her people and her times."[15] In a way, she chronicles the challenges black people faced during the era of Reconstruction:

> We have Frederick Douglass's history of slavery as he knew and experienced it. But of the storm and stress immediately after the Civil War, of the Ku Klux Klan, of ballot stuffing, wholesale murders of Negroes who tried to exercise their new-found rights as free men and citizens, the carpetbag invasion about which the South published much that is false, and the Negroes' political life in that era – our race has little of its own that is definite and authentic.[16]

As she neared the end of her life, Wells wanted to leave behind a corrective legacy, something definite and authentic, and to offer her life as a symbol of the struggle for freedom and a black *voice*. As a journalist and antilynching activist, Wells lived a life in opposition to the enforced silencing and misrepresentation of the black voice. She faced the very real danger that she herself would be killed for debunking the myth that black men raped white women.

Wells also revealed the flip side of the sexual double standard, the fact that many a "respected" white leader of a southern lynch mob was himself the father of a mixed-race child forced on a black woman. In any case, Wells, as a writer and editor for the *Memphis Free Speech*, refused to be silent, and she advanced a withering critique of race and gender relations. In her 1892 essay, "Southern Horrors, Lynch Law in All Its Phases," Wells wrote: "The miscegenation laws of the South only operate against the legitimate union of the races; they leave the white man free to seduce all the colored girls he can, but it is death to the colored man who yields to the force and advances of a similar attraction in white women."[17] Words like these inspired an angry white mob to destroy the type of Wells's press, put a price on her head, and force her into exile in the North.

A mother and a worker for universal suffrage, Wells often came into conflict with both black men and white suffragists who disagreed with her point of view and her right to speak and agitate for black and women's causes. It is therefore no wonder that Wells felt compelled to tell her free story, which not only provides a view of her times but also justifies her unconventional and heroic life. Wells's daughter, Alfreda Duster, understood the importance of the volume and submitted it to various publishers over a period of thirty-five years before it appeared in a series John Hope Franklin edited for the University of Chicago Press. Though Wells had completed *Crusade for Justice* thirty-five years earlier, it appears in print at the beginning of the 1970s, followed closely by the activist autobiographies of Angela Davis, Elaine Brown, and Assata Shakur. The retrieval of this work published almost four decades after it was written represents the recovery of part of the "lost ground" of black women's autobiography.

Another part of this "lost ground" may be uncovered by taking a serious look at works of performers and entertainers often written in collaboration with a second party. Scholars often turn away from such works out of a concern for authenticity, although many aspects of these criteria are met. Music is one of the spheres of culture where the oral tradition and written literature collide and/or embrace. Surely, the voices of Ethel Waters, Marian Anderson, Nina Simone, and Tina Turner should be included in our collective thinking about what constitutes the autobiographical tradition of black women. Pushing the traditional boundaries of genre makes it possible to see fresh relationships between the artist, the material written or performed and the community.

It is significant that three of these collaborative autobiographies bear a song as title. Waters's *His Eye is on the Sparrow* (with Charles Samuels, 1950), Anderson's *My Lord, What a Morning* (with Howard Taubman, 1956), and Simone's *I Put a Spell on You* (with Stephen Cleary, 1993) are more familiar to many readers as the names of songs than as titles of autobiographies, and when Tina Turner's *I, Tina* (with Kurt Loder, 1986) was released as a movie, it was called *What's Love Got to Do with It?* after her autobiographical song of the same title. Each evokes a sense of orality and a reminder of the influence of oral traditions, especially, in this case spirituals, gospel, and the blues. From this "insider–outsider" position, the subjects bring additional perspectives on the black and female experience.

Both Waters and Anderson grew up in Philadelphia, but whereas Anderson was protected and raised by a loving family, Waters's experience, as represented in *His Eye is on the Sparrow*, was considerably more raw:

> I never was a child.
> I never was coddled, or liked, or understood by my family.
> I never felt I belonged.
> I was born out of wedlock, but that had nothing to do with all this.
> To people like mine a thing like that just didn't mean much.
> Nobody brought me up.[18]

Indeed, Waters's book and the two by Simone and Turner have some "sensational" aspects. But the autobiographies of all three women reflect their experiences as survivors of abuse and neglect who emerge triumphant despite challenges in their home life and from the dominant culture.

"By the time I was seven," Waters, the original star of *Shuffle Along*, writes, "I knew all about sex and life in the raw. I could outcurse any stevedore..." (p. 1). Waters was also a blues singer. Yet when she played the character of Hagar in Du Bose Heyward's *Mamba's Daughters*, she prayed for strength to tell what she saw as the story of her mother, who delivered Ethel at age thirteen after being raped by a neighborhood youth while Ethel's grandmother was at work: "Momweeze was always as unhappy as Hagar, and as lonely. Playing that role gave me new insight into the depthless nature of her loneliness, and also the loneliness that I've known ever since I was born" (p. 253). Even after her Broadway successes, Waters was haunted by the very real problem of finding for her mother a mental health facility that would treat women of color. And like Marian Anderson and others of their generation, Waters suffered insults and needless inconvenience when traveling, especially when she performed on the segregated Theatre Owners Booking Agency (TOBA) circuit in the South. Her story offers a personal narrative of a vernacular performance landscape peopled by Florence Mills, Josephine Baker, Canada Lee, Bill Robinson, Darryl Zanuck, Carl Van Vechten, and others; it has *a voice*, and that voice has left a legacy, not only in writing autobiography, but also in documenting the history of black theatre and music history.

Anderson, of course, is popularly remembered for her publicly defiant act of singing on the steps of the Lincoln Memorial on Easter Sunday, April 10,

1939, after being denied access to the Daughters of the American Revolution (DAR) owned Constitution Hall in Washington, DC, but her life as portrayed in autobiography stands for so much more than that. Indeed, Anderson's ascent is nothing short of phenomenal. From her early training in the choir of her church, through her family's struggle for economic survival after the death of her father, and her increasing determination to acquire more formal training and eventually to perform opera and German *Lieder*, this too is the story of a forerunner. But the volumes have their differences. Whereas Ethel Waters represents primarily a connection with the blues and vernacular culture, Marian Anderson makes her mark in the rarified air of classical music. She did not sing the blues, and when she did sing African American spirituals, the very manner in which she performed them emphasized their universal appeal, "complex simplicity" and timeless elegance. The spiritual, emanating from the mouth of this woman who always sang with her eyes closed, as if praying, became visible as a true form of American classical music. But this triumph has its price. For an audition with one of her early teachers, a Mr. Giuseppe Boghetti, Anderson sang the spiritual "Deep River":

> At that first audition, I should add, Mr. Boghetti had given me a scale to sing after I had finished "Deep River." Once I began to appear regularly at his studio I found out why. He had discovered unequal tones in that scale, and he set to work to iron out the unevenness. It gradually dawned on me that, although I had worked with two teachers, I had not yet reached the point where I had relinquished my wholly natural and spontaneous manner of singing for a consistently controlled method. [19]

Whereas Waters's autobiography has those qualities of naturalness and spontaneity, Anderson's has the same evenness of tone and the same "consistently controlled method" throughout, partly perhaps, because of the collaborator, but also, perhaps, because of what Anderson herself chose as a dignified self-defining persona. While still a deeply intriguing read, it comes off "stiff" in comparison to most other autobiographies by black women performers.

Nina Simone's *I Put a Spell on You* crosses over into the subgenre of political autobiography; like its author, the book defies categorization. Simone, also known as "the High Priestess of Soul," played "popular songs in a classical style with classical technique."[20] Like the precolonial African griot-troubadour-poets, who went in front unafraid to lead warriors into battle with their words, Simone contributed inspired protest songs to the civil rights struggle of the 1960s. In addition, many of Simone's autobiographical songs transcend her individual perspective and become vehicles for the collective consciousness of the civil rights movement as well as rituals of remembrance for fallen heroes, black and white, and often black and female. As such, the collected body of Simone's work, with written autobiography and songs taken together, offers an unusual opportunity to view the autobiographer as performer, both on the stage and on the page, in the context of her larger community.

Like Marian Anderson, Simone, née Eunice Kathleen Waymon, who grew up in Tryon, North Carolina, got her first musical training in the church. Her father, a barber, worked many different jobs, depending upon the state of his health. Eunice often took care of her father, making him milkshakes when he could consume nothing else; the two had a special relationship. Meanwhile, her mother worked as a maid outside the home and Eunice was largely raised by her older sister, Lucille, and Eunice's relationship with her mother faltered because she scarcely saw her.

Even though Tryon was a segregated community, Eunice gained support for her talents from both blacks and whites. In fact, Mrs. Miller, the woman for whom her mother worked, paid for the entire first year of Eunice's music lessons with Mrs. Massinovitch, her first piano teacher. After the end of that first year, Mrs. Massinovitch arranged a scholarship fund for Eunice, and, when the time came, she helped her find a more advanced teacher to prepare Eunice for conservatory and raised enough money to send her to Juilliard for a year. Eunice Kathleen Waymon was classically trained and hoped to enter the Curtis Conservatory in Philadelphia as a scholarship student after her year at Juilliard, but she was turned down by the school, which had no black students but which had auditioned her, because it was reluctant to take on a girl who was black, poor, and unknown.

Marian Anderson had earlier been turned down by a prestigious conservatory in the same city, but she dismisses the incident in her autobiography, saying that the school no longer exists and that its name does not matter. Simone mentions Anderson in describing her own situation, but does not directly allude to Anderson's earlier rejection.[21] What kind of an institution calling itself a conservatory of music could dismiss Marian Anderson or Nina Simone? In both cases, the undeserved rejection was devastating – the worst part was Eunice's loss of self-esteem. Eventually, the answer trickled down from the circle of Anderson's friends, and Eunice felt for the first time, the sting of discrimination. This discrimination was different from being forced to eat her melted cheese sandwich on the steps of the Tryon Country Store on the way to her music lessons with "Miz Mazzy" while whites sat at the counter; Eunice had accepted that. Turned away by the Curtis Conservatory, Eunice had the idea of playing the Midtown Bar in Atlantic City, but knew her mother, now a Methodist preacher, would sanction her for being "in the world," so she presented herself under the stage name "Nina Simone" and immediately developed a following. She saved her money and continued her Juilliard studies. In time, she would marry Don Ross, described as "a white boy, a good looking man with a slow smile and charm" and move to New York City. Don, a salesman, preferred hanging out with beatnik poets to working, and, predictably, the marriage failed. A second marriage, to Andy Stroud, a black former police detective described as a jealous and abusive husband, would also fail. Simone moved out of the tiny apartment she had shared with Don, got her own place, and eventually attracted the mentorship of Langston Hughes, James Baldwin, Lorraine Hansberry, and others who educated her on the nascent black protest movement.

Of her friendship with Hansberry, Simone writes, "we never talked about men or clothes or other such inconsequential things when we got together. It was always Marx, Lenin and revolution – real girls' talk" (p. 87). Real girls' talk, for real black women like Nina Simone and Lorraine Hansberry, includes topics both political and pressing, far removed from the usual beauty shop connotations. Simone would later commemorate Hansberry's life and work by writing and performing the song "To Be Young, Gifted and Black" taken from the title of Hansberry's last and unfinished play. In this song, Simone sings about being "haunted" by her youth, a possible reference to her Curtis Conservatory experience.

In "To Be Young, Gifted and Black," the High Priestess of Soul not only praises her lost friend, she reaches out to another generation to provide the same sort of encouragement and direction offered in much of black women's writing. A griot, troubadour and poet for the children of the civil rights era, she lifted our spirits and girded our armor as we faced fire hoses, police dogs, bombings, and assassinations. Ultimately, Simone's autobiography *I Put a Spell on You* is not only the record of a life but also a challenge to transcend the madness and the trauma of the American racial nightmare in acceptance of one's gifts – a call to lead and to serve.

These same images, the beloved patriarchs of non-violence lying dead in pools of their own blood and photographs of peaceful marchers beset by fire hoses and German shepherd police dogs, determined new directions for the black liberation in America including a political and cultural identification with Africa and with black liberation struggles around the globe. Coining a phrase first used by Richard Wright to interrogate the global "color curtain" and later to celebrate independence in Ghana, West Africa, the "Black Power" movement was born, like a phoenix rising from the ashes of the martyred dead.

"Black Power" was committed to freedom from oppression, especially capitalism and racism, yet ironically the struggle for freedom from sexual oppression and gender bias took a back seat. Within this arena, black women activists were challenged by threats of death, beatings, rape, mutilation, and separation from their children and families. Sometimes the challenges came from outside, from the police, the FBI, and jailers, but, ironically, at other times, the violence, both sexual and otherwise, came from within the organizations they served and from the men they loved. It is not surprising, therefore, that there are, to date, only three book-length autobiographies by women Black Power activists in print; these are *Angela Davis: An Autobiography* (1974), Assata Shakur's *Assata* (1987), and Elaine Brown's *A Taste of Power: A Black Woman's Story* (1992). In her prize-winning monograph, *Autobiography as Activism: Three Black Women of the Sixties*, Margo Perkins reads these works as "extensions of the writers' political activism" (cover):

> Angela Davis, Assata Shakur, and Elaine Brown exemplify a radical current in African American political resistance. Their individual and collective commitment to revolutionary activism is evident in the kind of autobiography each produces. Like other leftist radicals, Davis, Shakur and Brown seek through their work (as both activists and writers) to alter mass consciousness by disrupting the status quo in a way they believe will lead to progressive social transformation.[22]

In the tradition of Frederick Douglass and Harriet Jacobs, these modern captivity narratives express a transcendent liberatory impulse and brave defiance; however, these authors inherit more the stuff and substance of a continuing struggle than a particular autobiographical form. Perkins observes that "[t]hemes and motifs traceable from the emancipation narratives" of fugitive slaves, especially "the struggle for literacy and the commitment to self-education it necessarily entails," run through the life stories of these women whose immersion in organized resistance movements led them to become fugitives. However, she notes, "even had Davis, Shakur and Brown not read these or other such texts, their experiences under racist oppression, as well as their participation in African American collective consciousness, would have been sufficient to create noteworthy parallels between their texts and those of their forebears."[23]

Angela Davis, the target of a national "manhunt" in a murder case in which she was finally found not guilty, felt that her real crime was being an intellectual and a Communist allied with black liberation struggles. Assata Shakur was pursued on the New Jersey Turnpike, shot, and later beaten by police. "They kept me under those blinding lights for days," writes Shakur, today living in exile in Cuba. "I felt I was going blind. I was seeing everything in doubles and triples. When Evelyn, my lawyer, came to see me, I complained. Finally, after Evelyn accused them of torture, they turned the lights off at eleven. But every fifteen minutes or so they would shine a huge floodlight into the cell."[24] She also reminds the reader that under the Thirteenth Amendment to the Constitution, slavery is still legal in prisons: "Well, that explained a lot of things. That explained why jails and prisons all over the country are filled to the brim with Black and Third World People, why so many Black people can't find a job on the streets and are forced to survive the best way they know how. Once you're in prison, there are plenty of jobs..." (p. 64). Enslaved in New Jersey jails in the twentieth century, Shakur conceives her daughter while locked down with Kamau, a brother member of the Black Liberation Army, after they were barred from the courtroom during trial. Weary from the isolation of solitary confinement, they enjoy each other's company and take advantage of the privacy, even though Shakur is facing a possible life sentence. Shakur defiantly refuses to identify the father: "I'll tell them that this baby was sent by the Black creator to liberate Black people. I'll tell them this baby is the new Black messiah, conceived in a holy way, come to lead our people to freedom and justice and to create a new black nation" (p. 123).

Elaine Brown, the first woman to lead the Black Panther Party, tells the story of a different experience. Brown details her beating and sexual abuse by Huey P. Newton, her lover and supposed comrade, and the violent "discipline" forced upon sister Panthers by men who resented the presence of women in leadership roles. She began to fight back:

> There would be no further impositions on me by men, including black men, including Black Panther men. I would support every assertion of human rights by women – from the right to abortion to the right of equality with men as laborers and leaders. I would declare that the agenda of the Black Panther Party and our revolution to free black people from oppression specifically included black women.
>
> I would denounce loudly the philosophies of the Karengas, who raised the name of Africa to justify the suppression of black women. I would lambaste the civil-rights men who had dismissed the importance of women like Fannie Lou Hammer and Ella Baker and Daisy Bates and even Kathleen Cleaver. I would not tolerate any raised fists in my face or any Black Power handshakes, or even the phrase "Black Power," for all of it now symbolized to me the denial of the black woman in favor of the freedom of "the black man."
>
> I would reclaim my womanhood and my place.[25]

Reclaiming her womanhood and her place was a dangerous proposition. Eventually, she fled with her daughter Erika into the night, traveling light, seeking sanctuary with her mother in Los Angeles. Though she lived in Oakland, she flew from San Francisco, employing multiple strategies of disguise and concealment reminiscent of the escape of a Frederick Douglass or a Harriet Jacobs. The ironic difference is that she is fleeing her own "comrades," her own "brothers and sisters." "Freedom," writes Brown, "That was all I could think about in those first seconds away from the Black Panther Party" (p. 449). On the final page of her modern day narrative of liberation, Brown dreams the dream of the outraged mother, the dream of a better life for her child: "One night just before bed / She shocked me when she said / What would happen if I died / 'Cause no one cared / When black girls cried – / Oh, Erika, my little baby, / Erika, my little child, / Erika, there is no maybe / I'll change the world for you / In just a little while ..." (p. 456).

These black women activists publicly theorize their lives in an attempt to reach others and to win them to liberation causes; autobiography becomes a political tool in their hands. Angela Davis, for example, "had come to envision" her effort as a "political autobiography that emphasized the people, the events and the forces in my life that propelled me to my present commitment."[26] She hoped to inspire "more people – Black, Brown, Red, Yellow and white ... to join our growing community of struggle" (p. xvi). But Perkins astutely notes another purpose, as the publication of autobiography also becomes a form of protection:

> Not only does the ability to read and write facilitate individual physical and psychic liberation, it also opens up the possibility of amassing an audience. During a period when both Davis and Shakur were extremely vulnerable to political neutralization and/or detention stemming from their activities, for example, their writing of an autobiography was a useful means of protecting themselves from renewed harassment and persecution ... In making the public aware of their predicament, they endeavored to amass potential support and also to undermine the ability of the state to retaliate against them in secrecy.[27]

The same is potentially true for Elaine Brown, who ultimately comes to fear the Black Panther Party almost as much as "the state." The black women activists and political autobiographers are, as Perkins observes, not only "writing their lives," but *writing for their lives.*[28] Thus, autobiography, and political autobiography in particular, becomes both sword and shield for these black women activists. Indeed, Angela Davis, Assata Shakur, and Elaine Brown inscribe their lives in the symbolic language of autobiography to advance the cause of black liberation, to bear witness, to offer analysis, provide direction, to help create a better world, and, ultimately, to save their own lives. They are the survivors amidst many who were lost along the way, and their twentieth-century narratives of emancipation chart the psychic course of a latter-day underground railroad.

Autobiographies and memoirs that are primarily literary in their form and intent confront still a different set of challenges. Such works include Katherine Dunham's *A Touch of Innocence* (1959), *I Know Why the Caged Bird Sings*

(1970) by Maya Angelou, *Generations* (1976) by Lucille Clifton, Audre Lorde's *Zami: A New Spelling of My Name* (1982), and *Soldier: A Poet's Childhood* (2000) by June Jordan. Though almost all of these writers are involved in activist struggles, the emphasis here is primarily on the developmental aspects of coming to consciousness of self as black women and artists.

Those looking to Katherine Dunham's *A Touch of Innocence* (1959), a forerunner in this genre, for a glimpse of her life as dancer, choreographer, and anthropologist will be disappointed, for this is not the story of this eminent woman's public life but rather a poignant and personal story written in a form that dares analysis and defies genre. Unlike most autobiographers who write in the first person and who promise to write the truth, Dunham writes in the third person and says that her book is *not* an autobiography:

> This book is not an autobiography. It is the story of a world that has vanished, as it was for one child who grew up in it – the Middle West in the boom years after the First World War, and in the early years of the Depression. And it is the story of a family that I knew very well, and especially of a girl and a young woman whom I rediscovered while writing about the members of this family. Perhaps from their confused lives may come something that will serve as guidance to someone else, or something that will at least hold attention for a while as a story.[29]

Perhaps these anomalies account for the fact that *A Touch of Innocence* has been written about so infrequently. After all, it is difficult to include a work in the genre of autobiography when the author specifically says that it is a work of fiction, a story about someone else, and when she writes in the third person, as if to prove it. The Katherine Dunham of the "novel" still has mother and father and siblings and nieces and nephews named just like those in the author's real life, but meanwhile the writing reflects the trauma Dunham suffered in being tormented and beaten by her father, who kept the boys away and then touched his daughter in inappropriate ways: "These same hands now stroked the flesh above her thigh, seeking farther: hands of a lover in first caress" (p. 282).

Writing at the time of publication, critic J. Saunders Redding called *A Touch of Innocence* "a harrowing book" (book jacket). Judging from the readers' responses to the rape in *I Know Why the Caged Bird Sings* a decade later, it is probably fair to say that the book's odd form as well as the portrayal of her father and the threat of sexual violation contribute to the book's failure to receive more critical attention. *A Touch of Innocence* does, in fact, presage the coming of Angelou's autobiographical volumes. In addition to sharing the theme of sexual abuse, both *A Touch of Innocence* and *I Know Why the Caged Bird Sings* display the same intense involvement with nature that characterizes the autobiographies of Zora Neale Hurston, Era Bell Thompson, and many other gifted autobiographers. Also, either book could be read as a work of fiction; if the reader is not aware that the work is the portrait of a life, both Marguerite and Katherine could be looked at as fictional characters. The most important difference is that Angelou, the Marguerite of *I Know Why the Caged Bird Sings*, overcomes her troubles and rises above them. Katherine, in *A Touch of Innocence*, remains a tragic figure, unlike the Katherine Dunham who emerges to make major contributions to anthropology, dance, and other performance genres. Perhaps, it is the meaningful work, following the theory of psychiatrist Viktor Frankl,[30] that keeps both autobiographers sane; writing itself might also be viewed as part of the healing process.

Autobiographers Lucille Clifton and June Jordan also suffered at the hands of abusive fathers. Clifton's biographer, M. J. Lupton, writes that Clifton was sexually abused but not raped by her father, Samuel Sayles. Jordan was not molested sexually but she was beaten by both parents, often pummeled by her father's fists. Jordan portrays the violence in her home as capricious and sporadic. Granville Ivanhoe Jordan and Samuel Sayles were also physically and psychologically abusive to their wives. According to Lupton:

> Clifton claims that her mother had burned her poems because her husband Samuel didn't want her to publish them; "a lot of people now might not understand that, but then a wife obeyed." She remembered her father saying, "Ain't no wife of mine going to be no poetry writer." His prohibition, which had a tremendous effect on the young Lucille, is perhaps the reason she kept on writing. Supposedly Sam's "favorite," she resented the way he treated Thelma. Clifton said, "I can forgive my father for driving us crazy. He was driven crazy, you know. *But* I cannot forgive him for driving my mother mad. And she was probably always on the edge."[31]

Jordan's mother, Mildred Fisher Jordan, eventually goes over that edge and commits suicide, though not in the pages of *Soldier*.

This is the first generation of black women autobiographers to address suicide, always a taboo subject in the black community. Lorde, like Jordan, the child of West Indian immigrant parents, was also routinely beaten in the family home by both parents. While Lorde herself is not sexually abused in the home, she recounts the story of her friend, Gennie, who committed suicide after being repeatedly sexually abused by her father, who had appeared after a long absence. "What kind of a jackabat woman ... and to let her go off with that good-for-nothing call himself father," intones Lorde's Grenadian born mother.[32]

Jordan and Lorde also write about the process of *becoming* poets. Jordan's book is subtitled *A Poet's Childhood*, and Lorde writes "How I Became a

Poet" in *Zami: A New Spelling of My Name*, which she calls her "biomythography." The brutal beatings by her father notwithstanding, in becoming a poet, Jordan acknowledges the role of her father, who treated June like a son and subjected his "soldier" to the discipline of memorizing and reciting long poems as well as military training.[33] Lorde, on the other hand, praises and identifies with her mother, "When the strongest words for what I have to offer come out of me sounding like words from my mother's mouth, then I either have to reassess the meaning of everything I have to say now, or re-examine the worth of her old words" (p. 30). She also wrote, "I am a reflection of my mother's secret poetry as well as her hidden angers" (p. 32). In contrast, Jordan's identification with her father presents itself as a tragic dislocation, especially when we know that he had virtually removed his wife Mildred, June's mother, from the parenting process. The specter of Mildred Maude Fisher's suicide looms large.

Both Jordan and Lorde become activists around such human rights issues as police violence, open education, health care and women's rights; each poet uses her art to raise the conscience of an audience, especially with regard to black identity, human rights, women's issues, and gender preference: both women are bi-sexual, mothers, and lovers of women as well as men, each will eventually succumb to breast cancer after a valiant struggle for survival.

But this is not that story; these volumes represent voyages of discovery in uncharted waters and for each a recognition, a coming to consciousness of self in a world that does not treasure, nurture, or protect black women. Interestingly enough, Jordan and Lorde both fall in love with young women of similar descriptions, each is named Kitty. Jordan describes her summer camp counselor, the one she awakened to find lying on top of her one morning:

Pretty Miss Kitty was dark-skinned like my Uncle Teddy:

> Dark chocolate like you could just about drink it thick and smooth and sweet and not quite steaming from a cup you'd want to hold and smell and stare at and nobody bother you about that. I followed her around.   (*Soldier*, p. 240)

And Lorde's description:

> Kitty was still trim and fast-lined, but with an easier looseness about her smile and a lot less make-up. Without its camouflage, her chocolate skin and deep, sculptured mouth reminded me of a Benin bronze.   (*Zami*, p. 244)

Since all three of these women were relative contemporaries living in and around New York City, it is conceivable that the two Kittys are one and the same person, but with both Lorde and Jordan gone, now only Kitty herself can solve that mystery. *(Kitty, please come forth!)* Either way, Kitty was so sublime in every aspect that Lorde transformed her into a goddess:

> And I remember Afrekete, who came out of a dream to me always being hard and real as the fine hairs along the under-edge of my navel. She brought me live things from the bush, and from her farm set out in cocoyams and cassava. (*Zami*, p. 249)

But if Lorde's childhood ends with the discovery of her lesbianism in the arms of Afrekete, Jordan's ends when she is sent off to prep school by train, without either mother or father to support her:

> My mother didn't see me off.
> My father brought me to the railroad
> station by himself.
> Just outside Track 22, we faced each other:
> "Okay! Little Soldier! G'wan! G'wan!
> You gwine made me proud!"
> And I could hear nothing else.
> And I wondered who would meet my train. (*Soldier*, p. 261)

Who would cheer the weary traveler, who would meet June Jordan's train? Ironically, *Soldier: A Poet's Childhood*, comes very near the end of Jordan's life, and as the young woman of the memoir begins her journey into adulthood, Jordan, then dying after a long struggle with breast cancer, contemplates another journey into the unknown: "And I wondered who would meet my train." Even if there is some sacred meeting place at the end of the line, some big campground or bush arbor on the other side of the river, we can each only anticipate our ending, which remains unknowable. Challenged by the knowledge of her impending death, Jordan becomes one of the first black women autobiographers to contemplate the impermanence of life. Powerful, eerie, and evocative, the final words of Jordan's narrative go some distance in suggesting the problematic nature of the final journey as well as the anxiety of not knowing who will meet our train.

The expanding generations of black women writers push the limits of autobiography and life writing; anticipating their radiance is almost as problematic as anticipating the final journey, but we have intimations of the greatness of an evolving tradition of black women's autobiography and life writing in the works of Lorene Cary, Meri Nana-Ama Danquah, Rosemary L. Bray, Rebecca Walker, Deborah McDowell, and others whose work exemplifies finding and or recreating oneself in moments where one is challenged by race or gender, sexuality, intimate family relations, and motherhood, including, at times, the decision not to become a mother. Interracial parents, preparatory schools, interracial dating, abortion, and depression become new themes. At other times, the black woman autobiographer looks back to look forward and to provide encouragement, direction and guidance, as in Rosemary L. Bray's *Unafraid of the Dark: A Memoir*:

I know who I am. More important, I know who I was and who I became; I understand the journey from there to here. I am the great-great-granddaughter of slaves and the granddaughter of sharecroppers and the daughter of poor, proud angry people determined to make more of me than they could of themselves.

I understand that there is a world of people determined to make me ashamed, make me embarrassed, make me forget what I know to be true. I understand that such people never go away. But I have been given priceless gifts I have no right to squander; a family, a once-committed nation, the luxuries of education and political awareness, opportunity and time. Most of all, I understand that these things were mine for a reason: to secure for others what was secured for me.[34]

Reading, writing, marching, singing, dancing, loving, daring, black women autobiographers exchange their letters for liberation.

NOTES

1. Joanne M. Braxton, *Black Women Writing Autobiography: A Tradition Within a Tradition* (Philadelphia: Temple University Press, 1989), pp. 5–10.
2. Audre Lorde, "The Master's Tools Will Never Dismantle the Master's House," *Sister Outsider: Essays and Speeches by Audre Lorde* (Trumansburg, NY: The Crossing Press, 1984).
3. Belinda, "Belinda: or the Cruelty of Men Whose Faces Were Like the Moon," *American Museum and Repository of Ancient and Modern Fugitive Pieces, Prose and Poetical*, vol. 1, June 1787.
4. Hannah More (attributed), "The Sorrows of Yamba or the Negro Woman's Lamentation," Electronic Text Center, University of Virginia Library http://etext.lib.virginia.edu/etcbin/toccernew2?id=AnoSorr.sgm&images=images/mode ng&data=/texts/english/modeng/parsed&tag=public&part=1&division=div1
5. Phillis Wheatley, "On Imagination," from *Poems* (1773) www.4literature.net/ Phillis_Wheatley/Poems/
6. William L. Andrews, Introduction, *Six Women's Slave Narratives* (New York: Oxford University Press, 1989), p. xxxiii.
7. Angelyn Mitchell, *The Freedom to Remember: Narrative, Slavery and Gender In Contemporary Black Women's Fiction* (New Brunswick, NJ: Rutgers University Press, 2002), p. 38.
8. Andrews, Introduction, *Six Women's Slave Narratives*, p. xxxiii.
9. Braxton, *Black Women Writing*, p. 30.
10. Susie King Taylor, *Reminiscences of My Life in Camp With the U.S. 33rd Colored Troops* (1902; New York: Arno Press, 1968).
11. Andrews, Introduction, *Six Women's Slave Narratives*, p. xxxiii.
12. Ibid., p. xxxi.
13. Sue E. Houchins, Introduction, *Spiritual Narratives* (New York: Oxford University Press, 1988). Houchins establishes the literary kinship of these "sisters" with an earlier tradition of "visionary sister autobiographers who wrote during the Middle Ages and the Counter-Reformation – e.g., Christina Markyate

(twelfth century), Julian of Norwich (1342–c. 1420), Margery Kempe (c. 1373–1438), and Teresa of Avila (1515–1582)." She cites the allegedly "unlettered" Maria Stewart in affirming this connection:

> In the 15th century, the general spirit of this period is worthy of observation. We might have then seen women preaching and mixing themselves in controversies. Women occupying the chairs of Philosophy and Justice; women haranguing in Latin before the Pope; women writing in Greek and studying Hebrew; Nuns were Poetesses, and women of quality Divines; and young girls who studied Eloquence, would with sweetest countenances, and most plaintive voices exhort the Pope and the Christian Princes ... Women in those days devoted their leisure hours to contemplation and study. (p. xxxvi)

14. Braxton, *Black Women Writing*, p. 73.
15. Ibid., p. 109.
16. Ida B. Wells, *Crusade for Justice: The Autobiography of Ida B. Wells* (Chicago: University of Chicago Press, 1970), p. 4.
17. Ida B. Wells, *Southern Horrors: Lynch Law in All Its Phases* (New York: Arno Press, 1969; originally published 1892), p. 2. Quoted in Braxton, *Black Women Writing*, p. 118.
18. Ethel Waters, *His Eye is on the Sparrow* (Kingsport, TN: Kingsport Press, 1950), p. 1.
19. Marian Anderson, *My Lord, What a Morning* (New York: Viking, 1956), p. 50.
20. Nina Simone, *I Put a Spell on You* (New York: De Capo, 1993), p. 68.
21. Simone mentions Anderson at another time – ironically she remembered Anderson's 1939 Constitution Hall protest concert as being on Independence Day – in a sense, it was Independence Day for Anderson and for many Americans, especially black Americans, who celebrated her defiance and her artistry on that day.
22. Margo Perkins, *Autobiography as Activism: Three Black Women of the Sixties* (Jackson: University of Mississippi, 2000), p. 22.
23. Ibid., p. 27.
24. Assata Shakur, *Assata: An Autobiography* (Chicago: Lawrence Hill Books, 1987), p. 67.
25. Elaine Brown, *A Taste of Power: A Black Woman's Story* (New York: Anchor, 1992), p. 368.
26. Angela Davis, *Angela Davis: An Autobiography* (New York: International, 1974), p. xvi.
27. Perkins, *Autobiography as Activism*, p. 27.
28. Ibid., p. 27.
29. Katherine Dunham, *A Touch of Innocence* (New York: Harcourt Brace, 1959), "A Note to the Reader."
30. Viktor Frankl, a Jewish physician-psychiatrist and psychotherapist who lived in Vienna, Austria, escaped the Holocaust by resisting identification with the will of the master (and the master class), by doing deeds, creating work, and defining his own attitude toward unavoidable suffering – by maintaining a spiritual or inner life.
31. Mary Jane Lupton, *Lucille Clifton: Her Life and Letters* (New York: Praeger, 2006), p. 14.

32. Audre Lorde, *Zami: A New Spelling of My Name* (Freedom, CA: Crossing Press, 1982), p. 68.

33. June Jordan, *Soldier: A Poet's Childhood* (New York: Basic Civitas, 2000). Jordan describes a household where both she and her mother receive physical and verbal abuse from her father.

34. Rosemary L. Bray, *Unafraid of the Dark: A Memoir* (New York: Random House, 1998), pp. xvi–xvii.

8

MADHU DUBEY

"Even some fiction might be useful": African American women novelists

Octavia Butler's science-fiction novel *Parable of the Sower* (1993) depicts a dystopian future society riven by racial and class war. Anticipating the impending collapse of her social world, the novel's protagonist Lauren Olamina assembles a survival kit that contains (among other items) various kinds of reading material, including novels. "Even some fiction might be useful," says Lauren,[1] and she turns out to be right, as the books she has salvaged supply valuable information that helps her survive hunger and thirst as well as social chaos. The life-saving power of fiction emerges as a recurrent motif in African American women's novels published from the mid nineteenth to the early twenty-first century. Harriet Wilson, the first black woman to publish a novel, explained in her author's preface that she wrote *Our Nig* (1859) in a desperate bid to raise money to save the life of her child. The most celebrated black woman novelist, Toni Morrison, describes the novel as a form that "should be beautiful, and powerful, but it should also *work*."[2] African American women have critically refashioned a variety of genres, from neoslave narratives to science fiction, sentimental romances to ghost stories, in their effort to make novels that work in practical as well as imaginary ways.

Novels by African American women have attained unprecedented levels of commercial success and academic recognition by the turn of the twenty-first century, yet reconstruction of this literary tradition still remains a work in progress. What is now believed to be the first novel written by an African American woman, Hannah Crafts's *The Bondwoman's Narrative*, was recovered and published in 2002, nearly a hundred and fifty years after it was written. The first published novel by an African American woman, Harriet Wilson's *Our Nig*, was printed at the author's expense in 1859, but sank into complete obscurity until its rediscovery during the 1980s. In their prefaces, both of these novelists voice strong discomfort about the very act of writing. In order to enter the sphere of literary culture, mid-nineteenth-century black women felt obliged to write within two influential genres, the slave narratives sponsored by the abolitionist movement and the sentimental novels popular among white women. Yet these genres, which centered around male slaves or white ladies, were not exactly amenable to the literary intentions of early black women writers. The anxiety of authorship expressed by Crafts and Wilson arose in part from their ambivalence toward the two predominant literary genres of their time.

The Bondwoman's Narrative reads as an incoherent mélange of genres, including fugitive slave narrative, sentimental romance, gothic fiction, and the novel of passing. This odd assemblage of genres has the ultimate effect of unsettling conventional literary representations as well as social hierarchies of race and gender. Crafts plays a sly variation on the slave narrative and sentimental novel genres, presenting the tales of two white ladies, both slave owners, who are blackened and thereby divested of their racial and class privileges. Hannah's first mistress turns out to be a mulatta passing for white who is forced to flee the plantation once her racial identity is exposed. Another slave mistress, Mrs. Cosgrove, becomes black through a more comic turn of events, as her obsession with preserving her fair complexion leads her to use a white face powder that unaccountably turns her skin black. Unaware of this transformation, Mrs. Cosgrove goes to petition a powerful gentleman on behalf of her husband, only to be curtly told that it is "not customary to bestow offices on colored people."[3] These examples of racial passing, whether narrated in a melodramatic or farcical register, clearly mock the absurdity of a social system founded on racial difference. Hannah Crafts takes unmistakable delight in creating a topsy-turvy fictional world of fugitive slave mistresses and ladies in blackface.

Harriet Wilson is more straightforward in her aberration from the slave narrative and sentimental novel genres. *Our Nig* represents a rare instance of an antebellum African American literary text that does not take slavery as its focus. The novel's depiction of indentured servitude in the North, marked by the hard labor and brutal bodily punishment generally associated with slavery, utterly confounds the abolitionist equation of racial oppression with the southern institution of slavery. Wilson is equally explicit about the ways in which the experience of poor black women deviates from the model of femininity idealized in sentimental novels. Due to her race and poverty, Frado is disqualified from prevalent norms of female development, embodied in the character of Jane, a frail and helpless white girl whose only crisis in the novel revolves around the question of how she should best exercise her free choice in marriage. In contrast, Frado is defeminized by the hard labor she is forced to perform and her marriage, to a man who impregnates and abandons her, only exacerbates her social and economic insecurity.

The grim story of Frado's experience of work, marriage, and motherhood is mitigated only by the novel's inspirational account of her spiritual and intellectual development. Frado's slow conversion to Christianity imparts a strong sense of justice and free will, eventually inspiring her to challenge her mistress's cruelty and injustice. As Frado secretly reads the Bible, her little room in her mistress's house is transformed into a "safe retreat."[4] Reading helps Frado cultivate an inner life and instills aspirations for self-improvement and autonomy that are repeatedly thwarted by her material circumstances. The image of Frado converting her cramped servant quarter into a safe retreat vividly captures the dilemma of the early black woman writer who literally lacked a room of her own, to adopt Virginia Woolf's celebrated phrase for the financial independence necessary for the development of women's literary culture. Despite a life of homelessness and penury, Harriet Wilson did manage to seize the agency of authorship, but her preface to *Our Nig* evinces her keen sense of unease in doing so. Anticipating that her literary ambitions would be censured by her audience, Wilson defensively insists that her purpose in writing a novel is to try to earn the means to support her child. Far from being a leisure activity or even a vehicle of moral elevation, the writing of fiction for a working-class black woman is presented here as a pressing economic necessity.

It should come as no surprise that the secure possession of a room or house of one's own provided the foundation for the outpouring of African American women's literary creativity at the turn of the twentieth century. A range of novelists, including Frances Harper, Pauline Hopkins, Amelia Johnson, Emma Kelley-Hawkins, and Katherine Tillman, described in intricate detail the comfort, beauty, and order of domestic spaces. The domestic romance, as Claudia Tate labels this genre of black women's fiction,[5] showcased the ability of at least a certain class of African American women to attain the gentility, respectability, and refinement idealized in the nineteenth-century cult of true womanhood. Home spaces in these novels serve as sites for the reconstitution of family, allowing black women to assume the roles of wives and mothers that were proscribed by slavery. However, while enshrining domesticity as the proper sphere for women, novelists such as Frances Harper or Pauline Hopkins play a unique twist on the sentimental romance, blurring the boundaries between private and public spheres by inventing home spaces that are hubs of intellectual and political debate. Ma Smith's boarding house in Hopkins's novel *Contending Forces* (1900) is the most striking example of an expanded domestic realm, with its sewing-circle meetings where participants spiritedly discuss public matters pertaining to the welfare of black women.

This sort of fictional recreation of the domestic domain was made possible by a climate of intense political activism among African American women. In the Women's Era, or the post-Reconstruction decades of the 1880s and

1890s, black women entered the public sphere by writing, lecturing, and agitating on behalf of various political campaigns, including suffrage, equal rights, and antilynching legislation. This was also the period when African Americans self-consciously turned to the writing of literature, and novels in particular, as an effective way to press the case for racial equality. Authorial prefaces and notes appended to novels published during this period repeatedly reaffirmed the new role of the novel as a vehicle of political advancement, with Frances Harper asserting that she wrote *Iola Leroy* in order to "awaken ... a stronger sense of justice" in her readers, and Pauline Hopkins likewise stating that *Contending Forces* was "actuated by a desire ... to raise the stigma of degradation from my race."[6] In order to accomplish these political objectives, Harper and Hopkins selectively appropriated the conventions of sentimental romance fiction.

As suggested by Harriet Wilson's diffidence about writing as a means of economic sustenance, confident assumption of literary authority has always been tied up with class privilege. Whereas Wilson bitterly parodied the genteel femininity idealized in sentimental novels, writers such as Harper and Hopkins shored up their moral and political authority by subscribing to the bourgeois cult of true womanhood. The characterization of Harper's Iola Leroy and Sappho Clark, the heroine of *Contending Forces*, as exemplars of moral virtue and Christian piety was intended to counter the history of sexual degradation that shadowed African American women well into the twentieth century. While enslaved, Sappho and Iola are subjected to rape and attempted sexual assault, but this is not shown to compromise in any way their moral rectitude for, as pithily expressed by a female character in *Contending Forces*, "We are virtuous or non-virtuous only when we have a *choice*" (p. 149). Because racist allegations about the "natural" depravity of black women were widely circulated to rationalize their sexual exploitation, Harper and Hopkins created black heroines who are thoroughly desexualized and white male villains who embody wanton lust. The sentimental novel, with its starkly melodramatic confrontations between virtue and villainy, female innocence and male aggression, offered these writers an effective means of redressing the sexual violations of slavery.

In keeping with the conventions of the sentimental romance, both *Iola Leroy* and *Contending Forces* end with marriage, affirming their heroines' achievement of bourgeois respectability, but their treatment of marriage also clarifies their divergence from the norms of proper womanhood. All the significant married couples presented in the two novels are cemented by a commitment to racial uplift rather than romantic love. Iola values her husband not as a provider or protector but as her intellectual equal and partner in public service to the race. Much of the novel traces Iola's struggle to secure financial independence through employment and there is no indication that marriage will consign her to a lady's life of leisure. In a further departure from the sentimental novel, the marriage plot in *Iola Leroy* offers Harper a vehicle for asserting pride in black identity and community. Before she meets her future husband, Iola receives a marriage proposal from the white Dr. Gresham, who urges her to capitalize on her white appearance and to pass into a life of ease that was not available to many African Americans in the immediate aftermath of slavery. Declaring that the "best blood in [her] veins is African blood" (p. 208), Iola refuses to pass for white, and she turns down Dr. Gresham's offer of material prosperity on the grounds that she would rather "serve the race which needs [her] most" (p. 235).

The sentimental romance and racial uplift strands of *Iola Leroy* appear to blend together so seamlessly because both are driven by a commitment to bourgeois codes of value and conduct. In the post-Reconstruction era, when basic civil and political rights were being stripped away from African Americans, the racial uplift mission sought to inculcate bourgeois norms of behavior in the masses of black people as a way of proving the race's fitness for citizenship. Accordingly, we find characters like Iola and her brother Harry, who epitomize intellectual and social refinement, traveling through the poor Black Belt regions of the South preaching the benefits of literacy, temperance, and marriage. To present-day readers, the uplift agenda of these novels seems riddled with contradictions, as declarations of racial pride come from heroes and heroines who are almost always light-skinned enough to pass for white. These characters' avowed identification with the black community is belied by the fact that their genteel comportment and language conspicuously set them apart from the ordinary black folk whose speech is rendered in orthographically mutilated dialect. The contradictions of racial uplift ideology are at times explicitly acknowledged in these novels, such as when the working-class, dialect-speaking character of Mrs. Robinson in *Contending Forces* mocks the elite black women engaged in racial uplift as "them white-folkesy colored ladies" (p. 186).

As if amplifying Sister Robinson's remark, Nella Larsen's novel *Quicksand* (1925) presents a searing critique of the racial hypocrisy of uplift ideology. The southern institution of Naxos, where the novel begins, is dedicated to training morally upstanding citizens who must suppress all visible signs of racial difference in their quest for bourgeois propriety. Larsen's quirky protagonist Helga Crane leaves Naxos and moves first to Chicago and then New York in search of wider horizons, but finds the life of race men and women in the urban North to be equally stultifying. While flaunting their loyalty to the race, members of the Harlem elite such as Anne Grey blindly mimic the manners of white ladies and gentlemen and treat the ordinary black folk they are trying to uplift as objects of condescension and charity. The Talented Tenth's preoccupation with bourgeois respectability bears severely repressive implications for black female sexuality, as illustrated by Robert Anderson's prudish recoil from his sexual desire for Helga. The first novel to present a black female character as a sexual being, *Quicksand* decisively breaks from the traditions of both racial uplift and sentimental romance.

Ironically deflating the lofty aspirations of these traditions, *Quicksand* inaugurates the New Negro realism of the 1920s, which called for exactly this kind of departure from genteel literary representations of black life. Yet literary histories of the African American novel have often aligned Larsen with the rearguard camp of the Harlem Renaissance, associated with idealized romances of black middle-class life and pitted against the earthy folk realism of the vanguard, as exemplified in the writings of Claude McKay or Langston Hughes. The only rationale for this sort of categorization lies in Larsen's refusal to romanticize the black folk as repositories of primal vitality and natural sexuality. In her reappraisal of Larsen, Barbara Christian suggests that African American women writers could not endorse the 1920s fad of racial primitivism, because its emphasis on a natural black sexuality was too uncomfortably reminiscent of racist discourses originating in slavery, discourses that, as shown in the novels of Frances Harper and Pauline Hopkins, had sanctioned systematic sexual violence against black women. That such discourses of black female sexuality were by no means obsolete is made clear in *Quicksand* when Helga is propositioned by a white man who discerns the "soul of a prostitute" behind her ladylike exterior.[7] The damaging consequences of racial primitivism for black women's bodies become all too clear by the end of the novel, when Helga, acting on her sexual desires, marries a preacher, follows him to a conservative southern folk community, and ends up with her body ravaged by repeated childbirth.

Helga's alienation from the genteel and folk traditions dramatizes the dilemma of the early twentieth-century African American woman novelist whose attempt to explore black female sexuality gets mired between the extremes of prudery and primitivism. Neither of the two predominant racial discourses of her day – racial uplift or New Negro realism – offers Larsen an adequate medium for her subject. Not surprisingly, then, the most frank fictional treatments of black female sexuality during the 1920s occur when black women pass for white. It is quite telling that in the era of racial pride that was the Harlem Renaissance, the two most prominent black women writers published novels of racial passing – *Plum Bun* by Jessie Fauset and *Passing* by Nella Larsen, both published in 1929. Predictably, in both novels the women who identify as black, Irene Redfield and Virginia Murray, are dedicated to racial uplift and bourgeois domesticity and are, as a result, thoroughly desexualized. Conversely, sexual agency is afforded only to those female characters who choose to reject the race and pass for white. At the end, the sexually adventurous woman is either punished, as when Clare Kendry literally falls to her death at the end of *Passing*, or domesticated as wife and loyal race woman, like Angela Murray in Fauset's novel. Although it ultimately affirms the ideals of both domestic romance and racial uplift, *Plum Bun* presents a harshly realist and even cynical picture of the rampant commodification of black female sexuality during the 1920s, as is clear even from the title ("Market") of the section in which Angela engages in an illicit affair with a wealthy white man. With greater subtlety, Larsen presents her two main female characters as doubles, revealing the upright (and uptight) race woman's latent longing to stray from established standards of sexual and racial conduct. While *Plum Bun* closes with Angela's return home, secure in her sense of domestic and racial belonging, *Passing* yields no such stable understanding of racial or gender identity.

Although the passing novel seems vulnerable to easy condemnation for featuring mulatto characters that aspire to be white, the transgressive purposes of the genre are unmistakable when situated in its own time. Racism in the nineteenth and early twentieth centuries was grounded on pseudoscientific claims of biological difference between the races, claims that are voiced by white male characters in novels such as *Iola Leroy* and *Passing* who boast of their infallible ability to detect the tell-tale signs of black blood even in those who appear to be white. Both novels expose the absurdity of such claims and the arbitrariness of the one-drop rule by focusing on mulatto characters who can easily pass for white. In response to scientific racism, earlier novelists such as Pauline Hopkins had invoked the biblical phrase "of one blood" to insist on the common origin of all the human races and on the reality of racial miscegenation in the United States,[8] thereby contesting white supremacist discourses of racial purity. Of course, it was not only at the level of discourse that racial boundaries were being fiercely defended; from the post-Reconstruction period onward, social separation of the races had become entrenched through institutionalized segregation. The literary figure of the mulatto who easily crossed the borders between black and white social worlds offered an implicit critique of racial segregation. The social and economic mobility of the character passing for white underscored the actual disqualification of African Americans from the ostensibly race-neutral promise of the American Dream.

In the passing novels of Fauset and Larsen, racial inequities are compounded for black women, who can secure social and economic mobility only through marriage. Although Fauset's novels are often labeled domestic romances because they present marriage as the culmination of female desire, their romance is tempered by a realist, pragmatic assessment of the financial benefits of the institution. Larsen is more overtly critical of the marriage plot, especially in *Passing*, where domestic stability and social status are bought at the expense of sexual ardor and emotional intensity. Extending Larsen's interrogation of the ascent narrative,[9] Zora Neale Hurston's *Their Eyes Were Watching God* (1937) presents marriage as a utilitarian arrangement that stifles all possibilities of romance and sexual passion. But whereas Larsen's novels register the absence of legitimate sexual outlets for black middle-class women, *Their Eyes* frankly celebrates its heroine's discovery of sexual passion outside marriage. In contrast to Helga Crane, whose search for sexual fulfillment through immersion in southern folk life is shown to be utterly debilitating, Hurston's Janie Starks finds not only love but also her own voice and identity during her sojourn with Tea Cake in the black folk community of the Everglades. *Their Eyes* is the first novel by a black woman to use the language of nature – the metaphor of the blossoming pear tree – to describe black female sexual desire, and perhaps this was made possible by the fact that 1920s racial primitivism, with its disturbing implications for black women, had waned by the time Hurston's novel was published in 1937.

Their Eyes inaugurates a new genre, of the folk romance, in African American women's fiction, a genre that would drop out of literary history until its recovery by Alice Walker during the 1980s. The folk romance boldly departs from the narrative conventions of the sentimental romance. Class descent is the condition of possibility for Janie's romance with Tea Cake, and the romance narrative must be delinked from the narrative of social ascent through marriage in order to rechart the journey of sexual discovery. But even more powerful than Janie's romance with Tea Cake is Hurston's romance with black southern folk culture, a romance that bears profound implications for the language and form of the novel. The genteel aspirations of the novel of racial uplift were inscribed in a clear-cut linguistic hierarchy, with the proper English spoken by the black elite serving as the norm against which the dialect of ordinary black folk appeared as a visual and grammatical aberration. Although some racial uplift novels such as Frances Harper's *Iola Leroy* contain passages appreciating the sophisticated language of the black folk (notably, the chapter on the "mystery of market speech"),[10] folk speech was always filtered through the standard English of the omniscient narration. *Their Eyes* breaks with this linguistic convention through its use of free indirect discourse, or a style that integrates first- and third-person narration. As the voice of the omniscient narrator is inflected with the idioms of the novel's characters, black folk speech gains a new legitimacy as an aesthetic medium.

Hurston's portrayal of black folk culture came under fire when Richard Wright, in his review of *Their Eyes Were Watching God*, castigated it as a primitivist romance that suppressed the realities of racial and economic oppression in the South. But Hurston quite deliberately defined her literary ambitions in opposition to the genre of racial protest epitomized by Wright. Asserting that she did not "belong to the sobbing school of Negrohood,"[11] Hurston chose to portray black southern life from the inside, as it were, exploring its cultural vitality and its internal conflicts of color, class, and gender rather than its dehumanizing confrontations with white racism. With the benefit of hindsight, Hurston's lyrical evocation of southern folk culture can be seen as an urgent act of historical commemoration, an effort to preserve in literature an agrarian way of life that was being eroded by modernization. The decade following the publication of *Their Eyes Were Watching God* witnessed the second great wave of black urban migration out of the South, and the social and cultural conflicts sparked by urbanization formed the central concern of African American novelists of the 1940s and 1950s. New Negro optimism about urbanization as a means of full black participation in American life proved difficult to sustain in the 1940s, as patterns of residential segregation and employment discrimination in northern cities became increasingly entrenched and visible. The most prominent African American women novelists of this time – Ann Petry, Dorothy West, and Gwendolyn Brooks – all wrote failed ascent narratives assessing the psychological and cultural costs of urbanization.

In West's *The Living Is Easy* (1948), these costs are dramatized through city-dweller Cleo Judson's contradictory understanding of the meaning of the South. Cleo's quest for upward mobility demands blind emulation of upper-crust white Boston society and contemptuous distance from the working-class culture of recently arriving black southern migrants. But even as Cleo regards the South as the source of a vulgar blackness that must be disowned in the interests of social ascent and racial assimilation, she simultaneously longs for the South of her childhood, which she selectively remembers as a site of female ancestry. Cleo's efforts to recreate this imaginary South in the city (by relocating all her sisters to Boston) fail disastrously and, in an intricate plot twist, the disintegration of her family romance is tied up with the refusal of the Boston black elite to ally themselves with a southern antilynching campaign. The novel sketches a complex symbolic geography, qualifying romanticized views of the South as ancestral home and the urban North as a promised land of opportunity.

Ann Petry's *The Street* (1946) metaphorically narrows the distance between racial oppression in the urban North and the rural South by describing city streets as the "North's lynch mobs."[12] As with Cleo Judson, Lutie Johnson's ascent aims directly result in her alienation not only from family and community, but also from her own sexuality. The sexual frigidity of both characters is meant not only to bolster their sense of class superiority but also to shield them from an urban market economy in which black women can gain power only in exchange for their sexuality. Through its literal and figurative treatment of prostitution, *The Street* directly links the commodification of black female sexuality in modern cities with the rape of black women during slavery. The circular and repetitive narrative shape of Lutie's efforts to escape her destiny as sexual prey discredits any notion of urbanization as a process of progressive advancement for African American women. Lutie's intensifying sense of suffocation in the narrow spaces of urban ghetto life is entirely unabated by memories or fantasies of the rural South as an elsewhere to the modern city. In this and other respects, *The Street* closely adheres to the conventions of naturalist fiction, which reinforces its critique of socio-economic oppression by denying its characters any real or imaginary outlets. Likened to a caged animal in a zoo or a rat in a maze, Lutie ends up, like Richard Wright's Bigger Thomas, exercising agency only through repeated and futile acts of violence.

The protagonist of Gwendolyn Brooks's *Maud Martha* (1953) inhabits an urban environment as grey and confined as any to be found in naturalist fiction, as she battles mice and cockroaches in her kitchenette apartment in Chicago's segregated south side. In one such scene, Maud's imaginary excursion into the inner life of a trapped mouse moves her to spare its life. This fine detail crystallizes the difference between Petry's naturalism and Brooks's modernism, which endows the drabbest urban life with rich interiority and poetry. Like Cleo and Lutie, Maud starts out aspiring for upward mobility. Her ascent ambitions take the form of a yearning for gentility and domestic beauty, which is thwarted by her shabby urban surroundings. But Brooks's modernist style transmutes a story of material disenchantment into a portrait of the artist as an ordinary black woman. The impressionistic form of the novel, consisting of brief, fragmented vignettes, offers a perfect medium for Maud's aesthetic sensibility, which finds beauty in the fleeting moments and wayward details of everyday life. Maud's delight in dandelions as "yellow jewels for everyday"[13] finds an echo nearly two decades later, when Pecola, the protagonist of Toni Morrison's *The Bluest Eye* (1970), similarly frustrated in her pursuit of conventional beauty, seizes upon dandelions as "the codes and touchstones of her world, capable of translation and possession."[14]

In this respect, *Maud Martha* anticipates the black female aesthetic that would take shape in African American women's novels during the "second renaissance" of the 1970s. Alice Walker's essay, "In Search of Our Mothers' Gardens," identifies everyday life as the realm of black female artistry; as their access to high art was restricted by racism, sexism, and poverty, black women perforce channeled their artistic energy into domestic activities such as gardening or quilting. Walker's search for her mothers' gardens, or for historical precedents for her own literary ambitions, ultimately led to her rediscovery of Zora Neale Hurston, inaugurating what might be called a southern folk aesthetic in African American women's fiction published since the 1970s. This aesthetic is best understood as a complicated response to the Black Arts movement of the 1960s, which at once catalyzed and constrained the literary production of black women writers. With its slogan of "Black is beautiful," the Black Arts movement sought to reverse long-standing Western definitions of blackness as a stigmatic sign of inferiority. While initiating a radical revaluation of black cultural identity, the nationalist Black Aesthetic discouraged literary explorations of class, gender, sexuality, and other differences that might threaten a unitary conception of racial solidarity. It is surely telling that very few African American women published novels during the 1960s, the heyday of black cultural nationalism. This was due in part to the fact that Black Arts advocates preferred the performative genres of drama and poetry as more capable of politically engaging a mass audience.

For African American women writers of the 1970s, the genre of the novel offered a flexible and capacious vehicle for questioning the Black Arts agenda, especially its monolithic and exclusively race-centered models of identity and community. Through their fragmented plot lines and multiple points of view, novels such as Toni Morrison's *The Bluest Eye*, Alice Walker's *Meridian* (1976), and Toni Cade Bambara's *The Salt Eaters* (1980) explored alternate notions of community as a terrain of intraracial differences and conflicts. *The Bluest Eye* exposed the hollowness of "black is beautiful" rhetoric from the vantage point of a little girl whose dark skin makes her a perfect scapegoat for her community's racial self-hatred, and whose quest for the blonde-haired, blue-eyed ideal of female beauty culminates in madness. Through its imagery of "funk," *The Bluest Eye* reaches for a different ideal of beauty that critically adapts the nationalist Black Aesthetic, which affirmed urban vernacular culture as the source of an authentically black art. African American women novelists of the 1970s and 1980s retained the Black Arts emphasis on oral culture, but redirected it toward the female folk practices of the rural South, perhaps in an effort to displace the stridently masculine and urban tenor of Black Aesthetic discourse.

In a wide range of novels, including Morrison's *Song of Solomon* (1977), Bambara's *The Salt Eaters*, Walker's *Meridian* and *The Color Purple* (1982), Ntozake Shange's *Sassafras, Cypress, and Indigo* (1982), and Gloria Naylor's *Mama Day* (1988), the South is represented as the site of cultural ancestry and memory. This emphasis on historical continuity must have seemed urgently necessary at a time when past traditions, and especially those associated with the racially oppressive history of the South, were being disavowed in the interests of political change. In *Meridian*, radical student activists committed to revolutionary change end up destroying the Sojourner tree, which through its very name suggests that the historical past contains female models of resistance that can nourish the political movements of the present and future. Not long after the magnolia tree is chopped down, Meridian turns her back on the nationalist movement in the urban North and journeys South in search of a different sort of politics grounded in historical memory. Delving into the history of her own foremothers, Meridian learns that her great-grandmother prevented her husband from building his farm over a Native American burial mound, land hallowed by the presence of departed ancestral spirits. Toni Cade Bambara's *The Salt Eaters*, which was also published in the immediate aftermath of the Black Arts era, similarly portrays the South as an ancestral ground. At the center of the novel stands the Southwestern Community Infirmary, whose mission is to preserve folk practices and traditions. Among these is the ritual ceremony of laying on of hands, conducted by the ancestral figure of Minnie Ransom with the aid of her spirit-guide Old Min, which helps cure Velma Henry of her psychological and political malaise. Black women's novels of this period contain a gallery of ancestral figures, such as Toni Morrison's Pilate or Gloria Naylor's Mama Day, who keep alive the southern black folk traditions of storytelling, song, and conjuring.

In her influential essay, "Rootedness: The Ancestor as Foundation," Toni Morrison describes the recurring theme of ancestry in African American fiction as a yearning for "conscious historical connection" (p. 344). As is clear from Walker's search for her mothers' gardens, this yearning for historical connection is also a desire for a tradition that might authorize the literary production of late twentieth-century African American women novelists. Taking their cue from Walker and Morrison, many black feminist literary critics writing during the 1980s emphasized the folk provenance of this literary authority, drawing on practices such as conjuring or specifying to capture the distinctive qualities of black women's fiction.[15] In "Rootedness," Morrison writes that she tries to infuse the genre of the novel with "unorthodox novelistic characteristics" in order to render it distinctively black. Among these, Morrison highlights her efforts to inflect the print genre of the novel with the idioms and rhythms of black oral culture and to reclaim a uniquely black "cosmology" that conjoins supernatural and mundane levels of reality (p. 342). These twin impulses are at the core of the remarkable formal experimentation found in African American women's novels published during the 1980s.

Alice Walker's *The Color Purple*, for example, pays tribute to her revered foremother, Zora Neale Hurston, by extending her adaptation of black southern folk culture into print literature. In *Their Eyes Were Watching God*, even as the more conventionally authoritative omniscient narration is saturated by black folk speech, the folk language of the novel's characters is still subsumed by third-person narration. Celie's story is subject to no such linguistic mediation and is narrated entirely in the southern vernacular of her own first-person voice. Walker's experiments with narrative voice were made possible by Gayl Jones's novels published during the 1970s, *Corregidora* (1975) and *Eva's Man* (1976), which first validated black women's vernacular speech as a literary language in its own right. Jones developed the genre of the blues novel and Walker reworked the epistolary novel, or the novel narrated in the form of letters, in order to seize literary agency for subjects who have been denied the privilege of authorship. In both cases, the tradition of print literature had to be oralized before it could serve as an expressive medium for black female subjectivity.

It is no coincidence that Celie's and Ursa Corregidora's search for an authentic literary voice is also a struggle for sexual autonomy. Celie responds to repeated incestuous rape by writing letters that are addressed to God but always remain unsigned, indicating her difficulty in imagining herself as a writing subject who can assume a human readership. As the novel progresses, Celie starts to address her letters to her sister Nettie and the novel begins to include letters from Nettie to Celie, establishing a literary genealogy in which writing becomes a reciprocal exchange among black women. In constructing her novel in the form of letters, Walker appropriates the literary conventions of the Victorian epistolary novel, which typically narrated a sentimental tale of heterosexual assault and eventual seduction. Celie's letters, too, begin by recounting violent heterosexual assault but end up testifying to her growing erotic seduction by a woman blues singer, Shug Avery, who initiates Celie's perception of sexuality as a source of pleasure rather than victimization. Blues music is often hailed as the first cultural medium that allowed black women to represent themselves as sexual subjects. Although most blues lyrics focus on the travails of heterosexual love, some women blues singers such as Gertrude "Ma" Rainey also voiced their sexual desire for women, making the blues an exceptionally supple instrument for exploring black female sexuality.

In Gayl Jones's *Corregidora*, Ursa's blues-singing voice gains resonance after her husband's sexual violence forces her to undergo a hysterectomy. Her suddenly missing womb forces Ursa to revaluate the reproductive conception of black female sexuality that has been imposed on her by three generations of her maternal ancestors. For the Corregidora women, giving birth is a form of cultural as well as biological reproduction, enabling them to pass down through the generations their experience of sexual violation during slavery. Alienated from this ancestral tradition by her lack of a womb, Ursa gropes for a new understanding of black female sexuality but is relentlessly drawn back to the past as her abusive relationship with her husband continues to be plagued by the sexual history of slavery. The novel ends with a dialogue between Ursa and her husband Mutt, narrated in the repetition-with-variation structure of a blues stanza, which voices their conflicting emotions of love and hate, pleasure and pain, exemplifying the unique capacity of blues music to express the unresolved contradictions of heterosexual desire. Not only the final confrontation between Ursa and Mutt but the novel as a whole follows the three-part blues structure of incremental repetition, with Ursa's story developing as a critical variation on the history of her maternal slave ancestors. The blues genre of *Corregidora* allows for a complex relation between modern black women and ancestral tradition, a relation marked by interrogation as much as identification.

In the two decades following the publication of *Corregidora*, African American women's novels would be haunted by the presence of slave ancestors and would persistently turn to oral tradition as the only reliable source of historical memory. The Corregidora women place so much importance on transmitting their oral testimony to future generations because their master has burnt all written records of their enslavement. In Gloria Naylor's *Mama Day*, the slave ancestor Sapphira Wade lives on in the realm of oral legend rather than historical record. The only written trace of her existence is a bill of sale inserted into her slavemaster's ledger, but age and water damage make it impossible for her descendants to decipher her name. The faded bill of sale in Naylor's novel, like the burnt historical evidence in *Corregidora*, attests to the erasure of black women's experience from the official archives of slavery, prompting both Jones and Naylor to turn to oral tradition as a supplementary source of historical knowledge.

Even those novels that are inspired by surviving historical documents about actual black female slaves, such as Sherley Anne Williams's *Dessa Rose* (1986) or Toni Morrison's *Beloved* (1988), exhibit a deep distrust of the historiography of slavery. Each novel contains a master's text, or a written document that actively contributes to the ideological reproduction of slavery. In *Beloved*, Schoolteacher's notebook lists the animal and human characteristics of the slaves, and historian Adam Nehemiah in *Dessa Rose* is the author of a tract on the proper management of slaves and of a journal perpetuating the most demeaning caricatures of slaves as happy darkies. Both novels clarify the ways in which writing itself served as a crucial justification for slavery: people of African descent were disqualified from human status and therefore held to be fit for slavery because of their lack of written cultural traditions. In response, nineteenth-century fugitive slaves seized on writing as a means of demonstrating the slave's humanity and fitness for citizenship. By the late twentieth century, as national integration of African Americans remained incomplete, the genre of the neoslave narrative began to probe the emancipatory hopes invested in print literacy by early African American writers. In her preface to *Dessa Rose*, Sherley Anne Williams writes that "Afro-Americans, having survived by word of mouth ... remain at the mercy of literature and writing; often, these have betrayed us."[16] Neoslave narratives such as *Dessa Rose* or *Beloved* affirm instead the oral traditions of slaves, such as the songs that covertly help Dessa to escape from prison or Baby Suggs's sermon at the Clearing, as vehicles of physical and psychological freedom.

In her preface to *Dessa Rose*, Williams goes on to say that she "loved history" until she came to realize that "there was no place in the American past [she] could go and be free" (p. x). Disenchanted with the historical archive, late twentieth-century African American women writers turn to blatantly fictive genres such as science fiction or the ghost story in order to emphasize the difficulties of arriving at the real truth of the slave experience. In *Kindred* (1977), for example, Octavia Butler uses the device of time travel to force her protagonist Dana to confront the lingering immediacy of the historical past. Dana's travels back to the era of slavery reveal the limitations of the knowledge she has gleaned from reading history books, and her jarring movement between past and present compels readers to question our modes of access to the past of slavery. *Beloved* poses an equally daunting challenge, urging readers to believe that Sethe's murdered daughter has literally returned from the dead. Beloved's vampiric hunger for stories about slavery suggests that, until the past finds narrative representation, it will continue to prey upon the present. Through Beloved's deterioration into a succubus straight out of a supernatural horror story, Morrison represents slavery as a trauma that defies rational comprehension. Neoslave narratives by black male writers, such as Ishmael Reed's *Flight to Canada* (1976) or Charles Johnson's *Oxherding Tale* (1982) and *Middle Passage* (1991), also bend the rules of realist fiction, but what distinguishes Morrison's and Butler's uses of this genre is their focus on black women's unique experience of reproductive slavery. In fact, Butler's *Wild Seed* (1988) casts a man of African descent as a breeder of slaves, perhaps to highlight all the more sharply the gendered dimensions of reproductive slavery. An example of the emergent genre of speculative fiction, *Wild Seed* features a female slave who resists her destiny as breeder through the magical practices of shape-shifting and animal metamorphosis. Flagrantly flouting the rules of realist fiction, novels such as *Beloved* and *Wild Seed* call attention to their own status as literary inventions, emphasizing the mediation involved in all present efforts to reconstruct the past of slavery.

In their break with realism and their self-conscious attention to problems of representation, late twentieth-century neoslave narratives depart not only from the mid-nineteenth-century fugitive slave narratives but also from earlier historical novels of slavery such as Margaret Walker's *Jubilee*, published in 1966. Narrative realism forms a crucial component of the peculiar burden of literary and racial representation that has long been imposed upon African American writers. In the interests of political progress, African American writers have been compelled to present their narratives not only as accurate reflections of social reality but also as representative of the experience of the race as a whole. Some writers believe that the African American novel is finally being released from this burden of racial representation at the turn of the twenty-first century. In his article "Black to the Future," detective fiction writer Walter Mosley noted the belated entry of African American novelists into popular genres such as science fiction, claiming that this was made possible only because writers began refusing the imperative to write always and only in realist genres protesting racial oppression.[17]

Mosley's observations are borne out by the profusion of popular genres in contemporary African American women's fiction. The remarkable commercial success of Terry McMillan's romance novels, *Disappearing Acts* (1989) and *Waiting to Exhale* (1992), revealed the existence of a sizeable market for accessible and entertaining fiction by African American women. Contemporary black women novelists are writing in a broad array of popular and middle-brow genres, including speculative and science fiction, romances and chick lit, erotica and detective fiction, family sagas and uplift novels. Instead of claiming to speak for and to black women as a whole, these novels deal with discrete segments of black female experience, reflecting the splintered nature of racial identity and community in the post-civil rights era. Some novelists, such as Terry McMillan, take the race of their characters for granted and write unapologetically about the love and sex lives of privileged black women, reversing the long-standing equation, in African American literature, of middle-class status, sexual prudery, and racial inauthenticity. Others, such as Barbara Neely in her detective novel *Blanche Among the Talented Tenth* (1994), satirize the foibles and hypocrisies of the black elite. Tananarive Due's *The Between* (1995) explores black bourgeois malaise through the speculative-fiction device of otherworldly intrusions into mundane reality. An equally diverse set of intentions and representations is evident at the other end of the class spectrum, where we find a novel such as Sister Souljah's *The Coldest Winter Ever* (1999), a cautionary tale about ghetto-fab ethics and aesthetics, along with uplifting narratives of ascent out of poverty like Sapphire's *PUSH* (1996).

Even as African American women novelists are branching out in a multitude of new directions, certain continuities persist. Precious, the protagonist of Sapphire's novel, views education in print literacy as the best means of acquiring the economic independence necessary to raise her child. Affirming the urgent practical uses of reading and writing, *PUSH* recalls Harriet Wilson's *Our Nig*, which similarly presents writing as a response to financial exigency, a last-ditch attempt to save a child's life. Sapphire's novel closes with a group of destitute women of color forging subjectivity and community out of their jointly authored "Life Stories." The life-saving value of print literacy is also emphasized by the subtitle of Lauren Olamina's journal – "The Books of the Living" – in Octavia Butler's *Parable of the Sower*. Both Sapphire and Butler loop back to the origins of the African American literary tradition, restaging the classic slave-narrative scenario of literacy obtained by stealth. Other recent novels by black women, such as Gayl Jones's *Mosquito* (2000) and Pearl Cleage's *Babylon Sisters* (2005), are also renewing the mid-nineteenth-century genre of the slave narrative to serve distinctly contemporary uses. The enslaved in these novels by Butler, Cleage, Jones, and Sapphire include welfare mothers, illegal immigrants, domestic laborers, and sweat-shop workers – the multiracial female underclass spawned by global capitalism. Whether they are sex-trade workers or debt slaves to multinational corporations, whether they are organizing domestic workers or underground railroads for Mexican immigrants, the women in these novels are shown to be passionately driven by the pursuit of print literacy. The literacy class in *PUSH*, the fugitives who listen to Lauren reading aloud from her "Books of the Living" in *Parable of the Sower*, the Babylon Sisters Book Club in Cleage's novel, and the Daughters of Nzinga in Jones's *Mosquito* offer striking examples of multiracial and largely female communities bound together by the act of reading. Updating the slave-narrative quest to suit changing political and cultural needs, these fictive reading communities project a vital social role for the novel in the twenty-first century.

NOTES

1. Octavia Butler, *Parable of the Sower* (New York: Warner Books, 1993), p. 56.
2. Toni Morrison, "Rootedness: The Ancestor as Foundation," *Black Women Writers (1850–1980): A Critical Evaluation*, ed. Mari Evans (New York: Anchor Books, 1984), p. 341.
3. Hannah Crafts, *The Bondwoman's Narrative* (New York: Warner Books, 2002), p. 173.
4. Harriet E. Wilson, *Our Nig; or, Sketches from the Life of a Free Black* (1859; New York: Vintage, 1983), p. 87.
5. Claudia Tate, *Domestic Allegories of Political Desire* (New York: Oxford University Press, 1992).

6. Frances E. W. Harper, *Iola Leroy* (1892; Boston: Beacon, 1987), p. 282; Pauline E. Hopkins, *Contending Forces* (1900; New York: Oxford University Press, 1988), p. 13.

7. Nella Larsen, *Quicksand and Passing* (New Brunswick, NJ: Rutgers University Press, 1986), p. 87.

8. This is the title of Pauline Hopkins's novel, *Of One Blood*, originally published in serial form in *The Colored American Magazine* between March 1901 and November 1903.

9. The ascent narrative in African American literature focuses on a quest for upward mobility. Usually set in the urban North, these narratives feature individualist protagonists whose attainment of bourgeois status comes at the cost of alienation from black folk culture and community. See Robert Stepto's definition of the ascent narrative in *From Behind the Veil: A Study of Afro-American Narrative* (Urbana and Chicago: University of Illinois Press, 1979), p. 167.

10. The quoted phrase is part of the title of the first chapter of *Iola Leroy* (p. 7).

11. Zora Neale Hurston, "How It Feels to Be Colored Me" (1928), rpt. in *I Love Myself When I Am Laughing ...: A Zora Neale Hurston Reader*, ed. Alice Walker (New York: Feminist Press, 1979), p. 153.

12. Ann Petry, *The Street* (1946; Boston: Beacon, 1974), p. 323.

13. Gwendolyn Brooks, *Maud Martha* (New York: Harper, 1953), p. 2.

14. Toni Morrison, *The Bluest Eye* (New York: Simon & Schuster, 1970), p. 41.

15. For example, see *Conjuring: Black Women, Fiction, and Literary Tradition*, ed. Marjorie Pryse and Hortense J. Spillers (Bloomington: Indiana University Press, 1985); and Susan Willis, *Specifying: Black Women Writing the American Experience* (Madison: University of Wisconsin Press, 1987).

16. Sherley Anne Williams, *Dessa Rose* (New York: Berkley Books, 1986), p. ix.

17. Walter Mosley, "Black to the Future," *New York Times Magazine*, November 1, 1998, p. 34.

9

KEITH D. LEONARD

African American women poets and the power of the word

One way to understand African American women's poetry – its historical evolution, its aesthetic beauty, its political power – is to start with the story of creation. According to biblical tradition, Adam was granted the power to name and this power was one measure of his authority over Eve, his wife, and Eve's predecessor, Adam's lesser-known wife Lilith. By naming everything in the world, Adam was defining what could be known and therefore controlling the nature of reality. That was his power. Legend also has it that Lilith, created from the clay like Adam rather than from his rib as Eve had been, would not relinquish the power of the word and subordinate herself to Adam simply because he was male. For her resistance, she was banished from Eden and cursed to devour her children. This story has been cited by well-known feminist critics Sandra Gilbert and Susan Gubar as an analogy for the difficulties women writers in Britain faced in seeking to speak for themselves in the face of a patriarchal society that privileged the status and culture of men.[1] Not only was literary genius and its power to name defined in terms of male sexual potency, Gilbert and Gubar argue, but such definitions, when added to the conventions of aesthetic beauty that rendered women as objects, led women writers to doubt the legitimacy of their own imaginations. Placed in the context of the United States, this story illuminates how, with the effects of racism added to patriarchy, this dynamic of expression and exclusion, misnaming, self-doubt, and banishment becomes an even more devastating challenge to self-knowledge and creativity. In the face of a patriarchal American society rooted in a system of slavery and then segregation that named the African as a non-person and that devised laws and practices to keep those Africans in subordinate positions, African American women could have been like Lilith, banished by the society into a self-devouring silence.

But from slave poets Lucy Terry and Phillis Wheatley to contemporary spoken-word artists like Sapphire and Jill Scott, African American women have been unified by their faith in the power of poetic language to assert their personal truths in defiance of the exclusionary privileging of male thought and expression by claiming the power to name themselves against the silencing dynamics of a male-dominated society. Empowered by poetry's association with the emotions and intuition that patriarchal societies often devalue, African American women poets "adopted, adapted and transformed" the definitions of motherhood, sexual identity, love, beauty, and spirituality in order to liberate themselves.[2] So even though poets writing during slavery, like Wheatley or Frances Ellen Watkins Harper, imitated the poetic forms and themes of the patriarchal British tradition that threatened to silence them, they used the ideals of that tradition – especially its sentimentality and its Puritan morality – to claim their denied humanity and to build coalitions with politically sympathetic whites, assimilating the racist culture of the slaveholding society in order, paradoxically, to defy it. Early twentieth-century African American women poets, likewise assimilating mainstream culture to defy it, were also very mindful of the compromises of this approach, critiquing their own traditionalism by illuminating how conformity to its conventions came at great cost to identity, desire, and love. By the middle of the twentieth century, therefore, the next generation of poets had diversified their artistic repertoire by using black folk cultural forms – like jazz or the sermon – and black folk language in order to articulate alternative notions of artistic genius, aesthetic beauty, motherhood, sexual identity, and spirituality. In fact, by the Black Arts movement during the era of civil rights, African American women poets, like their male counterparts, had rejected traditional forms and assimilationist politics altogether, turning instead exclusively to the forms of black culture in order to push their ideas of artistry, sexual identity, and spirituality even further beyond the dictates of white society. And subsequent poets have been liberated by that radicalism to use African American ethnic culture to articulate fuller and more egalitarian notions of human selfhood than either assimilation or cultural nationalism could allow. By telling the stories of their hearts and minds in verse, in other words, African American women poets produced a body of poetry beautiful and empowering in its intricate rewriting of cultural conventions, a liberating self-definition central to American literature.

In essence, as African American poet, essayist, and activist Audre Lorde put it, "poetry is not a luxury" for African American women because this act of speaking, of naming one's own reality, has been an act of self-assertion as important as protests, lawsuits, and marches for redefining how African American women live in American society.[3] Readers of this poetry must therefore understand how, by engaging with the stereotypes and ideologies – the naming practices – of their time, African American women poets ultimately asserted that, as Hortense Spillers aptly put it, "In order for me to speak a truer word concerning myself, I must strip down through layers of attenuated meanings ... and there await whatever marvels of my own inventiveness."[4] Like Spillers, readers of this verse must therefore comprehend the history of the oppressive "meanings" by which society negatively defined – or "named" – African American women in order to recognize not only how inventive these poets were in representing their intellectual and emotional lives in response, but also how those representations materially defied the simplistic political characterizations that pervaded the dominant culture. As Spillers argues, the documents and imagery of the dominant culture have consistently implied or asserted that the racist allegations about the African's lesser intelligence, about deviant sexuality, and about the lack of a soul were particularly true of African women and that, even more than black men, African American women were inferior to and absolutely different from whites, the negative shadow self by which the mainstream society could positively define itself. Such negative labels and stereotypes include, among many others, the sexual vixen, the welfare mother, the self-sacrificing matriarch who gives her all for others, the mammy figure who "mothers" her white master or mistress, and even seemingly empowering images like Cleopatra Jones or the female gangsta rapper, images which actually parallel violent male fantasies rather than creating new female ones. In each case, the white mistress or heroine had her virtues allegedly enhanced by her contrast with these stereotypical black women characters. Such stereotypes pervade the conventions of poetry in which European cultural heritage and beauty standards are also privileged. By working within and against these images and stereotypes, African American women enacted the inventive self-creation that rejected silence and gave voice to the full complexity of black female selfhood.

What matters about African American women poets, then, is how they used poetry to represent the complex emotional and intellectual lives of black women, rewriting these exclusionary norms from the inside out. Reading this poetry as protest, as is sometimes done, misses some of this complexity. Without protest, Lucy Terry, the first African American woman poet, announced with her poem "Bars Fight" (1746) the presence of an articulate black woman among some of the earliest British colonists, a presence erased in most histories. Well known for her public-speaking ability, Terry orally passed down this poem that chronicles a battle between British settlers and Native Americans, recording herself along with the massacre of the colonists. Wheatley's 1773 volume *Poems on Various Subjects Religious and Moral* is important for more than being the first volume of poetry published by a person of African descent in the New World. In addition to announcing her presence, Wheatley used her mastery of neoclassical poetics and of the dominant culture's expectations for religious women to prove her capacity for imagination and, by extension, any African's ability for intellect and culture, whether slave or free. Similarly, Harper's many volumes of poetry gain much of their force from her mastery of traditional ballad stanzas, her persona as a traditional female moral authority, and her abolitionist activism, all of which depend on her assimilation of conventional notions of femininity.

In other words, Wheatley's and Harper's empowering use of poetic conventionality and religious conservatism prefigures the liberating practices of poetic self-naming used by black women poets well into the twentieth century. Guided by her owners, John and Susanna Wheatley, Wheatley modeled her poetry on that of Alexander Pope, a British poet famous for writing poems steeped in the Greek and Roman classics, and on that of British poet John Milton whose *Paradise Lost* famously transformed the biblical story of the fall from paradise into an epic poem. Given her preference for European poets over African culture, Wheatley has been accurately criticized for seldom positively affirming her African heritage. However, even her most controversial poem, "On Being Brought from Africa to America," enacts Wheatley's paradoxical racial affirmation by rewriting racist Christianity from the inside. After declaring her gratitude for being brought from the "dark abodes" of her "pagan" Africa to the light of Christianity, Wheatley declares to her white readers that she is not the only African capable of such transformation: "Remember, *Christians*, Negroes black as Cain / May be refin'd and join th'angelic train." According to Wheatley, who is sometimes credited for sarcasm in this poem, the African's capacity for religious conversion is obvious and constitutes his or her humanity. Though this assertion accepts the racist notion that Africans needed to be Christianized in order to be human, Wheatley complicates it in other poems by uniting her spirituality and her African past by calling herself an "Ethiop," a term that evokes a biblical prophecy about Ethiopians raising their hands to God.[5] Not the sellout that some of her earliest critics called her, Wheatley suggested that her creativity and her identity fulfilled biblical prophecies about her African heritage. Her imitative inventiveness therefore rewrites some "attenuated meanings" of racism.

Seventy years later, Harper similarly assimilated the culture of her day in order to use her spirituality to confront slavery and racism. The first famous African American female protest poet, Harper derived her fame in part from the fact that she had mastered the ballad style of British and Anglo-American folk poets in order to portray herself as a poet of the people. She enhanced this status by manipulating the era's "separate spheres" ideology of gender relations in which the public world of men was thought to be entirely separate from the domestic world of women and in which women were responsible for the morality of the home, a morality that could be corrupted by participation in public life. Embracing this stereotypical persona, Harper portrayed herself as a woman of conventional moral values whose rectitude proved that Africans had the same private morals as whites even as it allowed Harper to prod the complacent consciences of her largely white female audiences in the forbidden public realm. With such a claim of public voice through private moral authority, Harper read her poems aloud at predominantly white abolitionist rallies, turning the British ballad – usually based in a story of homespun truths – into an act of political critique. Unlike Wheatley, whose use of sentimentalism simply proved common human emotions, Harper evoked those common emotions in order to call for action in defense of those who could not defend themselves.

Not alone in this practice, Harper defined her poetic persona using moral rationales similar to those used by abolitionist leaders and suffrage activists like Mary Church Terrell and Ida B. Wells, and by the many African American women's clubs of this era – groups of middle-class black women who sought to improve the lives of black people through social services.[6] Harper's anti-racist artistic version of these otherwise conservative ideals is exemplified by the first stanza in one of her most famous poems, "The Slave Mother": "Heard you that shriek? It rose / So wildly on the air, / It seemed as if a burden'd heart / Was breaking in despair." Calling on her abolitionist audience to "hear" the suffering of slave women, Harper posits the emotional ties of motherhood as a defining source of human unity, asserting that, though the slaveholding society denied that Africans had maternal instincts, slave women "named" themselves as mothers by the anguish they articulated in their shrieks when they were separated from their children by greedy slaveholders who sold them. Breaking down the alleged boundary between public and private, Harper affirmed how enslaved African women experienced the same conventional familial ties and motherly yearnings as free white women and that those ties form the foundation of abolitionism. And after slavery was over, Harper maintained a similar persona in her poems on temperance which sought to eliminate alcohol from the life of the newly freed African citizens. She also became the first African American poet to use folk language in her poems, creating a sage named Aunt Chloe, a wise folk hero who offered homespun truths about how to use the vote and which political party to support. As such, Harper's poetic mastery transformed traditional femininity and morality into characteristics of an early militant feminism in which private morals validated what were for the time radical public definitions of freedom and equality.

From the turn of the century up to the 1920s, however, African American women poets of the next two generations were dubious about whether or not this traditional femininity that Harper embraced could validate their senses of self, even though it could support militant feminist defenses of slave mothers.

These poets explicitly confronted the internal conflicts created by the assimilation that was so empowering for Wheatley, Harper, and many African American club women by considering how beauty and romantic love as they were portrayed in traditional poetics were limiting and needed to be rewritten in light of race politics and black female identity. These poems used irony and African American folk culture to reveal how imaginative independence was sometimes sacrificed for the artistic and moral authority available through assimilation and that whatever public freedom could come from such activism would be undermined by how these conventions limited the ways in which women could understand themselves. Many of these women have been associated by scholars with the Harlem Renaissance, that flowering of African American literary culture in and around Harlem in the 1920s, even though many of them started publishing well before then and even though Harlem literati did not always take these women seriously. The association is apt, nonetheless, because these women participated actively in the movement's debates about how to represent the new ethnic community that they believed, along with the men, was being born in Harlem in the 1920s, the "New Negro" as they called it. Like Harlem Renaissance men, these women artists disagreed over whether they should prove that they were cultured in traditional bourgeois terms by writing in Anglo-American artistic styles or demonstrate the distinctiveness of African American culture by transforming jazz and the blues and folk language into poetry. Also, like the men, they explored the role of individuality for defining ethnic identity and political agency, though their emphasis on gender identity complicated their relationship to the movement. While supporting husbands, raising children, and pursuing same-sex love affairs, these poets rejected the notion that they could only be voices of righteousness. They wanted to be themselves.

Probably the most famous poet of this era, Georgia Douglas Johnson exemplifies this shift from the assimilation of conventional religious beliefs, femininity and moral leadership toward self-affirmation through the individuality that could be expressed in lyric poetry. A musician, playwright, novelist, teacher, and mother, Johnson wrote love lyrics whose form closely resembled that of Harper's poetry while being purposefully removed from Harper's public stance and her engagement with race politics. Coming of age in the decades before the Harlem Renaissance, and living primarily in Washington, DC, rather than in New York City, Johnson at first had priorities quite different from that collection of writers. As she put it in a 1941 letter to fellow Harlem Renaissance poet Arna Bontemps, "Whenever I can, I forget my special call to sorrow and live as happily as I may. Perhaps that is why I seldom elect to write racially. It seems to me an art to forget those things that make the heart heavy. If one can soar, he should soar, leaving his chains behind."[7] Instead of writing racially in her first volume, *The Heart of a Woman* (1918), then, Johnson focused on how lost love, yearning for connection, and nostalgia revealed the dynamic emotional lives of women, especially older women left lonely by their conformity to conventional femininity or women whose same-sex desire conflicted with the expectations associated with being a bourgeois "lady." Still, Johnson conducted literary salons from her DC home for Harlem writers, hosting almost all of the famous figures of the movement. Along with Jessie Fauset, who wrote poetry and edited *The Crisis*, the NAACP's magazine which published Harlem Renaissance poetry, and Anne Spencer, who likewise brought the Harlem Renaissance out of Harlem to salons in Lynchburg, Virginia, Johnson insinuated herself into a movement that sometimes neglected her. Johnson's work was not welcome among the new publishers in New York City who helped foment the Harlem Renaissance because it did not conform to their ideas of what they called "Negro material." She had to publish her first two volumes of poetry on her own.

Rather than primarily trying to claim moral leadership, then, Johnson distinguished herself as a master of one of the chief strategies of this era's women poets: the dramatization of internal conflict. The inner conflicts that Johnson portrays are as much artistic as they are social, more gendered than racial, as they link a woman's love life to her capacity to imagine, especially once Johnson bowed to public pressure to write about race. After the publication of *The Heart of a Woman*, Johnson was criticized by Alain Locke and W. E. B. Du Bois, two primary commentators of the Harlem Renaissance, for not engaging with issues of race. Acknowledging as she put it to Bontemps that "lest we forget, we must now and then come down to earth, accept the yoke and help draw the load," Johnson published *Bronze* in 1922, a volume dedicated almost exclusively to poems of race protest.[8] No wonder Johnson concluded her most famous poem, "The Heart of a Woman," with the following lines: "The heart of a woman falls back with the night, / And enters some alien cage in its plight, / And tries to forget it has dreamed of the stars, / While it breaks, breaks, breaks on the sheltering bars."[9] Even before confronting Locke's and Du Bois's reviews, in other words, Johnson revealed how the imaginative woman faced serious limitations for self-expression, whether one reads the "sheltering bars" in the poem as the metaphorical safety of the home against the actual physical dangers of night, the traditional roles of wife, mother and host that Johnson played for her politically successful husband, or the "safe" subjects of race protest. As Nathan Huggins observed, such subjects led Harlem Renaissance writers to spend much of their energy – perhaps too much – trying to prove themselves within European-based conventions of bourgeois respectability, a "race doubt" about the validity of their own culture that, for Johnson, was also clearly a "gender doubt."[10] Effectively speaking for the educated women of an enlarging black middle class, Johnson associated the yearning for lost love with the yearning for independent selfhood by pointing out how the "sheltering bars" of conventionality were falsely protective and how the woman's heart breaks itself trying to "soar" away from a shelter it nonetheless accepts. Ambivalently appreciating the limiting safety of her respectable existence, the woman speaker mourns her lost adventures.

Some of Johnson's contemporaries sought to envision alternatives to this divided self and its sheltering bars of bourgeois and artistic conformity, but many of them had even more difficulty being heard than Johnson did. The expectation to protest racism has led scholars, even ones who celebrate these women, to neglect the full range of their artistic self-definition just as their contemporaries did. In fact, without the fairly recent publication of *Shadowed Dreams: Women's Poetry of the Harlem Renaissance*, edited by Maureen Honey, many of the era's most intriguing poets – like Mae V. Cowdry, Angelina Weld Grimké and Helene Johnson – would have been lost. And Honey clearly felt obliged to spend much of her introduction to the volume trying to demonstrate that these women's "non-racial" poetry was in fact race protest. Sometimes this approach leads to insights – about the use of color imagery, for example – but sometimes it downplays issues that were of greater concern to the poets. It would be better to recognize how, like Johnson, few of the women of this era got support from mainstream publishers and, like Johnson, that lack of support was likely motivated by the fact that they found issues of gender and sexual identity to be more compelling than race politics. In fact, Alice Dunbar-Nelson, a writer who is too often remembered only for being the wife of African American poet Paul Laurence Dunbar, wrote several of her poems about this kind of exclusion. In "I Sit and Sew," for example, the poem's speaker bemoans the fact that women could not join the Union Army in the Civil War along with African American men though their desire for freedom was just as strong. The poem also contains Dunbar-Nelson's complaint that a woman's artistry – sewing – and therefore her person are perceived as less important in this patriarchal society than men's wars and their claims of being heroes.

Even though publishing outlets were unsympathetic to them and though audiences have sometimes resisted or ignored their gender politics, then, these poets enacted remarkably intricate practices of self-reflection and self-definition that extended Wheatley's, Harper's, and Johnson's conventional self-naming into new artistic avenues. Often, the speakers of their poems, like the poet herself, embraced the celebration of nature characteristic of famous male Romantic poets like John Keats and used that celebration to validate their own stereotypically female qualities. For example, in addition to writing poems which hint at lesbian love and that rewrite heterosexual love conventions, Cowdry affirms herself through a connection to nature: "I want to wake and find / That I have slept the day away. / Only the nights are kind now … / With the stars … moon … winds and me … ." The yearning in this poem for refuge in nature from the "day" – which could signify scrutiny, public life, work life – is a signature romantic gesture. Rather than protesting racism, Cowdry is using these conventions to associate her identity with positive symbolic meanings of the wind, moon, and stars. Reading the poem "racially" is possible, with the "light" of day being "white," but it is more productive to see a subtly affirming version of the traditional association of women with mother earth. While such poems reinforce stereotypical associations of women with nature, they grant mother earth a voice and a mind distinct from the usual objectification in the patriarchal tradition.

Thus, Honey is right to suggest that the poetry of this era was "animated, not entirely by an imitative impulse, but rather by a defiant sensibility reflective of the rebellious women who wrote it."[11] For example, instead of accepting the male gaze of love poetry in which the male writer imposes his perspective on the objectified love interest, these poets either applied that perspective to female lovers or demonstrated how the female being written about could resist its objectification. For example, according to scholar Gloria Hull, Angelina Weld Grimké led a buried life despite the fact that her father was the acknowledged black nephew of famous white abolitionists, the Grimké sisters, a buried life that derived in part from her lesbian desire. In poems like "A Mona Lisa," Grimké transformed this desire into a critique of how love poetry limited the representation of female subjectivity. The poem's first section expresses the speaker's desire to enter "the leaf-brown pools / That are your lashes" and "I should like to sink down / And down / And down…" Instead of the traditional male poet expressing admiration for female beauty, this poem displays a female speaker – who may be the Mona Lisa of the title – expressing her desire for similar inspiration from a woman as an art object. But the speaker is torn, questioning her own practice by speculating on the consequences of such objectification: "Would my white bones / Be the only white bones / Wavering back and forth, back and forth / In their depths?" The eyes of the objectified love interest can in fact destroy those who gaze upon it because they are swallowed up by the depths that they have failed to recognize, an internal life that refutes false notions of static, passive female beauty. Those who fail to see the depth become bones, the relic of a limiting past. The poem is thus a powerful plea for women to be exhumed from the deadening expectations of passive beauty that lock them within the sheltering bars of love poetry.

In fact, this turn inward was one of the most important empowering gestures and one of the most significant artistic innovations of mid-twentieth-century African American women's poetry. Though the women poets of the Harlem Renaissance did not always benefit as much from the Harlem Renaissance as their male counterparts, the most important poets of the next generation – Margaret Danner, Gwendolyn Brooks and Margaret Walker (Alexander) – wrote similarly introspective verse, both for the individual and for the community, verse that garnered substantial mainstream support and acclaim. This generation of women poets is usually understood as enacting what scholars have come to call "Afro-modernism" or "African American modernism," an aesthetic vision arguably initiated by Harlem Renaissance women poets and culminated in this generation. These three poets used rigorous and intricate poetic form derived from both European literary and African American folk traditions and complex poetic personae to explore the rich internal lives of African American characters as their consciousnesses come in conflict with and are shaped by external circumstances. Unlike most of their predecessors, for whom the "I" in a poem was likely to be the poet herself, in other words, Brooks, Walker, and sometimes Danner inhabited many different characters, ranging from Brooks's south Chicago neighbors to the prophetic voice of some of Walker's poetry. Like such Anglo-American modernist poets as T. S. Eliot and Ezra Pound, then, Brooks, Walker, and Danner seek to revise the "old certainties" of the Western tradition, including Christianity, ideals of human progress, and individualism by showing how African Americans, individually and collectively, rewrote these ideals on their own terms. As Mark Sanders would put it, such Afro-modernism consisted of the representation of "historicity, of change, development ... and ... both social and psychic complexity."[12] Sometimes discussed as cultural masking, following the work of Houston Baker, this approach is better understood in Sanders's terms, in which Afro-modernist poetry could show that black people have full, rich, even ambivalent personalities that defy racist notions that black culture and personhood are the static opposite of the always-progressing western culture. By showing the parallel progress of African American culture, these women poets, like many women early in the civil rights movement, sought to justify social integration by highlighting the basis of a shared consciousness.

For Danner and Walker, this modernism consisted of an oracular poetic voice. Known almost as much for her Detroit Writers group called "Boone House" and her editorial work with Dudley Randall as for her verse, Danner distinguished herself by carefully crafted lyrics whose speakers tended to articulate themes pertaining to Baha'í religious faith – which unified all the world's religions under one god, regardless of race or nationality or religious tradition – and to African heritage by acting as a wise elder to Danner's own grandson. She was among the first African American poets, male or female, to write knowledgeably about African heritage in poetry. In "Inheritance for Muffin," for example, Danner declares that she cannot leave Muffin monetary gold but she can leave him "this exquisitely carved Benin Bronze," "this Senufo Firespitter mask," and "these modern bones so superbly carved" that they remind misguided viewers of "Rome and other classic places" though they were made on Beale Street. The first African American winner of the Yale University Younger Writers prize, Walker created an introspective communal voice in her best-known poem "For My People" from her 1942 same-titled volume, an oracular black voice who spoke more literally for the people than even Harper did. It is a voice modeled on the black folk sermon, probably based in part on the voice of Walker's father, a well-educated minister. The poem traces black history from slavery to Walker's present and concludes

> Let a beauty full of healing and a strength of final clenching be pulsing in our spirits and our blood. Let the martial songs be written, let the dirges disappear. Let a race of men now rise and take control.

Such proclamations, while written in the male-centered language of our culture, validate African American culture on its own terms rather than exploring its ambivalent relationship with other cultures. With each stanza an almost self-contained prose poem, "For My People" is written in a form all its own, one presented as if it had grown up organically from the culture and heritage that it discusses. As with Danner's poems about Africa, Walker's poems produced an empowering communal self affirmation, a truly "New Negro" no longer ambivalent about the value of black culture for art or identity.

More like the European modernists than either Walker or Danner were, Brooks provided the richest version of this modernism by presenting in her poetry various characters going through the process of making order out of the chaos of experience and potentially resolving inner conflicts into a momentary equilibrium of an affirmed identity. In this way, Brooks's portraits of her neighborhood in Chicago rejected the notion that blackness was static by showing how a communal ethnic identity was always in the process of growth. In "Negro Hero," for example, Brooks creates a persona modeled on a real-life African American soldier named Dorie Miller who, in the segregated army, had been forbidden to participate in combat in World War II until the Japanese bombed Pearl Harbor. Written from his first-person perspective in a free-verse form that rejects traditional patterns of meter and rhyme, the poem enacts the individualized way in which he comes to believe in himself enough to reject the traditions of segregation that he once accepted in order to defend the nation that excluded him. And in "Of DeWitt Williams on his way to Lincoln Cemetery," Brooks combines the four-line structure of the traditional English ballad with the ethos of the blues and the transcendent lyrics of the spirituals in order to show how, with these overlapping song forms, the community transforms its funeral rites for "a plain black boy" into a heroic folk tale celebrating his (and its) attempt to wring what joy is available out of a deprived existence. And her Pulitzer-Prize-winning volume *Annie Allen*, which made Brooks the first African American winner of this prize, traces the birth, adolescence, adulthood, and motherhood of the title character as she grows into greater self-awareness and political consciousness. In all of these works, Brooks implies that, as one scholar put it, "the acceptance of themselves by blacks must finally be their salvation, both politically and personally," and uses highly formalized poetic styles to enact the ambivalent process by which such self-acceptance leads to social integration.

In fact, Brooks's longstanding themes of African American self-acceptance make her doubly important to this tradition because, in addition to exemplifying the modernist virtuosity that won her the Pulitzer Prize, Brooks also had the political savvy and artistic foresight to recognize that this need for self-acceptance might be better served by eschewing integration for cultural separatism. She was at the Fisk University Writers Conference of 1967 when the new generation of radical activist writers, proponents of the Black Power movement, declared that her brand of modernist cultural introspection and formal innovation did not go far enough to serve the interests of the black community. The emerging Black Arts movement, as it came to be called, committed themselves instead to producing poetry exclusively for black audiences and for the sake of political revolution by representing unambiguous affirmative values and clear political perspectives. For example, Nikki Giovanni, Sonia Sanchez, and Jayne Cortez recorded themselves reading poetry with musical accompaniment in order to spread the new ideals of black cultural nationalism, the idea that African Americans need to define themselves in exclusively black terms of black folk life and African heritage. Rather than blues musicians, who were seen as too passive in their existential confrontation with pain, they paired themselves with jazz musicians who were lionized for their revolutionary uses of improvisation to break the rigid and oppressive structures of Western music. Moreover, West African cultures were celebrated for being the primary source of African American culture and the model of cosmologies that privilege community over bourgeois individualism, the artist as political leader over the artist as a removed aesthete.

This shift in the artist's role led to some enforced homogeneity among black writers in the interest of sometimes limiting political ideals, and it too often privileged the needs and voices of black men. This shift, nonetheless, led to some of the most substantial formal innovations in the practice of self-naming among African American women poets. At first, the Black Arts movement reinforced the binary logic created by white supremacy that declared black people and white people to be absolutely different from one another and inherently opposed. Believing that European culture was exclusively a "white" culture that was inherently oppressive to black people, especially black men, these writers built separate black literary institutions to protect black writers from what they considered to be oppressive literary standards in which the so-called universals of literature were really affirmations of European heritage and white western bourgeois perspectives. These institutions included writing workshops like the ones Brooks led for Chicago area writers and large-scale organizations like the Combahee River Collective, a black women's feminist organization that, among other things, rejected the tendency of the mainstream feminist movement to neglect the issues of racism and poverty. Within this separatist mindset, African American women made themselves more knowledgeable about systems of political power rather than relying on changing individual hearts and minds. Many also did thorough historical research and rooted their verse in a comprehensive knowledge of current international political events, especially from a pan-African perspective, of the need for Africans of all nations to be united with each other and with African Americans. Sometimes called identity politics, this approach to culture was based on the idea that communal cultural identities were the fundamental sources of meaning in the world and that, therefore, social identities – not philosophical conceptions of a deep self – should be paramount in self-definition. Artistically, this led to what came to be called the Black Aesthetic. Characteristic of this remarkably innovative artistry were: a revision or rejection of traditional English syntax and punctuation; a broader rejection of conventional poetic topics of love, etc., than the Harlem Renaissance offered; the replication of musical forms such as jazz in verse; the privileging of performance over publication, immediacy over canonization; the adaptations of African and African American folk tales and religious traditions to verse; and an expansion of the black oracular voice.

These heavy-handed, sometimes overly masculine, doctrines paradoxically liberated African American women's creativity. Though the movement has rightly been critiqued for its sexist emphasis on validating African American men and for its homophobia, it did provide the foundation for two major components of contemporary African American women's poetry: the use of the oral tradition, including black music and the black sermon, to construe the poet as a griot – an African communal storyteller – or a political exhorter; and the turn to African cultural resources to articulate a distinctive and liberating African American spirituality. Adopting an oracular voice at once more personal and grander than Margaret Walker, Giovanni enjoins her readers in poems like the 1968 "Of Liberation" to remake their consciousnesses for the sake of political activism first by pointing out that "'the last bastion of white supremacy / is in the Black man's mind'" and concluding that "Everything comes in steps: / Negative step one: get the white out of your hair / Negative step two: get the white out of your mind." Advocating communal unity for the sake of political power, Giovanni calls for this unity by writing poems celebrating black heroes ranging from Malcolm X to James Brown, by writing topical poems that advocate particular political positions on current events presumably best suited for black people, and by identifying the cultural sensibility by which black people can live and black poets can continue to write. As she famously put it in "For Saundra," "maybe i shouldn't write / at all / but clean my gun / and check my kerosene supply // perhaps these are not poetic / times / at all." An affirmation of the integrity of the poet who writes for the sake of changing material circumstances rather than for the sake of a "beautiful green tree poem," Giovanni's poem typifies how women of this movement characterized a definite interrelation between poetry and activism. Such an attitude toward poetry motivated Maya Angelou to produce some of the most accessible, most directly affirming, and most popular poetry in the United States, including eventually a poem for the inauguration of President Bill Clinton. In fact, her direct simplicity and faith in black women's strength continues to speak to audiences of all races, ethnicities, and nationalities. And at its root is this shift from introspective intricacies of Afro-modernism to the direct affirmations of the Black Aesthetic.

This simple but complex oracular voice became as much a spiritual as a political voice, articulating a historical vision that was as much myth as history. For example, Sonia Sanchez wrote "A Blues Book for Blue Black Magical Woman" in which she used sound effects to create an incantatory tone analogous to West African ululating for grief and joy, an incantation that linked African American women to a mythic ancestor:

> as I ride my past on horseback
> tasting the thirst of yesterday tribes,
> hearing the ancient / black / woman
> me, singing   hay-hay-hay-hay-ya-ya-ya
>   hay-hay-hay-hay-ya-ya-ya

Like most poets of this generation, Sanchez sees these revisions of poetry as part of a reclaiming and a rewriting of the past that had to be central to present self-affirmation, especially if that rewriting allows African American women to reclaim an ancestor-goddess as the source of voice, of name and of spirit. Cheryl Clarke called this the death of the lyric for black women because these poets were no longer interested in the kind of individuality and internal conflict that interested Johnson and Brooks, and that was predicated on the notion of an internally coherent individual self that these poets believed to be derived from oppressive capitalist individualism. For Sanchez, an individual black self had its existence only in relationship to and as an extension of communal attitudes and heritage. African American women, for example, should understand the African woman's keening in grief and joy because their social identities were derived from the same historical and cultural sources, a myth of historical unity that presumed an essence of blackness throughout history.

Though this notion of a black essence has been rejected by contemporary theory, the concept has nonetheless led to the complex notions of black spirituality that came to be alternative to that essentialism, and which serve as the foundation for sophisticated notions of black identity as cultural multiplicity. The women who transformed that simplistic essence into a more complex mythic self did so by articulating alternative notions of spirituality that linked sexuality and the body to the divine. Audre Lorde's famous conception of the erotic is a case in point. She imagines that a "disciplined attention" to feelings and intuition – aspects of the woman's self devalued in patriarchal culture in favor of intellect and reason – would allow women to understand themselves and then act in the world. According to Lorde, for African American women, "the erotic is a resource within each of us that lies in a deeply female and spiritual plane, firmly rooted in the power of our unexpressed or unrecognized feelings," a capacity for insight and for joy that "forms a bridge … which can be the basis for understanding much of what is not shared [between people] and lessens the threat of their difference."[13] Though sometimes criticized as essentialist, this commitment to intuition, to deep and unexpressed feelings, and to a notion of spirituality rooted in those feelings led Lorde, in her volume *Black Unicorn* (1978), to create a complex historical vision rooted in the androgynous gods of the Yoruba tradition. She used that history to represent how identity is always in process, an idea that defies its roots in a black essence. Not a utopian myth of transformation or transcendence, though, Lorde's myth of artistic, cultural, historical, and spiritual origins uses non-standard grammar and syntax to unite the so-called "masculine" characteristics of rationality and "feminine" characteristics of intuition, heterosexual motherhood and lesbian community, into one complex, self-contradictory consciousness, what Lorde calls "the house of difference." Her work urged her readers to inhabit and make real an imagined cultural space in which individuals accept all of the different aspects of themselves as always coexisting in productive conflict, a practice that will allow them to accept themselves and others. Following similar lines of thought, Lucille Clifton, Alice Walker, and Ntozake Shange similarly demonstrate how, in the face of the historical predatory behavior of men, mothers and daughters develop complex cultural wisdoms that unite African, European, eastern, and middle eastern cultural resources into female identities based in contradiction and multiplicity. And for each of these women poets, this multifaceted black female self depends on uniting spirit to body, sexuality to the divine, a fundamental coherence that emerges in the imagination and in art from the tensions within the self.

The result of these innovations of thought was a more complex existence, one capable of validating its own multiplicity as affirmation rather than internal conflict, historical complexity rather than black essence. Rejecting the binary logics of white supremacy and the most simplistic versions of identity politics, contemporary African American women's poetry elaborates on the value of multiplicity for ethnic identity. Poets like Clifton published volumes of verse in which they explore, for example, how a hysterectomy affects notions of sexuality, womanhood, and motherhood. The poem implies that womanhood has multiple meanings that do not entirely depend upon the capacity to reproduce or the genteel sexual norms that govern procreation, moving beyond biological conceptions of motherhood to the multiple emotional connections implicit in Clifton's ideals of a pan African spirituality. Moreover, the Black Arts movement rejection of "white" cultural forms and ideals paradoxically made those forms and ideals more available to African American women poets, as women poets since the 1970s have self-consciously divorced those forms from an exclusive European tradition in part by taking it for granted, as Pulitzer Prize winner Rita Dove does, that European culture belongs as much to her as to white Americans. Also, African American women have been fuller participants in such important African American literary institutions as the Darkroom Collective, including Natasha Tretheway, Sharan Strange, and Vera Beatty, and the Cave Canem retreat, founded by Toi Derricote and Cornelius Eady. This collection of writers have distinctive styles, distinctive manifestos for their art, and thus cannot be too simply unified under one movement the way Black Arts movement poets could. In fact, Black Arts movement poets joined in this commitment to multiplicity in institution-building, as in June Jordan's course, "Poetry for the People," at the University of California, Berkeley. The course was open to poets and would-be poets of all ethnic backgrounds and skill levels, and each year the course published a book.

In effect, then, contemporary African American women poets inhabit the broadest range of aesthetic principles in the tradition's history, finding numerous empowering names for the experiences and perspectives of a broad range of

African American women. With a much greater number of educated women and more social and artistic outlets for their work, African American women poets have achieved their fullest voices, their greatest capacities for affirming self-naming. At one end, poets like Marilyn Nelson and Rita Dove, the second ever African American Pulitzer Prize winner, have returned to traditional forms and used them to articulate so-called universal ideals within the context of African American culture. Nelson was a finalist for the National Book Award in 1997 for *The Fields of Praise: New and Selected Poems*. Nelson's poetry is characterized by standard literary language and traditional poetic forms whose alleged "whiteness" seems no longer to be an issue. Dove, the winner of the Pulitzer Prize in 1987 for her 1986 volume, *Thomas and Beulah*, which used a range of forms but primarily literary language, similarly turned to a sonnet sequence in producing *Motherlove*, a volume that explores the trials, traumas, and triumphs of mother–daughter relationship through the myth of Persephone and Demeter. These two poets express no anxiety about adapting so-called European culture to their aesthetics, whether writing about raceless characters like mythological families or, as Nelson does, about southern heritage. At the other end of the spectrum are Harryette Mullen's postmodern concerns with the limits of language to convey meaning. Rather than creating notions of identity that could defy racism, in other words, Mullen turns the reader's attention to the dynamics of language itself in order to examine quite self-consciously how language reinforces social and cultural power. Even the idea of an affirming black self, Mullen's poetry suggests, can trap women in limiting roles, as in the "Black Queen" of Black Nationalism, a figure as passive and objectified as the love object in traditional poetry. In her volume *Muse & Drudge*, for example, Mullen evokes various stereotypes, like muse and drudge, and explores the weight of cliché for reinforcing those stereotypes: "intimidates intimates / polishing naked cactus / down below a bitter buffer / inferno never froze over." The poem reminds us that sound matters and that meaning is always being constructed and is not inherent. Such an acknowledgement allows for the play that resists stereotype by leaving us always unsettled by the pleasure we take in making meaning stick. If it never sticks, perhaps we can avoid being oppressive.

But perhaps the most impressive and innovative component of the contemporary scene is the diversification of oral tradition for the sake of the multifaceted black female self. These innovative approaches include the work of poets like the hip-hop inflected Jessica Care Moore, who uses her Moore Black Press to publish her own transcriptions of her performance poetry onto the page. Like hip hop, these poems take on the subject matter of life in the poor inner cities and adapt folk language into an appeal to young people to claim their voices. A leader among poets invested in the democratic implications of spoken-word poetry and open-mike nights, Care Moore affirms the voices of ordinary black women, even those whose lives seem to reinforce stereotypes. The welfare mother, rather than being a stereotype, becomes a fully fleshed and even articulate figure, as does the crack addict, the blues singer, and the teenager. Honorée Fanonne Jeffers returns to the blues in much the same way that Dove and Nelson return to formalism. In a volume called *Outlandish Blues*, Jeffers adopts the attitude that the music, rather than merely bemoaning pain, constitutes a heritage by which contemporary self-affirmation can happen. Professor and poet Elizabeth Alexander likewise embraces history and heritage and writes to that communal history through the history of her family in poems written in the language and tone of family oral legend. Sapphire, author of acclaimed novel *Push*, also uses her poetry and performance to confront an America fragmented by war in a way that reinvigorates the traditional theme of the self-transformation that happens when one traces one's spiritual path back to one's roots, a theme common in African American novels. Even musicians like Jill Scott incorporate the conventions and attitude of spoken-word oracles and combine them with the personal introspection characteristic of Harlem Renaissance poetry to tell stories of love, self-validation, and the traumas of pursuing love in modern times. Such is the beauty of neosoul, as it is called, a spoken-word inflected soul music performed by Scott, Erykah Badu, Floetry, and India Arie, among others.

In these ways, African Americans have resisted the silence of Lilith. In negotiating the representations of African American women in mainstream popular culture, African American women poets have rewritten that culture, sometimes marginally, sometimes radically, in order to find ways to articulate the dramas of heart, mind, and spirit of African American women everywhere. And in articulating that drama, African American poets provided some powerful revisions of traditional poetic conventions that were adopted by other poets, making their work a coherent tradition. Culminating in the democratic spoken-word venue, African American women's poetry transformed its faith in the power of poetic language and the value of personal experience, creating a tradition of egalitarian values affirmed by its diversity of voices. It is, as Lorde suggested, the affirmation of the deepest values of African American women expressed in a language that empowers us all.

NOTES

1. Sandra Gilbert and Susan Gubar, *The Madwoman in the Attic: The Woman Writer and the Nineteenth-Century Imagination* (New Haven, CT: Yale University Press, 1979), pp. 35–42.
2. Hazel Carby, *Reconstructing Womanhood: The Emergence of the Afro-American Woman Novelist* (New York: Oxford University Press, 1987), p. 15.

3. Audre Lorde, "Poetry is Not a Luxury," *Sister Outsider* (Freedom, CA: The Crossing Press, 1984), p. 36.

4. Hortense Spillers, "Mama's Baby, Papa's Maybe: An American Grammar Book," *Black and White and in Color: Essays on American Literature and Culture*, ed. Hortense Spillers (Chicago: University of Chicago Press, 2003), p. 203.

5. Psalms 68:31.

6. Gerda Lerner, "Early Community Work of Black Club Women," *Journal of Negro History* 59 (1974), 158–67.

7. Gloria T. Hull (ed.), *Color, Sex, and Poetry: Three Women Writers of the Harlem Renaissance* (Bloomington: Indiana University Press, 1987), p. 179.

8. Ibid.

9. Georgia Douglas Johnson, *Selected Works of Georgia Douglas Johnson* (New York: G. K. Hall, 1997), p. 13.

10. Nathan Huggins, *Harlem Renaissance* (New York: Oxford University Press, 1971), p. 65.

11. Maureen Honey, ed., *Shadowed Dreams: Women Poets of the Harlem Renaissance* (New Brunswick, NJ: Rutgers University Press, 1989), p. 3.

12. Mark Sanders, *Afro-Modernist Aesthetics and the Poetry of Sterling Brown* (Athens: University of Georgia Press, 1999).

13. Lorde, "Poetry Is not Luxury," pp. 55–56.

10

OLGA BARRIOS

African American women in the performing arts

When I write about place, I'm writing about family, about us, still trying to rebuild and redefine our families after the ravages of enslavement. I'm still trying to create a place that feels like home when we are so far from home.
(Pearl Cleage)[1]

Each of us is our own author, director, producer and star. In each moment, we have the power, the unalienable right to alter our actions and reinterpret the circumstances of our lives. In each moment, we have the freedom to speak, *write and invent our own scripts*.
(Barbara Ann Teer; emphasis added)[2]

Introduction

Throughout the history of performing arts, self and community have been inextricably linked to African American women's incessant search to find the place they needed, and, as black women, were not allowed to have in North American society. Angela Davis's use of the term "aesthetic community of resistance"[3] can apply to the alternative and transformative models presented by African American women playwrights and performers within a range of womanist sites built in their works. After the 1970s, when the black women's artistic movement grew especially strong, the community of black women began to expand into what today can be considered a pan-African movement that includes African American, African, and Caribbean[4] as reflected in these women's creations for the stage.

When referring to African American women in the performing arts, Lorraine Hansberry and Alice Childress (playwrights) or Katherine Dunham (dancer/choreographer) would probably be the first names that come to mind as forerunners of contemporary female playwrights and per-formance artists. Nevertheless, although it was in the late 1950s when African American playwrights began to receive acknowledgement, it was not until the 1970s that they became fully recognized by scholars and critics; and it has only been after the 1980s and 1990s that more and more African American women playwrights and performers from the first half of the twentieth century have come to light thanks to the extensive research conducted by scholars such as James V. Hatch, Ted Shine, Leo Hamalian, Kathy A. Perkins, and Elizabeth Brown-Guillory. These scholars have published various anthologies that include a significant number of the plays written by African American women before 1950.[5]

The incessant social and artistic movements against injustice and discrimination led by African American men and women gave rise to the North American and international women's movement at the end of the nineteenth century and during the 1970s. Antilynching movements contributed to the late nineteenth-century women's movement, and the civil rights movement and Black Arts movement contributed to the birth of the 1970s women's liberation movement. However, the history of African Americans, permeated by their constant struggle against oppression to achieve freedom and civil rights, made it even more difficult for African American women to opt for a public genre that had been almost exclusively reserved for men: the performing arts, whether directing, performing, and/or writing a play. These performance artists, however, have played an active role in the African American tradition by always being at the front of the struggle against injustice. The first black abolitionist woman Maria W. Stewart, writer and orator, in a manifesto written in 1831, proposed physical force to achieve freedom and encouraged black women to obtain formal education for their own independence as well as for their people's achievement of further political advancement;[6] abolitionist and activist Harriet Tubman helped many slaves to escape to the North; Frances Ellen Watkins Harper took her poetry to the people as poets of the 1960s would do during the Black Arts movement.

African American women, many of whom were performance artists, led the antilynching movement, made speeches and wrote on racial and gender rights – i.e. Sojourner Truth and Frances E. W. Harper. The first poems and narratives by African American women pioneered the perspective of double victimization, both black and female, in literary genres, which has continued to be central in all works written and performed by black women artists. The roots of black feminism, then, can be found in the women's narratives and autobiographies written by African American women at the end of the nineteenth century. Playwright Anna Julia Cooper, for instance, wrote a collection of speeches and essays in 1892 in a volume entitled *A Voice from the South* in which feminist black thought was articulated and advanced. A few years later during the Harlem Renaissance, playwright Eulalie Spence (a black Caribbean woman) wrote an essay "On Being Young – a Woman – and Colored" (1925) equally considered to be a landmark for its powerful critique on a society that "devalued women and blacks."[7] On the other hand, together with Cooper, Mary Church Terrell – also a playwright – and Ida B. Wells-Barnett founded the National Association for Colored Women in 1896, which demonstrates how the women of this era set the basis for future African American women's activism.[8] Either with their pen, their oratory or their organizational skills, African American women artists have always demanded justice and fought for their community's freedom as they eradicated stereotypical notions held against their community in general and against black womanhood in particular.

Throughout their history of unremitting endurance since slavery times, African American women never accepted the subjugated position into which they were placed, working indefatigably to find a womanist space that allowed them and their community to feel both free and whole, and the performing arts was the ideal alternative site to that purpose. Considering the development of the artist, black feminist Barbara Christian focuses on the position of the African American woman as one who needed "to generate her own definition to survive for she found that she was forced to deny essential aspects of herself to fit the definitions of others."[9] It is out of a political continuum of black women that a womanist ideology emerged, as defined by Alice Walker in her book *In Search Of Our Mothers' Gardens* (1983) as a philosophy that shows women who love each other sexually or non-sexually, and focuses on women's culture and emotions, music and dance. The Combahee River Collective expands on the concept offered by Walker and asserts that as feminists they "believe in collective process and a non-hierarchical distribution of power within [their] own group and in [their] vision of a revolutionary society."[10] Walker and the Combahee River Collective clearly establish community and self with strong links to the performing arts as inseparable in their conception of black feminism.

Similarly, Judith L. Stephens argues that African American women artists have developed a cultural legacy of self-sufficiency and collective, and their networks working through all historical periods "provide a site for examining a 'womanist consciousness' in which the concepts of self and community are not seen as separate entities."[11] African American women, such as playwright Georgia Douglas Johnson, were leaders of the antilynching movement during the 1920s. They wrote and performed against lynching, and these creations became a "source of womanist/feminist" theater.[12] Since the early twentieth century, African American theater writers and performers have continued to maintain a womanist site, incorporating their family, their community, their bodies, and their selves. They have never forgotten, though, that African American women's liberation is just one aspect "of the need to liberate the total society from dehumanization," being always aware that it is the social system that must change.[13]

The new sites created by African American women for the stage are usually female-centered which, according to Gloria Hull, "constituted a first line of resistance."[14] Those sites presented in their theatrical pieces become transgressive as they help revise, reconstruct, and broaden African Americans' history. They also provide space where women are able to construct their identity and to develop their personal, social, and sexual needs. In addition, those sites offer healing for the women characters, for the actors who rehearse in that woman-centered space, and for the reader/audience that is introduced to and participates in new alternative models. Since the nineteenth century, most of these new sites designed by African American women in their theatrical creations have incorporated songs, music, dance, children's games, poetry, and/or prayers, and, in more recent works, different types of technology (slides, video projections, microphones, etc.). This combination of artistic elements parallels the creative compositions of African American dancers Katherine Dunham and Pearl Primus who incorporated lyrics, poetry, and oral literature into their choreographies, which Dunham considered part of the African aesthetic.[15]

Many of the African American women playwrights and performers have founded their own theater/performance companies, directed, performed, and/or produced their own work as well as helped design and establish new theater buildings within the black community. This is the case with Barbara Ann Teer who founded the National Black Theatre in 1968, still in operation. Even during the Harlem Renaissance, at a time when black women were not especially trained for the theater, they ventured to direct and produce their plays in school halls, kitchens, library basements, lodges, yards, churches.[16] One of the best advocates in community theater at this time was Eulalie Spence, who initiated a movement that left the trend of the "plays to be read" written by the majority of her contemporary colleagues.[17] Therefore, these playwrights followed Du Bois's philosophy about black theater: it should be written by, about, for black people and performed near the black community.

Plays, usually regarded as a corpus of drama, are pieces to be performed by actors on the stage in front of an audience. The significance of the oral tradition within African American history is obvious for it has pervaded all literary genres (i.e. transference of the rhythms of music and speech, and/or the call and response pattern to the written text), and in many cases, those literary works (narrative or poetry) have been read aloud to large audiences. Consequently, it could be deduced that drama (as a text to be performed) or any other creation for performance should be the genre par excellence in which the elements of the African American oral tradition would be especially highlighted. In this regard, referring to African American drama and performance, Sandra Richards reminds us that when examining a dramatic written text, the critic must analyze the text but also the "absent potential," and "offer informed accounts of the latent intertexts" likely to be produced in performance, "which increase and complicate meaning."[18] As will be examined later, African American women playwrights and performers have established a clear and distinctive tradition that, even when preserving western patterns (such as the linear storyline format), these are usually disrupted by the inclusion of components such as music, songs, dance, prayers, or simply by leaving the end of their plays open. These disruptive elements actually reverse the western traditional passive role of the audience into an active and participatory one – through the call and response technique, or by an open-ending story that intends to raise the audience's consciousness and make them think, react, and/or bring change to their lives. Therefore, these women artists have expanded the traditional theatrical space into a new one in permanent motion that reveals new alternatives and possibilities: new sites that have shattered a traditional racist and sexist space by introducing and representing gender issues which welcome a different interaction with men;[19] and an open site that offers an active role to the audience re-mapping, thus, the geography of the performing arts.

Playwrights and performers before 1950

It is significant to mention that before 1930, one hundred male and female African Americans had written 350 plays,[20] and only recently have these plays found inclusion in African American theater anthologies. African American women's early plays have cast new light on North American life and culture by offering a new perspective and more integral picture of African Americans from the point of view of women. Most of these early plays are one-act, female-centered plays that use the domestic home (a kitchen or dining room) as the main setting (in rural and urban areas) and usually as a shelter against external racism. The male figure is generally absent from the household, either because he has died, has been lynched, is working outside, or has been abandoned by his wife; and if this male figure is present he is either crippled – as in Eulalie Spence's *Her* (1927) – or is countered by a wife presented as the strong figure – as in Spence's *Fool's Errand* (1927). Characters are not stereotypes and are usually black (except in the case of May Miller's white characters in *Nails and Thorns*, 1933) although the effects of white racism upon the family are present. Most of these works are either propaganda or folk plays, or a combination of both. One of the issues that most concerns these playwrights and that repeats in many of their plays is lynching, either as the main theme or as backdrop of the story. Other issues also selected by the playwrights are poverty, education, class, slavery, historical black heroes/heroines, or the black church. In all cases, though, they show how, in spite of adversity, black families survive, united, and nurtured by love in the only safe place where they can feel at ease: their home. In addition, all the plays incorporate either sacred (spirituals or gospel) or secular (folk) music that comments on the action of the play or leave the ending open for the audience to interpret it. Consequently, the style and structure of these plays are transgressive since these components disrupt the linear structure of traditional drama, broadening the possibilities of the theatrical event with the creation of new models.

After the production and success of Angelina Weld Grimké's *Rachel* (1916), many other women continued to write protest plays, most of which specifically dealt with lynching. However, *Rachel* aroused considerable controversy among African American intellectuals and writers over whether plays should deal with propaganda or folk issues. W. E. B. Du Bois defended the propagandistic plays to raise consciousness among the black community against racism, founding the Krigwa Players. On the other hand, Professors Montgomery T. Gregory and Alain Locke of Howard University supported folk plays representing the black experience in order to reach a wider audience, and founded the Howard Players as their platform. The Howard Players actually helped African American women in their initial training and playwriting and contributed to the production of their plays in northern areas of the US. Likewise, Du Bois, editor of *The Crisis*, and Charles S. Johnson, editor of *Opportunity*, launched literary contests for one-act plays to be published in those magazines.[21] Most of these early plays by African American women are available to us today because they were published in one of those premier black journals.

The pioneers

Referring perhaps to the tradition begun by Angelina Weld Grimké with *Rachel*, Christine Gray asserts that African American women playwrights started in 1916 to become "actively engaged in writing serious plays for the non-musical stage."[22] However, the first African American playwright that we have a record of is Pauline Elizabeth Hopkins (1859–1930) – also a novelist and singer – who wrote one of the first black musical dramas that would actually bring to a close the racist ideologies and stereotypes displayed in the minstrel tradition of the eighteenth century. The minstrel show began with "Jim Crow white performers in black face mimicking black speech, music, dance and culture." When black minstrel troupes appeared, they had to "imitate their imitators and kept the same stereotypes" that whites had created about them.[23] However, by the year 1880, minstrelsy was disappearing. That same year Hopkins's *Peculiar Sam, or the Underground Railroad, A Musical Drama in Four Acts* was first performed.

Peculiar Sam was produced by the author's family company – the Hopkins Colored Troubadours – starring Hopkins's stepfather, her mother, and Pauline Hopkins herself, and the then well-known Hyers Sisters and a chorus of over sixty people. The show toured for over a year, playing from coast to coast, introducing black male and female performers who were not wearing burnt cork on their faces.[24] The play was highly innovative at the time as it presented a group of slaves led by Sam through the Underground Railroad from a US southern plantation to Canada. In addition, the play included all manner of spiritual and folk songs and dance incorporating a new element to it: the call-and-response pattern, which changed the role of the minstrel show's passive audience into an active one.[25] Moreover, Martha Patterson underscores that *Peculiar Sam* left aside the stock characters of minstrelsy to acknowledge "subjectivity and social mobility".[26] Patterson also observes that the male protagonist, Sam, rebels against slavery and counters the Jim Crow stereotypical jumping figure of the minstrel with that of the African American folk trickster who would use the image whites expected from him to meet his needs. Sam's peculiarity, then, comes from his refusal to remain a slave.[27] Caricatured black vernacular is used at the beginning, but by the end of the play, Sam and his sister Juno (who becomes a teacher) speak standard English, illustrating the patterns of the minstrel (caricatured black vernacular) and their revision (the introduction of standard English to show that blacks were perfectly capable of using it). This important linguistic component disrupted the stereotype associated by whites with the black community who, as characters, were always portrayed speaking a caricatured black dialect. The play also shows the characters' black pride and reverses the tragic mulatto figure (Virginia) into affirming her black identity by marrying black Sam. By the end of the play, all the characters are dignified and respectable citizens.

If Hopkins takes the audience/reader on a journey into freedom, *Aunt Betsy's Thanksgiving* (c. 1914) by Katherine D. Chapman Tillman (1870–193?) introduces us to a poor but warm and safe black home composed of grandmother, Aunt Betsy, and her twelve-year-old granddaughter, Ca'line. *Aunt Betsy* shows Tillman's command in using both black dialect for black characters and standard English for the only white character, a lawyer, who actually helps the family. Through Aunt Betsy, we learn that Caroline's mother, Nellie, abandoned her alcoholic and abusive husband, leaving mother and daughter behind so that she could find a job. By the end of the play, Nellie returns with a new husband (who never appears on stage), purchases the house her mother lives in, and moves to live with her, Caroline, and her new husband, thus reuniting her family. Various significant issues are emphasized in this play: on the one hand, an independent woman repudiates her husband for not respecting or treating her appropriately; on the other, a strong and caring old woman who keeps struggling against poverty and whose vulnerability is symbolized by her broken leg. This vulnerable image of Aunt Betsy counters the stereotypical image of the black mammy as a powerful, strong, and seemingly happy woman.[28]

But without question, the most significant playwright of the early twentieth century was Angelina Weld Grimké (1880–1958). Her play *Rachel* is considered to be the first black non-musical play, written, produced, and publicly performed by African Americans. *Rachel* is a four-act play that, as stated in its program, became "the first attempt to use the stage for race propaganda in order to enlighten the American people relative to the lamentable condition of ten millions of Colored citizens in this free republic [the US]" from a woman's perspective.[29] Grimké attempted to reach the conscience and heart of white mothers by depicting a young girl, Rachel, who in the face of the brutal lynching her father suffered at the hands of a white mob and the continuous racism and discrimination suffered by black children on the part of white children and teachers, decides not ever to marry nor ever to have children.

Rachel was transgressive in a series of revisions and redefinitions that it presents. Rachel and her middle-class family as well as the other black characters all speak standard English rather than dialect; and the black family is depicted as self-sufficient and refined. Further, Rachel rejects traditional gender roles when she decides not to marry or to become a biological mother. This departure from social norms "grants [Rachel] the insight to lead a rebellion by way of symbolic power."[30] However, before making the decision of never becoming a biological mother, she adopts a little child (Jimmy) when he is left alone after his parents' death. Jimmy's adoption by Rachel brings to front the African philosophy of an extended family where women become *othermothers*,[31] thus transcending the western concept of a nuclear family. Consequently, Grimké constructs a family unity whose home becomes a shelter and a healing site that counters and resists the external cruelties of racism and tightens the bonds among members of the black community. Furthermore, *Rachel* not only shaped racial discourse and stated the basis for future African American plays on this issue, but was also an attempt to build a bridge between blacks and whites[32] – something that more recent playwrights such as Lorraine Hansberry, Robbie McCauley, or Anna D. Smith have continued to do. It is significant that *Rachel* was produced again in 1990 at Spelman College in Atlanta, Georgia, with good audience reception,[33] suggesting that seventy years after it was written, the play still tackles current social issues that concern the dynamics of North American society.

From the Harlem Renaissance to 1950

The Harlem Renaissance was a time of vast theater productions, especially thanks to the efforts of African American intellectuals such as Du Bois, Gregory, and Locke, who encouraged and supported many of the plays written by the African American women of the time. Among the most prolific women playwrights were Georgia Douglas Johnson, May Miller, Eulalie Spence, Zora Neale Hurston, and Mary Burrill. However, there were many other women whose plays were also significant either for their revolutionary styles – i.e. Marita Bonner and Regina M. Anderson – or for their controversial issues exposed with special mastery – i.e. Alice Dunbar Nelson and Myrtle Smith Livingston. Following the years of the Harlem Renaissance, the most outstanding figure in theater was Shirley Graham together with two female dancers/choreographers who would open the door to other African Americans in concert dance: Katherine Dunham and Pearl Primus.

Among the issues most repeated in the plays and performance creations by the African American women of these years were lynching, miscegenation, and the segregated military. That lynching was one of the main themes of these plays is understandable since 3,589 blacks (including eighty-three women, several of whom were white) were lynched between 1882 and 1927.[34] In many cases the issue of lynching is combined with the black soldier's dilemma as is the case of *Mine Eyes Have Seen* (1918) by Alice Dunbar-Nelson (1875–1935) and *Aftermath* (1919) by Mary P. Burrill (1884–1946). Dunbar-Nelson delivered antiwar speeches all throughout the country as well as addressing issues on women's rights. In *Mine Eyes Have Seen* she depicts a family composed of two brothers (the eldest is crippled) and a sister. When the youngest brother, Chris, learns that he has been drafted to fight in World War I and remembers that their father was shot by whites for defending his home, he initiates a debate on whether his duty is to remain and take care of his family or to go to war on behalf of a nation that robs him of his dignity. Two neighbors, an Irish woman and a Jewish woman, join in the debate. By the end, the eldest brother and his sister beg Chris to consider love of humanity above time, race or sect, encouraging him to fight for those French mothers who must be also suffering. The end of the play shows Chris reflecting on that position and probably resigned to go to war.

Burrill's *Aftermath*, however, promotes an armed black revolution as the only solution to bring oppression and racism to a close. The play shows an old mother, Mam Sue, and her granddaughter Millie dressed in black for Millie's father's recent death by lynching while John, Millie's brother, was fighting in the war. When John returns home and learns about his father's lynching, he decides to take his pistols and find the murderers. *Aftermath* is a very power-ful piece where contrasts play an important part to sustain the author's position. Thus, the play starts with Mam Sue sewing a many-colored patch-work quilt, a symbol of black culture which could stand for a solid bond among its members and for their joy of life, in contrast with Mam Sue's and Millie's mourning, dressed in black, symbolizing the pain caused by white racism. In addition, another subtle contrast is posed when John, dressed in his military uniform, arrives from war and leaves his two pistols on the same spot where the Bible was seen at the beginning of the play. This move foreshadows John's final action, symbolizing that praying is not enough and action must be taken by blacks to defend themselves from injustice and racist practices such as lynching.

Georgia Douglas Johnson (1880–1966), a specialist in music – violin, piano, voice, and harmony – and songwriter, also protested against lynching in many of her plays. Like Burrill in *Aftermath*, in *A Sunday Morning in the South* (1925), Johnson juxtaposes the church bells and hymns that can be heard from a Sunday morning service with the lynching of a young black man – proven to be innocent of the charges against him – by a white mob, thus condemning white Christian hypocrisy. In other plays, such as *Blue-Eyed Black Boy* (c. 1930), Johnson combines lynching and miscegenation. In this play, a mulatto young man is about to be lynched and his mother sends someone with a ring she gives him to see the governor and ask him to save her son, clearly hinting that the governor is the father of the young man, which he actually does. Miscegenation is an issue that Johnson carefully examines in *Blue Blood* (1926), showing the origins of it and possible risks run by mulattoes who fall in love, since both might be children of the same white father without being aware of it – as depicted in this play. Likewise, but in a more blatant position, Myrtle Smith Livingston (1902–73), in her play *For Unborn Children* (1926), clearly opts against the mixing of races. The male protagonist, Leroy, is a mulatto who is about to marry a white woman in the South. When his grandmother and sister learn about this marriage, they show their strong opposition by making him think about what might happen to his *unborn children* in a racist society. The play ends with Leroy willingly going to meet the lynching mob which is searching for him as a sacrifice for those *unborn children*.

Even after the Harlem Renaissance, the theme of lynching was still chosen by African American women in music and dance. In 1939, Billie Holliday made popular the poem "Strange Fruit" by white poet Lewis Allan, and in 1943, African American choreographer and dancer Pearl Primus premiered a dance composition in New York against lynching by using the same poem. Most of Primus's dance compositions were considered protest dances, with which she intended "not to entertain but to help people better understand each other."[35] A similar attempt to build a bridge of dialogue and understanding between different cultural groups could be found in another playwright of the Harlem Renaissance, May Miller (1899–1995), as presented in her play *Nails and Thorns* (1933), where she depicts a white family and the tragic effects of racism and lynching upon them – Miller was one of the few playwrights to include interracial casts in her plays. As educator, Miller was concerned about black history as well and wrote several plays on historical figures such as Haitian revolutionary Henri Christophe and African American abolitionist Harriet Tubman.

Like protest plays, folk plays – focusing on the black experience – were also very popular. Some of the most significant were *Color Struck* (1925) – incorporating a cake-walk contest – by Zora Neale Hurston (1891–1960); *Riding the Goat* (1929) – with class conflicts and conflicts between self and community traditions and class – by May Miller; *Fool's Errand* (1927) – a humorous side of the black church busybodies – by Eulalie Spence (1894–1981); and *Climbing Jacob's Ladder: A Tragedy of Negro Life* (1930) – an extraordinary and powerful piece that shows the central role of the black church in social organization – by Regina M. Anderson (1901–93).

Apart from the completely new perspective offered by these women's plays on the African American community, some of them introduced truly innovative staging techniques for their time. Marita Bonner's *The Purple Flower* (1926) is a surrealist depiction of the condition of blacks (Us) living at the bottom of the hill, and the exploitation and oppression that whites (White Devils) living at the top exert on blacks without allowing them to go up the hill. Eulalie Spence's *Her: A Mystery Play* (1927), depicts the story of an apartment haunted by the spirit of a Philippine woman who committed suicide because her husband would never allow her to have her own space. This haunting is a beautiful metaphor for a woman's need to have her own space where she can grow and develop as a free human being as well as a metaphor for a woman's strong spirit that continues living even after death. Zora Neale Hurston's *Color Struck* and Regina A. Anderson's *Climbing Jacob's Ladder: A Tragedy of Negro Life* are two plays that use what could be called *metaperformance* since the audience can see another audience on stage watching and participating within the performance they have gone to see. Hurston's play shows several short scenes of blacks rehearsing various dances and enjoying themselves on a train heading to a cake-walk dance contest where they will participate. Besides, the audience will see the contest that would actually encourage their participation. Likewise, in Anderson's play, the audience can see a whole congregation/audience of black people in a black church (young, old, poor, middle class, groups of friends, and so on) and both congregation and theater audience will be able to participate following the call-response pattern, with their songs, applause, humming, or other sounds. Hurston and Anderson expand the stage space into the audience, establishing a new site that situates actors and audience together in the same acting space.

Following the years of the Harlem Renaissance, Shirley Graham (1896–1977), who married W. E. B. Du Bois in 1951, was the most prolific African American woman playwright. She was a feminist, theater director and biographer, played piano and organ, sang spirituals, composed and conducted musical scores. Apart from her well-known play on mothers in slavery, *It's Morning* (1940), she also wrote *Tom-Tom: An Epic of Music and the Negro* (1932), which traces African music through the United States. An epic on the history of blacks' survival throughout two centuries of oppression in the New World, it was the first all-black opera to be produced on a large scale, including a professional cast of approximately five hundred actors. Graham's musical background is always present in her plays; thus, in *It's Morning*, there are spirituals and dancing or singing at the rhythm produced by slaves cutting wood with an ax. The play emphasizes the importance of music for the black community during slavery to help alleviate their burdens. The protagonist, Cissie, when learning that her adolescent daughter has been sold to be taken to another plantation with another master, decides to take her daughter's life rather than see her suffering and being abused for being a slave. If Graham revises the cruelty of slavery and its effects upon the black mother in 1940, Grimké in *Rachel* shows that after slavery racism still had destructive effects upon young women who eschewed motherhood rather than having children who will suffer from segregation and injustice. Most of the plays of this time place the mother and/or grandmother as central figures who would do whatever necessary to protect their children and family/home from external racism and injustice against them.

Playwrights and performers from 1950 to the present[36]

The process of independence initiated by various African countries during the 1950s greatly influenced the period of struggle for civil rights in the United States. Likewise, the courage of an African American woman who in 1955 refused to give up her seat to a white passenger on a bus in Montgomery, Alabama, sparked a bus boycott that galvanized the civil rights movement led by Dr. Martin Luther King and others. Moreover, this movement contributed to the birth of the Black Arts and Black Theater movements of the 1960s, proclaiming a black aesthetic based on the African American tradition to be separate from that established by western parameters. Encouraged by both the civil rights and the Black Arts movement, the 1970s would witness the rise of the gay and women's liberation movements, which would be broadened and enlightened by black feminist thought formulated by African American, Caribbean, and African women writers and intellectuals.

The 1950s witnessed the birth of two great African American playwrights considered by many critics the forerunners of the Black Arts and Theater movements of the 1960s: Alice Childress and Lorraine Hansberry. In the 1960s, two African American women who followed the philosophy of the Black Arts/Theater movements were Sonia Sanchez and Barbara Ann Teer; and another playwright, Adrienne Kennedy, introduced a new revolutionary theatrical style which, although not truly understood at the time, would become a precedent for African American women artists in the following decades. In the 1970s, Ntozake Shange continued Kennedy's experimental style, incorporating black women's condemnation of sexism suffered within the black community and a declaration of their needs. Other innovative playwrights and performers of the 1970s were Alexis De Veaux, Aishah Rahman, Sybil Kein, Adrian Piper (who performed in the streets and other public places), Edwina Lee Tyler (percussionist), and Bernice Johnson Reagon (founder of all-black female ensemble Sweet Honey in the Rock, which used African American traditional sacred and secular music accompanied by different musical instruments, performance, and words).

The African American playwrights and performers whose works have appeared since the 1980s are the products of the previous and revolutionary decades. These women artists have continued the tradition of their ancestors with new perspectives, writing styles, and performing techniques such as solo performances, dance theater, the use of technology, or experimental theater. Among the most significant in experimental theater are Thulani Davis, Suzan-Lori Parks, Robbie McCauley, Judith Alexa Jackson, Anna Deavere Smith, Urban Bush Women, Kia Corthron, or poet/performer Sapphire. Another significant playwright of this time who considers herself a nationalist and radical feminist is Pearl Cleage. In the line of Thulani Davis and Glenda Dickerson, Cleage's plays revise and reconstruct African American women's history in a combination of classical realism and Brechtian distancing technique – the audience is taken to the past and that distance in time from their present is intended to involve them in active and transformative thinking. A great number of these African American artists blend different skills, since many – such as Shange, McCauley, or Smith – are not only writers (poets and playwrights) but also performers, dancers, actors, or musicians, and at times directors and performers in their own productions. As happened with the African American women playwrights and performers of the 1920s and

1930s, many of these contemporary artists have collaborated with one another on different projects, maintaining thus a historical tradition of African American women's collective work.

From 1950 to 1980: civil rights, Black Arts and women's movements

Alice Childress and Lorraine Hansberry have probably been the most well-known and recognized African American playwrights during and since the 1950s. Together with the works of African American dancers/choreographers Katherine Dunham and Pearl Primus, Childress's and Hansberry's plays provided fertile ground for the forthcoming and always transgressive and alternative artistic creations of successive African American women writers and performers. Just as in the 1940s, Primus had used the poem "Strange Fruit" to create a piece on lynching, in 1953 Dunham created the ballet *Southland* inspired by the same poem. In this ballet, the lynching of a man was actually dramatized on stage when it was performed in Santiago (Chile), intending to show the injustices suffered by African Americans in the US and, thus, preventing "further destruction and humiliation." The US State Department insisted that she remove the lynching scene, but Dunham refused by saying she would only remove it "when lynching ceased in the United States."[37] Consequently, Dunham's ballet was never staged in the US.

Dunham's artistry and courage in denouncing the injustices endured by African Americans were paralleled during the 1950s by Childress's and Hansberry's theatrical pieces. Alice Childress (1916–94) mastered various skills related to performing as an actor, playwright, and theater director, using her pen to condemn the stereotypical roles black actors were forced to play in films as well as on the stage – i.e. *Trouble in Mind* (1956, Obie Award) and *Florence* (1950). Among her many plays, there are two especially well known, *The Wedding Band* (1966), which analyzes the implications and consequences of interracial love in the South, and *Wine in the Wilderness* (1969), in which Childress depicts what it means to be black, poor, and female in the US, exposing how sexism, racism, and classism are inextricably connected while offering a revised notion of black womanhood.[38] Most of Childress's plays focus on working-class characters, and although written in what might be considered a realism style, she disrupts it by including African American traditional music, liturgy of black church, folk and fantasy elements, as well as African mythology. It is also significant that Childress has been the only African American woman playwright whose plays have been written, published, and produced for four consecutive decades.

A Raisin in the Sun (1959) made Lorraine Hansberry (1930–65) the first African American woman playwright to reach Broadway and the first African

American playwright to win the New York Critics Circle Award. Hansberry wrote her play mindful of the historical and revolutionary times of the civil rights movement, since Lena, the mother and head of the black family in the play, decides to move out of a ghetto in order to find a better place/home that meets the needs of her family, which only seems available within the range of white neighborhoods. In her play, Hansberry continues Childress's line in eradicating black stereotypical characters by presenting a family who symbolizes the black community and the many different points of view and personalities that can be found in it. In addition, Hansberry's plays show her concern about race relations, as she demonstrated in *The Sign in Sidney Brustein's Window* (1965), believing that dialogue between blacks and whites was necessary. However, by the end of her life she was convinced that words were insufficient, and action was also needed to achieve African Americans' rights, as presented in her unfinished piece *Les Blancs* (produced in 1970). Although *Les Blancs* takes place in Africa, Hansberry clearly distances the story to make her audience think about what should be done in their own country. Like previous black women playwrights in the US, she revised and reconstructed different black historical periods and heroes in her writing, such as slavery (*The Drinking Gourd*, 1961), or historical black leaders such as Haitian revolutionary Toussaint L'Overture (*Toussaint: A Work in Progress*, 1961).

Childress's and Hansberry's stories are usually presented in a linear form, and their themes are socially oriented, maintaining their concern for the African American community as the backdrop of their theatrical creations. On the contrary, the pieces written by Adrienne Kennedy (1931–) are built upon a more experimental style and focus on the psychological states of mind of her characters. Kennedy opened a new door for African American theater by building a completely new theatrical site on which she valiantly dared to expose the terrible pain of her black characters split between the black and white worlds. Abandoning any possible closeness to traditional realism, she opted for a symbolic style more appropriate to expose her characters' states of mind. This is the case with Sarah's internal struggle in her play *Funnyhouse of a Negro* (1964, Obie Award). *Funnyhouse* depicts Sarah's confusion and pain at being unable to find her right place, so she creates her own rooms filled with icons from the western culture and vivid images inspired by the African masks Kennedy saw during a trip to the Congo while writing this play. Mulatto Sarah stands as a symbol for the battleground on which blacks and whites are unable to reconcile, and incapable of bearing the pain, Sarah decides to commit suicide. Kennedy uses her own dreams (actually nightmares) to show the destructive effects caused by a racist society in a surrealistic/expressionistic style and in a very powerful and poetic language. *Funnyhouse* was produced at the time of the Black Arts movement that promoted black pride, but the play was considered outside the parameters defended by black intellectuals. However, no other African American writer of that time was as daring as Kennedy in depicting and voicing the individual internal pain suffered by many blacks. Kennedy's exorcism of pain would actually facilitate other African American women playwrights and performers to follow her example. These playwrights, such as Sonia Sanchez and Ntozake Shange, would start not only expressing their pain but also their rage and their needs as women.

Sonia Sanchez (1934–), one of the few women considered part of the Black Arts and Theater movement, was mainly a poet who used to read her poetry during the 1960s. Like Kennedy, she turned away from classical realism and used her poetry to create theater, giving birth to *poemplays* written in a very visual language. But in contrast to Kennedy's plays, Sanchez's plays were written in consonance with the aesthetic pursued by the artists of the Black Arts movement, as reflected in her one-woman monologue *Sister Son/ji* (1969). Presented in a surrealistic style, the play shows a fifty-five-year-old woman's struggle that stands as a metaphor for that of African Americans throughout history in the US and is, according to Elizabeth Brown-Guillory, "one of the most significant portrayals of the Black Power Movement of the 1960s."[39] Moreover, Sanchez also uses the stage to address black men and ask them to respect black women, as presented in *The Bronx Is Next* (1968).

Likewise, following the philosophy of the Black Arts and Theater movements, in 1968 Barbara Ann Teer abandoned commercial theater and opened an alternative and transformative space for black theater within the African American community by founding the National Black Theater of Harlem. Teer proposed a ritual form for her theatrical creations since ritual can be considered collective and participatory. Teer chose Harlem for she saw "the transformative potential of Harlem as well as a need for new patterns and innovative rituals."[40] And not satisfied with that, years later she erected a circular theater playhouse to become the physical evidence of her philosophy in favor of ritual, a collaborative theatrical form that opened space for the audience as part of its productions (an endeavor already begun by other black women playwrights during the Harlem Renaissance). Most of Teer's theatrical pieces have originated out of collective work – this is the case with their work on Gwendolyn Brooks's poem "We Real Cool" – and almost always combine dance, music, and drama. Teer explains that spirituals are among the musical pieces she usually includes in her performances because "they feed the spirit" of people[41] as proven throughout African American history.

By dissecting the mind of her characters, Kennedy had begun a process of individual healing that was continued and extended by Sanchez and Teer to the black community. Ntozake Shange (1948–), on the other hand, focused specifically on black women whose healing required breaking the silence of past generations and giving voice to their rage and their womanly needs. Her internationally acclaimed play, *for colored girls who have considered suicide/ when the rainbow is enuf* (1976), transforms the stage into a healing site for seven women who tell the audience the painful experiences that actually took them to the point of considering suicide. If, in Kennedy's *Funnyhouse*, Sarah's loneliness leads her to suicide, in Shange's play, women find the courage to exorcise their pain thanks to their strong bond – this piece was also created collectively. It is that emotional bond that helps these seven women break their silence, abandon their lack of self-esteem, and reach the point in which they can celebrate divinity within themselves – "i found god in myself & i loved her/i loved her fiercely."[42] That emotional bond is paralleled by an emotional language composed of poetry, music, and dance presented on a bare stage filled with the rainbow colors of these women's outfits. Apart from having pioneered "black feminist thought-in-action to theater,"[43] Shange introduced a new theatrical technique: the *choreopoem*. She incorporated her writing and performing skills (as poet, novelist and dancer) into the stage, following the trend already established by Kennedy and broadening the possibilities of finding new transformative sites for black women and theater.

If dance and music are integral components of Shange's *choreopoems*, music is an essential element in the plays by Aishah Rahman as part of what the playwright calls *jazz aesthetic*. Rahman's *jazz aesthetic* shows the various levels of characters' reality – the unborn, the living, and the dead – while it intends to express in drama "multiple ideas and experiences through language, move-ment, visual art and spirituality simultaneously."[44] Simultaneity is essential in her play *Unfinished Women Cry in No Man's Land While a Bird Dies in a Gilded Cage* (1977), in which she juxtaposes a woman's screams while giving birth with a note blown by Charlie Parker (Bird). *Unfinished Women*, symbo-lizing the live music on stage, is staged on split space to depict on one side pregnant teenagers contemplating whether to give their children up for adop-tion, and, on the other, Bird's last days of life. Presenting a combination of styles, including avant-garde, the absurd, surrealism, farce, satire, and ritual, Rahman has also written a musical tragedy, *Lady Day* (1972) on Billie Holiday, and *The Mojo and the Sayso* (1989) – based on the tragic shooting by the police of a ten-year-old child. As her ancestors sought to do, Rahman widened the range of possibilities for the stage space.

From 1980 to the present: an extended family of women

Since the 1980s, not only have African American women continued the path of re-mapping the geography of the stage, but they have also sought new spots that are an extension of that space. They have shown that the stage is a space that always remains in motion. A great number of works by contemporary African American playwrights can be included within the category of experimental theater/performance, such as Robbie McCauley's creations. McCauley is especially well known for her play *Sally's Rape* (1989, Obie Award), which connects the past of slavery with present history and tries to create a bridge between races through the two – black and white – actors on stage, while including the audience as the third actor of the show. Judith Alexa Jackson has created another experimental piece entitled the "high-tech of Anita Hill" *WOMBmanWars* (1992). Both McCauley and Jackson are writers and performers, and they use different technological devices, such as video cameras, slides, and microphones for actors and for the audience. Lisa Jones also uses technology in her plays, as in *Combination Skin* (1986), a deconstructive exploration of the tragic mulatto theme set to the rhythm of a television contest show in order to find *a place* for mulatto women. On the other hand, Thulani Davis has excelled in musical opera with *The Life of Malcolm X* (1985), written to be sung using the rhythms of Malcolm X's speeches that, according to the author, sound similar to jazz. Saphire (Ramona Lofton), dancer, writer, and poet, performs her autobiographical poetry that shows the cruel legacy of child abuse as well as demanding new places for women's sexuality and the transgender movement. Kia Corthron, on the other hand, is one of the few playwrights to have written on black mothers in jail, i.e. her play *Cage Rhythm* (1993). And, finally, there is the dance theater group founded by Jawole Willa Jo Zollar in 1984, Urban Bush Women, who have especially focused on the body of the black woman as a site of restoration and a source of strength. They have especially concentrated on healing the raped body. Moreover, through dance – as in their piece *Batty Moves* (1995) – they have tried to recuperate and to emphasize black women's hip movement so characteristic of black Caribbean rhythms as an expression of sensuality and spirituality.[45]

Out of the tapestry of African American playwrights after the 1980s, three of them have received special acclaim: Suzan-Lori Parks, Anna Deavere Smith, and Pearl Cleage. Parks and Smith could be included within the category of experimental theater whereas Cleage's plays present a more linear storyline. Although clearly influenced by Adrienne Kennedy's style and imagery and Ntozake Shange's deconstruction of the English language, Suzan-Lori Parks takes this experimental trend to a higher extreme. The titles of her plays give a hint of her use of language: *The Death of the Last Black Man in the Whole Entire World* (1990), or *Imperceptible Mutabilities in the Third Kingdom* (1990, Obie Award). In Parks's plays, language becomes subject and theme,[46] "a physical act. Something that happens in your entire body ... Words are things that move our bodies." Parks's creations intend to challenge both the actor's and the audience's imagination.[47] Her plays also show how people are fixed in a specific place by a language that has been imposed on them and seek to free themselves from the "weight of words."[48] In addition, Parks examines history for she is concerned about the *holes*, the absences of black people in history. According to Liz Diamond, who has directed most of Parks's plays in close connection with Parks, Parks's plays contain two stories, reminiscent of jazz, suggesting that her plays be read as musical scores.[49] Futhermore, Parks explains the "rep" and "rev" strategy used in her work, the repetition and revision of history that can be seen in *The American Play* (1993), where characters and historical events happen first as tragedy, second as farce, and then as theater of the absurd. This "rep" and "rev" strategy, Parks states, "keeps the spectator/reader ever-vigilant, looking for something missed in the last repetition while scrutinizing the upcoming revision." Her plays depict the world as a complex and multidimensional place.[50]

Anna Deavere Smith's experimental pieces are solo performances in which many different characters are impersonated by her. The mastery of her acting is essential in the production of her shows.[51] Different characters are inter-viewed by Smith on a specific and controversial issue. When the audience listens to each character's point of view, multiple versions of truth, they realize the unresolvable contradictions found within them.[52] Two of her most acclaimed pieces won an Obie Award, *Fires in the Mirror: Crown Heights Brooklyn and Other Identities* (1992) and *Twilight: Los Angeles 1992* (1993). Sydné Mahone emphasizes that Smith's performances fore-ground the "power of oral tradition" and the "power of the solo artist to become the voice of the people."[53] Smith explains the title of *Fires in the Mirror*: "The fire images in the title of the show represent many small, dormant fires of social unrest, which can flare up as a result of high-speed friction. The mirror is the stage, reflecting the fires back to us."[54] Regarding *Twilight*, Smith states it is "a call to the community ... I wanted to be part of their examination of the problems. I believe that solutions of these problems will call for the participation of large and eclectic groups of people." She also believes that in the United States people have reached a stage where silence must be broken about race, and many people should be encouraged to participate in the dialogue.[55] Smith, then, places herself on the same side as Robbie McCauley, who also believes in the need for the audience's participa-tion in a dialogue on racial issues.

If Smith's works pose a special emphasis on performance, those of Pearl Cleage underline the power of the written word and storyline to be told. Cleage considers herself a black nationalist and radical feminist who is determined to continue in the struggle "against racism, sexism, classism and

homophobia."[56] Her determination is especially manifest in her play *Flyin'*
West (1992), a new perspective on the history of the US west from a black
woman's point of view, which shows a group of late nineteenth-century black
women controlling their own lives. This play was inspired by a note Ida B.
Wells published in a Memphis newspaper during the 1890s, after a lynching
and a riot. Wells encouraged African Americans to leave their homes in the
South and move to the West in search of freedom and new land. The
protagonists of this piece are three sisters and Ms. Leah, an old woman
who was born into slavery. Cleage, then, creates a womanist space where
there is no room for intruders who might want to abuse them and break the
women's achieved harmony. The older sister Sophie always carries her rifle,
and when she is ready to kill her younger sister Minnie's abusive husband,
Ms. Leah counsels her about a better method slave women used to kill abusive
masters and that would prevent her from going to jail. It is Ms Leah, then,
who will help to finish with the abusive intruder's life by preparing a pie
with her *special* secret recipe. Interestingly enough, soon after the death of
Minnie's husband, Minnie gives birth to a baby girl who will continue
strengthening and broadening that womanist tradition already established
in her home. Cleage builds a special female-centered site in *Flyin' West*
through which she redefines the concept of family and kinship. Cleage offers
the image of an extended family of women that actually create a home where
they can feel free and safe, and where they can grow and love each other
without hierarchies. Cleage asserts that with her plays she offers analysis,
establishes a context and clarifies a point of view intended to incite her
audience or readers to action.[57] Continuing the circle of womanist spaces
created by African American women performance artists, *Flyin' West* is a
vital link in the performative circle where contemporary African American
performance artists look to the past for inspiration as they construct new
womanist sites for the present and for the future.

NOTES

1. Pearl Cleage, "Pearl Cleage," *Essence* (September 2003) www.findarticles.com
2. Karen Malpede, "Barbara Ann Teer: An Interview," *Women in Theatre: Compassion & Hope*, ed. Karen Malpede (New York: Drama Book Publishers, 1983), pp. 220–30.
3. Angela Davis, *Women, Culture and Politics* (New York: Vintage, 1990), p. 201.
4. Patricia Liggins Hill, *Call and Response: The Riverside Anthology of the African American Literary Tradition* (Boston and New York: Houghton Mifflin, 1998), p. 1804.
5. See James V. Hatch and Ted Shine (eds.), *Black Theatre USA: Forty-five Plays by Black Americans, 1847–1974* (New York: Free Press, 1974) and *Black Theatre USA: Plays by African Americans*, vol. I, *The Early Period, 1847–1938* (New

York: Free Press, 1996); James Hatch and Leo Hamalian (eds.), *The Roots of African American Drama: An Anthology of Early Plays, 1858–1938* (Detroit: Wayne State University Press, 1991) and *Lost Plays of the Harlem Renaissance 1920–1940* (Detroit: Wayne State University Press, 1996); Kathy A. Perkins (ed.), *Black Female Playwrights: An Anthology of Plays before 1950* (Bloomington: Indiana University Press, 1989); Kathy A. Perkins and Judith Stephens (eds.), *Strange Fruit: Plays on Lynching by American Women* (Bloomington: Indiana University Press, 1998); Elizabeth Brown-Guillory, *Wines in the Wilderness: Plays by African American Women from the Harlem Renaissance to the Present* (Westport, CT: Greenwood Press, 1990).

6. Hill, *Call and Response*, p. 226.
7. Brown-Guillory (ed.), *Wines in the Wilderness*, p. 1.
8. Hill, *Call and Response*, p. 553.
9. Barbara Christian, *Black Feminist Criticism* (New York: Pergamon, 1985), p. 161.
10. Combahee River Collective, "A Black Feminist Statement," *All the Women Are White, All the Blacks Are Men, But Some of Us Are Brave*, ed. Gloria T. Hull, Patricia Bell Scott, and Barbara Smith (New York: Feminist Press, 1982), p. 21.
11. Judith L. Stephens, "The Harlem Renaissance and the New Negro Movement," *The Cambridge Companion to American Women Playwrights*, ed. Brenda Murphy (Cambridge: Cambridge University Press, 1999), p. 100.
12. Judith L. Stephens, "Lynching Dramas and Women: History and Critical Context," *Strange Fruit*, ed. Perkins and Stephens, p. 5.
13. Molara Ogundipe-Leslie, *Re-creating Ourselves. African Women and Critical Transformations* (Trenton, NJ: Africa World Press, 1994), pp. 214–15.
14. Gloria T. Hull, "Researching Alice Dunbar-Nelson: A Personal and Literary Perspective," *All the Women Are White*, ed. Hull *et al.*, p. 193.
15. Lynne Fauley Emery, *Black Dance: From 1619 to Today*, 2nd revised edition (Princeton, NJ: Dance Horizons, Princeton Book Company, 1988), p. vii.
16. Perkins (ed.), *Black Female Playwrights*, p. 16.
17. Brown-Guillory, *Wines*, p. 40.
18. Sandra Richards, "Writing the Absent Potential: Drama, Performance and the Canon of African-American Literature," *The Routledge Reader in Gender and Performance*, ed. Lizbeth Goodman and Jane de Gay (London and New York: Routledge, 1998), p. 156.
19. Barbara Smith quoted in Maggie Humm, *The Dictionary of Feminist Theory* (Upper Saddle River, NJ: Prentice Hall, 1999), p. 26.
20. Christine Gray, "Discovering and Recovering African American Women Playwrights Writing before 1930," *The Cambridge Companion to American Women Playwrights*, ed. Murphy, p. 244.
21. Perkins (ed.), *Black Female Playwrights*, pp. 4–6.
22. Gray, "Discovering and Recovering," p. 244.
23. Hatch and Hamalian (eds.), *The Roots of African American Drama*, p. 30.
24. Whites who mimicked blacks in their performances used burnt cork on their faces and black actors had continued the same custom in minstrelsy.
25. Martha Patterson, "Remaking the Minstrel: Pauline Hopkins's *Peculiar Sam* and the Post-Reconstruction Black Subject," *Black Women Playwrights: Visions of the American Stage*, ed. Carol P. Marsh-Lockett (New York and London: Garland, 1999), pp. 48–9.

26. Ibid., p. 13.

27. Ibid., p. 13.

28. For further information on the representation of old women countering the mammy stereotype, see Trudier Harris, "Before the Strength, the Pain," in *Black Women Playwrights*, ed. Marsh-Lockett.

29. Ann Allen Shockley, *Afro-American Women Writers, 1746–1933: An Anthology and Critical Guide* (New York: Meridian, New American Library, 1989), p. 375.

30. Carol Dawn Allen, *Peculiar Passages: Black Women Playwrights, 1875 to 2000* (New York: Peter Lang, 2005), p. 65.

31. For further information on *othermothering* see Stanlie James, "Mothering," *Theorizing Black Feminisms: The Visionary Pragmatism of Black Women*, ed. Stanlie James and Abena Busia (New York: Routledge, 1994).

32. Allen, *Peculiar Passages*, pp. 62–63.

33. Hatch and Shine (eds.), *Black Theatre USA*, p. 135.

34. Kathy A. Perkins, "The Impact of Lynching on the Art of African American Women," *Strange Fruit*, ed. Perkins and Stephens, p. 16.

35. Quoted in Emery, *Black Dance*, p. 266.

36. For an annotated bibliography on contemporary African American playwrights, see Dana A. Williams, *Contemporary African American Female Playwrights* (Westport, CT: Greenwood Press, 1998).

37. Perkins, "The Impact of Lynching," pp. 17–18.

38. Brown-Guillory, *Wines*, p. 108.

39. Ibid., p. 154.

40. Barbara Lewis, "Ritual Reformulations: Barbara Ann Teer and the National Black Theatre of Harlem (1998)," *A Sourcebook of African-American Performance: Plays, People, Movement*, ed. Annemarie Bean (London and New York: Routledge, 1999), p. 72.

41. Malpede, "Barbara Ann Teer," p. 229.

42. Ntozake Shange, *for colored girls who have considered suicide / when the rainbow is enuf* (New York: Bantam, 1977), p. 67.

43. Sydne Mahone (ed.), Introduction, *Moon Marked and Touched by Sun: Plays by African American Women* (New York: Theater Communications Group, 1994), p. xxv.

44. Ibid., p. 284.

45. WAC, Urban Bush Women Hyperessay. www.walkerart.org/pa/ubw/choeog.html.

46. K. A. Berney, "Suzan-Lori Parks," *Contemporary Dramatists*, ed. K. A. Berney (London: St James, 1994), p. 190.

47. Mahone (ed.), *Moon Marked*, p. 242.

48. Berney, "Suzan-Lori Parks," p. 188.

49. Steven Drukman, "Doo-a-Diddly-Dit-Dit: An Interview with Suzan-Lori Parks (1995)," *A Sourcebook of African-American Performance*, ed. Bean, pp. 284, 297, 298.

50. Ibid., pp. 285, 294.

51. See Kathy A. Perkins and Roberta Uno (eds.), *Contemporary Plays by Women of Color: An Anthology* (London and New York: Routledge, 1996), p. 265.

52. Carol Martin, "The Word Becomes You: An Interview with Anna Deavere Smith (1993)," *A Sourcebook of African-American Performance*, ed. Bean, p. 267.

53. Mahone, Introduction, *Moon Marked*, p. xxxi.
54. James V. Hatch and Ted Shine (eds.), *Black Theatre USA: Plays by African Americans*, vol. II, *The Recent Period: 1935–Today* (New York: Free Press, 1996), p. 492.
55. Perkins and Uno, *Contemporary Plays*, p. 280.
56. Cleage, "Pearl Cleage," p. 46.
57. Ibid., p. 46.

11

DIANNE JOHNSON

African American women writers of children's and young adult literature

There was a time when an entry on children's and young adult literature (both encompassed under the term "children's literature") never would have been included even in a volume such as the *Cambridge Companion to African American Women's Writing*. This was the case because, for a very long time, African American children's and young adult literature has been triply marginalized. There are several reasons for this marginalization – first because it was designed for an audience of children, second, because it is created by African Americans,[1] and third because it has been considered largely women's work. Fortunately, there is a growing group of committed, reputable scholars, both African American and non-African American, and largely female, who are making it their life's work to document the literary history of the long-standing body of children's and young adult literature produced by African American women writers. Rudine Sims Bishop's *Shadow and Substance: Afro American Experience in Contemporary Children's Fiction* (1982) is now a classic. In 1998, *African American Review*, one of the leading scholarly journals in African American literary studies, devoted an issue to children's literature.[2] Michelle Martin's *Brown Gold: Milestones of African-American Children's Picture Books, 1845–2002* is one of the more recent literary histories of this genre. Still, there is little scholarly work that focuses exclusively on black women's writing for children.

The history of black women writing children's literature begins at least as far back as 1887 when Mrs. Amelia Johnson founded an eight-page monthly magazine for children called *The Joy*. In addition, she published the children's novels *Clarence and Corinne, or God's Way* in 1889 and *The Hazeley Family* in 1894. The protagonists in these books, apparently, were European American. These books were published by the white-owned American Baptist Publishing Board. The black-administered National Baptist Publishing Board began its publication program for Negro youth in 1896. Perhaps Amelia Johnson wrote titles for them that have yet to be rediscovered. There is still much recovery to be accomplished.

But how do we talk about Amelia Johnson without talking about Paul Laurence Dunbar's *Little Brown Baby* (1895)? How do we talk about Leila A. Pendleton's *An Alphabet for Negro Children* (date unavailable) without discussing Silas X. Floyd's *Floyd's Flowers, or Duty and Beauty for Colored Children* (1905)? How, and why, do we separate the contributions of W. E. B. Du Bois from the contributions of Jessie Fauset to the pivotal children's magazine *The Brownies' Book* (1920–21)? Unfortunately, these women have been overshadowed. The importance of celebrating women's contributions cannot be overemphasized. Fauset's life and work is a perfect example of how women's work has been devalued over time. A core figure of the Harlem Renaissance, Fauset remains a figure whose name is not recognized nearly to the same extent as writers such as Langston Hughes or Du Bois. So although both African American men and women have been involved in the development of the literature, it is worth giving especial attention to some of the women who might be overlooked in more general explorations.

Some would argue that Jessie Fauset, as one of the editors/managers of *The Brownies' Book* (the children's counterpart to the NAACP's *Crisis*), is one of the people most responsible for the way that African American children's literature has developed over time. This is largely due to her part in formulating the objectives of the magazine. These objectives include goals such as "to make colored children realize that being 'colored' is a normal beautiful thing," "to make them familiar with the history and achievements of the Negro race," and "to teach them delicately a code of honor and action in their relations with white children."[3]

These objectives are simultaneously astounding and obvious. For example, consider how sad it is that someone had to articulate the thought that our bodies, our own skins, are normal and beautiful. But more to the point, how sad it is that the objectives outlined in 1920 are still entirely relevant in the early twenty-first century. In fact, the spirit of most of the objectives has never changed substantively, regardless of who was articulating them. It is interesting, for instance, to note that a group organized in the early 1970s, Black Creators for Children, wrote what they called a manifesto which explicated their motivations for doing the work in which they were engaged. These motivations are similar to those of *The Brownies' Book* creators in many ways. For example, the Black Creators identified collectivity as one of the principles of African struggle and liberation – a struggle in which they saw children's books playing a major role. They related their work to this principle this way: "The work should help the child establish a positive image of African people throughout the world, so that he can develop a positive sense of self as an individual who participates responsibly in the building and maintaining of his immediate family and community, and of his African community as a whole."[4] So clearly, Jessie Fauset and *The Brownies' Book* are important in being one of the first people and first publications to put some of these central, lasting ideas into writing and practice – ideas that show up again and again over the years.

Children's literature is a unique art form. It is a highly collaborative form that often includes both words and visual images. Unfortunately, there are not many contemporary black female picture-book illustrators. Some notable ones are Pat Cummings, Melodye Rosales, Jan Spivey Gilchrist, Carole Byard, Synthia Saint James, Michelle Wood, and Veronique Tadjo. Quilt artist Faith Ringgold's work is especially intriguing in that she has translated her story-quilts, with stories written right on the fabric, into the picture-book form. Aminah Brenda Lynn Robinson's *A Street Called Home* is a completely original creation that documents the lives of individuals that make up an actual Ohio community. But Ringgold, Robinson, and the others are only eight names in an American publishing industry that releases over five thousand children's books each year. I can only speculate on the reasons for this dearth of black female book artists. But there is every reason to think that this situation is related, again, to this idea of women's work. One way that writing becomes women's work is that it is an activity that is possible, that is do-able. One needs monies to attend art school, but the only materials necessary to write are pencil and paper. But whether writing or creating visual art, one needs time and a certain appreciation for the value of artistic production. The cultural, racial, and economic intersections are clear: Upper-class women (often white), have the required leisure time often not available to uneducated, working-class, black women.

Obviously, there are still gender-related issues that need to be addressed to continue changing the landscape of American children's literature in relationship to writers and artists of color. This was one of the goals of Jessie Fauset and *The Brownies' Book* almost a century ago. Recognizing the importance of visual images and the ways in which African Americans were represented (and misrepresented) in popular culture, it was the policy of the magazine to use the art of black artists whenever possible. They considered this their contribution to the development of "modern Negro art." So the artists listed above are the artistic descendants of women such as Laura Wheeler Waring and Hilda Rue Wilkinson, whose art was published regularly in *The Brownies' Book*. Their representations of black people depicted them with authenticity and with dignity.

This basic issue of representation has been an ongoing one. And it has not been uncomplicated. For instance, as far back as *The Brownies' Book* African American communities have been struggling with concerns such as color stratification and hair texture that raise questions of class and aesthetics: what is beautiful? Who is beautiful? Who defines beauty? How is it commodified? One of the classic books that address these issues is Camille Yarbrough's *Cornrows* (1979), which poetically connects black Americans' ways of caring for and styling their hair with their African ancestry and their history across continents. Natasha Tarpley's *I Love My Hair* (1998) is another title in what is now almost a subgenre about black hair. Also at issue, unfortunately, is the idea of blackness itself. Dinah Johnson's *Black Magic* (2008) is a meditation on that color/idea. Eleanora Tate's *Thank You Dr. Martin Luther King, Jr!* (1990) and Sharon Flake's *The Skin I'm In* (1998) are recent books that deal head on with young female characters who are uncomfortable with their dark skin complexions. Both issues come together in Carolivia Herron's *Nappy Hair* (1997) which caused the biggest controversy in the past twenty years in the children's book publishing world.

Meant by the author as a celebration of nappy hair, the book embodies a host of mixed messages. Why, a young reader might wonder, do the angels consider nappy hair so negative that they would plead with God not to bestow it upon the little girl in the story? Why would the (personified) nap be sitting in Africa waiting to be enslaved and go to America? The problematic questions do not stop there. On the positive side, Herron's call-and-response structured text is a beautiful example of that cultural form. The text is full of rhythm and energy and a certain kind of authenticity. Part of the problem with its public reception was, in fact, its authenticity – the extent to which it aired dirty laundry, exposing for any and all readers the kinds of discussions about hair that go on in many black families. But given the sensitivity of the subject matter, Joe Cepeda never should have been chosen as the illustrator. His artistic style is too close to caricature for comfort and the images are disastrously close to the buffoon-like stereotypes of the early twentieth century. Clearly, the *Nappy Hair* controversy raises countless issues that are in some way central in any discussion of black children's literature, particularly issues of representation and authenticity.

Some have argued for African American children's literature that is positive and counteracts the negative stereotypes of the past, images dating back before the era referred to as "The All-White World of Children's Books," the title of a 1965 *Saturday Review of Books* article by Nancy Larrick. But there is quite a difference between writing that is positive and writing that is authentic, though they are not necessarily mutually exclusive. The desire for material that is positive is understandable. But the consequences must be considered. Taken too far, can relating only positive stories and representations result in sugar-coating? And can sugar-coating be just as harmful, in the final analysis, as the negative images? Authenticity, on the other hand, is more interesting, more complicated, and more honest. And I think this is what many people mean when they say they want positive images.

One of the women most instrumental in changing the "all-white world of children's books" was Augusta Baker (1911–98). She began her career with the New York Public Library (NYPL) in 1934 at the Harlem Branch on 135th Street and spent the last thirteen years, 1961–74, as Coordinator of Children's Services for the entire NYPL system. Along with other library professionals, she was instrumental in convincing editors and publishing houses to broaden their lists of authors and illustrators, to do more than darken existing illustrations, without changing the stories. One of the undertakings that Augusta Baker is remembered for is her publication *The Black Experience in Children's Books* (earlier entitled *Books about Negro Life for Children*). Inclusive of titles by both black and non-black authors and illustrators, Baker eventually appended a list identifying them by race because parents, teachers, and others who used the bibliography wanted to know the racial identities, one might suppose, in order to guarantee authenticity, to some extent. In choosing books, and not having time to read every book in full before purchase, people use clues as to the value of any particular book. One clue to the value, in terms of authenticity, is the background of the artist. People are making a bet that a book written by a black writer, about black hair, is somehow "better" or more authentic than one by someone not of the represented culture.

Another cue/clue that people are looking for when selecting children's books is award seals. The major awards for American children's literature are the Caldecott Medal (for distinguished art in a picture book) and the Newbery Medal (for authors of the most distinguished American books for children). Both of these honors are bestowed by the powerful and prestigious American Library Association. Awarding since 1922, the American Library Association did not award a Newbery Medal to an African American writer until 1975 when the incomparable Virginia Hamilton won for *M.C. Higgins, the Great*. Two years later in 1977, the remarkable writer Mildred Taylor won for *Roll of Thunder, Hear My Cry*. A black writer did not win the Newbery again until 2000, when Christopher Paul Curtis won for *Bud, Not Buddy*. The problem is evident; work by African American writers is recognized much too infrequently.

Because of the lack of recognition for writers and illustrators of African American children's literature, the Coretta Scott King Award was established in 1969 largely due to the efforts of African American librarians Glyndon Greer and Mabel McKissick, among others. Winning this award has helped to launch the careers of many notable African American writers and illustrators. In 1995, the CSK committee began giving the John Steptoe Award for

New Talent, recognizing books by writers and illustrators just starting out in the field. There are arguments for and against awards: they can become political in nature, they lead people to believe that the winners are the only worthy books any given year. And the arguments go on. But it is undeniable that they make a difference to those selecting books and to those making profits from the books that get attention.

The Coretta Scott King Award is not the only important recognition in the development of African American children's literature. The Council on Interracial Books for Children has been at the forefront of activism in the world of children's books. They began their annual writers' contest in 1969. Among their winners are Kristin Hunter, author of *The Soul Brothers and Sister Lou* (1968), a bold statement during the Black Arts era; Sharon Bell Mathis, author of *Listen for the Fig Tree* (1974), an early celebration of Kwanzaa; and Mildred Taylor, author of the *Roll of Thunder* series, dealing with issues of land ownership, class, education, and more. Taylor went on to win the Newbery and other prestigious awards. In fact, Taylor's *Song of the Trees*, which won the CIBC writers' contest, was the genesis of the series. Contests such as this have always been important as they often highlight new or emerging talent.

In addition to the contest, the goals of the Interracial Council on Books for Children are important. In addition to supporting multicultural literature, they also addressed the issue of sexism in children's books forcefully through their publication, *The Bulletin of the Council on Interracial Books for Children*.[5] The importance of organizations such as CIBC putting in written form their philosophies, in relation to race or gender or other concerns, cannot be overemphasized. Likewise, the support systems and networks formed through these organizations are invaluable. Black Creators for Children is a case in point. One of their stated objectives was "[t]o provide a forum and resource center for the exchange of ideas and to facilitate the coordination of talents among writers, illustrators, and other members of the black community concerned with literature and arts for black children."[6] Some of those "other members" are people such as librarians and editors and publishers. Almost everyone who participated in this group, including the late Tom Feelings and the late James Haskins, went on to make considerable contributions to the world of children's literature. But two members in particular who deserve note especially in the context of black women and African American children's literature are Bernette Ford and Cheryl Willis Hudson. Bernette Ford went on to become one of the few editors of African American descent working in the field of children's literature. She had a long career with Scholastic Books and has gone on to found her own company, Color-bridge Books. Cheryl Hudson, along with husband Wade Hudson, became the founder of the only truly successful independent publishing house of books for African American children, Just Us Books. An individual such as Andrea Davis Pinkney, member of the Jerry Pinkney family dynasty, successful writer and powerful children's book editor/publisher (few of whom are African American) stands upon their shoulders. In addition to writers, illustrators, editors, and publishers, there are black women who are activists in other ways. The indefatigable Toni Trent Parker is the founder of Black Books Galore, an organization that promotes black children in any way possible, whether through publishing guides to the literature, sponsoring reading clubs, or holding massive literature festivals in major cities around the United States.

One other organization that deserves mention is the Children's Defense Fund (CDF), the vision of founder Marian Wright Edelman. At the CDF meeting site at the Former Alex Haley Farm in Clinton, Tennessee, the organization has established the Langston Hughes Library, whose mission is intimately related to the preserving and promoting of African American children's literature. To that end, Edelman hopes to use the resources of her organization to design and support continuous programming relating to black children's literature. These efforts include retreats for African American writers and illustrators of children's books, book festivals for families, readings, other special events, and roundtables that bring together artists, scholars, teachers, librarians, publishing professionals, and others who are child advocates. The Library itself has the goal of becoming the leading repository of African American and African diaspora children's literature in the world.

Clearly, without women's work and women's vision, there would be no African American children's literature. One reason that the efforts of Marian Wright Edelman and the Children's Defense Fund's efforts are significant is because of the organization's mission, which is, in part, "to ensure every child a Healthy Start, a Head Start, a Fair Start, a Safe Start, and a Moral Start in life." This is so important because if a child is not healthy or safe, it is next to impossible for her to concentrate on reading a book, let alone be fully engaged in or inspired by literature. And too often, we do not consider the total child.

At the same time, there has been an emphasis, throughout the history of black children's literature, on the self-esteem of children. While self-esteem is important, and outstanding children's literature can enhance the self-esteem of young readers, building self-esteem should not be the reason that black children read black children's literature. They should read it, as well, to enjoy outstanding art and what it has to offer – illumination, interpretation, inspiration, exploration, education, and the joy to be gotten from enjoying the power and magic of words. All of the women mentioned in this chapter cared about the quality of African American children's literature. Their efforts support the creation, dissemination, and celebration of that quality literature. And they do this by wearing many hats.

Cheryl Hudson, Toni Trent Parker, and Marian Wright Edelman, for example, are not only activists on various levels, but authors as well. Through their writing, they have become part of a long line of African American women who have devoted at least part of their professional lives to creating literature for young people. Interestingly, many of the pioneers in the field usually thought of as writers of adult titles, as well as contemporary writers such as Toni Morrison and Marilyn Nelson, also write for children. This fact is significant because it suggests that African American writers have recognized for a long time that the separation between children's and adult literature is, in some ways, artificial; that a good story is a good story. Furthermore, they recognize the power and function of literature to accomplish certain objectives, such as the revising of histories that have been mistold. Thus, African American children's literature is full of biographies of historical figures and reexaminations of historical eras and events.

One of these early writers is Ann Petry, known for her best-selling adult novel, *The Street* (1946); she is also the author of several books for young readers, including a few biographies and the memorable *Tituba of Salem Village* (1955). This was bold historical fiction, exploring the life of a native Barbadian woman who found herself implicated in the Salem witch trials. Petry confronts some of the most complex, often misunderstood, issues of culture and identity politics. Who decides who belongs? Who defines the outsider, and what role does race play? More specifically, what is a witch? How do issues of gender play into this definition? How do the ideas of witchcraft and blackness relate to each other?

In addition to raising these kinds of issues, Petry's book also makes clear that the experiences of peoples of various parts of the African diaspora are intimately related. This is a thread that runs through the entire history of black children's literature, beginning with the Africentric perspectives represented in *The Brownies' Book*, through the picture books of Lucille Clifton. Her character Everett Anderson says in *Some of the Days of Everett Anderson* (1970), "I already know where Africa is / and I already know how to count to ten. / I went to school every day last year. / Why do I have to go again?"[7] For him, as it should be for all African American children, knowledge of Africa is just as basic as arithmetic. Consciousness of Africa runs through the novels of Rosa Guy, to Merle Hodge's *For the Life of Laetitia* (1993), to Simi Beford's *Yoruba Girl Dancing* (1992), Jaira Placide's *Fresh Girl* (2002), and Edwidge Danticat's *Behind the Mountains* (2002). These women do not romanticize the diaspora or relationships between black peoples from various parts of the world. Rosa Guy's trilogy, which includes *The Friends* (1973), *Edith Jackson* (1978), and *Ruby* (1979), is a case in point, exploring the deep and profound tensions between West Indians and US black people in the multicultural New York City.

Geography is important not only in the context of the African diaspora but within the United States itself. The southern US has been very important to African Americans. Mildred Taylor is perhaps the black woman writer most associated with exploring black experiences in the southern states. Her unforgettable Cassie Logan is one of the strongest young female protagonists in the history of American children's literature. Her family's struggle to keep their land is at the foundation of the entire series revolving around them. The stories are that much more poignant when readers know that the written stories are based upon the storytelling of Taylor's actual family, especially her father David. The stories are inclusive of the lives of generations, both well before and after the civil rights movement – a movement that is important to people the world over. And Taylor's writing is important to people world-wide. In the 2002 novel *Fresh Girl* by Haitian writer Jaira Placide, the main character, an aspiring writer herself, opens the book she's reading, *Roll of Thunder, Hear My Cry* by Taylor: "Jilline's grandfather saved it especially for me to read. Mr. Hunter is a retired policeman and works at the Flatbush public library."[8] Mildred Taylor's stories address issues such as family relationships, Jim Crow, education, land ownership, responsibility to community, and more. And they clearly establish the South as a kind of homeland/sacred site for black Americans and others.

The traditional journey in African American literature is from south to north, from slavery to freedom. Many black women writers of literature for young people have done a magnificent job of documenting this journey. Joyce Hansen comes to mind immediately. Though she writes engaging, appealing contemporary fiction that has stayed in print for decades, her historical fiction is exceptional. At least one of her books, *The Captive* (1994), originates in Africa. And her *African Princess: The Amazing Lives of Africa's Royal Women* (2004) is luscious in both language and visual images. But her particular expertise rests in the history of slavery – the Underground Railroad, Reconstruction. One of her most beautiful and, as always, meticulously researched books is *I Thought My Soul Would Rise and Fly: The Diary of Patsy, a Freed Girl* (2005), part of Scholastic's "Dear America" series. It asks all of the questions about what happens on that journey toward freedom, both physically and psychologically. Do we make the journey northward? Do we choose new names? The main character, Patsy, in fact, decides to name herself partly after Phillis Wheatley, one of the first African American women of letters.

Another of Hansen's books, *Breaking Ground, Breaking Silence: The Story of New York's African Burial Ground* (1998), reminds readers not to idealize the North, just as they should not idealize Africa. As many forget, or never know, the North was not always a place of freedom. There is a history of legal slavery in the northern states and after the passage of the Fugitive Slave Law of 1850, any black person said to be an escaped slave could be arrested and released to the custody of the claimant. Co-authored by the Howard University archeologist who excavated the site, *Breaking Ground, Breaking Silence* recovers an important historical moment and complicates our understandings of what the North and South stood for, what freedom means, and how the black people buried on that site lived their everyday lives.

The geographical area not often associated with black people is the American West. But writers such as Mildred Pitts Walter, Angela Johnson, and especially Joyce Carol Thomas have written poignant stories set there. Johnson's *Toning the Sweep* comes to mind immediately. It recounts the journey of a grandmother figure from the South, after the death of her husband during the civil rights movement, to Little Rock, California. The echoes of the movement are clear, yet Ola experiences a new kind of freedom in the West. Interesting, too, is the fact that she arrives in the West driving her red convertible. This is a major symbolic revision, as cars and physical mobility are usually identified with men. Women in black literature have often journeyed psychologically, rather than physically, because of various restrictions, including children. But Angela Johnson and her character Ola give a new model, on this count and others.

Joyce Carol Thomas is a highly underrated writer of fiction, poetry, and drama. She is a successful anthologist as well; *A Gathering of Flowers: Stories about Being Young in America* is a rich collection of multicultural young adult literature and *Linda Brown, You Are Not Alone: The Brown v. Board of Education Decision* commemorates the fiftieth anniversary of that judgment, in the voices of writers from various backgrounds. One of her unique contributions, related to the western setting of much of her work, is her exploration of the bonds between African Americans and Native Americans. Another wonderful contribution is her novel *When the Nightingale Sings*, a revision of the Cinderella story. This is notable because she makes the story her own, transforming the Cinderella character into a gospel singer and the prince character into a suitor who is attracted to her because of what he can tell about her spirit through hearing her voice. Thomas's story is not about being saved by a prince charming on a white horse. It is about human connections and spirituality. Hers is a truly successful example of creating something original out of a universal, ages-old ur-text rather than making an uninspired imitation of a story that says nothing about

African American culture. Of course, there is much diversity in the experiences of Africans in America and her work is a testament to this.

Other writers too, such as Rosa Guy, have been instrumental in complicating our thinking about blackness in more sophisticated ways. For example, people often use the term "the black experience," implying that all black people are alike, denying the multiple dimensions of our experiences. Guy's novel *The Music of Summer* is a powerful analysis of class dynamics in black American communities, asking questions about how socio-economic status, educational status, skin color, and other factors affect not only our lives in this society as a whole, but our interactions with each other. Language, too, is one of these issues that creates and exacerbates various tensions. Some readers are not always comfortable with literature whose characters speak in language that is "in character." Specifically, some might object to the use of black English (AAVE/African American Vernacular English) in fiction. But honest writers such as the prolific and accomplished Lucille Clifton have their characters speak in the language that is realistic to their circumstances and appropriate to various contexts.

Language raises questions of both literature and literacy. Some would suggest that children learn how to read and write most effectively, and gain a greater degree of satisfaction from the literature, when working with their own vernacular grammars and lexicons. And black English, like all languages, has its own aesthetic power and a long tradition within the history of African American literature. June Jordan's *His Own Where* (1971) is perhaps one of the earliest examples of a young adult novel written completely in black English, part artistic statement and part political statement. Lucille Clifton's standpoint on the language is simply that she creates literature, not grammar books.[9] These questions are becoming more and more vital to ask in the twenty-first century, as the gap between the haves and the "have nots" is increasing and some of the gains of the civil rights movement are eroding. Young African Americans need new, broader, more sophisticated understandings of "literacy," inclusive of technological and cultural literacies – how to read and negotiate the world.

Children's literature written by African American women has always confronted hard issues. Issues such as slavery, the civil rights movement, education, and family ties are the foundation of the literature. But there is a whole subgenre that might be called contemporary realism, or perhaps more accurately, urban realism. The genesis of this category goes back at least to the 1973 publication of Alice Childress's *A Hero Ain't Nothin' But a Sandwich*, which dealt with the subject of teenage drug abuse, a topic that was still somewhat taboo in young adult literature at that time. Told through the alternating voices of several characters including the young addict, his mother, his teacher, and others, the book is an in-depth, sensitive exploration of the situation. Childress's *Rainbow Jordan* (1981) dealt with foster children, yet another important social issue. As the decades have passed, attitudes about what is considered appropriate subject matter for both children's and young adult literature have expanded enormously. For example, Jacqueline Woodson's *Visiting Day* is a children's picture book about a child visiting her father in prison. For older readers, she has written *I Hadn't Meant to Tell You This*, which deals with issues of incest and abuse as well as interracial friendship. Her novel *From the Notebooks of Melanin Sun* chronicles a young boy's dealing with his mother's lesbian relationship. Angela Johnson's *First Part Last* is about a teenage father who is raising his infant daughter. Hope Anita Smith's *The Way a Door Closes* deals with a family abandoned by the father. Rita Williams-Garcia's *Like Sisters on the Homefront* begins with a mother forcing her teenage daughter, already a mother, to have an abortion. Sharon Draper, a former high school teacher whose writing career soared after winning a writing contest and a Coretta Scott King new talent award, is, arguably, the queen of contemporary African American young adult literature. At the 2004 CSK Award Breakfast, she shared a letter from a young fan who wrote, in part, "I just wanted to let you know how reading your books has changed my life. You make me think before I do stupid stuff." Clearly, the landscape of children's and young adult literature is vast, diverse, constantly expanding, and making a real difference to real readers. In addition to the deserving writers who have gone unnamed in this chapter are new voices such as Hope Anita Smith, Janet McDonald, Brenda Woods, and others we will come to know in the future.

Diverse, too, is the range of literary styles/forms in which black women writing for children create. African American children's literature includes fiction, biography, short stories, and drama. Nikki Grimes creates a fresh form with a book such as *Bronx Masquerade*, a novel told through a combination of poetry and narrative, and perhaps most importantly, celebrates the power of words and writing. The body of work that comprises African American children's and young adult literature encompasses history, historical fiction, and contemporary realism as well. In the late 1970s and early 1980s, the prolific and versatile Rosa Guy experimented with a form that has not been employed often by black women writers for children with her series of mysteries centered around the character Imamu Jones. The first book in the series, *The Disappearance* (1979), is dedicated to Louise Meriwether, author of the classic *Daddy Was a Number Runner* (1971), set in Harlem as are Guy's books.

The pioneer Virginia Hamilton, as part of her expansive body of work, even wrote science fiction (the Justice trilogy is made up of *Justice and Her*

Brothers, Dustland, and *The Gathering*) and fantasy; there is nothing like her diasporic, folkloric, fantastic, epic novel *The Magical Adventures of Pretty Pearl*. Practically creating a language of her own in some of her books, Hamilton is one of the black women writers for young people who absolutely understands and communicates the essence, if there is such a thing, of African American heritage and heart. In addition to other recognitions, she was the first American writer for children honored with the lucrative, no strings attached MacArthur Foundation Award, given to people from every discipline whose work is seminal, cutting edge, and simply exceptional. Angela Johnson is the other African American female writer who has won this award.

An equally prolific and accomplished writer is Patricia McKissack (who often collaborates with her husband Fred). Perhaps more than any other writer for children and young adults, McKissack deserves recognition for the sheer volume (and sustained quality) of her body of work, which numbers over one hundred titles. Her books cover the entirety of black history through biographies, historical fiction, and non-fiction. Her body of writing includes picture books, folklore, Bible stories, and even science. Like the title of her hilarious and insightful *The-Honest-to-Goodness Truth*, Patricia McKissack's life's work has been to tell the truth, as fully as possible, about African American experience across time, place, and perspective.

Black women writers for young people have created an incredible, enduring tradition. Among their subject matter, not surprisingly, are the life stories of other black women, writers as well as those whose lives followed other paths. Two noteworthy books by accomplished author Tonya Bolden exemplify what could almost be called a preoccupation. *The Book of African American Women: 150 Crusaders, Creators, and Uplifters* as well as *33 Things Every Girl Should Know: Stories, Songs, Poems, and Smart Talk by 33 Extraordinary Women* are significant contributions to the tradition. And indeed it is a tradition. In Angela Johnson's *Toning the Sweep*, teenaged Emily, the protagonist, says this about her grandmother's community of chosen family: "I think about how everybody Ola knows here has a story. Daddy says that everybody has one and their stories are all a part of us."[10] The tradition of black women writing for children and young adults is a testimony to that thinking and an acknowledgement and celebration of as many stories as can be told. It is a testament, too, to being part of a community of African American people and other African American women writers. In an essay entitled "Feminist Discourse/Maternal Discourse: Speaking With Two Voices," Marianne Hirsch points out the significance of critic Mary Helen Washington's foregrounding the "connection between the black woman writer's sense of herself as part of a link in generations of women, and her decision to write."[11] The black woman writer is part of a family, in terms of family and community, and also in the context of literary history.

In yet another book inscribed by one black women writer to another, the soulful and celebrated Eloise Greenfield opens her classic volume *Honey I Love* with an epigraph from Sharon Bell Mathis's *Teacup Full of Roses*: "It's a love place. A real black love place." The title poem ends with the words "But I love / I love a lot of things, a whole lot of things / And honey, / I love you, too."[12] Black women writers love their readers. This means that they are honest in spirit, meticulous in their research, responsible in their intentions, hopeful for their readers' lives, and masterful in their artistry. They understand the power of children's literature. For even in this age of technology, most children acquire the skills of reading and writing, as well as a degree of cultural literacy from children's and young adult books. They are confident that through their writing, young people will come to love – in a profound way – a lot of things, a lot of experiences. It is no exaggeration to say that the tradition of black women writers for children and young adults is created from and resides in a love place. How fortunate for both American and international literatures.

NOTES

1. The definition of African American children's literature is a contested one. Some scholars argue that this category includes literature written by people not of African descent but which is grounded in an African American cultural or historical context. For the purposes of this chapter, the term African American children's literature refers only to children's literature written by black people. This said, there are certain exceptions. For example, Diane Dillon, who is European American, has illustrated classic African American picture books in collaboration with her African American husband, Leo Dillon.
2. Dianne Johnson (ed.), *African American Review* (Spring 1998).
3. Dianne Johnson-Feelings (ed.), *The Best of The Brownies' Book* (New York: Oxford University Press, 1996), p. 337.
4. Black Creators Archives, 1976, unpublished.
5. Beryl Banfield, "Commitment to Change: The Council on Interracial Books for Children and the World of Children's Books," *African American Review* (Spring 1998).
6. www.justusbooks.com/tips/page 15b_tips.html (unpublished elsewhere)
7. Lucille Clifton, *Some of the Days of Everett Anderson* (New York: Henry Holt, 1987).
8. Jaira Placide, *Fresh Girl* (New York: Wendy Lamb Books, 2002), p. 35.
9. Personal communication.
10. Amelia Johnson, *Toning the Sweep* (New York: Orchard, 1993), p. 17.
11. Marianne Hirsch, "Feminist Discourse/Maternal Discourse: Speaking with Two Voices," *Mother/Daughter Plot: Narrative, Psychoanalysis, Feminism* (Bloomington: Indiana University Press, 1989), p. 176.
12. Eloise Greenfield, *Honey, I Love* (New York: Crown, 1978), unpaged.

12

MARILYN SANDERS MOBLEY

African American women essayists

To read the earliest essays of African American women writers is to discover that black women have always been keenly aware of the radical power of the word to transform their own lives and those of their community. It is perhaps no surprise that many of them chose the essay as the genre that would best enable them to address their concerns – be they spiritual, social, or political – in the public sphere. The first question that comes to mind, of course, is why would women of African heritage on American soil choose the essay rather than other available genres for putting pen to paper? There is no single answer to this question because the realities that propelled each woman to write and to choose the essay as the medium to communicate her ideas were varied. It could be argued, however, that the genre of the essay, by its very nature, connects an author with an audience through some stated issue of importance, with an expressed goal of engaging that audience through public discourse on paper about that issue in a way that invokes a response from the community of readers. It could further be argued, that the ways in which black women had been silenced, marginalized, and denied a voice in the public sphere, by both black men and white people of both genders, made the essay a convenient mode of subverting and circumventing the power of those who were otherwise not open to their thoughts and ideas. African American women could write their speeches and essays, sometimes in words excerpted from their own journals, diaries, and letters, not only to give voice to their thoughts and ideas, but also to express the breadth and depth of those ideas without the literary concerns that fiction, poetry, drama or other forms of *belles lettres* might create for them. Free from having to embellish their ideas through language and structures particular to other genres, black women chose the essay to employ the power of the word in a more direct unencumbered way for their audiences. The essay, then, was a liberating genre for African American women writers – a genre where they had freedom of expression and where their radical and sometimes revolutionary ideas could have full sway. Indeed, the essay has had and continues to have an appeal for a number of African American women writers as the best genre for their spiritual, intellectual, political, and cultural work. As literary and cultural critic Carla Peterson discovered, a number of early black women activists sought through public speaking and writing to be "doers of the word," by using their own words and the Bible – that is, the word of God – to inform, teach and persuade.[1] Thus, many black women writers considered the essay to be one of the most effective genres for addressing many of the realities with which black people, in general, and black women, in particular, in America and throughout the African diaspora have had to contend.

The expository power of this non-fiction genre has enabled even some of the best-known fiction writers, such as Zora Neale Hurston, Alice Walker, and Toni Morrison, to articulate some of their concerns more directly in the public sphere than they could through the art of fiction. Unfortunately, the essay as a genre was once significantly overshadowed by other literary genres, and essays written by African American women were once neglected while those written by African American men (such as Richard Wright, Ralph Ellison, and James Baldwin, in particular) were more widely anthologized and, thus, better known. Tracing the use of the essay from some of its earliest nineteenth-century practitioners – such as Maria Stewart and Anna Julia Cooper – to some of its most recent exemplars such as bell hooks and Julianne Malveaux, we discover the power of the word in one of its most provocative forms, and we can map the ways in which the tendency to neglect this genre has gradually been corrected both in and outside of the academy. As Beverly Guy-Sheftall asserts in *Words of Fire: An Anthology of African American Feminist Thought*, we now know that whether the women actually identified themselves as feminists or not, their expressed concerns, particularly at the intersection of race and gender, reveal that there has been "a continuous feminist intellectual tradition in the nonfictional prose of African American women."[2] Sometimes the work of African American women essayists has complemented that of African American male essayists. At other times, their work has consciously filled in gaps, spoken back to, and negated the misrepresentations of black women found in the texts of others, be they black men, white men, white women, or others. Indeed, in the writing of African American women essayists, we see the ways in which they have been engaged in their own personal and collective struggle against oppression in all its interlocking forms. Moreover, an overview of the essays written by black women reveals the intellectual and rhetorical power that these texts have had and continue to have influencing communities, the nation, and the world in nearly every area of life one might imagine.

Understanding language as social action, African American women have used the non-fiction genre of the essay as a site of resistance where they could experience self-empowerment as authors, intellectuals, cultural workers, and freedom fighters in their own right. To venture into the world of African American women essayists is to discover a form where black women initially reflected on their religious conversions to Christianity, the development of their faith, and the connection between their spiritual lives and the situation of black people in America. As is the case with most formerly enslaved Africans who first gained access to literacy through first hearing and then reading the Bible, black women employed the essay to tell their own personal stories of faith and conversion to the religion of the slaveholder. What these early essays, framed through the lens of faith, reveal, however, is that these women did not possess a blind faith that made them oblivious to the plight of their people. Instead, their faith empowered and emboldened them both to speak truth to power by protesting enslavement, oppression, and discrimination, and by inspiring others to join them. With their faith as a kind of moral compass for the rightness of their arguments, the early essayists confronted the difficult topics of their day using both the requisite literary style of the sentimental era and the tone that their situation demanded. Over time, the more overt religious sentiments that grounded the early essays dropped away as more secular frameworks began to shape black women's arguments for the public sphere. By the late twentieth and early twenty-first centuries, however, the pendulum swings back to sacred concerns, making space for such religious scholar/activists as Katie Geneva Cannon. Nevertheless, regardless of where they locate their arguments on the sacred–secular continuum or on the continuum between protest and affirmation, African American women writers have found in the essay a unique vehicle for expressing their responses to the social and political realities of pivotal moments such as slavery, Reconstruction, and the civil rights movement in American history.

As the first American woman to lecture in public on political issues to racially mixed audiences, Maria Stewart (1803–79) is recognized as the first African American woman writer to use the essay. In her essay "Religion and the Pure Principle of Morality, the Sure Foundation on Which We Must Build" (1831), she quickly shares the story of her own birth and early childhood, her thirst for knowledge, her education at Sabbath Schools, her short marriage and subsequent life as a widow, her conversion to Christianity, and her public confession of faith. Though her essay begins with the autobiographical information sometimes associated with the slave narratives, which recent scholars have asserted should be renamed "emancipatory narratives," she shifts to direct her comments to her fellow Africans.[3] Reminding them that they are formed and fashioned in the image of God and therefore endowed with "reason and strong powers of intellect" (p. 29), she also reminds her readers of the African diaspora that the God she worships is able to protect her from her enemies, especially those who would rise up against her for speaking her mind. In the body of her essay, she directs her comments to "daughters of Africa" (p. 30), imploring them to awake and arise that they may be virtuous women, loving wives, and responsible mothers of future generations. At one point she even advises: "Let every female heart become united, and let us raise a fund ourselves; and at the end of the one year and a half, we might lay the corner-stone for the building of a High School, that the higher branches of knowledge might be enjoyed by us" (p. 37). Focusing first on what African women and men in America can do to change their own circumstances rather than on what America should do to desist from its ill-treatment of them, the essay admonishes her people, saying "if no one will promote or respect us, let us promote and respect ourselves" (p. 37). The essay then shifts to a long prayer about the spiritual battlefield at hand and to the political landscape on which black people find themselves in the space between their African past and their present moment as enslaved persons. Alternating between two audiences – Africans in America and the white Americans who were denying black people the rights of liberty and the pursuit of education, economic independence, and the means to shape their own destinies – as early as 1831, Maria Stewart inaugurated a powerful tradition of black women essay writers. This tradition was informed by the black jeremiad used by such activist preachers as David Walker addressing instead the particular needs and responsibilities of black women. Using the language and rhetorical style of the Bible with which her audiences were familiar, she employed the essay subversively to challenge both the oppressor and the oppressed. As a result, she used biblical discourse in ways that those who introduced the community of the enslaved to Christianity could never have predicted.

Two other early African American women essayists of note – Jarena Lee (1783–1849) and Charlotte Forten (1837–1914) – both illustrate the ways in which women navigated the challenging space between their private lives and the public sphere in the nineteenth century. Lee, often regarded as the first African Methodist Episcopal (AME) preacher, narrates in her spiritual auto-biographical work – *The Life and Religious Experience of Jarena Lee* (1836) and *The Religious Experience and Journal of Mrs. Jarena Lee* (1849) – the story of her religious conversion and calling to preach and her frustration with church hierarchical structures that sought to contain her calling. Although Bishop Richard Allen supported her ministry and invited her to join him from time to time on the preaching circuit, he did not advocate for her to be ordained. Thus, because ordination was withheld from her and other women, her ministry was first delayed and then practiced outside the boundaries of the organized structure of the AME church. As an evangelist and itinerant preacher, therefore, her essay writing created a space for her commentary on women's rights and the unequal practices of the church. Charlotte Forten was married to a minister – Rev. Francis Grimke – and though she is more often recognized as a poet, she was also an abolitionist and essayist, whose essay "Life in the Sea Islands" (1864) provides an example of the somewhat distant ethnographic gaze of a black woman who had been born free. Writing at first from the liminal space between black and white communities, she later takes a strong interest, both as a teacher and advocate for teachers, in the education of the newly freed African American community and begins writing about the education activities of the Freedmen's Bureau. Both Lee and Forten produced essays that reveal the ways in which African American women's letters, diaries, journals, and sermons were safe spaces to express their deepest concerns and to shape public opinion.

At the end of the nineteenth century and Reconstruction, the essays of black women writers began to reflect the changing situation and concerns of African American people. The hybrid nature of earlier texts – with their combined focus on the personal spiritual journeys of the author and the freedom struggle of black people – gave way to essays that focused solidly and more stridently, not just on the social, educational, and political needs of the newly freed communities of formerly enslaved people, but also on the particular needs of women. Nowhere is this changing focus more apparent than in the essays of Anna Julia Cooper (1858–1964), whose *A Voice from the South* (1892) is one of the most important documents of the African American literary and womanist traditions. In fact, many scholars refer to Cooper's book-length collection of essays as the first black feminist text, best represented by her now famous statement of feminist advocacy, "Only the BLACK WOMAN can say 'when and where I enter, in the quiet, undisputed dignity of my womanhood, without violence and without suing or special patronage, then and there the whole *Negro race enters with me*'" (p. 31). Significantly, Cooper's analysis of black life in America at the intersection of race and gender at the end of one century and at the dawn of another was as prophetic as W. E. B. Du Bois's *The Souls of Black Folk* (1903), with its compelling analysis of race and society.[4] Taking on racism, sexism, and even American imperialism, Cooper boldly challenged interlocking forms of oppression. In her introduction to the Schomburg Library of Nineteenth-Century Black Women Writers edition of Cooper's essays, Mary Helen Washington indicates that Cooper's bold critique does not make her exempt from occasionally slipping into the domestic discourse of her day, which identified women with house and home and ideologies of true womanhood.[5] Given that these ideologies were shaped and perpetuated primarily by white women's experience of privilege and widely subscribed to by white men, such slips were not surprising, though they highlighted the very different circumstances of black women. In fact, it could be argued that black women employed and understood domestic discourse in very different ways from white women. Nevertheless, for the most part, *A Voice from the South* presents a sustained argument for women in general, and for African American women, in particular. Indeed, Cooper's profound understanding of how the women's movement needed the voice of black women who "confronted ...both [the] woman question and [the] race problem" (p. 134), made her an articulate spokesperson for two movements. Moreover, she did not shy away from a critique of racism and sexism in the church. Noting that the consistent failure to invite black people to church gatherings convened precisely to determine and promote the welfare of black people made the "whole machinery devoid of soul" (p. 37), and noting that Black women were "indispensable to the evangelization of the race" (p. 42), Cooper shifted religious discourse from the personal to the political at a critical moment in black American history. In fact, in naming "womanhood as a vital element in the regeneration" (p. 9) of her people, she placed black women at the center of black progress, as agents of change. She argues against the kind of binary oppositional thinking that would keep either the races or genders polarized by explaining:

> It would be subversive of every human interest that the cry of one-half the human family be stifled. Woman in stepping from the pedestal of statue-like inactivity in the domestic shrine, and daring to think and move and speak, – to undertake to help shape, mold, and direct the thought of her age, is merely completing the circle of the world's vision. Hers is every interest that has lacked an interpreter and a defender. Her cause is linked with that of every agony that has been dumb – every wrong that needs a voice. (p. 122)

In addition, by calling for "women who are so sure of their own social footing that they need not fear leaning to lend a hand to a fallen or falling sister" (p. 33), she gives voice to an ethic of care and social uplift that would characterize and distinguish the black women's club movement of which she was a part. In many ways, her essays were not just descriptive, but prescriptive and prophetic of a coming era of black women leaders.

In an essay entitled "The Higher Education of Women," Cooper advocates for a kind of gender symmetry, arguing "that there is a feminine as well as a masculine side to truth; that these are not related as inferior and superior, not as better and worse, not as weaker and stronger, but as complements – complements in one necessary and symmetric whole" (p. 60). She moves from this premise to offer a historical overview of women whose stories had been suppressed, but whose intellectual and artistic gifts had contributed to what Du Bois refers to as the "kingdom of culture" (p. 9). Arguing that the failure to give women credit for what they had contributed and could contribute had crippled the nation, she chronicles the outmoded thinking that hampered national progress, at the same time admitting that the nation may not have been ready to reconcile the notion of intelligent women with the institution of marriage. She concludes the essay on the education of women with a series of imperatives that the nation "let our girls feel that we expect something more of them than that they look pretty and appear well in society" (p. 78), and that "money be raised and scholarships founded in our colleges and universities for self-supporting, worthy young women, to offset and balance the aid that can always be found for boys" (p. 79). A woman who enjoyed the benefits of college at Oberlin, who went on to serve as the principal of M Street High School in Washington, DC, who earned a Ph.D. from the Sorbonne, and who later attended the first Pan-African Conference in London in 1900, Cooper provides insight into how a black woman intellectual regarded the so-called Woman's Era of the 1890s.

Contemporary readers of Cooper's essays might be surprised at the cultural critique that informs the second half of her book. She not only takes on American imperialism and the treatment of and response to Native Americans, but she also takes on issues of race and representation in American literature. Specifically challenging authors George Washington Cable and William Dean Howells, for example, she explains that she is not suggesting they cannot write about black people, but "that a man whose acquaintanceship is so slight that he cannot even discern diversities of individuality, has not right or authority to hawk 'the only true and authentic' pictures of a race of human beings" (p. 206). Throughout her critiques, Cooper anticipates her sister scholars who will dominate literary and scholarly circles of cultural criticism nearly one hundred years later.

Near the end of *A Voice from the South*, Anna Julia Cooper takes on socio-economic issues of wealth, poverty, privilege, and class as critical to the progress of black people and the nation as a whole. By so doing, she anticipates the writing of her contemporary – journalist and woman's rights activist, Gertrude Bustill Mossell (1855–1948). In her collection of essays entitled *The Work of the Afro-American Woman* (1894), Mossell continues the cultural work that Cooper began in the period between the end of slavery and Reconstruction by addressing the socio-economic issues of black women in all walks of life, regardless of their class, profession, or education. Mossell published this collection under the name of Mrs. N. F. Mossell, using the initials of her husband, Nathan Francis Mossell. At the front of the volume is a photo of herself with her two young daughters and the words that the book is dedicated to them, "praying that they may grow into a pure and noble womanhood" (p. 4). In their discussion of this dedication, both Joanne

Braxton and Claudia Tate acknowledge the discursive strategy that Mossell employs to mediate the intraracial and gender politics of her day.[6] In other words, she adheres to gender conventions of the era by subsuming her name under her husband's name, by foregrounding her role as a wife and mother, and by presenting herself rhetorically as a self-effacing woman. By employing this discursive strategy to introduce a text that will go on to challenge those very gender politics, she creates a space for herself as an essayist who is simultaneously a "race woman" and an activist for the growing women's movement.

By acknowledging how emancipation, the period known as the Woman's Era, the women's suffrage movement, and the Woman's Christian Temperance Union all contributed to making "the uplifting of the womanhood of this race a more hopeful task than might otherwise have been," Mossell opens her essay with a kind of roll call of black women – including Cooper – whose achievements in various professions (among them medicine, journalism, business, religion, and education) were worthy of recognition and commendation. Indeed, Mossell sees her work as chronicling these achievements for posterity's sake in an era in American history where they would most likely have gone unnoted. As she says, "The women of this race have always been industrious, however much the traducers of the race may attempt to make it appear otherwise" (p. 22). In her tribute to Sojourner Truth, Mossell praises her for laboring for years in the "Anti-Slavery, Woman's Suffrage and Temperance movements" and for being a woman of "magnificient [sic] presence, great power and magnetism" (p. 29). She also recognizes black women philanthropists, naming Ida B. Wells as one of the nation's greatest philanthropists of record at that time. The tribute Mossell pays to Wells in her essay is not just a commendation of her good work, however, but also a history of the consequences Wells endured because of her steadfast decision to be an outspoken critic of lynching and other forms of racial terrorism. Moreover, Mossell recognizes that not all black women had the opportunity to flourish in professions outside house and home. Referring to "uncrowned queens of the fireside who have been simply home-keepers, raising large families...and those whose work lies around us with its sweet fragrance" (p. 47), Mossell's eclectic text, which Braxton accurately says is "part intellectual history, part advice book, and part polemic" (p. xxix), attempts to create an inclusive space for all black women, regardless of their socio-economic or educational status. What emerges from reading Mossell's volume of essays, then, is an image of black women in sisterhood not only in the struggle against oppression in all its myriad forms, but also in the struggle to create a space for their work in literature, the arts, and elsewhere.

Chronicling African American literary production from the period of enslavement and the struggle for freedom and literacy to late nineteenth-century publications of fiction, non-fiction, drama, poetry, and song, Mossell uses her essay in her role as cultural archivist. In "A Sketch of Afro-American Literature," Mossell asserts "the intellectual history of a people or nation constitutes to a great degree the very heart of its life. To find this history, we search the fountain-head of its language, its customs, its religion, and it politics expressed by tongue or pen, its folkore and its songs" (p. 48). Citing the painstaking path to literacy from the moment when it was "against the law for an Afro-American to be found with a book, and a felony to teach one the alphabet" (p. 52), to the "matchless oratory" (p. 52) of Frederick Douglass and the "true poetic fire" of Phillis Wheatley, Mossell writes this essay not only to record the work that had come before, but to inspire a new generation of writers and black intellectuals. Indeed, in the essay "The Opposite Point of View," it is clear she seeks to inspire a radical paradigm shift in thinking about marriage, family, and the politics of home. Beginning by stating "[h]ome is undoubtedly the cornerstone of our beloved Republic" (p. 115), she then begins a systematic chipping away at long-held beliefs about courtship, marriage, and family life, and offers a critique of the gender politics that challenge all three. Cognizant of the domestic minefield into which she has entered, she quips that while "[m]any wonder that so many people separate...[her] wonder is that so many remain together" (p. 118). Mossell's observations of court-ship and marriage lead her to conclude that both men and women, not just women, need instruction on making a house into a home. With a decidedly womanist viewpoint, she advocates for equality in marriage at a time when the success or failure of a marriage was largely considered a woman's responsibility. In a statement meant to challenge orthodox views of marriage she says: "keeping a clean house will not keep a man at home; to be sure it will not drive him out, but neither will it keep him in to a very large extent. And you...that are being taught daily that it will, might as well know the truth now and not be crying your eyes out later" (p. 120). She does not leave women and men in suspension, however, about the alternative to the unequal gender politics that have prevailed as it relates to marriage, family, and home. She concludes:

> The home should be founded on right principles, on morality, Christian living, a due regard to heredity and environment that promise good for the future. With these taken into consideration, backed by love, or even true regard, with each having an abiding sense of duty and a desire to carry out its principles, no marriage so contracted can ever prove a failure. (p. 125)

Contemporary readers may be surprised to learn that such a bold assessment of marriage challenging the conventional attitudes about a woman's place and role in the domestic sphere was published as early as 1894.

It may be equally surprising to learn that nearly forty-five years before Virginia Woolf wrote her groundbreaking essay, "A Room of One's Own" (1939), Mossell wrote "A Lofty Study" (1894), about a writing woman's need for "a study of one's own" (p. 128). Recognizing the economic and spatial constraints that some women faced in their efforts to accommodate their work as writers, she recommends that women "have at least your own corner in some cheerful room" (p. 128). This short essay is significant, not just because it anticipates the now familiar suggestion of a more famous British woman author, but also because it advocates for women's literary aspirations in the 1890s and identifies the terms under which those literary aspirations could flourish inside the domestic sphere. While it is not possible to acknowledge all the African American women who were writing during the era Mossell refers to as the era of "universal scribbling" (p. 126), it is impossible to leave the period without acknowledging the essays of the famous anti-lynching crusader, investigative reporter, and activist journalist, Ida Wells-Barnett (1862–1931), whose radical words riveted the attention of the nation and the world to racial violence, inequalities in education, and injustice wherever she found it.

In such essays as *A Red Record* (1895), and "Lynch Law in America" (1900), Wells-Barnett proved herself to be not only an powerful journalist, but a staunch civil rights and woman's activist who was not afraid to use the power of the spoken and written word to be an agent of change in the face of American racism, sexism, and injustice toward her people.[7] At risk to her own life, she named lynching as a "national crime" (p. 70) that sustained itself by "unwritten law" (p. 70), fueled by the terrorist behavior of white supremacist groups such as the Ku Klux Klan and the refusal of American citizens to protest its barbarity. She became famous, not only for speaking out against lynching, but also for creating a database of its many occurrences, along with the excuses for its occurrence. Citing the three most common justifications for lynching black men – the fear of "race riots," the audacity of black people "to exercise their right to vote" (p. 71), and the protection of white women against black men – Wells-Barnett systematically debunked each of these, saving her strongest critique for the latter. By so doing, she simultaneously debunked the patriarchal myth of pure white womanhood by revealing the ways in which white women colluded with racial injustice done in the name of protecting them often naming acts that were not committed or that were not criminal in nature. She is astute, however, to acknowledge that she is not claiming that all black people or that all black men are always, already innocent of any and every wrongdoing. In response to anyone naïve enough to hold this presupposition, she writes: "We have associated too long with the white man not to have copied his vices as well as his virtues" (p. 74). She concludes, instead, that what is needed are fair trials, equal protection under the law and readers who will respond to her words by (1) disseminating the facts contained in her book of essays "to the end that public sentiment may be revolutionized"; (2) by "having churches, missionary societies, Y.M.C.A.'s, W.C.T.U.'s and all Christian and moral forces ... in religious and social life, pass resolutions of condemnation and protest every time a lynching takes place"; (3) by inspiring intelligent Southern people to consider the error of their ways by refusing to invest capital "where lawlessness and mob violence hold sway"; (4) by thinking and acting independently until the Nation lives by its own "precepts and theories of Christianity" (pp. 603–4); and (5) by supporting legislation (proposed by Congressman Blair in 1894) to have a thorough investigation of "alleged assaults by males upon females through-out the country during the ten years ... preceding the passing of this joint resolution" (p. 604). Convinced that knowledge is power and that the Christian world would rise up against lynching and other injustices against black people, Ida Wells-Barnett used her editorial essays in the *Memphis Free Speech* and other publications to inspire like-minded Americans of all races to join the struggle against one of the most devastating manifestations of insti-tutionalized racism and white supremacy.

The period between Reconstruction and the onset of the Harlem Renaissance was a period of tremendous progress for African American women as public intellectuals, activists, and leaders on the national and international front. Though she was known more for work on the lecture circuit than in print, as an educator, staunch suffragist, and one of the founders of Delta Sigma Theta Sorority, Mary Church Terrell (1863–1954) published her speeches in *Voice of the Negro* (1904). One of those speeches, "The Progress of Colored Women," is noteworthy, not so much as an essay, but for its celebration of African American women's achievements. Black women were "lifting as they climb, onward and upward as they go, struggling and striving and hoping that the buds and blossoms of their desires may burst into glorious fruition."[8] The phrase "lifting as they climb" would later become the motto of the National Council of Negro Women (originally referred to as the National Association of Colored Women) and would inspire other women in the National Black Women's Club movement, including Cooper and Wells-Barnett, to empower themselves, their sisters, and the race as a whole. During the period between the Harlem Renaissance and the civil rights and Black Power movements, many African American women writers came on the scene, and many were turning to poetry and fiction in large numbers. Nevertheless, many continued to employ the essay for various forms of cultural work, including Elise Johnson McDougald (1885–1971), Alice Dunbar-Nelson (1875–1935), Sadie Tanner Mossell Alexander (1898–1989), Zora Neale Hurston (1891–1960), and Amy Jacques Garvey (1896–1973).

McDougald's rather short essay, published in Alain Locke's *Survey Graphic* (1925), might otherwise go unnoticed except that it was one of the first published essays to identify and foreground the so-called double jeopardy of race and gender that black women faced in America. In her essay, "The Double Task: The Struggle of Negro Women for Sex and Race Emancipation," she argues that for women of African descent, "pressure has been exerted upon her, both from without and within her group. Her emotional and sex life is a reflex of her economic station."[9] Recognizing that African American women have made great strides, she advocates that women engage in more militant, robust activism in response to the "contempt from the world" (p. 382) and to their dual oppression. As both a teacher and journalist, McDougald notes the pattern that "their feminist efforts are directed chiefly toward the realization of the equality of the races, the sex struggle assuming a subordinate place" (p. 382), and views her essay ultimately as a call for raised consciousness among black women throughout the nation, regardless of their education or class status, about "the needs and demands of [their] family, community, and race" (p. 382). Though known primarily for her poetry, teaching, activism in the Black Women's Club movement, and her tumultuous marriage to poet Paul Lawrence Dunbar, Alice Dunbar-Nelson expresses in her essay "The Negro Woman and the Ballot" (1927) her disappointment with the six years of women's franchisement that she and her sisters had enjoyed.[10] Accusing black women of getting comfortable with access to the vote by adding "to the overhead of the political machinery, without solving racial problems" (p. 87), she challenges younger women to resist the intergenerational pull to fall in line with their male relatives, friends, and elders, by voting according to their conscience, not only for their own sake, but also for the "future of [their] children" (p. 88).

Like Dunbar-Nelson, Amy Jacques Garvey is partly known for her marriage to a famous man. As the second wife of Marcus Garvey, the Black Nationalist leader, spokesman of the Harlem Renaissance, and founder of the Universal Negro Improvement Association, Amy Garvey distinguished herself, not only by advocating for a nationalist rather than an integrationist perspective, but also by having a global, pan-Africanist vision of the black struggle. Seeing the black struggle as a global liberation struggle, in the essay "Our Women Getting into the Larger Life," she praises women for progress made, but encourages them to take note of the "worldwide movement" of women. In "Women as Leaders," acknowledging the unique role of women as mothers, she praises them for "extending this holy influence outside the realms of home, softening the ills of the world by their gracious and kindly contact."[11] Shifting her discourse from praise of black women's efforts to an impatient warning to unsupportive black men, she closes by reminding them that "Ethiopia's queens will reign again, and her Amazons protect her shores and people. Strengthen your shaking knees and move forward, or we will displace you and lead on to victory and to glory" (p. 94). Sadie Tanner Mossell Alexander was concerned with the financial status of black women. Though she was the first African American woman to receive a doctorate in economics (University of Pennsylvania, 1921), the race and gender discrimination of the period prohibited her from securing work as a social scientist that was commensurate with her education. Rather than permanently discouraging her, this treatment inspired her instead to return to school, this time for a law degree, but as labor and intellectual historian Francille Rusan Wilson explains, Alexander would come to know the pain of race and gender discrimination from two professions, despite her Ivy League credentials.[12] Establishing her argument with census data, personal interviews and other research, Alexander documents "[n]ot only are the wages of Negro women lower than those of white women, but Negro women as a whole are confined to simpler types of work, and are not engaged in highly skilled labor" (p. 98). Aware of conservative views both within and outside the race that would be critical of women earning a wage outside the home, she says, "The derogatory effects of the mother being out of the home are over balanced by the increased family income, which makes possible the securing of at least the necessities of life and perhaps a few luxuries" (p. 98). Alexander's essay reveals that, as early as the 1920s, the nation was no less polarized about a woman's role than in previous years, but the presence of highly educated, knowledgeable African American women was changing public discourse and simultaneously creating new spaces for women as writers, leaders, and workers.

Nowhere are the vicissitudes of public discourse more apparent than in the essays of Zora Neale Hurston, the anthropologist, folklorist, and fiction writer whose literary career spanned over four decades. In essays that took on issues of race, gender, black vernacular and other elements of black cultural expression, democracy and even the world of publishing in tone and style as flamboyant as she was, Hurston became the foremost public intellectual of the Harlem Renaissance. In "How It Feels to Be Colored Me" (1928), she self-consciously and intentionally takes on those who had grown to expect black writers to protest either their own racial plight, that of the race, or both. The contrary disposition for which she became famous is expressed in a counterstatement to this racialized expectation when she states:

> I am colored but offer nothing in the way of extenuating circumstances except the fact that I am the only Negro in the United States whose grandfather on the mother's side was *not* an Indian chief... But I am not tragically colored. There is no great sorrow dammed up in my soul, nor lurking behind my eyes. I do not mind at all. I do not belong to the sobbing school of Negrohood who hold that nature somehow has given them a lowdown dirty deal and whose feelings are all hurt about it. Even in the helter-skelter skirmish of a little pigmentation more or less. No, I do not weep at the world – I am too busy sharpening my oyster knife.[13]

While not oblivious to the identity of black people as former slaves, she offers an amusing glance at her detractors – both black and white – admitting that it is "exciting to hold the center of the national stage, with the spectators not knowing whether to laugh or to weep" (p. 153). Claiming rather stridently that she sometimes has "no race" but is simply "[t]he cosmic Zora" who "belong[s] to no race or time," but is the "eternal feminine with its string of beads" (p. 155), Hurston endured a great deal of criticism for these views, which placed her decidedly outside the boundaries of the predominant racial discourse and dialogue of her day. Many challenged the veracity of her statements, knowing that she had endured racial discrimination at Barnard College, where she was allowed to attend class, but not live in the residence halls. Others certainly must have challenged the sensitivity of using the public stage for such sentiments when the masses of black people were living under the effects of the Jim Crow South, with which she was familiar as a daughter of the South, as her essay, "My Most Humiliating Jim Crow Experience" (1944) attests, even though it takes place in New York. With her usual ironic wit, she takes on Jim Crow in the essay "Crazy for This Democracy," but from a more global perspective, offering critiques of the World War II imperialism, colonialism, and the lack of democratic principles in the United States.[14] Stating that she accepts "this idea of Democracy" and that she is "all for trying it out" (p. 166), she nevertheless asserts "the only thing that keeps [her] from pitching headlong into the thing is the presence of numerous Jim Crow laws on the statute books of the nation" (p. 167). Taken together, her essays actually offer examples of the double-consciousness that Du Bois described in 1903 "of always looking at one's self through the eyes of others, of measuring one's soul by the tape of a world that looks on in amused contempt and pity" (p. 8). But Hurston boldly looks back at America's racism, with her own contempt and pity, and understands this dual vision as a gift of discursive mediation between two worlds, not as weighted disadvantage.

In a later essay "What White Publishers Won't Print" (1950), Hurston seems to engage in a kind of metacriticism that looks self-reflexively at the field that has helped shape her public identity, but that has also been guilty of its own discriminatory, racist practices as it regards black life and culture.[15] Focusing on the "gap in the national literature" (p. 169) and its lack of interest in representing the "internal lives and emotions" of black people or "any non-Anglo-Saxon peoples within our borders above the class of unskilled labor" (p. 169), for that matter, Hurston expresses her most harsh critique of race discrimination in this essay. Granted, by the time she publishes this essay, she had had her own racial skirmishes with patrons, the publishing world, and even fellow artists. Nevertheless, she employs this essay to expose the routine ways in which white publishers offer short shrift to the realities of black life and culture, and by so doing, shortchange the American reading public of literary complexity and depth in the representation of black people and other minorities. She evinces awareness that her proposal of greater breadth and the knowledge that comes with it will "destroy many illusions and romantic traditions which America probably likes to have around" (p. 173), but she argues that the reliance on narrow stereotypes has left the national imagination impoverished and ignorant. Thus, despite her earlier claims that she is not "tragically colored," Hurston, near the end of her career, advocates not only for the race and for writers, but for the nation, and its need to know the full humanity of its fellow American citizens beyond the limitations of stereotype. In advocating the need for Americans to deepen their understanding of how race operates in America, Hurston anticipates the essays of Nobel laureate Toni Morrison, who interrogates in *Playing in the Dark: Whiteness and the Literary Imagination* (1992) and in "Home" (1998) the ways in which "to enunciate and then eclipse the racial gaze altogether."[16]

After Hurston, one of the most important essayists prior to the civil rights and Black Arts movements writing of the 1960s and beyond is playwright, political activist and cultural critic Lorraine Hansberry (1930–65). Her short life meant that her literary reputation revolved primarily around the success of one play – *A Raisin in the Sun* (1959), but her identity as a radical feminist voice is apparent in the unpublished essay "Simone de Beauvoir and the Second Sex: An American Commentary, 1957."[17] Hansberry's assessment of de Beauvoir's groundbreaking text is itself groundbreaking for its leftist critique, its feminist stance about beauty, dress, homemaking and mothering, and even its racial politics in describing the "national neuroses" (p. 139) as the tradition and continuing habit of "othering" and routinely ignoring "half of its people" (p. 136). Although Hansberry did not get the opportunity to finish the essay, it offers an impressive portrait of a black woman intellectual at home in the life of the mind at the critical moment in time when the civil rights movement became the Black Power movement and when other women were more reticent in their response to de Beauvoir's book.

When we turn to the last four decades of the twentieth century and the beginning of the twenty-first century, we enter a highly prolific period of essay writing for African American women writers. From Frances Beale's "Double Jeopardy: To Be Black and Female," to Toni Cade [Bambara]'s "On the Issue of Roles," both published in the 1970 anthology of voices called *The Black Woman: An Anthology* edited by Cade, black women used the essay to discuss variations on earlier themes but, as Cade says in her introduction, "Unlike the traditional sororities and business clubs, they seem to use the Black Liberation struggle rather than the American Dream as their yardstick, their gauge, their vantage point."[18] The landmark essay of scholar/activist Angela Davis, "Reflections on the Black Woman's Role in the Community of Slaves" (1971), was written while she was still in prison on false charges of conspiracy and murder, later dropped in 1972.[19] In the tradition of black women activists of the previous century, Davis has raised her voice on issues ranging from education, injustice, prison reform, welfare, and women's liberation, to disarmament and world peace. As she indicates in this essay, she did not envision confining her paper to "the era of slavery," but as she "began to think through the issue of the black matriarch," she realized, "it had to be refuted at its presumed historical inception" (p. 200). The result of her thorough exploration of the myth of the black matriarch is that she simultaneously debunked the so-called "Moynihan Report," which had attempted to reify the myth, stating, "The designation of the black woman as a matriarch is a cruel misnomer" (p. 202) as she made the case for the black woman by interrogating the "dialectics of her oppression" (p. 205).[20] Davis's essay offers a revisionist history, not only of the undocumented acts of resistance and rebellion against slavery that characterized the lives of black people during their enslavement in America, but it also examines the "dialectics of [the Black woman's] oppression" (p. 205) as a counterstatement to prevailing oversimplifications, misinformation, and untruths. Thus, Davis's essay ushered in an entire era of revisionist cultural and literary history, in which black women scholars, activists, and artists would begin correcting erroneous stories by telling the untold stories of black women's lives.

The context in which black women began telling and retelling their stories through their essays was fraught with contention. As white women became more vocal with the women's liberation movement, simultaneous with more black women gaining access to higher education and demanding that colleges and universities be responsive to their presence, African American women wrote essays that challenged racism and sexism as the interlocking systems of oppression that they are. Hence, the groundbreaking volume *All the Women Are White, All the Blacks Are Men, But Some of Us Are Brave: Black Women's Studies*, edited by Gloria T. Hull, Patricia Bell Scott, and Barbara Smith, captured the spirit of two movements at once when it was published in 1982. The volume also captured the spirit of black women's critique of institutional racism among the ranks of white women and the so-called women's movement. As a result, Barbara Smith's "Toward a Black Feminist Criticism" (1977) was a pivotal essay for African American women seeking to intervene in an ongoing discourse on the part of white women that did not take the intersections of race, gender, and class and Black women's lived lives into account.[21] In her essay, Smith not only breaks silences about racism within the white women's movement, but she also denounces homophobia within black communities and the emerging black women's movement, thus naming and creating space for more attention to the work of black lesbian women writers and critics. Expressing her desire that others will follow her example in breaking such silences, Smith acknowledges that her ultimate goal is to feel less alone in her struggle, and to know better "how to live" and "how to dream" (p. 173).

A few years earlier, Michele Wallace's essay "Anger in Isolation: A Black Feminist's Search for Sisterhood" (1975) would anticipate Smith's search for a community of black women writers and critics who would not be afraid to challenge misogyny within the black community.[22] Though very young when she chose to write this essay and to start a "black women's consciousness-raising group" (p. 226) which would result in her founding the National Black Feminist Organization, Wallace gives voice to the desire for "an environment in this society remotely congenial to our struggle" (p. 227). The archival work of uncovering, recovering, telling, and retelling black women's lives probably explains the recurrence of the word "search" in the titles of so many essays written by African American women during the 1970s and 1980s. Recognizing, although as a poet and fiction writer, that the genre of the essay could enable gender statements that other genres had not yet made, Alice Walker, in "In Search of Our Mothers' Gardens" (1974) gave voice to sentiments and concerns long unarticulated.[23] The central question of the essay remains poignant even today:

> What did it mean for a black woman to be an artist in our grandmother's time…? How was the creativity of the Black woman kept alive, year after year and century after century, when for most of the years Black people have been in America, it was a punishable crime for a Black person to read or write? And the freedom to paint, to sculpt, to expand the mind with action, did not exist. (pp. 233–34)

This essay and its answers to these questions create a space for Walker, not only to tell the untold stories of her ancestors, but also to inspire an emerging generation of black women artists, scholars, and writers to realize how their stories are connected to those of their mothers. Credited with coining the word womanist for black feminist ideology and thought, she writes:

> so many of the stories that I write, that we all write, are my mother's stories. Only recently did I fully realize this: that through years of listening to my mother's stories of her life, I have absorbed not only the stories themselves, but something of the manner in which she spoke, something of the urgency that involves the knowledge that her stories – like her life – must be recorded. (p. 240)

Near the end of her essay she sums up the value of discovering her mother's stories and those of other women whose lives preceded her own: "Guided by my heritage of a love of beauty and a respect for strength – in search of my mother's garden, I found my own" (p. 243).

As African American women continued to speak from their own concerns rather than react to the concerns of others, the discursive nature of their essays changed. Emboldened by greater visibility for and interest in their creative and critical production, black women began using the essay to break new silences. Nowhere is this new ground more apparent than in the essays of the award-winning author Toni Morrison. Though celebrated for her fiction, she has consistently throughout her literary career produced powerful literary and cultural criticism in her essays, beginning with "What the Black Woman Thinks about Women's Lib" (1971) to "Rootedness: The Ancestor as Foundation" (1984), including, but not limited to her ground-breaking essay, "Unspeakable Things Unspoken: The Afro-American Presence in American Literature" (1989). Morrison breaks new ground, not only by arguing that the black presence in so-called American texts can be gleaned, foregrounded, and critiqued, but also by challenging the very presumptions upon which the construction of whiteness is based. Morrison uses this essay, which is arguably one of her best for its provocative brilliance, to critique the lack of adequate scholarship concerning her own fiction, to intervene in 1980s debates about the so-called American literary canon, and to provide close readings of the first line of each of her first five novels.[24]

Morrison's essays provide insight not only into her own writing, but also into African American life and culture, particularly black vernacular language and music. Noting her expressed desire to unsettle the reader, to create space for her readers to come into her texts, and "practice language [as]...a search for and deliberate posture of vulnerability to those aspects of Afro-American culture that can inform and position" (p. 33) her work, Morrison uses the essay to explore the cultural work that her fiction performs and to argue for the kind of critical attention that she and other writers crave. In addition to Toni Morrison, African American women essayists include Julianne Malveaux, the black economist who has written on everything from the status of black women in the workplace to politics and education, Katie Geneva Cannon, the black womanist theologian, who celebrates her feminist ancestors in the ministry at the same time that she discusses the sacred-secular continuum in black women's literature; and June Jordan (1936–2002), who, like Audre Lourde (1934–92), took on issues of black female sexuality and gender politics when others were less willing to do so. The work of sociologist Patricia Hills Collins, especially in her essay "The Social Construction of Black Feminist Thought" (1989), provided black women with a consistent language for discussing their epistemological frameworks, and did so by referencing the public intellectual work of nineteenth-century activist predecessors such as Sojourner Truth, Anna Julia Cooper, and Ida Wells-Barnett, to name a few.

By many assessments, the African American woman who has most consistently and prolifically used the essay for the last three decades to speak truth to power, to engage a larger audience in the public sphere with issues that affect the black community is bell hooks. In collection after collection of essays, she has written from a decidedly black and feminist perspective and has offered new and cutting-edge perspectives on a wide range of topics, including gender politics inside the domestic sphere, black masculinity, the representation of black people in the film industry, and education. In one of her earliest essays "Black Women: Shaping Feminist Theory" (1984), hooks confesses to her own personal need to navigate the linguistic waters of what to call oneself carefully within the gendered politics of the feminist movement. Always choosing her words carefully, she prefers to identify herself as "a black woman interested in the feminist movement,"[25] to avoid the either/or oppositional thinking to which the uncritical adaptation of others' language can lead. Not wishing to be co-opted into making familiar choices as to whether one is a black first and a woman second, or vice versa, hooks admonishes black women to engage in the feminist struggle critically, challenging even those who would pose such choices. Moving from the gender politics of the public sphere to the gendered and racial politics of the domestic sphere, her later essay "Homeplace (a site of resistance)" (1990) illustrates hooks's ongoing project of using cultural essays to comment on both her own personal life and the untold lives of black people. Not shy about sharing stories of family and personal relationships in the service of the larger struggle, hooks's use of the word love reveals how the personal is connected to the political. From *Salvation: Black People and Love* (2001) to *Communion: The Female Search for Love* (2002) to *The Will to Change: Men, Masculinity, and*

Love (2004), perhaps more than any other contemporary public intellectual in the field of cultural studies, bell hooks has used the essay to shift the cultural dialogue to the emotional and spiritual needs of the black community, not blind to political realities, but informed by them. Bringing head and heart together, her essays take her readers where the first purveyors of the essay sought to go as well, to a place where all people, but especially black women, could know a sense of community and would experience what it means, not only to survive, but to thrive.

NOTES

1. See Carla L. Peterson, *"Doers of the Word": African-American Women Speakers & Writers in the North [1830–1880]* (New York: Oxford University Press, 1995).
2. Beverly Guy-Sheftall (ed.), *Words of Fire: An Anthology of African-American Feminist Thought* (New York: New Press, 1995), p. xiii. Guy-Sheftall admits that her anthology is in no way comprehensive, that it purposely omits many essays that focus primarily on literature, and that literary scholars such as Cheryl A. Wall, Deborah McDowell, Mary Helen Washington, and Henry Louis Gates, among others began the pioneering work of publishing on the creative expression of black women writers. Likewise, this chapter attempts to focus, not just on literature per se, but instead to offer an overview of the multiple spheres in which African American women have employed the essay as the genre of choice for their writing.
3. See Angelyn Mitchell, *The Freedom to Remember: Narrative, Slavery, and Gender in Contemporary Black Women's Fiction* (New Brunswick, NJ: Rutgers University Press, 2002).
4. See Paula Giddings, *When and Where I Enter: The Impact of Black Women on Race and Sex in America* (New York: Perennial, 1984) for a text that was inspired by Cooper's words and the cultural work of various black women in the areas of civil rights, women's rights, human rights, labor, government, and education. Also see W. E. B. Du Bois, *The Souls of Black Folk* (1903; New York: Vintage Books, 1990).
5. See Mary Helen Washington's Introduction to Anna Julia Cooper, *A Voice from the South* (New York: Oxford University Press, 1988).
6. See Joanne Braxton's Introduction to Mrs. N. F. Mossell, *The Work of the Afro-American Woman* (New York: Oxford University Press, 1988) and Claudia Tate, *Domestic Allegories of Political Desire: The Black Heroine's Text at the Turn of the Century* (New York: Oxford University Press, 1992), pp. 132–38.
7. Ida B. Wells-Barnett, "From *A Red Record*," *The Norton Anthology of African American Literature*, ed. Henry Louis Gates, Jr. and Nellie Y. McKay (New York: Norton, 1997), pp. 595–606 and "Lynch Law in America," *Words of Fire*, ed. Guy-Sheftall, pp. 69–78.
8. "The Progress of Colored Women," *Words of Fire*, ed. Guy-Sheftall, p. 68.
9. Elise Johnson McDougald, "The Task of Negro Womanhood," *The New Negro: Voices of the Harlem Renaissance*, ed. Alain Locke (New York: Touchstone, 1925), p. 379.
10. "The Negro Woman and the Ballot," *Words of Fire*, ed. Guy-Sheftall, pp. 85–88.

11. Amy Jacques Garvey, "Our Women Getting into the Larger Life" and "Women as Leaders," *Words of Fire*, ed. Guy-Sheftall, pp. 91–92 and 93–94 respectively.

12. See Francille Rusan Wilson's essay "All of the Glory...Faded...Quickly: Sadie T. M. Alexander and Black Professional Women, 1920–1950," *Sister Circle: Black Women and Work*, ed. Sharon Harley and The Black Women and Work Collective (New Brunswick, NJ: Rutgers University Press, 2002), pp. 164–83.

13. Zora Neale Hurston, *The Hurston Reader* (New York: HarperCollins, 1999), pp. 152–53.

14. See ibid., pp. 165–68.

15. Ibid., pp. 169–73.

16. Toni Morrison, *Playing in the Dark: Whiteness and the Literary Imagination* (New York: Vintage, 1992) and "Home," *The House That Race Built*, ed. Wahneema Lubiano (New York: Vintage, 1998), 9.

17. *Words of Fire*, ed. Guy-Sheftall, pp. 125–42.

18. Toni Cade [Bambara], *The Black Woman: An Anthology* (1970; New York: Washington Square Press, 2005), p. 4.

19. *Words of Fire*, ed. Guy-Sheftall, pp. 199–218.

20. The Moynihan Report refers to a memorandum written by Daniel Patrick Moynihan, who, as assistant secretary of labor under President Lyndon Johnson, argued that the black community had succumbed to a "matriarchal structure" by nature of its female-headed families, which were by nature dysfunctional. While some dimensions of the report had merit for their exploration of poverty, many black scholars critiqued its failure to account for the survival strategies black people developed to cope with decades of racial oppression in American society. See Darlene Clark Hine, Stanley Harrold, and William C. Hine, *African Americans: A Concise History-Combined Volume* (Upper Saddle River, NJ: Prentice Hall, 2004), pp. 454–55.

21. "Toward a Black Feminist Criticism," *All the Women Are White, All the Blacks Are Men, But Some of Us Are Brave: Black Women's Studies*, ed. Gloria T. Hull, Patricia Bell Scott, and Barbara Smith (New York: Feminist Press, 1982), pp. 157–75.

22. *Words of Fire*, ed. Guy-Sheftall, pp. 220–27.

23. Alice Walker, *In Search of Our Mothers' Gardens* (New York: Harcourt, Brace, Jovanovich, 1983), pp. 231–43.

24. Toni Morrison, "Unspeakable Things Unspoken: The Afro-American Presence in American Literature," *The Michigan Quarterly Review* (Winter 1989), 1–34.

25. bell hooks, "Feminism: A Movement to End Sexist Oppression," *Feminist Theory: From Margin to Center* (Boston, MA: South End Press, 1984), pp. 17–31, p. 29.

13

CRYSTAL J. LUCKY

African American women writers and the short story

The year of John Brown's unsuccessful uprising at Harpers Ferry, writer, lecturer, and political activist Frances Ellen Watkins Harper launched African Americans' participation in the art of short story writing. Harper's short story "The Two Offers" (1859) appeared in the *Anglo-African*, a magazine published in New York from 1859 to 1865 by Thomas and Robert Hamilton with a view to educate, encourage, and provide a voice for black people in America. Emblematic of the work of racial uplift, the tale traces the lives of two young cousins, Laura Lagrange and Janette Alston, and the consequences of the one young woman's decision to pursue romantic love and marriage and the other's attempt to discover the full scope of her abilities and inner self. For Harper and African American writers who followed her, the short story provided a vehicle through which they could explore the complex realities of African Americans' lived experiences in a form shorter than that of the novel. As an African American woman writer, Harper opened a way for other black women to explore the tension between women's self-fulfillment and adherence to social convention implicit in Anglo-America's cult of true womanhood. There are those nineteenth- and twentieth-century African American women short story writers, like Harper, Pauline Hopkins, Zora Neale Hurston, Alice Walker, and Toni Morrison, who are perhaps better known for their accomplishments as novelists, poets, and essayists. Because of its accessibility, the short story invites innovation, an opportunity to experiment with style and form, voice and language. An exploration of the short story reveals black women's significant contributions to the aesthetic and political contours of the form over time.

Black women's short stories are a part of a long and rich tradition of African American women's published work that began with the poetry of Lucy Terry and Phillis Wheatley. Wheatley's noble attempt to formulate her thoughts and feelings in verse were met with both skepticism and disdain by white America. In his widely acclaimed *Notes on the State of Virginia*, Thomas Jefferson pronounces the African in America utterly devoid of any linguistic, rational, or creative capabilities – except those required to produce the simplest forms of single-toned music. He points to Wheatley's poetry as a superb example of non-poetry. In fact, he is so contemptuous of Wheatley's verse that he declares it "below the dignity of criticism" and summarily dismisses her work in two sentences.[1] Jefferson's influential speculations did more than lay the groundwork for building a case for the racialized inferiority of black people; they cast further doubt in the minds of those desirous of disproving the intellectual and artistic capabilities of black women.

As the Enlightenment gave way to nineteenth-century Victorian ideals, not only did black women writers feel compelled to insist that they were worthy of Christian salvation and possessed human souls, they were forced to defend their honor and sexual virtue by negotiating a space among varied positions: placing themselves on display for public scrutiny, obeying God's call to serve and minister, and responding to artistic impulse. Throughout the century, free black preaching, teaching, and political women alongside formerly enslaved women attempted to write themselves onto the face of the changing American tableau. Thus Jarena Lee, Zilpha Elaw, Maria Stewart, Frances Harper, Harriet Wilson, Alice Dunbar-Nelson, Victoria Earle Matthews, Angelina Weld Grimké, Ruth Todd, Anna Julia Cooper, and Pauline Hopkins sought to write, address public audiences, tell stories of freedom and enslavement, and assure African Americans that they could seek more than what white America was offering them through existing political and religious structures.[2] Short fiction enabled many of these women to reimagine themselves and their male counterparts more favorably than stereotype and popular opinion allowed. Early short stories by black women writers reexamined and reshaped the degrading and devastating images of the mammy, jezebel, sapphire, tom, buck, coon, and sambo, constructed to bolster racist and sexist political agendas, into the complex, nuanced, and multilayered people that they really represented.

Added to this were the challenges that American women faced generally in getting their work published and distributed widely to reading audiences. Nineteenth-century African American women struggled to an even greater degree to get their writing of various types recognized by male publishers. Confronted with the challenges of convincing them that their writing was indeed their own and could garner any reading audience at all, particularly if the work was not directly related to the perils of slavery, sexual and psychic violence, or traditional domestic themes of motherhood and marriage, many black women turned to short fiction. Publishing the longer, more expensive novel in the nineteenth century was often limited to those who could afford to pay to have their work published privately. Instead, the plethora of African American edited and published magazines and newspapers, although often short lived in the years immediately preceding and following the Civil War, were run by committed men and women who were determined to provide a venue for black people to have their political, ideological, and artistic voices heard. Both Harper and Hopkins, for example, published their short stories and poetry in the antebellum and post-Civil War black press years before publishing their respective canon-shaping novels, *Iola Leroy; or, Shadows Uplifted* (1891) and *Contending Forces: a Romance Illustrative of Negro Life North and South* (1900).[3]

With the exception of Frances Harper's "Two Offers" and "The Triumph of Freedom – A Dream" (1860), no short stories by black women appeared before 1895. The Woman's Era of the 1890s, however, ushered in an important period of black women's literary contribution. Scholars have noted that more works of fiction by black women were published between 1890 and 1910 than black men had published in the previous half-century.[4] At the turn of the century, Alice Dunbar-Nelson published *The Goodness of St. Rocque* (1899), the first collection of short stories by a black woman. One year later, Pauline Hopkins became a shareholder in a small publishing company in Boston, the Colored Co-Operative. From that company was launched *The Colored American Magazine*, the premier issue of which featured Hopkins's first story, "The Mystery within Us" (1900).[5] In 1903, Hopkins became the magazine's editor-in-chief and published the works of Harper, Grimké, and other lesser-known black women storytellers.

The post-World War I era witnessed the continued burgeoning of black artistic and cultural production. African American organizations, newspapers, journals, and magazines attempted to capture the possibilities of modernity and to offer the most complete story of the lives and circumstances of African Americans affected by southern violence, migration, northern racism, cosmopolitan style, and the Depression. *The Crisis*, published by the National Association for the Advancement of Colored People (NAACP), and *Opportunity Magazine*, published by the National Urban League, hosted short story contests, making short fiction central to the publications and commencing the careers of some of the most important African American writers of the twentieth century, like Hurston, Jessie Redmon Fauset, Dorothy West, and Gwendolyn Bennett. *Fire!!*, *Saturday Evening Quill*, and *Messenger* were all short-lived literary magazines that published short stories by African American women of the New Negro Renaissance. Central to the Chicago Renaissance of the 1930s and 1940s was the creation of *Negro Story Magazine* by Alice Browning and Fern Gayden in 1944. The magazine published stories by both professional and amateur writers. And in the dawn of the civil rights movement, Alice Childress's *Like One of the Family: Conversations from a Domestic's Life* appeared (1956). Comprised of vignettes outlining the life of a black working woman in New York City in the 1950s, the collection helped to usher in the important period of the 1960s and the Black Arts movement for black women short story writers.

Resisting exoticism and recognizing the centrality of black women's contributions to the work of civil and women's rights, black women short story writers continued to use individual women's voices and stories to speak for the larger community. Ushering in the next decade, Toni Cade [Bambara] edited the groundbreaking collection, *The Black Woman: An Anthology* (1970). In it, she collected the short stories of Alice Walker, Nikki Giovanni, and Paule Marshall, along with the original work of essayists and poets. The chorus of outspoken women tackled issues surrounding race and sex, body image, the economy, politics, labor, and love. She edited a second collection entitled *Tales and Stories for Black Folks* (1971) and a year later published her own collection of short stories, *Gorilla, My Love* (1972). Alice Walker's *You Can't Keep a Good Woman Down* (1971) and *In Love & Trouble* (1973), and Gayl Jones's *White Rat* (1977), along with the work of Julia Fields, Anita Cornwell, Diane Oliver, and Nikki Giovanni, marked the decade as powerful.

Through the end of the century, the short story has allowed African American women to explore the wide-ranging aspects of their history and quickly changing future in fictionalized form. The myriad voices that emerged in the 1980s and 1990s, from Tina McElroy Ansa to Becky Birtha, Barbara Neely to Octavia Butler, explore the full range of African American women's experiences involving familial dysfunction, illegal drugs, the gaining and passing on of intergenerational wisdom, the legacy of slavery, motherhood, and negotiating varied sexual identities. A decade after Bambara's seminal collection of black women's work appeared, Mary Helen Washington offered *Black-Eyed Susans and Midnight Birds: Stories by Contemporary Black Women Writers* (1980). The collection focused on stories written about black women, by black women, and thereby recognized black women as an appreciable reading audience. Terry McMillan, Judith and Martin Hamer, and Bill Mullen understood this as well with the publication of their respective collections, *Breaking Ice: An Anthology of Contemporary African American Fiction* (1990), *Centers of the Self: Stories by Black American Women from the Nineteenth Century to the Present* (1994), and *Revolutionary Tales: African-American Women's Short Stories from the First Story to the Present* (1995). Along with Ann Allen Shockley's *The Black and White of It* (1987) and Asha Kanwar's *The Unforgetting Heart: An Anthology of Short Stories by African American Women (1859–1993)* (1993), the stories of the final decades of the twentieth century initiate new discussions concerning the black woman's place in American society. Wanda

Coleman, Colleen J. McElroy, Rita Dove, Maxine Clair, and Edwidge Danticat have each published important collections of their own work.[6] Magazines, newspapers, and journals were and continue to be the primary publishing outlets for African American women fiction writers, and as such, short fiction has a wide readership.

Although it is tempting simply to investigate the writers and their works chronologically, it is interesting to consider the ways that the women's stories might be read thematically. For example, early writers of the form, like Victoria Earle Matthews, Harper, Nelson, Hopkins, and Grimké, considered black women's political and domestic contributions to the changing landscape of Africans in America in the years immediately preceding and following their emancipation from American slavery. They considered a range of topics, in many ways mirroring the ideas undertaken by black writers in other genres. As a member of the black intelligentsia and freeborn, Frances Harper was nonetheless trapped by the sexist and racist conventions of the society in which she lived and wrote. She concerned herself in her writing with the problems of both race and gender, the latter indicated clearly in "The Two Offers." The sentimental tone of the story points readers to consider the dilemma facing the black woman of the nineteenth century, to develop the "affectional nature" or to develop fully her complete person. Harper writes, for example,

> Talk as you will of woman's deep capacity for loving – of the strength of her affectional nature. I do not deny it. But will the mere possession of any human love fully satisfy all the demands of her whole being? You may paint her in poetry or fiction as a frail vine, clinging to her brother man for support and dying when deprived of it, and all this may sound well enough to please the imaginations of schoolgirls, or lovelorn maidens. But woman – the true woman – if you would render her happy, it needs more than the mere development of her affectional nature. Her conscience should be enlightened, her faith in the true and right established, and scope given to her heaven-endowed and God-given faculties.[7]

Didactic in tone, the story is overtly feminist, arguing not only for the natural abilities of women but the necessity for women to accept their "earthly mission as a gift from God and strive to walk the path of life with earnest and unfaltering steps" (*Brighter*, p. 106). Harper's narrator cautions women against loving the man who bows at their shrine as a willing worshipper and instead calls for an "affinity of minds," an "intercommunication of souls" (p. 109). The powerful voice of the narrator, read easily as Harper's own, articulates many of the feminist themes outlined in the writer's speeches and essays on abolition, civil rights, women's rights, and temperance.[8] Like Maria Stewart, Harper's Boston counterpart, Harper preached moral uplift and counseled the oppressed how to free themselves from their demoralized condition. Like the spiritual narratives written by nineteenth-century black preaching women, Harper's fiction houses sermons that espouse moral responsibility.

This spiritual theme is found also in Angelina Weld Grimké's "Black Is, as Black Does (A Dream)" (1900).[9] The story uses biblical imagery to comment on racial and social inequity in the United States. The first-person narrator falls asleep on a dark and rainy morning. Reminiscent of Dickensian allegory, the narrator, identified as neither male nor female, is led on a journey past a verdant meadow and babbling brook to see the "lovers of God," a heavenly city, those who are scheduled to receive judgment and punishment from God, and those who will receive eternal peace. The irony, of course, is that those who would seemingly receive good things on earth instead receive damnation from God, and those who appear ragged and dejected are actually in line for tremendous reward. Grimké – whose distinguished biracial family included slaves, slaveholders, free black people, and abolitionists – makes her point quite clearly: although black people are treated inhumanly on earth by racist whites, the tables will be turned in eternity. During the journey, the narrator recognizes a "lame, torn, and bleeding" man as part of the oppressed race, "for in America, alas! it makes a difference whether a man's *skin* be black or white. Nothing was said, but I perceived that he had been foully murdered" (*Revolutionary Tales*, p. 23). God speaks to him in a sweet voice and ushers him into beauty and light. On the other hand, when a self-assured gentleman stands before the "judgment bar," in answer to God's questions about the righteousness of the life he has led on earth, he responds smugly: "Yea, yea, Lord, and laughed" (p. 23). God immediately recognizes him as the one who has murdered the poor man who has previously received mercy. The man is banished from God's presence and leaves behind blood-stained footprints, indicting him as the culprit. Interestingly, Grimké employs male characters to present her melodrama of eternal punishment and reward, pointing to a moral imperative focused on the achievement of racial parity that might have superseded an immediate need for the writer to advance a feminist agenda.

Much of the early work by black women short story writers considers forgiveness as a potential antidote to racism. When the white man is condemned to eternal punishment in Grimké's story, the black man creeps back to the judgment seat to plead his murderer's case, crying "Forgive, oh, forgive my brother, for he knew not what he did" (p. 24). The narrator awakens, sobbing. A similar moral is offered in Victoria Earle Matthews's "Aunt Lindy: A Story Founded on Real Life" (1893).[10] The story was originally published as a book and was republished for the first time in Shockley's *Afro-American*

Women Writers 1746–1933 (1988). Aunt Lindy, the faithful nurse of a post-Civil War black community in Georgia, is unwittingly called upon to care for her former slave master when he is injured during a devastating fire. This same man has cruelly sold all of her children during her enslavement. When Aunt Lindy looks into his face, she struggles with her initial desire to let him die. Instead, she calls him a devil and interrogates him about her children. Despite her desire to harm him physically, the story ends with her hearing the message of forgiveness from the prayer meeting being held next door: "Vengeance is mine, ses de Lawd" (*Revolutionary Tales*, p. 18). She asks for strength and nurses her former master back to health. In sentimental fashion, the story resolves itself neatly with Aunt Lindy's reuniting with her lost family members. Like Charles Chesnutt's story "The Wife of His Youth," the story explores slavery's traumatic effects on the family and calls black people to take the high road.

For some writers, particularly those whose careers span the twentieth century, the short story allows for experimentation with magical realism, narrative voice, and language where the writers can consider the experiences of black Americans that simply do not fall along neatly demarcated lines of gender or experiences. Zora Neale Hurston, known as a novelist, playwright, essayist, and folklorist, was also a prolific short story writer. Her stories first appeared in *The Crisis* and *Opportunity* magazines and in other periodicals of the Harlem Renaissance. Her stories were collected posthumously by members of her family in *Spunk: the Selected Short Stories of Zora Neale Hurston* (1985) and later by scholars who began to appreciate the wealth of material found in her short fiction alone. Hurston's use of dialect in her work, focusing almost exclusively on the interior lives of black people in the rural southern Florida of her childhood, creates an intimacy for readers familiar with the tone and cadence of black speech and folkways. Her training as a linguist and ear for the stories of her past make Hurston's stories a pleasure to read. As well, affected by white disregard for black life and the multitude of legalized restrictions inflicted upon black people in the early twentieth century, most notably segregated schools, public facilities, and transportation, Hurston considered the wide range of legal and social possibilities in her literature. Through imagined narrative and linguistic possibilities, sometimes rendered with the help of ghosts, visual transformations, or mere implications, Hurston attempted to create new realities in the face of white hatred. Hurston's experimentation with language and altered realities brings about legal and social justice where whites would either find black claims of injustice ludicrous, below the dignity of the law, or plain funny.

In Hurston's story "Black Death," the opening lines set the tone for an insider/outsider dichotomy: "We Negroes in Eatonville know a number of things that the hustling, bustling white man never dreams of. He is a materialist with little care for overtones. They have only eyes and ears, we see the skin."[11] For Hurston and her rural black characters, ghosts, dreams, and premonitions are commonplace and often execute judgment where the established system will not. Repeatedly in the story, Hurston pits black intuitive knowledge against white cerebral knowledge and uses as a case in point the undoing of Beau Diddely, a waiter at a southern hotel who has come from the North. He meets up and begins keeping company with Docia Boger, a chamber-maid at the same hotel. The two spend a great deal of time together until Docia's mother discovers that "Beau should have married her daughter weeks before" (*Harlem's Glory*, p. 382). When mother and daughter confront Beau about her delicate condition, Beau gives the wrong answer: "Looka heah, Mis' Boger. I'm a man that's traveled a lot – been most everywhere. Don't try to come that stuff over me – what I got to marry Docia for?" (p. 383). After hurling a series of insults at Docia and her mother, claiming finally that neither should have believed him anyway since he was a married man, Beau storms off in a huff. As is often the case in African American literature, the wounded party, in this case Docia's mother, often consults a root worker or hoodoo man or woman. On one side of town, Beau tells of his conquest of Docia to the other hotel waiters and anyone who will listen; on the other side, Docia's mother receives strict instructions on how to receive justice, resulting in Beau's strange and sudden death. The final words of the story bear out Hurston's intentions: "And the white folks never knew and would have laughed had anyone told them. He who sees only with the eyes is very blind" (p. 386).

The case is similar for writer Octavia B. Wynbush who also published stories in *The Crisis* and *Opportunity* magazines in the early twentieth century. Her setting for most of her stories is the South, like Hurston, and her characters employ the speech of the folk. Her story, "The Noose," takes place in Louisiana and tells the tale of marital infidelity among rural blacks. In the beginning of the story, King, a man whose wife, Nomia, has been lured away by another man, named Jed, speaks tentatively with a second woman, Leora. Leora is disturbed, because on this day, Jed has been hanged for the murder of a third man, Jeems. As well, Jed has made an important decree before his death, "Dat whoever be guilty – he comin' back an' tie dat same noose aroun' his neck."[12] Leora is equally disturbed because Jed has maintained his innocence until his execution, despite the fact that "a judge and twelve jurymen said he done it" (p. 98). According to Jed, it has been a case of mistaken identity or circumstantial evidence. In fact, after waiting five years, King has killed Jeems to frame Jed for stealing Nomia and ruining King's marriage:

King groaned as he lived again through scenes which time had not erased for him. Jed's first long compliments to him on having a wife who could "sing like a mocking bird": his long visits to the then cheerful cabin, ostensibly to see the husband; the chattering of the plantation women – chattering that, when King approached a group, gave place to meaningful signs, sly looks and nudges; the shock of coming home one day to an empty cabin, to a note from Nomia, stating she had gone away with Jed. (p. 100)

After the frightened Leora leaves King alone with his reminiscences, the tired man goes to bed and has a chilling vision, "his shadow, huge, distorted, lay along the way and partly across the ceiling. The head emerged from a noose, one end of which sprang upward as if attached to a beam out of sight" (p. 101). Relieved but still frightened, King falls into a fitful sleep, one full of visions of Nomia's mocking face, Jeems "dropping like a log in the grass, dying without a sound" (p. 102), and Jed being taken from the courtroom after the pronouncement of a guilty verdict. As King awakens from his sleep, he feels something choking him around his neck. He clutches his throat, gags, and screams. After King fails to appear among his friends, four men go to his cabin, and "[o]n the bed they found him, his body rigid, his face set in mask of mortal terror. Over his face and around his neck were the broken filaments of a spider web" (p. 103). For these writers, elusive justice is found for those inside and outside the black community where whites are unable or unconcerned.

A different type of justice is meted in Toni Cade Bambara's story "My Man Bovanne," well known from her collection *Gorilla, My Love*.[13] The language of the familiar, informal narrator, Miss Hazel, assumes that the reader is intimate with black speech and a colloquial black aesthetic. Hazel is caught in the midst of conflicting depictions of black women, expressed most clearly through Bambara's use of language. Hazel connects with Bovanne instinctively, spontaneously, because she understands community and human nature. Neither Bovanne's blindness nor his humming is off-putting to Hazel, both of which become a metaphor in the story for an authentic blackness that is grounded in history, community, and love, not mere political rhetoric. Hazel is judged by her children as country and unsophisticated, even though she has never been south of New York. She is lambasted for being both the mammy and the whore, even though she is vulnerable to black men who get "messy" when her relationship to them is dissolved (*Gorilla*, p. 4). She is often at risk, needing Bovanne's expertise as a locksmith to protect herself from those who would harm her. By dancing with Bovanne, Hazel attempts to rescue him from ridicule and alienation in the midst of a social gathering, "this benefit for my niece's cousin who's runnin' for somethin' with this black party somethin' or other behind her" (p. 4).

Where one would expect friendship and collegiality among oppressed people seeking political parity, what exists instead is disrespect, disloyalty, and disunity. Hazel's adult children berate their mother for her behavior and her dress. They call Bovanne an uncle tom and criticize him for not wearing glasses to cover his blindness. They are distressed because they feel that their mother is ill-equipped to be presented as the coordinator of the party's Council of Elders, an advisory board. The irony here is that the younger people are the ones who are blind, for they have no respect for the elders or their advice. Although Hazel and Bovanne have been invited to the gathering because they are "grass roots," they are not respected as such. Understanding the generational shift, Hazel refuses to be disrespected, whisks Bovanne away from the party, and leaves the younger generation to make avoidable and devastating mistakes.

For those black women writers who cross literal and figurative borders, like Dorothy West, Terry McMillan, Octavia Butler, and Edwidge Danticat, the short story provides a literary space for reading the blurred boundaries of ethnicity and culture. And for Sherley Anne Williams, Paule Marshall, and Ann Petry, the consideration of history in the short story serves as a source for meditation on black women's treatment at the hands of black and white men and on the women's existence as more than convenient sexual and visual stereotype.

At the end of Williams's phenomenally important story "Meditations on History" (1976), the ethnographer, named Adam Nehemiah in her later novel *Dessa Rose* (1986), laments Dessa's disappearance from his physically and psychologically controlling grasp: "She is gone. Even the smallest clue – but there was nothing, no broken twig to point a direction, no scent which the hound could hold for more than a short distance. Gone. And I not even aware, not even suspecting, just – just gone."[14] Nehemiah, unnamed in the story, uses Dessa, whom he misnames Odessa, as his slave subject, data for his treatise, *Eradicating Them*. In their interviews, Dessa tells Nehemiah about her life on the plantation, describing her friendships with individual members of the slave community. She speaks explicitly of her love for Kaine that is cut short by the master's fury. She repeats the rich lyrics of spirituals and mournful songs, outlining their encoded meanings, but Nehemiah does not listen. He does not comprehend the difference between blacks' humming, moaning, and singing. For him, the details of the slave uprising serve as a good opening for a book, not the desire for human freedom. And he reduces Kaine's anger and his subsequent death at the hands of his master to a skirmish over a banjo. So where readers are not surprised by Dessa's escape from the Hughes plantation, aided by the subversive actions of fellow slave, Jemima, Nehemiah is astounded. The problem, of course, is that he hasn't listened, a problem Dessa intuitively understands as inherent for whites who systematically ignore black knowledge production. Whites "don't be hearin" blacks when they provide information that is based in belief systems that differ from those of European origin, that are instead interconnected through black and white forms of Christianity and West African religions (*Black-Eyed*, p. 253). Such practices bolster black agency during slavery and beyond but mean very little to whites who dismiss black people, in particular, black women, as wenches, whores, negresses, she-devils, viragos.

The final lines of the story serve as a metaphor for the disappearance of historically accurate information about black women's experiences, their relationships to other black women, to black men and to their children, their participation in political activities, and their ability to survive despite being dismissed, disregarded, disrespected, disallowed – just plain "dissed." The publication of Williams's story represented a watershed moment in the reclaiming of black women's history from the obscurity and inaccuracy of racist and sexist depictions of black women as ugly, asexual servants, hyper-sexualized temptresses, unfeeling mothers, violent criminals, and pitiless matrons. Barbara Christian notes in her essay "The Highs and the Lows of Black Feminist Criticism" that black women writers and critics found that "in order to move beyond prescribed categories we had to 'rememory' – reconstruct our past. But in the literary church of the sixties, such an appeal to history was anathema. Presiding at the altar were the new critic priests, for whom the text was God, unstained by history, politics, experience, the world."[15] Short story writers of the 1970s and 1980s like Williams, Marshall, Walker, and Petry participate in the process of Morrisonian rememory[16] and take up the call of activist writer Angela Davis in her essay, "Reflections on the Black Woman's Role in the Community of Slaves." They consciously repudiate as myth the "black matriarchy and the castrating black female" and resurrect the "black woman in her true historical contours."[17] "Meditations on History," "Reena," and "The Witness" serve as representative examples.

"Meditations on History" considers the lives of black women during slavery, their painful treatment at the hands of white slaveholders, their precarious existence during childbearing years, and notably, their loving relationships with black men. Refrains of "Say, hey now, hey now, sweet mamma, Don't you hear me callin you? Hey, hey, sweet mamma, this Kaine Poppa, Kaine Poppa calling his woman's name" (p. 234) echo throughout the story, calling the reader to witness tender moments between a black man and black woman outside of the intrusive gaze of slave masters and further "scenes of subjection."[18] Williams writes,

This was love talk that made her feel almost as beautiful as the way he touched her. She shivered and pulled at the coarse material of his shirt, not needing the anger or the other words, now, because his hands and mouth made her feel so loved. His skin was warm and dry under her hands and even though she could barely wait to feel all of him against all of her, she leaned a little away from him. "Sho you want to be wid this ol dirty woman? Sho you want –"

His lips were on hers, nibbling and pulling and the sentence ended in a groan. Her thighs spead for him, her hips moved for him. Lawd, this man sho know how to love. (p. 238)

Williams's descriptions are sensual, intimate, and act as a foil to the cold and impersonal accounts of the ethnographer that render Dessa and the community of black people with whom she has lived incapable of humanity, rational thought, strategic skill, or self-agency.

The triumph of Dessa at the end of the story, her disappearance without the trace of a twig or scent, is celebrated in the meditation and points to the potential for black women to reappear in critical moments of American history. Paule Marshall takes up that vision in her story "Reena" (1983). In a revision of the middle-eastern epic *Arabian Nights*, Doreen, nicknamed Reena, and Paulie, the first-person narrator, spend a long night reminiscing after the funeral of Reena's Aunt Vi, Paulie's godmother. Reena revisits the highlights of her young adult years, entertaining and instructing her interlocutor about twentieth-century black women's history. Like Scheherazade, who must relate a series of stories to her malevolent husband to delay her execution, Reena sustains her own life by both giving and finding meaning in her experiences and linking black women's history to that of the nation. As well, the younger women's presence in Aunt Vi's bedroom, seated on the "huge Victorian bed and the pink satin bedspread with roses of the same material strewn over its surface," validates the truth of the older woman's existence and further distinguishes "her otherwise undistinguished life," for "Aunt Vi had seldom slept in her bed or, for that matter, lived in her house, because in order to pay for it, she had had to work at a sleeping-in job which gave her only Thursdays and every other Sunday off."[19]

As the two women sit on Aunt Vi's bed, literally supported by the fruits of her back-breaking labor, they travel through the significant moments of the twentieth century, moments that would not be possible were it not for the selfless, thankless, vital work performed by unschooled black women laborers like Aunt Vi. In Reena's recounting of events and incidents that have taken place since the women's graduation from high school, Marshall weaves a collective identity for black women, "so much so that as the night wore on [Paulie] was not certain at times whether it was [Reena or Paulie] speaking" (p. 90). The women rehearse their history – the complacency of

black college students and their lack of political passion, the legacy of southern violence and generational shifts, color stratification and beauty standards,
divergent notions of acceptable black hair styles, educated blacks' affinity
with liberal whites, black women dating white men, employment discrimination, the psychologically damaging effects of racism, marriage to middle class
black men, divorce, and children. Their two voices blend into one, adopting
the "tone of a litany":

"Too threatening ... castrating ..."
"Too independent and impatient with them for not being more ambitious ...
contemptuous ..."
"Sexually inhibited and unimaginative ..."
"And the old myth of the excessive sexuality of the black woman goes out the
window ..."
"Not supportive, unwilling to submerge our interests for theirs ..."
"Lacking in the subtle art of getting and keeping a man." (p. 100)

As the night gives way to morning, the story comes full circle, back to Aunt
Vi's rose-covered bedspread and the difficulties that have comprised her life.
In a final attempt to rescue themselves as the night wanes, Reena declares
"our lives have got to make more sense, if only for her" (p. 105). To find that
meaning, Marshall points to Africa as a site for hope and the possibility of a
future that offers black women and their children place and history, wholeness and affirmation.

Those black women short story writers who choose history as a site for
artistic inspiration grapple with painful experiences in American and African
American collective memory. In Ann Petry's "The Witness" (1971), the
continued threat of lynching in the midst of northern integration sets the
tone for the story.[20] Charles Woodruff, a retired professor of English from a
historically black Virginia college, has been recruited to integrate a small
town in New York. Enlisted to work with a group of juvenile delinquents,
the children of the town's influential middle-class residents, Woodruff unwittingly becomes a part of the most dangerous nexus historically for black men
in America – white women in direct relationship with white men. Guided by
the voice of his deceased wife, Addie, Woodruff attempts to fit himself into the
alien community that is blanketed in snow in the dead of winter. As he
attempts to negotiate who he is as an educated, middle-class black professional, he is plagued by the precariousness of his being the "one" that the
Superintendent of Schools says the town has been looking for. Petry creates a
type of schizophrenia in Woodruff, representative of the Du Boisian twoness
experienced by blacks in America. He is deeply torn. On the one hand, he can
afford to buy a $500 coat that is "guaranteed to make you feel like a prince"

(*Heath*, p. 2112). On the other, as he stands in front of the location where he is scheduled to work with the students, he second guesses himself, thinking he must

> look like a lunatic, standing in the snow, stamping his feet and talking to himself. If he kept it up long enough, someone would call the state police and a bulletin about him would go clattering out over the teletype: "Attention all cruisers, attention all cruisers, a black man, repeat, a black man is standing in front of the Congregational church in Wheeling, New York; description follows, description follows, thinnish, tallish black man, clipped moustache, expensive (extravagantly expensive, outrageously expensive, unjustifiably expensive) overcoat, felt hat like a Homburg, eyeglasses glittering in the moonlight, feet stamping in the moonlight, mouth muttering in the moonlight. Light of the moon we danced. Glimpses of the mood revisited." (p. 2112)

Although Petry adopts the narrative voice of a black male protagonist, she overlays it with the warnings of the black female ancestral figure in an attempt to explore the challenges of American integration.[21] Woodruff knows that Addie would be displeased with him for spending so much on a coat, but she had also counseled him to "dress more elegantly than [his] students so they would respect [his] clothes even if they didn't respect [his] learning," a dilemma rarely faced by white men of letters (p. 2112). Like black men, black women are caught between the seduction of American capitalism, the disingenuous promises of the American dream, and the realities of American racism.

Moreover, as readers progress through the story, they are reminded of the importance of the often prophetic ancestral voice. Like Lutie Johnson in Petry's acclaimed novel, *The Street* (1946), Charles Woodruff fails to listen to the wisdom of those who have passed on.[22] In the story, Addie's voice is one of skepticism, foreshadowing the danger that Woodruff will encounter at the hands of the young white hoodlums who will kidnap him and force him to be a witness to the brutal gang rape of a young white woman. Standing in front of the church, stamping and muttering and listening to Addie, Woodruff senses danger but fails to avoid it. After the counseling session, Woodruff sees the seven young men trying to force Nellie, their young white "friend," into the car. Instead of following his intuitive wisdom, most often associated with the feminine, and going home "where it was quiet and safe, mind his own business – black man's business, leave this white man's problem for a white man," Woodruff encroaches on their activities (p. 2116). Even as he is questioning them and they continue to close in on him, he thinks of Addie, new-mown hay, and flower gardens, a direct contrast to the boys' smell of stale, shut-up classrooms. Referring to Woodruff as "ho-daddy," the young men blindfold and kidnap him in his brand new station wagon, break his glasses, bind him in his own elegant coat, and force him to touch Nellie's thigh and breasts. The young men then release Woodruff, identifying him as a witness.

In the final scene of the story, Woodruff decides to return to Virginia and not to tell the police about the violent crime he has "witnessed." With Nellie's presence in the car with the seven young men the next morning, Petry shrewdly comments on one of the failures of integration and the early challenges of feminism – the solidarity between white men and women that precludes allegiances that might be forged between white women and other oppressed people in America. If the reader is encouraged to elide Addie's voice with the sense of impending doom that encourages Woodruff to leave the white man's business to the white man, then Nellie's presence in the car after the rape sheds light on black men and women's temptation to remain disconnected from white women at the hands of reprehensible white men. The burden of history is weighty in these stories of white violence and black victimization.

The early years of the twenty-first century point to the continued vibrancy of the short story for African American women writers. Contemporary collections continue to open the scope of concerns and help to push literary boundaries. Becky Birtha's *For Nights Like This One: Stories of Loving Women* (1983) and *Lover's Choice: Stories* (1987) offer black lesbian relationships sympathetically portrayed. Meri Nana-Ama Danquah's *Shaking the Tree* (2003) includes both new fiction and memoir by black women, allowing readers to consider the ways that fiction and life writing intersect and overlap. It is still the case, as Harper envisioned nearly one hundred and fifty years ago, that black women are challenged to develop all of the faculties of the human soul, "because no perfect womanhood is developed by imperfect culture" (*Brighter*, p. 109). In contemporary imperfect culture, the short story still serves as a means for the exploration of perfect womanhood.

NOTES

1. See Thomas Jefferson, *Notes on the State of Virginia* (Richmond, VA: J. W. Randolph, 1853), p. 140.
2. For rich and useful discussions on the writing of nineteenth-century speaking, preaching, and writing black women, see Katherine Clay Bassard, *Spiritual Interrogations: Culture, Gender, and Community in Early African American Women Writers* (Princeton: Princeton University Press, 1999); Hazel Carby, *Reconstructing Womanhood: the Emergence of the Afro-American Woman Novelist* (New York: Oxford University Press, 1987); Joycelyn Moody, *Sentimental Confessions: Spiritual Narratives of Nineteenth-Century African American Women* (Athens: University of Georgia Press, 2001); Carla L. Peterson, *"Doers of the Word": African American Women Speakers and Writers in the*

North (1830–1880) (New York: Oxford University Press, 1995); Marilyn Richardson (ed.), *Maria W. Stewart, America's First Black Woman Political Writer* (Bloomington: Indiana University Press, 1987).

3. For a discussion of the history of the black press, see Frankie Hutton, *The Early Black Press in America, 1827–1860* (Westport, CT: Greenwood, 1993); Armistead Scott Pride and Clint C. Wilson II, *History of the Black Press* (Washington, DC: Howard University Press, 1997); and Todd Vogel, *The Black Press: New Literary and Historical Essays* (New Brunswick, NJ: Rutgers University Press, 2001).

4. Gloria T. Hull (ed.), *The Works of Alice Dunbar-Nelson* (New York: Oxford University Press, 1988), p. xvi.

5. Hopkins also published three serialized novels: *Hagar's Daughter: A Story of Southern Caste Prejudice*; *Winona: A Tale of Negro Life in the South and Southwest*; and *Of One Blood. Or, the Hidden Self.* See Pauline Hopkins, *The Magazine Novels of Pauline Hopkins* (New York: Oxford University Press, 1988) and Patricia Okker, *Social Stories: The Magazine Novel in Nineteenth Century America* (Charlottesville: University of Virginia Press, 2003).

6. Wanda Coleman, *"A War of Eyes" and Other Stories* (1988); Colleen J. McElroy, *"Jesus and Fat Tuesday" and Other Short Stories* (1987); Rita Dove, *Fifth Sunday: Stories* (1990); Maxine Clair, *Rattlebone* (1995); and Edwidge Danticat, *Krik?Krak!* (1995).

7. Frances Smith Foster (ed.), *A Brighter Day Coming: A Frances Ellen Watkins Harper Reader* (New York: Feminist Press, 1990), pp. 109–10.

8. See Bill Mullen (ed.), *Revolutionary Tales: African-American Women's Short Stories from the First Story to the Present* (New York: Laurel, 1995).

9. Rpt. in Mullen (ed.), *Revolutionary Tales.*

10. Ibid.

11. Lorraine Elena Roses and Ruth Elizabeth Randolph (eds.), *Harlem's Glory: Black Women Writing, 1900–1950* (Cambridge, MA: Harvard University Press, 1996), p. 381.

12. Ibid., p. 99.

13. Toni Cade Bambara, *Gorilla, My Love* (New York: Random House, 1972).

14. Sherley Anne Williams, "Meditations on History," *Black-Eyed Susans: Midnight Birds: Stories by and about Black Women*, ed. Mary Helen Washington (New York: Doubleday, 1990), p. 277.

15. Barbara Christian, "The Highs and the Lows of Black Feminist Criticism," *Reading Black, Reading Feminist: A Critical Anthology*, ed. Henry Louis Gates, Jr. (New York: Penguin, 1990), p. 48.

16. In Toni Morrison's novel *Beloved*, the protagonist, Sethe, explains the phenomenon of "rememory" as the reality of things and places that simply do not go away but continue to exist. See Toni Morrison, *Beloved* (New York: Dutton, 1996).

17. Williams, "Meditations on History," p. 230. Williams quotes from Davis's essay in the epigraph to "Meditations." See Angela Davis, "Reflections on the Black Woman's Role in the Community of Slaves," *The Angela Y. Davis Reader*, ed. Joy James (Malden, MA: Blackwell, 1998).

18. The phrase references the title of Saidiya V. Hartman's *Scenes of Subjection: Terror, Slavery and Self Making in Nineteenth Century America* (New York: Oxford University Press, 1997).

19. "Reena," *Black-Eyed Susans*, ed. Washington, p. 90.
20. Rpt. in Paul Lauter (ed.), *The Heath Anthology of American Literature*, 3rd edition (Boston: Houghton Mifflin, 1998).
21. For a definition of the ancestral figure in literature, see Toni Morrison, "Rootedness: The Ancestor as Foundation," *Black Women Writers (1950–1980): A Critical Evaluation*, ed. Mari Evans (Garden City, NY: Anchor, 1984), pp. 341–43.
22. For a rich discussion of the ancestral figure in migration literature, generally, and *The Street*, in particular, see Farah Jasmine Griffin, *"Who Set You Flowin'?": The African American Migration Narrative* (New York: Oxford University Press, 1995).

14

HERMAN BEAVERS

African American women writers and popular fiction: theorizing black womanhood

The arrival of new media often generates a gap between accepted or "high" texts and those new texts regarded with suspicion or simply labeled "low." The popular drama in Shakespeare's time was regarded as low and gradually achieved high status. Following a similar trajectory, the novel began as a low form and was gradually elevated to the level of literary art…But the rise of so many new media, recently, has threatened to leave us with a deep gap between what is thought of as "high" art or literature on the one hand, and "mass" or "popular" culture on the other.

– Robert Scholes, *The Crafty Reader*

Popular culture has always been where black people theorize blackness in America. It has always constituted the sphere where black people produce narratives of pleasure, oppression, resistance, survival, and heroic performances. The kinds of stories told in popular culture may be characterized as black feminist ("Think" and "Respect" by Aretha Franklin and "Ladies First" by Queen Latifah), theses on black unemployment ("Sitting on the Dock of the Bay" by Otis Redding), interpretation of black rights ("Pay Back" by James Brown), or black funk pleasure ("Little Red Corvette" by Prince).

– Manthia Diawara, "A Symposium on Popular Culture and Political Correctness"

Girlfriend fiction, Urban Romance, Black Erotica, Speculative Fiction, or Detective Fiction, all these terms can be used to describe the subgenres of popular fiction written by African American women writers in the twenty-first century. Though the last fifteen years has seen the publication of hundreds of titles, from major publishing houses and vanity presses, the existence of what is now understood as African American popular fiction dates back many decades and points to the existence of distribution networks not found in mainstream culture. As Suzanne Dietzel points out, African American writers hoping to get their books into the hands of black readers often exploited "those venues easily accessible to the black community such as barbershops and beauty parlors, and through author programs and corner stores, church fairs, and community festivals," in addition to the growing numbers of African American writers who have turned to self-publishing as a way onto the literary scene.[1] Moreover, popular fiction and its wide appeal to African American readers insists, in contradistinction to persistent cultural stereotypes attesting to the contrary, that African Americans read books. For example, the membership of the African American Literary Book Club is overwhelmingly (84 percent), female, middle-class, and college-educated.[2] And given the fact that women constitute the majority of readers overall, the popularity of these texts must be understood as a manifestation of historical circumstance, as opposed to being simple matters of taste.

However, though it is the case that African American women's fiction has never been more widely read, it is also the case that popular fiction, with its attendant subgenres of romance fiction, detective fiction, erotica, and speculative fiction, has only recently become of interest to literary critics and historians.[3] But in light of this, we are faced with important questions. First, doesn't the popularity of these texts raise the question as to whether works of popular fiction are worthy of critical attention? That is, do they possess a level of literary craft and thematic "heft" that would justify critical labor? Second, in light of the achievements of writers like Zora Neale Hurston, Toni Morrison, Alice Walker, and Gloria Naylor, whose works have received the accolades of mainstream critics and become established in the American literary canon, can we judge these works on their own terms or does critical practice demand that we understand them within the context of *belles-lettres*? For if this were the case, it would be easy to conclude that authors like Terry McMillan, Zane, Octavia Butler, Sister Souljah, Barbara Neely, Sheneska Jackson, and Benilde Little are producing fictions that *fail* to achieve literary excellence and thus they fail to constitute an intervention upon the distorted representations of black women's lives to be found in mainstream literature and media.

To reach such a conclusion, though, is to misunderstand the ways that popular culture has functioned in black communities. Perhaps one reason for the ambivalence surrounding the reception of popular fiction is because, as a manifestation of what is deemed mass culture, it seems to lack a political critique of those forces that continue to plague the black community. Distinctions between high and low culture often associate critically situated acts of reading with the former, while viewing popular texts as too formulaic in structure to demand anything more than a cursory level of attention. Indeed, popular culture is often constructed as the site of racist and sexist representations, which leads cultural commentators to conclude that a lack of control over representations of black life persists.

As Diawara imagines it in the second epigraph, popular culture is characterized by its ability to produce a wide variety of narratives. In so doing, such narrative variety produces a set of sophisticated reading strategies that belie the charge that popular fiction is characterized by a mindless adherence to plot and fantasy. Though African American writing has from its beginnings in the eighteenth century sought to argue for the humanity and worth of the African American subject, what becomes clear is that popular fiction – in its many forms – raises questions about the nature of cultural work. For it is often the case that popular forms of entertainment are viewed, as Wahneema Lubiano suggests, as sites where the "common sense" of the dominant culture, in the form of sexism, white supremacy, patriarchy, and homophobia is reproduced. Hence, popular fiction, as cultural content produced in accordance with industrial and corporate procedures that seek to limit production and labor costs, market to selected demographic sectors, and achieve the largest return on investment, is often viewed with distrust by literary critics, despite the fact that the sales of popular fiction subsidizes "serious" or literary fiction, which does not achieve the same success in the marketplace. But, in spite of this, the debate about the value of popular fiction persists. Hence, the question might be posed, can a novel by an African American woman writer, whose readers have heard about it at a hair appointment or during a church or club gathering, be taken seriously as an instrument that furthers the project of liberation? Do texts which make the achievement of sexual pleasure or material and emotional well-being central to the plot create the grounds for resistance?

What gives these questions such rhetorical force is the fact that cultural studies often views popular culture as a site best understood through negative assessments of the motivations, production values, and outcomes associated with texts whose main function is the creation of pleasure. As such, critics often view popular texts in terms of what Stanley Fish refers to as rhetorical textuality, where the text seeks to validate and satisfy readerly desires, eschewing the task of challenging or troubling the reader.[4] However, if we take seriously Tricia Rose's observation that cultural expressions "are rarely, if ever, consistently and totally oppositional," and accept her argument that popular entertainment can represent "contradictory and partial forms of cultural resistance," we might also conclude that popular fictions are far from being instances where readers encounter texts locked in a circuit of desire and consumption. Rather, we can read them on a dialectical grid, where what Scott McCracken describes as transgression and utopia are central to an understanding of what and how popular texts *mean*.[5]

First, it must be said that when readers encountered the category of African American women's fiction, they came to understand it as a category whose parameters were defined by literary critics seeking to expand the African American literary canon. What this meant for a generation of African

American feminist critics trained after the mid 1960s was that the only women writers whose work would receive any critical attention were those who could stand up to critical scrutiny from African American male nationalist critics who felt that the pursuit of a Black Aesthetic organized around totalizing notions of racial allegiance was central to any discussion of literary value.

Such a consideration becomes especially important in view of the relatively small number of African American women writers whose works have become canonized. In light of this, it is a mistake to uncouple popular fiction from "literary" fiction or *belles-lettres*. Though popular fiction is often dismissed because of its lack of literary craft, the manner in which it endorses dominant ideological formations, and its aim to service a niche in the literary marketplace rather than seeking to cross demographic boundaries, it seems clear that without the literary achievements of Zora Neale Hurston, Ann Petry, Nella Larsen, Jessie Fauset, and Pauline Hopkins in the early stages of the twentieth century and, of course, those of Toni Morrison, Toni Cade Bambara, Alice Walker, Gayl Jones, Ntozake Shange, Sherley Anne Williams, Gloria Naylor, and Rita Dove in the latter portion of the century, African American women's popular fiction, as represented by McMillan, Benilde Little, Zane, Octavia Butler, Barbara McNeely, and a host of others would not be possible. At the same time, to demand that these writers tailor their work to fit critical tastes is to treat them in an ahistorical fashion. One need only remember Richard Wright's spiteful review of *Their Eyes Were Watching God* (1937) to understand that what we now deem to be classics of African American letters were once widely dismissed by male critics.[6] Moreover, it could be that in the dazzling brilliance displayed by African American women writers like Morrison and Walker (both of whom have been awarded the Pulitzer Prize for their works), a critical narrative has emerged that deemphasizes the level of resistance to their work when it first appeared.

For example, in an essay entitled, "Inhibiting Midwives, Usurping Creators: The Struggling Emergence of African American Women in American Fiction," critic Sondra O'Neale is critical of Morrison, Walker, Jones, and Bambara for creating characters who, in her view, represent nothing more than an impulse to tell African American women's stories "from a perspective that the white woman can manipulate and approve."[7] O'Neale's essay dismissed what critics now routinely understand as complexity of characterization in these writers' work as mere pandering, as attempts to serve the "three masters" of African American women's literary enterprise, "militant and political African American literature, the requirements of white feminism, and the trendyism of the literary and academic establishment," rather than to draw upon the examples of African American women like Angela Davis, Ida B. Wells, and Daisy Bates and create characters in their image.

I return to O'Neale's essay to suggest that the kinds of objections raised in regards to contemporary African American women's popular fiction are, like O'Neale's essay, historically situated. At the time O'Neale's essay was published in 1986, African American female scholars were often ambivalent about their relationship to feminism, in part due to the often egregious acts of exclusion and erasure perpetrated by white feminists, but also due to their sense that racial allegiance trumped the need to establish working coalitions with white feminists. In the present moment, with a younger generation of African American women readers who have grown up with a wider set of entertainment choices, where African American women are more visible in cinema, music videos, and televisual narratives – many of which are aimed at African American audiences – the idea of having a sparsely populated list of African American female writers to choose from is antithetical to the notion of progress. This is not to say that there are not legitimate questions to be directed toward popular fiction – there are myriad questions that can be raised regarding the representation of contemporary female experience in these texts – but it is to insist that the kinds of objections raised about texts we now deem to be canonical upon their publication are suggestive of the ways contestation accompanies the emergence of literary trends. Further, it could be that O'Neale's objections to the fictions of Morrison, Walker, Bambara, Jones, and Hurston, that among them, they too often fail to produce African American heroines who embody the tradition of resistance and self-invention to be found among African American women in African American communities,[8] are what may be seen as a driving force in the emergence of African American women's popular fiction.

In order to accomplish a critical maneuver such as this, we must pay close heed to McCracken when he insists that popular fiction must be read at the interstitial site where world, reader, and text merge.[9] In light of the large number of African American women writers producing popular fiction, this is borne out in the work of Jacqueline Bobo, whose book *Black Women as Cultural Readers* attempts to situate black women as readers whose encounters with authors like Terry McMillan and Alice Walker, or the films based on their books, are historically situated, an instance where they constitute an interpretive community who, in sharing the reading or viewing experience, generate "a culture of resistance where there is a supportive female community."[10] As Bobo argues, "Black women in an interpretive community are also part of this movement. As cultural producers, critics, and members of an audience, the women are positioned to intervene strategically in the imaginative construction, critical interpretation, and social condition of black women."[11]

In other words, whether black women are reading popular authors like McMillan or more canonical figures like Alice Walker or Toni Morrison, they are involved in a set of practices whose overall result is to counteract the effect of negative images. This is not to say that they read popular fictions uncritically, with no sense of what makes a fiction successful or unsuccessful, but rather it is to insist: (a) that black popular writing indicates the manner in which reality is contested by interpretive communities of women at the local level, and (b) the act of reading for pleasure, within the context of wish-fulfillment, can be understood as a transgressive act that makes it possible to imagine – and reimagine – utopian circumstance. Hence, urban romances that end with successful couplings between black men and women are not, as some might argue, instances where black women subordinate their desires in order to capitulate to the demands of patriarchy. Rather, they often create novelistic closure by juxtaposing the couple's happiness against the demands of the material world.

I turn, here, to two examples from the urban romance genre to bear this out. At the close of Sheneska Jackson's *Li'l Mama's Rules*, the novel's protagonist, Madison McGuire, stands above her "first and only love," Chris, who is on his knees proposing marriage. The novel's plot includes Madison's ill-advised couplings with men she does not love, men who embody the violation of the eponymous "rules," the first of which we discover at the beginning of the novel is "Never invite them back to your place." Madison is a teacher at private school in Los Angeles and Chris, described as "chiseled, steak-eating, rugged, pass me a beer fine," is a doctor who has returned to Los Angeles to open a clinic in Watts.[12] By the time the plot reaches the marriage proposal, Madison discovers that she is HIV-positive, survives a suicide attempt, and begins to resurrect her relationship with the father who abandoned and disappointed her as a child. In the wake of Chris's proposal, Madison hesitates until, suddenly, she hears God's voice asking her, "What about what you deserve?" (p. 258).

Reaching the end of Benilde Little's *Good Hair*, Alice, a senior editor at *View* Magazine sits in a restaurant with Miles, a former boyfriend, trying to move on from what she believes is her failed engagement to Jack, a surgeon working at Mt. Sinai in New York. As Alice and Miles toast her new job at *View*, in walks Jack, who (much to Alice's amazement and Miles's dismay) sits down at their table and proceeds to order dinner, talking to Alice's former lover as if they are old friends. Watching them, Alice marvels at two successful African American men discussing "billions of dollars in baby talk" or "talking on and on about hematomas and other medical procedures."[13] But what comes about after the dinner is what actually catches Alice by surprise. Saying goodnight to Miles, Jack and Alice get into a cab and ride to the Upper West

Side, where Jack has purchased a condominium where he insists they will live. Three chapters later, Alice and Jack exchange their vows in the apartment and the novel ends with Alice's aunt popping a bottle of champagne. However, by the time this happy ending occurs, we have learned that Alice has been a victim of incest, that Jack has fathered an out-of-wedlock child with a former lover, and that Alice, ashamed of her working-class origins, has always concealed them behind the lie of a middle-class upbringing.

In both these circumstances, we find novels which present a female hero who perseveres and finally gets exactly what she wants. These good things happen, though, only after she has achieved a sense of self-acceptance and self-love. The couplings happen, therefore, not as a consequence of, but rather concurrent to, the character's development. If there is the sense that *Li'l Mama's Rules* and *Good Hair* share a common plot trajectory – African American women who endure adversity only to end up happily married – we need only consider this fact against the hundreds of novels, featuring white female protagonists, that end in similar ways. Of course, as Janice Radway suggests, just as it is wrong to dismiss the latter as being symptomatic of women's entrapment within the patriarchal myth of "happily ever after," it is equally wrong to reach this conclusion about Jackson's and Little's protagonists.

Indeed, as Suzanne Dietzel proposes, novels like *Lil' Mama's Rules* and *Good Hair* can be understood as contemporary black novels of manners. Here, we find plots that, with slight variations, depict the "emergence and consolidation of a growing black middle class."[14] What makes this such an important development is that this circumstance calls for the protagonist to maintain a link to the familial past. Hence, when we consider characters like Robin in McMillan's *Waiting to Exhale* (1992), we must weigh her failed relationships with men, who often exploit and humiliate her, against her devotion to her elderly parents. Or, as we read about Savannah Jackson, who relocates to Phoenix, which is often considered to be a space hostile to blacks, doubts about her judgment have to be weighed against the admiration we feel for her commitment to her mother's financial well-being, even as she resists the older woman's attempts to manage her romantic life.

Further, in novels like Sister Souljah's *The Coldest Winter Ever*, we encounter a narrator who has heretofore been absent from African American fiction. Winter Santiaga, the daughter of a drug dealer, Rickey Santiaga, has grown up living in the luxury her father's illegal activities make possible. Winter describes her father as "the smoothest nigga in the world," insisting that when "he came into a room, he made a difference." Though drugs and violence are important elements of *The Coldest Winter*'s plot, ultimately, this novel is best described along the lines of what McCracken calls the family saga. Growing up in the projects, Winter's whole family – uncles, cousins, and aunts – is involved with, or benefits from, her father's drug business. In a move that completely reimagines the novel of manners, Souljah imbues Winter with the instincts and attitudes associated with the "gangsta lifestyle."[15] And, indeed, it could be said that she undertakes to revise the mafia sagas of Mario Puzo. For, like those narratives, Winter's perceptions, her desires, her strategies for apprehending the world are a complete manifestation of her life among the urban criminal element. And equally important is the fact that Winter understands her life, and the privileges it holds, against the backdrop of the projects. Seen in this way, her life is as deeply invested in the search for respectability and security as the lives of protagonists in the more genteel manifestations of the novel of manners. She talks about her first sexual experiences, learns how to manipulate boys to get what she wants, buys the best in designer clothes and shoes, pays to have her hair done in an expensive hair salon, and views those who work to earn an honest living with contempt. When Rickey Santiaga is arrested and all his possessions seized by government agents, Winter's life of privilege comes to an abrupt end. Her mother, who has been lavished with everything her heart desires, becomes a crack-addicted victim, Winter's sisters are sent to live with foster parents, and Santiaga ends up in prison, serving two consecutive life sentences.

In *The Coldest Winter Ever*, we come to understand the ways that the transgressive and the utopian aspects of popular fiction are brought to bear. For in spite of the fact that Winter Santiaga's whole life is constructed around acts of conspicuous consumption, unsafe sex, drugs, alcohol, and violence, the achievement here is that the reader comes to identify with her struggle. But it is a mistake to interpret this as Souljah's attempt to glorify this lifestyle. Rather, this novel must be understood as a cautionary tale, the intensity of which grows stronger as the novel progresses, culminating when Winter herself is arrested, sent to prison for a fifteen-year sentence and forced to live the life of an incarcerated black woman. One is forced to admire Winter, not because she learns her lesson and commits herself to reform. Rather, one is struck by the absolute and total commitment she has to her own gratification, for it is clear that Souljah makes Winter a vehicle for social commentary, even as the reader (and here, one can imagine the audience of this novel to be young women between the ages of thirteen and twenty) can revel in the delights associated with her pursuit of pleasure and stimulation, notwithstanding the illegality of selling drugs.

Obviously, the challenge becomes one of how the writer manages to create a narrative that allows the reader to experience vicariously the intense desires and fantasies associated with lifestyles located outside the realm of propriety. This is especially so when one considers the popularity of Zane, who has authored a number of highly successful novels in the field of black erotica. In *The Heat Seekers*, we have Tempest who opens the novel by narrating a list of men she refers to as "Sorry mofos." Tempest describes Hezekiel as a man who "loved to get freaky and suck on my fingers, toes, and everything in between. I don't know if it was due to his grassroots upbringing in the foothills of Kentucky or not, but the brother was born with a platinum tongue... Whatever it was the brotha had mad skillz. Not skills, skillz. He used to make me scream out his name in forty-two different languages."[16]

Though it would be easy to dismiss the popularity of Zane's work as a manifestation of the black wench, the oversexed, promiscuous construction of antebellum slave owners, it is much more accurate to draw links to Janie Woods, the hero of Zora Neale Hurston's *Their Eyes Were Watching God*, who holds the distinction of being the first female protagonist in African American literature to develop her own ideas about female sexual pleasure and pursue them. Like Janie, Zane's characters are driven to discover the many forms their sexual desire can assume as well as the multiple ways it can be satisfied. What makes this important in the present moment, when the social mores of the Right continue to scapegoat black women as being sexual outlaws, is that Zane's fiction, at its core, affirms the black female body, insisting that female agency and pleasure-seeking are not mutually exclusive.

This is not the only intervention popular fiction makes on gender stereotypes. In the mysteries of Barbara Neely, we discover her hero, Blanche White, who doubles as a maid and a detective. Published by Penguin, a division of Random House, Neely's novels instantly reclaim and recast the mammy figure, who exists in mainstream American culture as the embodiment of service and self-denial, as a character who is self-constituting, intuitive, and, in the way of all detectives, culturally literate. Blanche is heavy-set, dark-skinned, and prone to pass bad checks (again, in ways that are reminiscent of famous detectives like Sam Spade and Mike Hammer, she has her brief flirtations with the wrong side of the law, but ultimately, her integrity is unimpeachable). But she is also, refreshingly, incredibly free of self-pity or self-hatred. What she manifests instead is a will to do well, both for herself and for her children. And along the way, her unshakeable integrity, her desire to see things through to the end, make her one of the most memorable characters in contemporary African American fiction. Mindful of the ways that black femininity is often portrayed as an analogue to white femininity, as exemplified by the slender, fair-skinned women to be found in music videos, Neely imbues Blanche with a love for her body that serves the function of signifying on the sexist impulses that circumscribe representations of the female body. But along with this, Neely deconstructs the invisibility so often attributed to black servants in Hollywood cinema, turning the kind of servility that respects, and indeed, protects racial and gender boundaries, on its head to become an enactment of both access and, by extension, transgressive agency. In the novel *Blanche on the Lam*, Blanche remembers an exchange with her Cousin Murphy, whom Neely describes as the one responsible for Blanche becoming Night Girl, her fantasy alter-ego. As Cousin Murphy explains to Blanche after she sees her crying because she has been teased about her dark skin:

> They jealous cause you got the night in you. Some people got night in 'em, some got morning, others, like me and your mama, got dusk. But it's only them that's got the night can become invisible. People what got night in 'em can step into the dark and poof – disappear! Go any old where they want. Do anything. Ride them stars up there, like as not. Shoot, girl, no wonder them kids teasing you. I'm a grown woman and I'm jealous too![17]

In this passage, we find Neely rewriting the impulse that led to Ellison's narrator in *Invisible Man* (1952), where his invisibility is best revealed in the presence of light, creating instead a character whose invisibility, signified by her dark complexion, becomes a metaphor for access. What makes this important in the post-civil rights, post-Black Power era is that Neely avoids essentializing Blanche; her "power" does not issue from the exterior surface that is her skin, which could be read, depending on a particular moment in history, as either a liability or a false source of power. Rather, Blanche's subjectivity arises out of her affinity with the night; it is interiorized power that continues to be central to her self-concept long after she has grown up and ceased to be Night Girl. What this likewise suggests is that a reader coming upon this passage is provided with a strategy to shore up their own self-concept; the idea of embodying the night ceases to be a fantasy and becomes instead a useful tool for the reader.

However, the most important element of Blanche White is the fact that Barbara Neely's decision to make her a maid is, at root, a signifying gesture on detective work. If we consider the detectives of Hammett and Chandler, or, for that matter, Doyle's Sherlock Holmes, each of them is skilled in the act of deduction. As McCracken points out, the detective "is a distinctive, modern individual, but one whose identity is defined in relation to his or her world."[18] Hence, the detective is often marked by his or her ability to merge with their surroundings, to become, in effect, one with chaos. As denizens of urban space, detectives are also figures of modernity because they act out the social contradictions to be found in legally constituted societies. What makes Blanche White such a radical intervention into the detective genre is that as a maid whose role it is to keep an orderly house, to hold dirt and clutter at bay, she nonetheless undertakes to solve the crime as it exists beneath the illusion of order. As McCracken states, "the modern detective negotiates between the idea of modern life as ordered and comprehensible and the fear that such an order is fragile, and a pre-existing disorder will break through."[19] Unlike the hero of Valerie Wilson Wesley's excellent detective novels, Tamara Hayles, who is an ex-police detective and therefore trained in investigative methods, Neely's Blanche's main asset is her mother-wit. In *Blanche on the Lam*, she concludes, "This is how we've survived in this country all this time, by knowing when to act like we believe what we've been told and when to act like we know what we know" (p. 73). Certainly, this comment can be understood in the context of double consciousness but it can also be understood in structuralist terms, which is to say that the inter-relatedness of Blanche White's jobs as a maid and her talent for detection function to help the reader to understand the legacy of slavery's persistence and the inequities of a capitalist society.

In creating characters like Blanche White or Gloria, writers like Barbara Neely and Terry McMillan make it possible for black female readers to identify with characters whose struggles with body image and self-acceptance mirror their own. And in making them capable of outrageous behavior, as Neely does with Blanche when she is caught "taking liberties" by enjoying a bath in her employers' bathtub, these novels make us aware of the spatial politics that inhere to black women's bodies. For, as we encounter protagonists who shop in the most exclusive stores, drive expensive cars, and own the best brand names, these narratives present us with characters who are mindful of the fact that they are viewed as either interlopers or outright intruders and who are skillful at negotiating the gap between white perceptions and reality. Hence, in *The Coldest Winter Ever*, when Winter Santiaga finds herself in a halfway house with no money, she relies on her wits to generate enough capital to buy clothes and treat herself to a night on the town by helping the other girls in the halfway house realize their own desires for nice clothes, fancy hairstyles, and a stronger self-concept.

What may make novels like Benilde Little's *Good Hair* and Sheneska Jackson's *Li'l Mama's Rules* attractive to readers, then, is not so much their explication of African American female experience on a historical grid writ large, as we find in Morrison's *Beloved* (1987), but their depiction of African American women's experiences in the post-civil rights era, as a figuration of black postmodernity. These novels provide us with characters who are often well-educated, upwardly mobile, and residing in clean, well-lighted places that they nonetheless find unfulfilling. But that unfulfillment often arises out of their struggles to negotiate a multiplicity of roles and settings. As McMillan insists, "The eighties said we [women] should feel okay by ourselves, but after a while it gets lonely. That's what I was saying [in *Waiting to Exhale*]."[20]

These women are, after many twists and turns of the plot, often rewarded with relationships with men following similar trajectories, or in lieu of a mutually exclusive relationship, enough in the way of material benefits that they can undertake the hard work of self-definition and self-recovery without fear of destitution. Though their anxieties may lead to self-destructive tendencies, what is more often the case is that the women in these fictions are blinded by their success, by the material trappings that come to replace self-knowledge and self-awareness. In heroic fashion, these protagonists often pull themselves back from the abyss by acknowledging, if only to themselves, what they want out of life. The authors, rather than telescoping the narrative outward in order to critique the double oppression wrought by racism and sexism, often eschew wholesale explications of the white world in favor of what Manthia Diawara has termed "the black good life." As Diawara describes it, the black good-life society

> refers to black people's right to a good life – i.e. the right not to have one's life-world colonized by systems that emancipate others. The black good-life society emphasizes the necessity for productive space which is accompanied by consumption, leisure, and pleasure in black people's relation to modernity.[21]

As Diawara imagines it, the black good life "nurtures black funk as a cultural space."[22] I want to propose that popular fiction is marked by its "funkiness." Not only because it often represents settings where celebrity, wealth, and consumption are in evidence as part of the black good life, but also because it revels in the carnivalesque. As Scott McCracken notes, one of the key areas for the transcoding that accompanies the carnivalesque is the body.[23] Hence, in looking at a novel like Benilde Little's *The Itch*, McMillan's *Waiting to Exhale* or Zane's *The Heat Seekers*, we find characters whose interactions in the world are mediated through their sexuality. If we consider the ways that African American fiction by women in the twentieth century often had to skirt representations of sexuality as they worked to create positive images of black women, characters like Natasha, Robin, or Tempest overturn this impulse, insisting that black women who demonstrate competence in their professional lives should not be dismissed for being unable or unwilling to have a monogamous relationship or to consummate such a relationship in matrimony. They embody the "funky" side of postmodernity; their lives are often fraught with reversals where they find wisdom in low places.

In this respect, we need to consider the ways that popular fiction, as it assumes the form of speculative fiction or the novel of suspense, can explore dystopian settings. In these fictions, the black good life is not in evidence and the characters find their biggest challenge to be one of simply surviving harsh circumstances. For example, Octavia Butler's *Parable of the Sower*, set in the year 2025, depicts a United States nearly overcome with poverty and crime. Families must reside inside gated communities, with razor wire on the walls to keep out criminals. States have closed their borders, conservative politicians have assumed control of the government and begun to prosecute anyone who dissents. In the midst of all this, we have the novel's narrator, Lauren Olamina, who is distinguished by the fact that she is an empath who experiences the pain of anyone in close proximity. Lauren has developed a personal philosophy, called Earthseed, which she develops in the pages of a journal filled with parables that insist that the greatest force on Earth is change. Eschewing Christianity, Lauren's philosophy is put to the test after the family compound is overrun by criminals who kill the other family members and set fire to the compound. Forced to flee, Lauren sets out for northern California, picking up individuals along the way who are survivors like herself, and who become intrigued by Earthseed. The novel ends with the group having settled outside one of the smaller California cities, trading with the locals, growing their own crops, and with Earthseed slowly taking root, becoming something akin to a religion.[24]

The term "speculative fiction" has much to do with the way writers like Butler utilize realist elements to create fictions which speculate on the shape the future will assume. In *Parable of the Sower*, Butler fashions a narrative by taking recognizable aspects of American life – e.g. the growing gulf between the haves and have-nots, communities destroyed by drug addiction, gun violence, gated communities organized to keep out the unwelcome – and pushing them to logical extremes. In so doing, she creates fiction that critiques the inhumanity of the present moment, creating a cautionary tale of substance and pathos.

But we might also extend the term "speculative" to a reading of Tananarive Due's first novel, *The Between*. Whereas Butler's *Parable of the Sower* (and the sequel, *Parable of the Talents)* functions, in the way of all science fiction, as a commentary on the present, Due's novel moves in the direction of the suspenseful and the supernatural. The novel turns on a powerful conceit. In a prologue set in 1963, Due introduces us to Hilton James with the novel's first words, "Hilton was seven when his grandmother died, and it was a bad time. But it was worse when she died again."[25] Coming home from school, Hilton finds his grandmother, Eunice Kelly, sprawled on the kitchen floor of their house. However, when he runs to a neighbor for help, he returns to find his grandmother at the stove stirring pots. Her actual death comes, though, when she saves Hilton from drowning, an act which leads to her own death.

The novel's prologue is suggestive of the idea that Hilton James's life exists within the context of borrowed time, as if by some magical intervention, the life that should have been lost has been spared. The novel's plot turns on the fact that Hilton's marriage to Dede, a recently appointed circuit court judge in Dade County, is entering a difficult time, such that Hilton agrees to see a marriage counselor. But things grow desparate when Dede receives a letter containing a death threat from Charles Ray Goode, a white man she prosecuted and sent to prison. The reader comes to understand that the novel's title refers to the fact that Hilton James's life is caught between the world of the living and the world of the dead. He begins to have a series of recurring dreams, in which his grandmother's voice calls him to come back to the shore as he swims in the ocean. But despite this, his greatest concern is protecting his family from Goode, who continues to threaten his family.

Due's skill as a storyteller is evident through her ability to fuse elements of African myth, African American folklore, and surrealism into a tale that speaks to the ways that reality, as we understand it, is impinged upon by a world of shadows that blurs the boundaries between wakefulness and dreaming, as if to suggest that human senses can become attuned to the liminal space between life and death, but it requires the kind of near-death experience Hilton James undergoes to open the way to such power. Using realist elements, like the racist hate mail from Goode, as a way to locate the reader in a particular time and place, one that is recognizable because of the way identity politics pervade Hilton and Dede's professional and personal lives, Due is able, like Butler, to create a narrative whose suspense is rooted in the powerlessness that is manifest as one tries to mine the unconscious for the code key to a set of interlocking ciphers.

Conclusion

Almost by definition, popular fiction is often deemed unworthy of consideration in matters of canon formation. Because it often relies on formulas that make its plots predictable, fiction in the urban romance category is often held up to critical ridicule because it seems to revel in a kind of political incorrectness. Though in the pages above, I have tried to intimate that an understanding of popular fiction is not to be found in notions of the "literary," but rather in terms of the transgressive or the ephemeral, where a "recycling" aesthetic often leads, as we see with Hollywood films, to the fusion of two or more narrative forms – e.g. as in the lesbian-gay vampire novel, or the science fiction novel that locates social commentary alongside fantasy – it is nonetheless the case that popular fiction often generates critical anxieties about literary value in the face of what many deem to be an incomplete process of canon revision.

However, it could be that rather than relying on New Critical methodologies that reify the notion that the category of "literature" must always be emblematic of difficulty and impenetrability, the task we face is not one of trying to identify the craft to be found in popular fiction. Rather, a more fruitful task, as Robert Scholes suggests, could be in developing a deeper appreciation of the various forms of what Scholes refers to as "crafty reading." Like Scholes, I wish to argue that we do not have to reject the notion that some texts are better than others.[26] We do, I think, have to acknowledge that the readers of popular fiction written by African American women writers are adept at holding the world, the text, and their sense of self in a critical tension that allows them to engage what they read in ways that may serve a didactic function in their lives as it also complicates what it means for them to experience pleasure. Seen in historical terms, we should pay close heed to Scholes's observation in the first epigraph at the beginning of this chapter. Indeed, if we consider writers like Hammett and Chandler whose works are now considered "literary," what becomes clear is that critics are not prognosticators; we cannot, with any certainty, estimate what sorts of conditions will arise to make a text that we now deem to be popular into a classic. What we do know is that reading for pleasure can be understood as an act of rehearsal in the ongoing drama of self-invention.

NOTES

1. Suzanne Dietzel, "The African American Novel and Popular Culture," *The Cambridge Companion to the African American Novel*, ed. Maryemma Graham (Cambridge: Cambridge University Press, 2004), p. 157.
2. Ibid., p. 167.
3. Ibid., p. 157.
4. Stanley Fish, *Self-Consuming Artifacts: The Experience of 17th Century Literature* (Berkeley: University of California Press, 1972), p. 1.
5. Scott McCracken, *Reading Popular Fiction* (Manchester: Manchester University Press, 1998).
6. See Valerie Smith, "Gender and Afro-Americanist Literary Theory and Criticism," *Speaking of Gender*, ed. Elaine Showalter (New York: Routledge, 1989).
7. Sondra O'Neale, "Inhibiting Midwives, Usurping Creators: The Struggling Emergence of African American Women in American Fiction," *Conjuring: Black Women, Fiction, and Literary Tradition*, ed. Minrose C. Gwin and Hortense Spillers (Bloomington: Indiana University Press, 1985), p. 144.
8. Ibid., p. 139.
9. McCracken, *Reading Popular Fiction*, p. 2.
10. Jacqueline Bobo, *Black Women as Cultural Readers* (New York: Columbia University Press, 1995), p. 27.
11. Ibid., p. 27.
12. Sheneska Jackson, *Li'l Mama's Rules* (New York: Simon & Schuster, 1997), p. 19.
13. Benilde Little, *Good Hair* (New York: Simon & Schuster, 1996), p. 216.
14. Dietzel, "The African American Novel," 168.

15. For discussion of the "gangsta" narrative and its relation to the gangster narrative, see Todd Boyd, *Am I Black Enough for You?: Popular Culture from the 'Hood and Beyond* (Bloomington: Indiana University Press, 1997), and his essays in Todd Boyd and Kenneth Shropshire, *Basketball Jones: America Above the Rim* (New York: NYU Press, 2000).
16. Zane, *The Heat Seekers* (New York: Downtown Books Simon & Schuster, 2002), p. 3.
17. Barbara Neely, *Blanche on the Lam* (New York: Penguin, 1992), p. 59.
18. McCracken, *Reading Popular Fiction*, p. 61.
19. Ibid., p. 52.
20. Quoted in Bobo, *Black Women*, p. 15.
21. Manthia Diawara *et al.*, "A Symposium on Popular Culture and Political Correctness," *Social Text* (1993), 7.
22. Ibid., p. 7.
23. McCracken, *Reading Popular Fiction*, p. 159.
24. Octavia Butler, *Parable of the Sower* (New York: Warner Books, 2000).
25. Tananarive Due, *The Between* (New York: Harper Collins, 1995).
26. Robert Scholes, *The Crafty Reader* (New Haven, CT: Yale University Press, 2001), p. xv.

Adshead-Lansdale, Janet. "Introduction to Part Seven." *The Routledge Reader in Gender and Performance*, ed. Lizbeth Goodman and Jane de Gay. New York: Routledge, 1998. 231–35.

Allen, Carol Dawn. *Peculiar Passages: Black Women Playwrights, 1875 to 2000*. New York: Peter Lang, 2005.

Anderson, Marian. *My Lord, What a Morning*. New York: Viking, 1956.

Andrews, William L. ed. *Classic African American Women's Narratives*. New York: Oxford University Press, 2003.

  ed. *Six Women's Slave Narratives*. New York: Oxford University Press, 1989.

  To Tell a Free Story: The First Century of Afro-American Autobiography 1760–1865. Urbana: University of Illinois Press, 1986.

Angelon, Maya. *Just Give Me a Cool Drink of Water 'Fore I Diiie*. New York: Random House, 1971.

Ashcroft, Bill, Gareth Griffiths, and Helen Tiffin. *Key Concepts in Post-Colonial Studies*. New York: Routledge, 1998.

  eds. *The Post-Colonial Studies Reader*. New York: Routledge, 1995.

Assiba D'Almeida, Irene. *Francophone Women Writers. Destroying the Emptiness of Silence*. Miami: Florida University Press, 1994.

Austin, Gayle. "Feminist Theories: Paying Attention to Women." *The Routledge Reader in Gender and Performance*, ed. Lizbeth Goodman and Jane de Gay. New York: Routledge, 1998. 136–42.

Awkward, Michael. *Inspiring Influences: Tradition, Revision and African American Women's Novels*. New York: Columbia University Press, 1989.

  Negotiating Difference: Race, Gender and the Politics of Positionality. Chicago: University of Chicago Press, 1995.

  ed. *New Essays on Their Eyes Were Watching God*. New York: Cambridge University Press, 1990.

Baker, Augusta, ed. *The Black Experience in Children's Books*. New York: New York Public Library, 1971.

Baker, Houston A. "Generational Shifts and the Recent Criticism of Afro-American Literature." *Within the Circle: An Anthology of African American Literary Criticism from the Harlem Renaissance to the Present*, ed. Angelyn Mitchell. Durham, NC: Duke University Press, 1994. 282–328.

  Long Black Song: Essays in Black American Literature. Charlottesville: University of Virginia Press, 1972.

Modernism and the Harlem Renaissance. Chicago: University of Chicago Press, 1987.

Singers of Daybreak: Studies in Black American Literature. Washington, DC: Howard University Press, 1974.

Workings of the Spirit: The Poetics of Afro-American Women's Writing. Chicago: University of Chicago Press, 1991.

Baldwin, James. *Notes of a Native Son*. New York: Dial Press, 1963.

Bambara, Toni Cade. "Black Theater." *Black Expression*, ed. Addison Gayle. New York: Weybright & Talley, 1969.

"Black Theater of the 60's." *Backgrounds to Black American Literature*, ed. Ruth Miller. New York: Chandler, 1971.

ed. *The Black Woman: An Anthology*. 1970; New York: Washington Square Press, 2005.

"Chosen Weapons." Review of *Civil Wars* by June Jordan. *Ms.* 10 (April 1981), 40–42.

Deep Sightings and Rescue Missions: Fiction, Essays, and Conversations. New York: Pantheon Books, 1996.

The Salt Eaters. New York: Random House, 1980.

Banfield, Beryle. "Commitment to Change: The Council on Interracial Books for Children and the World of Children's Books." *African American Review* (Spring 1998), 17–22.

Baptiste, Edward and Stephanie M. H. Camp, eds. "Introduction: A History of the History of Slavery in the Americas." *New Studies in the History of American Slavery*. Athens: University of Georgia Press, 2006.

Baraka, Amiri. "Bopera Theory." *Black Theatre: Ritual Performance in the African Diaspora*, ed. Paul Carter Harrison. Philadelphia: Temple University Press, 2002. 378–81.

The LeRoi Jones/Amiri Baraka Reader, ed. William J. Harris and Amiri Baraka. New York: Thunder's Mouth Press, 1991.

"The Revolutionary Theater." *Home: Social Essays*. New York: Apollo, 1996.

Baraka, Amiri and Amina Baraka, eds. *Confirmation: An Anthology of African American Women*. New York: William Morrow, 1983.

Barrios, Olga. The Black Theater Movement in the United States and in South Africa: A Comparative Approach. Dissertation, University of California, Los Angeles, 1991. Ann Arbor: University of Michigan, 1992.

"From Seeking One's Voice to Uttering the Scream: The Pioneering Journey of African American Women Playwrights through the 1960s and 1970s." *African American Review* 37.4 (2003), 611–28.

"Mujer y feminismo en las artes escénicas contemporáneas [Women and Feminism in Contemporary Performing Arts]." *Estudios multidisciplinares de Género*, vol. 1. Salamanca: Universidad de Salamanca, Centro de Estudios de la Mujer, 2004. 27–61.

"Mujer, sexualidad y familia en las artes escénicas contemporáneas de África y de la diáspora africana [Women, Sexuality and Family in the Contemporary Performing Arts of Africa and the African Diaspora]." *La familia en África y la diáspora africana: Estudio multidisciplinar / Family in Africa and the African Diaspora: A Multidisciplinary Approach*, ed. Olga Barrios and Frances Smith Foster. Salamanca, Spain: Ediciones Almar, 2004. 115–58.

Bartheleme, Anthony, ed. *Collected Black Women's Narratives*. New York: Oxford University Press, 1988.

Bassard, Katherine Clay. *Spiritual Interrogations: Culture, Gender, and Community in Early African American Women Writers*. Princeton: Princeton University Press, 1999.

Bassnett, Susan. "Introduction to Part Three." *The Routledge Reader in Gender and Performance*, ed. Lizbeth Goodman and Jane de Gay. New York: Routledge, 1998. 87–91.

Bean, Annemarie, ed. *A Sourcebook of African-American Performance: Plays, People, Movement*. New York: Routledge, 1999.

Bedford, Simi. *Yoruba Girl Dancing*. New York: Viking, 1992.

Bell, Roseann P., Bettye J. Parker, and Beverly Guy-Sheftall, eds. *Sturdy Black Bridges: Visions of Black Women in Literature*. Garden City, NY: Anchor Press, 1979.

Bellah, Robert N. *Habits of the Heart: Individualism and Commitment in American Life*. New York: Harper & Row, 1986.

Bennett, Michael and Vanessa Dickerson, eds. *Recovering the Black Female Body: Self-Representations by African American Women*. New Brunswick, NJ: Rutgers University Press, 2001.

Benston, Kimberly W. "The Aesthetic of Modern Black Drama: From Mimesis to Methesis." *The Theater of Black Americans: A Collection of Critical Essays*, ed. Errol Hill. Upper Saddle River, NJ: Prentice Hall, 1980. 62.

  Performing Blackness: Enactment of African-American Modernism. New York: Routledge, 2000.

Berney, K. A. "Suzan-Lori Parks." *Contemporary Dramatists*. London: St James Press, 1994. 187–90.

Billingslea-Brown, Alma. *Crossing Borders through Folklore: African American Women's Fiction and Art*. Columbia: University of Missouri Press, 1999.

Bishop, Rudine Sims. *Shadow and Substance: Afro-American Experience in Contemporary Children's Fiction*. Urbana, IL: National Council of Teachers of English, 1982.

Bloom, Harold. *Toni Morrison: Modern Views*. New York: Chelsea House Publishers, 1990.

Bobo, Jacqueline. *Black Women as Cultural Readers*. New York: Columbia University Press, 1995.

Boesenberg, Elia. *Gender, Voice, Vernacular: The Formats of Female Subjectivity in Zora Neale Hurston, Toni Morrison and Alice Walker*. Heidelberg: Universitätsverlag Winter, 1999.

Bonner, Marita. "On Being Young – a Woman – and Colored." *Frye Street & Environs: The Collected Works of Marita Bonner*. Boston: Beacon Press, 1987.

Bordo, Susan. "The Body and the Reproduction of Femininity." *Writing on the Body: Female Embodiment and Feminist Theory*, ed. Katie Conby, Nadia Medina, and Sarah Stanbury. New York: Columbia University Press, 1997. 90–110.

Boyd, Melba Joyce. *Discarded Legacy: Politics and Poetics in the Life of Frances E. W. Harper, 1825–1911*. Detroit: Wayne State University Press, 1994.

Braxton, Joanne M. *Black Women Writing Autobiography: A Tradition Within a Tradition*. Philadelphia: Temple University Press, 1989.

  Introduction. *Work of the Afro-American Woman*. New York: Oxford University Press, 1988.

Braxton, Joanne M. and Andrée Nicola McLaughlin, eds. *Wild Women in the Whirlwind: Afra-American Culture and the Contemporary Literary Renaissance*. New Brunswick, NJ: Rutgers University Press, 1990.

Bray, Rosemary L. *Unafraid of the Dark: A Memoir*. New York: Random House, 1998.

Brooks, Gwendolyn. *Blacks*. Chicago: David Co., 1987.

   Mand Martha. New York: Harper, 1953.

Brown, Elaine. *A Taste of Power: A Black Woman's Story*. New York: Anchor, 1992.

Brown, Fahamisha Patricia. *Performing the Word: African American Poetry as Vernacular Culture*. New Brunswick, NJ: Rutgers University Press, 1999.

Brown, Janet. "Feminist Theory and Contemporary Drama." *The Cambridge Companion to American Women Playwrights*, ed. Brenda Murphy. Cambridge: Cambridge University Press, 1999. 155–72.

Brown, Sterling A. "Our Literary Audience." *Within the Circle: An Anthology of African American Literary Criticism from the Harlem Renaissance to the Present*, ed. Angelyn Mitchell. Durham, NC: Duke University Press, 1994. 69–78.

Brown-Guillory, Elizabeth. *Their Place on the Stage: Black Women Playwrights in America*. Westport, CT: Greenwood Press, 1988.

   ed. *Wines in the Wilderness: Plays by African American Women from the Harlem Renaissance to the Present*. Westport, CT: Greenwood Press, 1990.

Bryant, Jacqueline K. *The Foremother Figure in Early Black Women's Literature: Clothed in My Right Mind*. New York: Garland Publishing, 1999.

Butler, Judith. "Peformative Acts and Gender Construction." *Writing on the Body: Female Embodiment and Feminist Theory*, ed. Katie Conby, Nadia Medina, and Sarah Stanbury. New York: Columbia University Press, 1997. 401–17.

Butler, Octavia. *Parable of the Sower*. New York: Warner Books, 1993.

Butler-Evans, Elliot. *Race, Gender, and Desire: Narrative Strategies in the Fiction of Toni Cade Bambara, Toni Morrison and Alice Walker*. Philadelphia: Temple University Press, 1989.

Cade, Toni, ed. *The Black Woman: An Anthology*. New York: New American Library, 1970, rpt. Washington Square Press, 2005.

Campbell, Jennifer. "It's a Time in the Land: Gendering Black Power and Sarah E. Wright's Place in the Tradition of Black Women's Writing." *African American Review* 31.2 (Summer 1997), 211–22.

Cannon, Katie Geneva. *Katie's Canon: Womanism and the Soul of the Black Community*. New York: Continuum, 1995.

Carby, Hazel. *Reconstructing Womanhood: The Emergence of the Afro-American Woman Novelist*. New York: Oxford University Press, 1987.

Carroll, Rebecca. *Sugar in the Raw: Voices of Young Black Girls in America*. New York: Three Rivers Press, 1997.

Carter, Alexandra. "Feminist Strategies for the Study of Dance." *The Routledge Reader in Gender and Performance*, ed. Lizbeth Goodman and Jane de Gay. New York: Routledge, 1998. 247–50.

Case, Sue Ellen. "Towards a New Poetics." *The Routledge Reader in Gender and Performance*, ed. Lizbeth Goodman and Jane de Gay. New York: Routledge, 1998. 143–48.

Chapman, Dorothy. *Index to Poetry by Black American Women*. Westport, CT: Greenwood Press, 1989.

Cherry, Gwendolyn *et al. Portraits in Color: The Lives of Colorful Negro Women.* Paterson, NJ: Pageant Books, 1962.

Christian, Barbara. *Black Feminist Criticism: Perspectives on Black Women Writers.* New York: Pergamon, 1985.

 Black Women Novelists: The Development of a Tradition, 1892–1976. Westport, CT: Greenwood Press, 1980.

 "But What Is It That We Think We're Doing Anyway: The State of Black Feminist Criticism(s) or My Version of a Little Bit of History." *Changing Our Own Words: Essays On Criticism, Theory, and Writing by Black Women*, ed. Cheryl A. Wall. New Brunswick, NJ: Rutgers University Press, 1989.

 "The Highs and Lows of Black Feminist Criticism." *Reading Black, Reading Feminist: A Critical Anthology*, ed. Henry Louis Gates. New York: Penguin, 1990.

 "The Race for Theory." *The Black Feminist Reader*, ed. Joy James and Denean Sharpely-Whiting. Malden, MA: Blackwell, 2000. 11–23.

 "Trajectories of Self-Definition: Placing Contemporary Afro-American Women's Fiction." *Conjuring: Black Women, Fiction and Literary Traditions*, ed. Marjorie Pryse and Hortense Spillers. Bloomington: Indiana University Press, 1985. 233–48. Rpt. in Christian, *Black Feminist Criticism.* 171–86.

Clarke, Cheryl. *"After Mecca": Women Poets and the Black Arts Movement.* New Brunswick, NJ: Rutgers University Press, 2005.

 "The Failure to Transform: Homophobia in the Black Community." *Home Girls: A Black Feminist Anthology*, ed. Barbara Smith. New Brunswick, NJ: Rutgers University Press, 2000. 190–201.

 "Lesbianism: An Act of Resistance." *Words of Fire: An Anthology of African American Feminist Thought*, ed. Beverly Guy-Sheftall. New York: New Press, 1995. 242–52.

Cleage, Pearl. "Pearl Cleage." *Essence* (September 2003) www.findarticles.com

Clifton, Lucille. *Good Woman, Poems and a Memoir, 1969–1980.* Brockport, NY: BOA Editions, 1987.

 Some of the Days of Everett Anderson. New York: Henry Holt, 1987.

Cole, Johnnetta B. "Black Women in America: An Annotated Bibliography." *Black Scholar* 3 (December 1971), 42–54.

Collier, Eugenia. "Fields Watered with Blood: Myth and Ritual in the Poetry of Margaret Walker." *Fields Watered with Blood: Critical Essays on Margaret Walker*, ed. Maryemma Graham. Athens: University of Georgia Press, 2001. 98–109.

Collins, Patricia Hill. "Social Constructions of Black Feminist Thought." *The Black Feminist Reader*, ed. Joy James and Denean Sharpely-Whiting. Malden, MA: Blackwell, 2000. 181–207.

Conboy, Katie, Nadia Medina, and Saraha Stanbury. "Introduction." *Writing on the Body: Female Embodiment and Feminist Theory*, ed. Katie Conboy, Nadia Medina, and Sarah Stanbury. New York: Columbia University Press, 1997. 1–12.

Conner, Marc. *The Aesthetics of Toni Morrison: Speaking the Unspeakable.* Jackson: University Press of Mississippi, 2000.

Connor, Kimberly. *Conversions and Visions in the Writing of African American Women.* Knoxville, TN: University of Tennessee Press, 1994.

Crafts, Hannah. *Bondwoman's Narrative.* New York: Warner Books, 2002.

Cummings, Pat. *Talking With Artists*. New York: Bradbury, 1992.

Curtis, Christopher Paul. *Bud, Not Buddy*. New York: Delacorte, 1999.

Dandridge, Rita. *Black Women's Activism: Reading African American Women's Historical Romances*. New York: Peter Lang, 2004.

"On Novels by Black American Women: A Bibliographic Essay." *Women's Studies Newsletter* (Summer 1978), 28–30.

Davies, Carole Boyce. *Black Women, Writing and Identity: Migrations of the Subject*. New York: Routledge, 1994.

Davis, Angela. *An Autobiography*. New York: International, 1974.

"Reflections on the Black Woman's Role in the Community of Slaves." *Black Scholar* 3 (December 1971), 3–15. Rpt. in *The Angela Y. Davis Reader*, ed. Joy James. Malden, MA: Blackwell, 1998.

Women, Culture and Politics. New York: Vintage, 1990.

Davis, Arthur P. *From the Dark Tower*. Washington, DC: Howard University Press, 1974.

"Gwendolyn Brooks: Poet of the Unheroic." *College Language Association Journal* 7 (1973), 114–25.

Davis, Thadious. *Nella Larsen: Novelist of the Harlem Renaissance*. Baton Rouge: Louisiana State University Press, 1994.

Davis, Thulani. "Don't Worry, Be Buppy: Black Novelists Head for the Mainstream." *Village Voice Literary Supplement* (May 1990), 26–29.

DeWeever, Jacqueline. *Mythmaking and Metaphor in Black Women's Fiction*. New York: St. Martin's Press, 1992.

Diawara, Manthia, *et al.* "A Symposium on Popular Culture and Political Correctness." *Social Text* (1993).

Dickerson, Glenda. "The Cult of True Womanhood: Toward a Womanist Attitude in African-American Theatre." *Performing Feminisms: Feminist Critical Theory and Theatre*, ed. Sue-Ellen Case. Baltimore: Johns Hopkins University Press, 1990. 109–18.

Dieke, Ikenna, ed. *Critical Essays on Alice Walker*. Westport, CT: Greenwood Press, 1999.

Dietzel, Susanne B. "The African American Novel and Popular Culture." *The Cambridge Companion to the African American Novel*, ed. Maryemma Graham. Cambridge: Cambridge University Press, 2004. 156–70.

Dollan, Jill. "The Discourse of Feminisms: The Spectator and Representation." *The Routledge Reader in Gender and Performance*, eds. Lizbeth Goodman and Jane de Gay. New York: Routledge, 1998. 288–94.

Douglas, Ann. *Terrible Honesty*. New York: Farrat, Straus, and Giroux, 1995.

Drukman, Steven. "Doo-a-Diddly-Dit-Dit: An Interview with Suzan-Lori Parks (1995)." *A Sourcebook of African-American Performance: Plays, People, Movement*, ed. Annemarie Bean. New York: Routledge, 1999. 284–306.

Dubey, Madhu. "A New World Song: The Blues Form of Corregidora." *Black Women Novelists and the Nationalist Aesthetic*. Bloomington: Indiana University Press, 1994. 72–88.

Du Bois, W. E. B. *The Crisis* (Nov. 1910), 10.

The Souls of Black Folk. 1903. Chicago: A. C. McClurg & Co., 1931.

duCille, Ann. *The Coupling Convention: Sex, Text, and Tradition in Black Women's Fiction*. New York: Oxford University Press, 1993.

"The Occult of True Black Womanhood: Critical Demeanor and Black Feminist Studies." *Signs* 19.3 (Spring 1994), 591–629.

Dunbar, Paul Laurence. *The Complete Poems of Paul Laurence Dunbar*. New York: Dodd, Mead & Co., 1940.

Little Brown Baby, ed. Bertha Rodgers, illust. Erick Berry. New York: Dodd, Mead & Co., 1895, 1940.

Dunbar-Nelson, Alice. "The Negro Woman and the Ballot," *Words of Fire: An Anthology of African-American Feminist Thought*, ed. Beverly Guy-Sheftall. New York: New Press, 1995. 85–88.

Dunham, Katherine. *A Touch of Innocence*. New York: Harcourt Brace, 1959.

Egar, Emmanuel. *Black Women Poets of the Harlem Renaissance*. Lanham, MD: University Press of America, 2003.

Elia, Nada. *Trances, Dances and Vociferations: Agency and Resistance in Africana's Women's Narratives*. New York: Garland Press, 2001.

Emery, Lynne Fauley. *Black Dance: From 1619 to Today*. 2nd rev. edn. Princeton, NJ: Dance Horizons, Princeton Book Company, 1988.

Ernest, John. *Liberation Historiography: African-American Writers and the Challenge of History, 1794–1861*. Durham, NC: University of North Carolina Press, 2004.

Evans, Mari, ed. *Black Women Writers (1950–1980): A Critical Evaluation*. New York: Anchor Books, 1984.

I Am a Black Woman. New York: William Morrow, 1970.

Exum, Pat Crutchfield, ed. *Keeping the Faith: Writings by Contemporary Black American Women*. Greenwich, CT: Fawcett Publications, 1974.

Fabian, Ann. "Hannah Crafts, Novelist; or, How a Silent Observer Became a 'Dabster at Invention.'" *In Search of Hannah Crafts: Critical Essays on the Bondswoman's Narrative*, ed. Henry Louis Gates and Hollis Robbins. New York: Basic Civitas, 2004.

Fabre, Geneviève. *Drumbeats, Masks, and Metaphor: Contemporary Afro-American Theatre*. Cambridge, MA: Harvard University Press, 1983.

Fanon, Frantz. *Black Skin, White Masks*. London: Pluto, 1986.

"The Fact of Blackness." *The Post-Colonial Studies Reader*, ed. Bill Aschroft, Gareth Griffiths, and Helen Tiffin. New York: Routledge, 1995. 323–26.

The Wretched of the Earth. 1961. Trans. Constance Farrington. New York: Grove Press, 1963.

Fauset, Jessie. *Plum Bun*. 1928; Boston: Beacon Press, 1990.

There Is Confusion. 1924; Boston: Northeastern University Press, 1989.

Fehrenbach, Robert. "An Early Twentieth Century Problem Play of Life in Black America: Angelina Grimké's *Rachel*." *Wild Women in the Whirlwind. Afra-American Culture and the Contemporary Literary Renaissance*, ed. Joanne Braxton and Andrée Nicola McLaughlin. New Brunswick, NJ: Rutgers University Press, 1990. 89–106.

Ferguson, Sally Ann H. "Christian Violence and the Slave Narrative." *American Literature* 68.2 (1996), 297–320.

Ferris, Lesley. "Introduction to Part Five: Cross-Dressing and Women's Theatre." *The Routledge Reader in Gender and Performance*, ed. Lizbeth Goodman and Jane de Gay. New York: Routledge, 1998. 165–69.

Fisher, Dexter, ed. *The Third Woman: Minority Women Writers in the United States*. Boston: Houghton Mifflin, 1980.

Fleischner, Jennifer. *Mastering Slavery: Memory, Family, and Identity in Women's Slave Narratives*. New York: New York University Press, 1996.

Floyd, Silas X. *Floyd's Flowers, or Duty and Beauty for Colored Children*. Atlanta: Hertel, Jenkins, 1905.

Foreman, P. Gabrielle. "Who's Your Mama? 'White' Mulatta Genealogies, Early Photography, and Anti-Passing Narratives of Slavery and Freedom." *American Literary History* 14.3 (2002), 505–39.

Foreman, P. Gabrielle and Reginald Pitts. Introduction to Harriet Wilson, *Our Nig; or, Sketches from the Life of a Free Black*. New York: Penguin, 2004.

Forte, Jeanie. "Realism, Narrative, and the Feminist Playwright – A Problem of Reception." *Feminist Theatre and Theory*, ed. Helen Keyssar. London: Macmillan, 1996. 19–34.

Foster, Frances Smith. "Changing Concepts of the Black Woman." *Journal of Black Studies* 3 (June 1973), 433–54.

 Witnessing Slavery: The Development of Ante-Bellum Slave Narratives. 2nd edn. Madison: University of Wisconsin Press, 1994.

 Written By Herself: Literary Production by African American Women, 1746–1892. Bloomington: University of Indiana Press, 1993.

Fulton, DoVeanna S. *Speaking Power: Black Feminist Orality in Women's Narratives of Slavery*. Albany: SUNY Press, 2006.

Gabbin, Joanne V., ed. *The Furious Flowering of African American Poetry*. Charlottesville: University of Virginia Press, 1999.

Garvey, Amy Jacques. "Our Women Getting into the Larger Life." *Words of Fire: An Anthology of African American Feminist Thought*, ed. Beverly Guy-Sheftall. New York: New Press, 1995. 91–92.

 "Women as Leaders." *Words of Fire: An Anthology of African American Feminist Thought*, ed. Beverly Guy-Sheftall. New York: New Press. 93–94.

Gates, Henry Louis, Jr. *Black Literature and Literary Theory*. London: Methuen, 1984.

 Foreword. *The Schomburg Library of Nineteenth-Century Black Women Writers*, gen. ed., Henry Louis Gates. 40 vols. New York: Oxford University Press, 1988–94. Vii–xxii.

 Figures in Black: Words, Signs and the Racial Self. Oxford: Oxford University Press, 1987.

 The Signifying Monkey: A Theory of Afro-American Literary Criticism. Oxford: Oxford University Press, 1988.

 The Trials of Phillis Wheatley: America's First Black Poet and Her Encounters with the Founding Fathers. New York: Basic Civitas, 2003.

Gates, Henry Louis and K. Anthony Appiah, eds. *Alice Walker: Critical Perspectives Past and Present*. New York: Amistad, 1993.

 Zora Neale Hurston, Critical Perspectives Past and Present. New York: Amistad/Penguin, 1993.

Gayle, Addison. *The Way of the New World: The Black Novel in America*. Garden City, NY: Doubleday, 1975.

Gerald, Carolyn F. "The Black Writer and His Role." 1969. *The Black Aesthetic*, ed. Addison Gayle, Jr. Garden City: Doubleday, 1971. 349–51.

Gere, Anne Ruggles and Sarah R. Robbins. "Gendered Literacy in Black and White: Turn of the Century African American and European Club Women's Writing." *Signs: Journal of Women in Culture and Society* 21.3 (1996), 643–78.

Giddings, Paula. *When and Where I Enter: The Impact of Black Women on Race and Sex in America.* New York: William Morrow, 1984.

Gilbert, Sandra and Susan Gubar. *The Madwoman in the Attic: The Woman Writer and the Nineteenth-Century Imagination.* New Haven, CT: Yale University Press, 1979.

Giovanni, Nikki. *Black Feeling, Black Talk, Black Judgement.* New York: William Morrow, 1970.

Goodman, Lizbeth. "Introduction: Gender in Performance." *The Routledge Reader in Gender and Performance*, ed. Lizbeth Goodman and Jane de Gay. New York: Routledge, 1998. 1–16.

Gray, Christine. "Discovering and Recovering African American Women Playwrights Writing before 1930." *The Cambridge Companion to American Women Playwrights*, ed. Brenda Murphy. Cambridge: Cambridge University Press, 1999. 244–53.

Greenfield, Eloise. *Honey, I Love.* New York: Crown, 1978.

Griffin, Farah Jasmine. "Minnie's Sacrifice: Frances Ellen Watkins Harper's Narrative of Citizenship." *The Cambridge Companion to Nineteenth-Century American Women's Writing*, ed. Dale M. Bauer and Philip Gould. New York: Cambridge University Press, 2001.

"Conflict and Chorus: Reconsidering Toni Cade's *The Black Woman: An Anthology.*" *Is It Nation Time? Contemporary Essays on Black Power and Black Nationalism*, ed. Eddie Glaude. Chicago: University of Chicago Press, 2002. 112–29.

"That the Mothers May Soar and the Daughters May Know Their Names: A Retrospective of Black Feminist Literary Criticism." *Signs* 32.2 (2007), 483–507.

"Thirty Years of Black American Literature and Literary Studies: A Review." *Journal of Black Studies.* November, 2004.

"Who Set You Flowin'?": The African American Migration Narrative. New York: Oxford, 1995.

Guy-Sheftall, Beverly, ed. *Words of Fire: An Anthology of Black Feminist Thought.* New York: New Press, 1995.

Haraway, Donna. "The Persistence of Vision." *Writing on the Body: Female Embodiment and Feminist Theory*, ed. Katie Conby, Nadia Medina, and Sarah Stanbury. New York: Columbia University Press, 1997. 283–95.

Harper, Frances E. W. *Iola Leroy.* 1892; Boston: Beacon Press, 1987.

Harper, Philip Brian. *Is It Nation Time? Contemporary Essays on Black Power and Black Nationalism*, ed. Eddie S. Glaude, Jr. Chicago: University of Chicago Press, 2002. 163–88.

Harris, Jessica. "The National Black Theatre: The Sun People of 125th Street." *The Theatre of Black Americans: A Collection of Critical Essays*, ed. Errol Hill. Vol. II. Upper Saddle River, NJ: Prentice Hall, 1980. 13–29.

Harris, Trudier. "Before the Strength, the Pain: Portraits of Elderly Black Women in Early Twentieth-Century Anti-Lynching Plays." *Black Women Playwrights: Visions on the American Stage*, ed. Carol P. Marsh-Lockett. New York: Garland Publishing, 1999. 25–42.

From Mammies to Militants: Domestication in Black American Literature. Philadelphia: Temple University Press, 1982.

Hart, Linda, ed. *Making Spectacle: Feminist Essays on Contemporary Women's Theater.* Ann Arbor: University of Michigan Press, 1992.

Hartman, Saidya. *Scenes of Subjection: Terror, Slavery, and Self-Making in Nineteenth Century America*. New York: Oxford University Press, 1997.

Hatch, James. "Some African Influences on the Afro-American Theatre." *The Theatre of Black Americans: A Collection of Critical Essays*, ed. Errol Hill. Vol. I. Upper Saddle River, NJ: Prentice Hall, 1980. 85–93.

Hatch, James V. and Leo Hamalian, eds. *Lost Plays of the Harlem Renaissance, 1920–1940*. Detroit: Wayne State University Press, 1996.

   The Roots of African American Drama: An Anthology of Early Plays, 1858–1938. Detroit: Wayne State University Press, 1991.

Hatch, James V. and Ted Shine, eds. *Black Theatre, USA: Forty-five Plays by Black Americans, 1847–1974*. New York: Free Press, 1974.

   Black Theatre USA: Plays by African Americans, vol. I, *The Early Period, 1847–1938*. New York: Free Press, 1996.

   Black Theatre USA Plays by African Americans, vol. II, *The Recent Period: 1935–Today*. New York: Free Press, 1996.

Hemenway, Robert. *Zora Neale Hurston: A Literary Biography*. Urbana: University of Illinois Press, 1977.

Henderson, Mae G., ed. *Borders, Boundaries, and Frames: Essays in Cultural Criticism, and Cultural Studies*. New York: Routledge, 1995.

   "Speaking in Tongues: Dialogics, Dialectics and the Black Women's Literary Tradition." *Changing Our Own Words: Essays on Criticism, Theory, and Writing by Black Women*, ed. Cheryl A. Wall. New Brunswick, NJ: Rutgers University Press, 1991. 16–37.

Henderson, Stephen E. Introduction. *Black Women Writers 1950–1980: A Critical Evaluation*, ed. Mari Evans. New York: Anchor Books, 1984. xxiii–xxviii.

   Understanding the New Black Poetry: Black Speech and Black Music as Poetic References. New York: William Morrow, 1973.

Hernton, Calvin C. *The Sexual Mountain and Black Women Writers: Adventures in Sex, Literature, and Real Life*. New York: Anchor Books, 1987.

Hill, Errol G. and James V. Hatch, eds. *A History of African American Theatre*. Cambridge: Cambridge University Press, 2005.

Hill, Patricia Liggins, ed. *Call and Response: The Riverside Anthology of the African American Literary Tradition*. Boston: Houghton Mifflin Co., 1998.

Hine, Darlene Clark, Stanley Harrold, and William C. Hine. *African Americans: A Concise History – Combined Volume*. Upper Saddle River, NJ: Prentice Hall, 2004.

Hine, Darlene Clark and Kathleen Thompson, eds. *A Shining Thread of Hope: The History of Black Women in America*. New York: Broadway, 1998.

Hirsch, Marianne. "Feminist Discourse/Maternal Discourse: Speaking with Two Voices." *Mother/Daughter Plot: Narrative, Psychoanalysis, Feminism*. Bloomington: Indiana University Press, 1989.

   "Knowing Their Names: Toni Morrison's *Song of Solomon*." *New Essays on Song of Solomon: The American Novel*, ed. Valerie Smith. New York: Cambridge University Press, 1995.

Holloway, Karla. *Moorings and Metaphors: Figures of Culture and Gender in Black Women's Literature*. New Brunswick, NJ: Rutgers University Press, 1992.

Honey, Maureen, ed. *Shadowed Dreams: Women's Poetry of the Harlem Renaissance*. New Brunswick, NJ: Rutgers University Press, 1989.

hooks, bell. *Ain't I a Woman: Black Women and Feminism*. Boston: South End Press, 1981.

Black Looks: Race and Representation. Boston: South End Press, 1992.

"Black Women: Shaping Feminist Theory." *The Black Feminist Reader*, ed. Joy James and T. Denean Sharpley-Whiting. Malden, MA: Blackwell, 2000. 131–45.

"Choosing the Margin as a Space of Radical Openness." *Framework* 36 (1990), 15–23.

"Feminism: A Movement to End Sexist Oppression." *Feminist Theory: From Margin to Center*. Boston: South End Press, 1984. 17–31.

Outlaw Culture: Resisting Representations. New York: Routledge, 1994.

"Revolutionary Black Women: Making Ourselves Subject." *A Howard Reader: An Intellectual and Cultural Quilt of the African-American Experience*, ed. Paul E. Logan. New York: Houghton Mifflin, 1997. 53–62.

"Selling Hot Pussy: Representations of Black Female Sexuality in the Cultural Marketplace." *Writing on the Body: Female Embodiment and Feminist Theory*, ed. Katie Conboy, Nadia Medina, and Sarah Stanbury. New York: Columbia University Press, 1997. 113–28.

Sisters of the Yam: Black Women and Self-Recovery. Boston: South End Press, 2005.

Talking Back: Thinking Feminist, Thinking Black. Boston: South End Press, 1989.

When Angels Speak of Love: Poems. New York: Atria Books, 2007.

"Writing the Subject: Reading *The Color Purple*." *Reading Black, Reading Feminist: A Critical Anthology*, ed. Henry Louis Gates, Jr. New York: Meridian, 1990.

Yearning: Race, Gender, and Cultural Politics. Boston: South End Press, 1990.

Hopkins, Pauline. *Contending Forces: A Romance Illustrative of Negro Life North and South*. Boston: Colored Cooperative Publishing, 1900.

Horton-Stallings, La Monda. *Mutha' is Half a Word: Intersections of Folklore, Vernacular, Myth and Queries in Black Female Culture*. Columbus: Ohio State University Press, 2007.

Houchins, Sue E. Introduction. *Spiritual Narratives*. New York: Oxford University Press, 1988.

Huggins, Nathan. *Harlem Renaissance*. New York: Oxford University Press, 1971.

Hull, Akasha Gloria. *Soul Talk: The New Spirituality of African-American Women*. Rochester, VT: Inner Traditions, 2001.

Hull, Gloria T. *Color, Sex, and Poetry: Three Women Writers of the Harlem Renaissance*. Bloomington: Indiana University Press, 1987.

"Researching Alice Dunbar-Nelson: A Personal and Literary Perspective." *All the Women Are White, All the Blacks Are Men, But Some of Us Are Brave*, ed. Gloria T. Hull, Patricia Bell Scott, and Barbara Smith. New York: Feminist Press, 1982. 189–95.

Hull, Gloria T., Patricia Bell Scott, and Barbara Smith, eds. *All the Women Are White, All the Blacks Are Men, But Some of Us Are Brave: Black Women's Studies*. New York: Feminist Press, 1982.

Humez, Jean. *Gifts of Power: The Writings of Rebecca Cox Jackson, Black Visionary, Shaker Eldress*. Amherst: University of Massachusetts Press, 1981.

Harriet Tubman: The Life and the Life Stories. Madison: University of Wisconsin Press, 2004.

Humm, Maggie. *The Dictionary of Feminist Theory*. Upper Saddle River, NJ: Prentice Hall, 1999.

Hurston, Zora Neale. "Characteristics of Negro Expression." 1934. *Within the Circle: An Anthology of African American Literary Criticism from the Harlem Renaissance to the Present*, ed. Angelyn Mitchell. Durham, NC: Duke University Press, 1994. 79–94.

    The Hurston Reader. New York: Harper Collins, 1999.

    Dust Tracks on the Road. 1942; New York: Harper Collins, 1991.

    Jonah's Gourd Vine. 1934; New York: Harper Collins, 1990.

    Their Eyes were Watching God. 1937; New York: Harper Collins, 1990.

Hutchinson, George. *The Harlem Renaissance in Black and White*. Cambridge, MA: Harvard University Press, 1995.

Hutton, Frankie. *The Early Black Press in America, 1827–1860*. Westport, CT: Greenwood Press, 1993.

Ikard, David. *Breaking the Silence: Toward a Black Feminist Criticism*. Baton Rouge: Louisiana State University Press, 2007.

Irigaray, Luce. "This Sex Which Is Not One." *Writing on the Body: Female Embodiment and Feminist Theory*, ed. Katie Conby, Nadia Medina, and Sarah Stanbury. New York: Columbia University Press, 1997. 248–56.

Jackson, Angela. "What is American About American Poetry?" *The Poetry Society of America*. www.poetrysociety.org/jackson.html

Jacobs, Harriet. *Incidents in the Life of a Slave Girl: Written by Herself*, ed. Jean Fagan Yellin. Cambridge, MA: Harvard University Press, 1987.

James, Joy and Denean Sharpley-Whiting, eds. *The Black Feminist Reader*. Oxford: Blackwell, 2000.

James, Stanlie M. "Mothering: A Possible Black Feminist Link to Social Transformation?" *Theorizing Black Feminisms: The Visionary Pragmatism of Black Women*, ed. Stanlie M. James and Abena P. A. Busia. New York: Routledge, 1994. 44–54.

James, Stanlie M. and Abena P. A. Busia, eds. *Theorizing Black Feminisms: The Visionary Pragmatism of Black Women*. New York: Routledge, 1994.

"Jawole Willa Jo Zollar, Biographical Essay." www.pbs.org/wnet/freetodance/biographies/zollar.html

Jefferson, Thomas. *Notes on the State of Virginia*. 1786; Richmond, VA: J. W. Randolph, 1853.

Johnson, Amelia. *Toning the Sweep*. New York: Orchard, 1993.

Johnson, Georgia Douglas. *Selected Works of Georgia Douglas Johnson*. New York: G. K. Hall, 1997.

Johnson, Yvonne. *The Voices of African American Women: The Use of Narrative and Authorial Voice in the Work of Harriet Jacobs, Zora Neale Hurston*. New York: Peter Lang, 1998.

Johnson-Feelings, Dianne, ed. *The Best of the Brownies' Book*. New York: Oxford University Press, 1996.

Jones, Gayl. *Corregidora*. New York: Random House, 1976.

    Liberating Voices: Oral Tradition in African American Literature. Cambridge, MA: Harvard University Press, 1991.

Jones, Sharon. *Rereading the Harlem Renaissance: Race, Class and Gender in the Fiction of Jessie Fauset, Zora Neale Hurston and Dorothy West*. Westport, CT: Greenwood Press, 2002.

Jordan, Jennifer. "Making the Connections: An Interview with Sonia Sanchez." *BMA: The Sonia Sanchez Literary Review* 8.1 (Fall 2002), 17–32.

Jordan, June. "The Difficult Miracle of Black Poetry in America or Something Like a Sonnet for Phillis Wheatley." *Wild Women in the Whirlwind: Afra-American Culture and the Contemporary Literary Renaissance*, ed. Joanne M. Braxton and Andrée Nicola McLaughlin. New Brunswick, NJ: Rutgers University Press, 1990. 22–34.

  Soulscript. New York: Harlem Moon, 2004.

  Things That I Do in the Dark: Selected Poetry. Boston: Beacon Press, 1977.

Kafka, Phillipa. *The Great White Way: African American Women Writers and American Success Mythologies*. New York: Garland Press, 1993.

Keehnen, Owen. "Artist with a Mission: A Conversation with Sapphire." www.glbtq.com/sfeatures/interviewsaphhire.html 1–3.

Kennedy, Adrienne. "A Growth of Images (1997)," *A Sourcebook of African-American Performance: Plays, People, Movement*, ed. Annemarie Bean. New York: Routledge, 1999. 216–18.

Keyssar, Helen. Introduction. *Feminist Theatre and Theory*, ed. Helen Keyssar. London: Macmillan, 1996. 1–18.

Killens, John Oliver. "The Black Writer vis-à-vis His Country." *The Black Aesthetic*, ed. Addison Gayle, Jr. Garden City, NY: Doubleday, 1971. 357–73.

King, Deborah. "Multiple Jeopardy, Multiple Consciousness: The Context of Black Feminist Ideology." *Words of Fire: An Anthology of African American Feminist Thought*, ed. Beverly Guy-Sheftall. New York: New Press, 1995. 294–318.

King, Woodie, Jr., ed. *The National Black Drama Anthology*. New York: Applause, 1995.

Kozel, Susan. "Multi-Medea: Feminist Performance Using Multimedia Technologies." *The Routledge Reader in Gender and Performance*, ed. Lizbeth Goodman and Jane de Gay. New York: Routledge, 1998. 299–303.

Kubitschek, Missy. *Claiming Heritage: African American Women Novelists and History*. Jackson: University of Mississippi Press, 1991.

Ladner, Joyce. *Tomorrow's Tomorrow, the Black Woman*. Garden City, NY: Doubleday, 1971.

Larrick, Nancy. "The All-White World of Children's Books." *Saturday Review of Books* 48 (1965), 63–65, 84–85.

Larsen, Nella. *Quicksand and Passing*. New Brunswick, NJ: Rutgers University Press, 1986.

Lauter, Paul, ed. *The Heath Anthology of American Literature*, 3rd edn. Boston: Houghton Mifflin, 1998.

Lee, Jarena. *Religious Experiences and Journal of Mrs. Jarena Lee: A Preaching Woman*. Nashville: Amec, 1992.

Lee, Valerie. *Granny Midwives and Black Women Writers: Double-Dutch Readings*. New York: Routledge, 1996.

Leonard, Keith D. *Fettered Genius: The African American Bardic Poet from Slavery to Civil Rights*. Charlottesville: University of Virginia Press, 2006.

Lerner, Gerda. "Early Community Work of Black Club Women." *Journal of Negro History* 59 (1974), 158–67.

Leseur, Geta. "One Mother, Two Daughters: The Afro-American and the Afro-Caribbean Female Bildungsroman." *Black Scholar* 17 (March/April 1986), 26–33.

Levin, Amy. *Africanism and Authenticity in African American Women's Novels.* Gainesville: University of Florida Press, 2003.

Lewis, Barbara. "Ritual Reformations: Barbara Ann Teer and the National Black Theater of Harlem." *A Source Book of African American Performance: Plays, People, Movement*, ed. Annemarie Bean. New York: Routledge, 1999. 68–82.

Lewis, David L. *When Harlem Was in Vogue.* New York: Knopf, 1981.

  W. E. B. Du Bois: Biography of a Race, 1868–1919. New York: Henry Holt, 1993.

Liddell, Janie and Yakini Kemp. *Arms Akimbo: Africana Women in Contemporary Literature.* Gainesville: University of Florida Press, 1999.

Lippard, Lucy. "*Catalysis*: An Interview with Adrian Piper (1972)." *A Sourcebook of African-American Performance: Plays, People, Movement*, ed. Annemarie Bean. New York: Routledge, 1999. 204–7.

Locke, Alain. "Literature By and About the Negro." *Opportunity.* June 1, 1938.

  ed. *Plays of Negro Life: A Source Book of the Native American Drama.* Westport, CT: Negro University Press, 1927.

Lorde, Audre. "The Master's Tools Will Never Dismantle the Master's House." *Sister Outsider: Essays and Speeches by Audre Lorde.* Trumansburg, NY: The Crossing Press, 1984.

  Zami: A New Spelling of My Name. Freedom, CA: Crossing Press, 1982.

Lott, Eric. *Love and Theft: Blackface Minstrelsy and the American Working Class.* New York: Oxford University Press, 1993.

Lowe, John. *Jump at the Sun: Zora Neale Hurston's Cosmic Comedy.* Urbana, IL: University of Illinois Press, 1997.

Lupton, Mary Jane. *Lucille Clifton: Her Life and Letters.* New York: Praeger, 2006.

Lyotard, Jean-François. *The Postmodern Condition: A Report on Knowledge*, trans. Geoff Bennington and Brian Massumi. Minneapolis: University of Minnesota Press, 1984.

Mahone, Sydne, ed. *Moon Marked and Touched by Sun: Plays by African American Women.* New York: Theater Communications Group, 1994.

Mairs, Nancy. "Carnal Acts." *Writing on the Body: Female Embodiment and Feminist Theory*, ed. Katie Conby, Nadia Medina, and Sarah Stanbury. New York: Columbia University Press, 1997. 296–305.

Malpede, Karen, ed. *Women in Theater: Compassion & Hope.* New York: Drama Book Publishers, 1983.

Mance, Ajuan. *Inventing Black Women: African American Women Poets and Self-Representation, 1877–2000.* Knoxville: University of Tennessee Press, 2007.

Marsh-Lockett, Carol P. *Black Women Playwrights: Visions of the American Stage.* New York: Garland, 1999.

Martin, Carol. "The Word Becomes You: An Interview with Anna Deavere Smith." *A Sourcebook of African-American Performance: Plays, People, Movement*, ed. Annemarie Bean. New York: Routledge, 1999. 267–83.

Martin, Jonathan D. *Divided Mastery: Slave Hiring in the American South.* Cambridge, MA: Harvard University Press, 2003.

Martin, Michelle. *Brown Gold: Milestones of African-American Children's Picture Books, 1845–2002.* New York: Routledge, 2004.

McCracken, Scott. *Reading Popular Fiction.* Manchester: Manchester University Press, 1998.

McDougald, Elise Johnson. "The Negro Woman and the Ballot." *Words of Fire: An Anthology of African American Feminist Thought*, ed. Beverly Guy-Sheftall. New York: New Press, 1995. 85–92.

"The Task of Negro Womanhood." *The New Negro: Voices of the Harlem Renaissance*, ed. Alain Locke. New York: Touchstone, 1925. 379.

McDowell, Deborah. *The Changing Same: Black Women's Literature, Criticism, and Theory*. Bloomington: Indiana University Press, 1995.

"'The Changing Same': Generational Connections and Black Women Novelists." *New Literary History* 18.2 (Winter 1987), 281–302.

Introduction. *Quicksand and Passing*. New Brunswick, NJ: Rutgers University Press, 1986.

"New Directions for Black Feminist Criticism." *Within the Circle: An Anthology of African American Criticism from the Harlem Renaissance to the Present*, ed. Angelyn Mitchell. Durham, NC: Duke University Press, 1994. 428–42.

McKay, Nellie Y. "The Souls of Black Women Folk in the Writings of W. E. B. Du Bois." *Reading Black, Reading Feminist: A Critical Anthology*, ed. Henry Louis Gates, Jr. New York: Meridian, 1990.

McKinley, Catherine E. and Joyce DeLaney, eds. *Afrekete: An Anthology of Black Lesbian Writing*. New York: Anchor/Doubleday, 1995.

McLendon, Jacquelyn. *The Politics of Color in the Fiction of Jessie Fauset and Nella Larsen*. Charlottesville: University of Virginia Press, 1995.

Melhem, D. H. *Gwendolyn Brooks: Poetry and the Heroic Voice*. Lexington: University of Kentucky Press, 1987.

Melrose, Susan. "Introduction to Part Four: 'What Do Women Want (in Theatre)?" *The Routledge Reader in Gender and Performance*, ed. Lizbeth Goodman and Jane de Gay. New York: Routledge, 1998. 131–35.

Miller, Jeanne-Marie A. "Black Women Playwrights from Grimké to Shange: Selected Synopses of Their Work." *All the Women Are White, All the Blacks Are Men, But Some of Us Are Brave*, ed. Gloria T. Hull, Patricia Bell Scott, and Barbara Smith. New York: Feminist Press, 1982. 280–96.

Mitchell, Angelyn. *The Freedom to Remember: Narrative, Slavery, and Gender in Contemporary Black Women's Fiction*. New Brunswick, NJ: Rutgers University Press, 2002.

Molette, Barbara. "They Speak: Who Listens? Black Women Playwrights." *Black World* 25 (April 1976), 28–34.

Moody, Joycelyn. *Sentimental Confessions: Spiritual Narratives of Nineteenth-Century African American Women*. Athens: University of Georgia Press, 2001.

Moore, Lisa. *Does Your Mama Know: An Anthology of Black Lesbian Coming Out Stories*. Decatur, GA: RedBone Publishing, 1997.

Mootry, Maria K. and Gary Smith, eds. *A Life Distilled: Gwendolyn Brooks, Her Poetry and Fiction*. Chicago: University of Illinois Press, 1987.

Moraga, Cherrie and Gloria Anzaldua, eds. *This Bridge Called My Back: Writings by Radical Women of Color*. Watertown, MA: Persephone Press, 1981.

More, Hannah (attributed). "The Sorrows of Yamba or The Negro Woman's Lamentation." Electronic Text Center. University of Virginia Library. http://etext. lib.virginia.edu/etcbin/toccernew2?id=AnoSorr.sgm&images=images/modeng&data =/texts/english/modeng/parsed&tag=public&part=1&division=div1.

Morrison, Toni. *Beloved*. New York: Knopf, 1987.

The Bluest Eye. New York: Simon & Shuster, 1970.

"Home." *The House That Race Built*, ed. Wahneema Lubiano. New York: Vintage, 1998.

Playing in the Dark: Whiteness in the American Literary Imagination. Cambridge, MA: Harvard University Press, 1992.

ed. *Race-ing Justice, En-gendering Power: Essays on Anita Hill, Clarence Thomas and the Construction of Social Reality*. New York: Pantheon, 1992.

"Rootedness: The Ancestor as Foundation." *Literature in the Modern World*, ed. Dennis Walder. New York: Oxford University Press, 1990. 326–32.

"Unspeakable Things Unspoken: The Afro-American Presence in American Literature." *Michigan Quarterly Review* 38.1 (Winter 1989), 1–35.

Morton, Patricia, ed. *Discovering the Women in Slavery: Emancipating Perspectives on the American Past*. Athens: University of Georgia Press, 1996.

Moses, Sibyl. *African American Women Writers in New Jersey, 1836–2000*. New Brunswick, NJ: Rutgers University Press, 2003.

Mosley, Walter. "Black to the Future." *New York Times Magazine*. Nov 1, 1998.

Mullen, Bill, ed. *Revolutionary Tales: African American Women's Short Stories, From the First Story to the Present*. New York: Laurel, 1995.

Mullen, Harryette. "The Black Arts Movement: Poetry and Drama from the 1960s to the 1970s." *African American Writers*, ed. Valerie Smith. 2nd edn. Vol. 1. New York: Scribner's, 2001. 51–64.

"Runaway Tongue: Resistant Orality in *Uncle Tom's Cabin, Our Nig, Incidents in the Life of a Slave Girl*, and *Beloved*." *The Culture of Sentiment: Race, Gender, and Sentimentality in Nineteenth Century America*, ed. Shirley Samuels. New York: Oxford University Press, 1992.

Murdy, Anne-Elizabeth. *Teach the Nation: Public School, Racial Uplift and Women's Writing in the 1890's*. New York: Routledge, 2003.

Murphy, Brenda, ed. *Cambridge Companion to American Women Playwrights*. Cambridge: Cambridge University Press, 1999.

Neal, Larry. "The Black Arts Movement." *Within the Circle: An Anthology of African American Literary Criticism from the Harlem Renaissance to the Present*, ed. Angelyn Mitchell. Durham, NC: Duke University Press, 1994. 184–98.

ed. *Black Fire: An Anthology of Afro-American Writing*. New York: William Morrow, 1968.

"Into Nationalism, Out of Parochialism." *The Theatre of Black Americans: A Collection of Critical Essays*, ed. Errol Hill. Vol. 11. Upper Saddle River: Prentice Hall, 1980. 95–102.

Visions of a Liberated Future: Black Arts Movement Writings, ed. Michael Schwartz. New York: Thunder's Mouth Press, 1989.

"The Writer as Activist–1960 and After." *The Black American Reference Book*, ed. Mabel M. Smythe. Englewood Cliffs, NJ: Prentice Hall, 1976. 767–70.

Nielsen, Aldon Lynn, ed. *Black Chant: The Languages of African American Postmodernism*. Cambridge: Cambridge University Press, 1997.

Ogundipe-Leslie, Molara. *Re-creating Ourselves. African Women and Critical Transformations*. Trenton, NJ: Africa World Press, 1994.

Ogunyemi, Chikwene Okonjo. *Africa Wo/man Palava. The Nigerian Novel by Women*. Chicago: University of Chicago Press, 1996.

Okker, Patricia. *Social Stories: The Magazine Novel in Nineteenth Century America.* Charlottesville: University of Virginia Press, 2003.

O'Neale, Sondra. "Inhibiting Midwives, Usurping Creators: Struggling Emergence of African American Women in American Fiction." *Conjuring: Black Women, Fiction, and Literary Tradition*, ed. Majorie Pryse and Hortense Spillers. Bloomington: Indiana University Press, 1985.

Orlandersmith, Dael. Foreword. *Beauty's Daughter, Monster, The Gimmick: Three Plays.* New York: Vintage Books, 2000.

Pagnattaro, Marisa. *In Defiance of the Law: from Anne Hutchinson to Toni Morrison.* New York: Peter Lang, 2001.

Painter, Nell I. *Sojourner Truth: A Life, A Symbol.* New York: Oxford University Press, 1997.

Patraka, Vicki. "Obsessing in Public: An Interview with Robbie McCauley." *A Sourcebook of African-American Performance: Plays, People, Movement*, ed. Annemarie Bean. New York: Routledge, 1999. 219–45.

Patterson, Martha H. "'Kin' of Rough Justice Fer a Parson:' Pauline Hopkins' *Winona* and the Politics of Reconstructing History." *African American Review* 32.3 (1998), 445–60.

"Remaking the Minstrel: Pauline Hopkins's *Peculiar Sam* and the Post-Reconstruction Black Subject." *Black Women Playwrights: Visions of the American Stage*, ed. Carol P. Marsh-Lockett. New York: Garland Publishing, 1999. 13–24.

Patton, Sharon F. *African American Art.* New York: Oxford University Press, 1998.

Patton, Venteria. *Women in Chains: the Legacy of Black Women's Fiction.* Albany, NY: State University of New York Press, 2000.

Perkins, Kathy A., ed. *Black Women Playwrights: An Anthology of Plays Before 1950.* Bloomington: Indiana University Press, 1989.

Perkins, Kathy and Judith Stephens, eds. *Strange Fruit: Plays on Lynching by American Women.* Bloomington: Indiana University Press, 1998.

Perkins, Kathy A. and Roberta Uno, eds. *Contemporary Plays by Women of Color: An Anthology.* London and New York: Routledge, 1996.

Perkins, Margo V. *Autobiography as Activism: Three Black Women of the Sixties.* Jackson: University of Mississippi Press, 2000.

Peterson, Carla L. *"Doers of the Word": African-American Women Speakers and Writers in the North (1830–1880).* New York: Oxford University Press, 1995.

Petry, Ann. *The Street.* 1946; Boston: Beacon Press, 1974.

Placide, Jaira. *Fresh Girl.* New York: Wendy Lamb Books, 2002.

Plato, Ann. *Essays: Including Biographies and Miscellaneous Pieces, in Prose and Poetry.* New York: Oxford University Press, 1988.

Pollack, Sandra and Denise Knight, eds. *Contemporary Lesbian Writers of the United States: A Bio-bibliographic Critical Sourcebook.* Westport, CT: Greenwood Press, 1993.

Pride, Armistead Scott and Clint Wilson. *The History of the Black Press.* Washington, DC: Howard University Press, 1997.

Pryse, Marjorie and Hortense Spillers, eds. *Conjuring: Black Women, Fiction, and Literary Tradition.* Bloomington: Indiana University Press, 1985.

Quashie, Kevin. *Black Women, Identity and Cultural Theory: (un)Becoming the Subject.* New Brunswick, NJ: Rutgers University Press, 2004.

Quashie, Kevin, Joyce Lausch, and Keith Miller, eds. *New Bones: Contemporary Black Writers in America*. Upper Saddle River, NJ: Prentice Hall, 2001.

Radway, Janice. *Reading the Romance: Women, Patriarchy, and Popular Literature*. Chapel Hill: University of North Carolina Press, 1986.

Ransom, Portia. *Black Love and the Harlem Renaissance: The Novels of Nella Larsen, Jessie Fauset, and Zora Neale Hurston, an Essay in African American Literary Criticism*. Lewiston, NY: Edwin Mellen Press, 2005.

Redding, J. Saunders. *To Make A Poet Black*. Chapel Hill: University of North Carolina Press, 1939.

Reed, E. Shelly. "Beyond Morrison and Walker: Looking Good and Looking Forward in Contemporary Black Women's Studies." *African American Review* 34 (Summer 2000), 313–28.

Regan, Stephen. "Reception Theory, Gender and Performance." *The Routledge Reader in Gender and Performance*, ed. Lizbeth Goodman and Jane de Gay. New York: Routledge, 1998. 295–98.

Reid, Margaret Ann. *Black Protest Poetry: Polemics from the Harlem Renaissance and the Sixties*. New York: Peter Lang, 2001.

Rhodes, Jane. *Mary Ann Shadd Cary: The Black Press and Protest in the Nineteenth Century*. Bloomington: Indiana University Press, 1998. xii.

Richards, Sandra. "Writing the Absent Potential: Drama, Performance and the Canon of African-American Literature. *The Routledge Reader in Gender and Performance*, ed. Lizbeth Goodman and Jane de Gay. New York: Routledge, 1998. 156–61.

Richardson, Willis, ed. *Plays and Pageants from the Life of the Negro*. Washington, DC: Associated Publishers, Inc., 1930.

Riley, Clayton. "On Black Theatre." *The Black Aesthetic*, ed. Addison Gayle, Jr. Garden City, NY: Doubleday, 1971. 295–311.

Robnett, Belinda. *How Long? How Long? African-American Women in the Struggle for Civil Rights*. New York: Oxford University Press, 1997.

Rodgers, Carolyn. *Songs of a Black Bird*. Chicago: Third World Press, 1969.

Rody, Caroline. *The Daughter's Return: African American and Caribbean Women's Fictions of History*. New York: Oxford University Press, 2001.

Roses, Lorraine and Ruth E. Randolph, eds. *Harlem's Glory: Black Women Writing 1900–1950*. Cambridge, MA: Harvard University Press, 1996.

Harlem Renaissance and Beyond. Boston: G. K. Hall, 1990.

Ross, Alec. "Sapphire: One of America's Best Emerging Writers Smacks the Smile off Our Faces." www.horizonmag.com/4/sapphire.htm. 1–3.

Ruffin, Josephine St. Pierre, ed. *Woman's Era*. Atlanta, GA: Lewis H. Beck Center for Electronic Collections and Services, 2002.

Rushdy, Ashraf. "The Neo-Slave Narrative." *The Cambridge Companion to the African American Novel*, ed. Maryemma Graham. Cambridge: Cambridge University Press, 2004. 87–105.

Russell, Sandi. *Render Me My Song: African American Women Writers from Slavery to the Present*. London: Pandora, 2002.

Ryan, Judlyn. *Spirituality as Ideology in Black Women's Film and Literature*. Charlottesville: University of Virginia Press, 2005.

Sale, Maggie. "Critiques from Within: Antebellum Projects of Resistance." *American Literature* 64.1 (December 1992), 695–718.

Sanchez, Sonia. *Sister Son/Ji. New Plays for the Black Theatre: An Anthology*, ed. Ed Bullins. New York: Bantam Books, 1969.

Sanders, Mark. *Afro-Modernist Aesthetics and the Poetry of Sterling Brown*. Atlanta: University of Georgia Press, 1999.

Santamarina, Xiomara. *Belabored Professional Narratives of African American Working Womanhood*. Chapel Hill, NC: University of North Carolina Press, 2005.

Sapphire (Ramona Lofton). *Femme Noir: A Web Portal for Lesbians of Color*. www. femmenoir.net/Leaders-Legends/Sapphire.htm

Sarr, Akua, ed. *Black Women Novelists' Contribution to Contemporary Feminine Discourse*. Lewiston, IL: Mellon, 2003.

"Sassy Urban Bush Women Performance Dance Theater Piece *HairStories* at UCSBC Campbell Hall." www.artsandlectures.ucsb.edu/pr/urban.htm

Saunders, James. *The Wayward Preacher in the Literature of African American Women*. Jefferson, NC: McFarland, 1995.

Schechner, Richard. "Anna Deavere Smith: Acting as Incorporation (1993)." *A Sourcebook of African-American Performance: Plays, People, Movement*, ed. Annemarie Bean. New York: Routledge, 1999. 265–66.

Scholes, Robert. *The Crafty Reader*. New Haven, CT: Yale University Press, 2001.

Shakur, Assata. *Assata: An Autobiography*. Chicago: Lawrence Hills Books, 1987.

Shange, Ntozake. *For colored girls who have considered suicide / when the rainbow is enuf*. New York: Macmillan, 1976.

Shaw, Fiona. Foreword. *The Routledge Reader in Gender and Performance*, ed. Lizbeth Goodman and Jane de Gay. New York: Routledge, 1998. xxiii–xxv.

Shockley, Ann. *Afro-American Women Writers, 1746–1933: An Anthology and Critical Guide*. New York: New American Library, 1989.

  "The Black Lesbian in American Literature." *Conditions: Five* 11 (Autumn 1979), 133–42.

Sievers, Stefanie. *Liberating Narrative: The Authorization of Black Female Voices in African American Women Writers' Novels of Slavery*. Piscataway, NJ: Transaction Publishers, 1999.

Simone, Nina. *I Put a Spell on You*. New York: De Capo, 1993.

Smith, Barbara. "Doing Research on Black American Women." *Women's Studies Newsletter* 4 (Spring 1976): 4–7.

  ed. *Homegirls: A Black Feminist Anthology*. New York: Women of Color Press, 1983.

  "Toward a Black Feminist Criticism." *Conditions: Two* 1 (October 1977), 25–44. Rpt. in *All the Women Are White, All the Men Are Black, But Some of Us Are Brave: Black Women's Studies*, ed. Gloria T. Hall, Patricia Bell Scott, and Barbara Smith. New York: Feminist Press, 1982. 157–75.

  The Truth That Never Hurts: Writings on Race, Gender, and Freedom. New Brunswick, NJ: Rutgers University Press, 2000.

Smith, Valerie. Introduction. *Incidents in the Life of a Slave Girl*, by Harriet Jacobs. New York: Oxford University Press, 1988.

  "Gender and Afro-Americanist Literary Theory and Criticism." *Speaking of Gender*, ed. Elaine Showalter. New York: Routledge, 1989.

  ed. *New Essays on Toni Morrison's Song of Solomon*. New York: Cambridge University Press, 1995.

Not Just Race, Not Just Gender: Black Feminist Readings. New York: Routledge, 1998.

Spencer, Anne. "Substitution." *Time's Unfading Garden: Anne Spencer's Life and Poetry*, ed. J. Lee Greene. Baton Rouge: Louisiana State University Press, 1977.

Spillers, Hortense J. "Afterword: Cross-Currents, Discontinuities: Black Women's Fiction." *Conjuring: Black Women, Fiction, and Literary Tradition*, ed. Marjorie Pryse and Hortense Spillers. Bloomington: Indiana University Press, 1985. 249–61.

"'All the Things You Could Be by Now, if Sigmund Freud's Wife Was Your Mother'": Psychoanalysis and Race." *Black, White, and in Color: Essays on American Literature and Culture*, ed. Hortense Spillers. Chicago: University of Chicago Press, 2003. 376–427.

"A Hateful Passion, A Lost Love: Three Women's Fiction." *Black, White, and in Color: Essays on American Literature and Culture*, ed. Hortense Spillers. Chicago: University of Chicago Press, 2003. 93–118.

"Mama's Baby, Papa's Maybe: An American Grammar Book." *Black, White, and in Color: Essays on American Literature and Culture*, ed. Hortense Spillers. Chicago: University of Chicago Press, 2003. 203–29.

Staples, Robert. *The Black Woman in America: Sex, Marriage, and the Family*. Chicago: Nelson-Hall, 1973.

Starling, Marion Wilson. *The Slave Narrative: Its Place in American History*, 2nd edn. Washington, DC: Howard University Press, 1988.

Steady, Filomina Chioma. "Women and Collective Action: Female Models in Transition." *Theorizing Black Feminisms: The Visionary Pragmatism of Black Women*, ed. Stanlie M. James and Abena P. A. Busia. New York: Routledge, 1994. 90–101.

Stephens, Judith L. "Lynching Dramas and Women: History and Critical Context." *Strange Fruit: Plays on Lynching by American Women*, ed. Kathy A. Perkins and Judith L. Stephens. Bloomington: Indiana University Press, 1998. 3–14.

"The Harlem Renaissance and the New Negro Movement." *The Cambridge Companion to American Women Playwrights*, ed. Brenda Murphy. Cambridge: Cambridge University Press, 1999. 98–117.

Stepto, Robert. *From Behind the Veil: A Study of Afro-American Narrative*. Urbana and Chicago: University of Illinois Press, 1979.

Stover, Johnnie. *Rhetoric and Resistance in Black Women's Autobiography*. Gainesville: University of Florida Press, 2003.

Tate, Claudia. *Black Women Writers at Work*. New York: Continuum, 1983.

Domestic Allegories of Political Desire: The Black Heroine's Text at the Turn of the Century. New York: Oxford University Press, 1992.

Psychoanalysis and Black Novels: Desire and the Protocols of Race. New York: Oxford University Press, 1998.

ed. "Gwendolyn Brooks." *Black Women Writers at Work*. New York: Continuum, 1983.

Taylor, Carol Ann. *The Tragedy and Comedy of Resistance: Reading Modernity through Black Women's Fiction*. Philadelphia: University of Pennsylvania Press, 2000.

Thomas, Joyce Carol, ed. *A Gathering of Flowers: Stories about Being Young in America*. New York: Harper & Row, 1990.

Thomas, Lundeana M. "Barbara Ann Teer: From Holistic Training to Liberating Rituals." *Black Theatre: Ritual Performance in the African Diaspora*, ed. Paul Carter Harrison. Philadelphia: Temple University Press, 2002. 345–77.

Traylor, Eleanor. "Re Calling the Black Woman." *The Black Woman: An Anthology*, ed. Toni Cade Bambara. New York: Washington Square Press, 2005. ix–xviii.

"Two Afro-American Contributions to Dramatic Form." *The Theatre of Black Americans: A Collection of Critical Essays*, ed. Errol Hill. Vol. 1. Upper Saddle River, NJ: Prentice Hall, 1980. 45–66.

Vogel, Todd. *The Black Press: New Literary and Historical Essays*. New Brunswick, NJ: Rutgers University Press, 2001.

Wade-Gayles, Gloria. *No Crystal Stair: Visions of Race and Sex in Black Women's Fiction*. New York: Pilgrim Press, 1984.

Walker, Alice. "The Civil Rights Movement: What Good Was It?" *In Search of Our Mother's Gardens: Womanist Prose*. San Diego: Harcourt Brace Jovanovich, 1983. 119–29.

ed. *I Love Myself When I Am Laughing...and Then Again When I Am Looking Mean and Impressive: A Zora Neale Hurston Reader*. New York: Feminist Press, 1979.

Revolutionary Petunias and Other Poems. New York: Harcourt, Brace, Jovanovich, 1993.

In Search of Our Mothers' Gardens: Womanist Prose. New York: Harcourt, Brace, Jovanovich, 1983.

"In Search of Zora Neale Hurston." *Ms.* 3.9 (1975), 74–90.

Walker, Ethel Pitts. "The American Negro Theatre." *The Theatre of Black Americans: A Collection of Critical Essays*, ed. Errol Hill. Vol. 11. Upper Saddle River, NJ: Prentice Hall, 1980. 49–62.

Walker, Margaret. *This Is My Century: New and Collected Poems*. Athens: University of Georgia Press, 1989.

Prophets for a Day. Detroit: Broadside Press, 1970.

Walker, Melissa. *Down From the Mountain Top: Black Women's Novels in the Wake of the Civil Rights Movement, 1966–1989*. New Haven, CT: Yale University Press, 1991.

Wall, Cheryl A., ed. *Changing Our Own Words: Essays on Criticism, Theory, and Writing by Black Women*. New Brunswick, NJ: Rutgers University Press, 1989.

Women of the Harlem Renaissance. Bloomington: Indiana University Press, 1995.

Worrying the Line: Black Women Writers, Lineage, and Literary Tradition. Chapel Hill: University of North Carolina Press, 2005.

Zora Neale Hurston: Folklore, Memoirs, and other Writings. New York: Library of America, 1995.

Zora Neale Hurston's "Their Eyes Were Watching God": A Casebook. New York: Oxford University Press, 2000.

Wallace, Michelle. *Black Macho and the Myth of the Superwoman*. New York: Warner Books, 1980.

Washington, Mary Helen. "The Black Woman's Search for Identity: Zora Neale Hurston's Work." *Black World* 21 (1972).

"Black Women Myth and Image Makers." *Black World* 23 (August 1974).

Introduction. *A Voice from the South*. New York: Oxford University Press, 1988.

Introduction. *Black-Eyed Susans: Classic Stories by and About Black Women*, ed. Mary Helen Washington. Garden City, NY: Anchor Books, 1975.

"'The Darkened Eye Restored:' Notes Toward a Literary History of Black Women." *Within the Circle: An Anthology of African American Criticism from the Harlem Renaissance to the Present*, ed. Angelyn Mitchell. Durham, NC: Duke University Press, 1994. 442–53.

Washington, Teresea. *Our Mothers, Our Poetry, Our Texts: Manifestation of Aje in Africana Literature*. Bloomington: Indiana University Press, 2005.

Waters, Ethel. *His Eye Is on the Sparrow*. Kingsport, TN: Kingsport Press, 1950.

Watson, Carole McAlpine. *Prologues: The Novels of Black American Women, 1891–1965*. Westport, CT: Greenwood Press, 1985.

Weathers, Mary. "An Argument for Black Women's Liberation as a Revolutionary Force." *Words of Fire: An Anthology of African American Feminist Thought*, ed. Beverly Guy-Sheftall. New York: New Press, 1995. 158–61.

Weixlmann, Joseph and Houston Baker. *Black Feminist Criticism and Critical Theory*. Greenwood, FL: Pineville Publishers, 1988.

Wells-Barnett, Ida. *Crusade for Justice: The Autobiography of Ida B. Wells*. Chicago: Chicago University Press, 1970.

"From *A Red Record*." *The Norton Anthology of African American Literature*, ed. Henry Louis Gates, Jr. and Nellie McKay. New York: Norton, 1997. 595–606.

"The Lynch Law in America." *Words of Fire: An Anthology of African American Feminist Thought*, ed. Beverly Guy-Sheftall. New York: New Press, 1995. 69–78.

"The Progress of the Colored Woman." *Words of Fire: An Anthology of African American Feminist Thought*, ed. Beverly Guy-Sheftall. New York: New Press, 1995. 68.

Southern Horrors: Lynch Law in All Its Phases. 1892; New York: Arno Press, 1970.

Werner, Craig. "On the Ends of Afro-American 'Modernist' Autobiography." *Black American Literature Forum* 24 (Summer 1990), 203–220.

Black American Women Novelists: An Annotated Bibliography. Pasadena, CA: Salem Press, 1989.

Wheatley, Phillis. *Memoir and Poems of Phillis Wheatley, a Native African and Slave*. Boston: Isaac Knapp, 1938.

Wilkerson, Margaret, ed. *Nine Plays by Black Women*. New York: New American Library, 1986.

"From Harlem to Broadway: African American women playwrights at mid-century." *The Cambridge Companion to American Women Playwrights*, ed. Brenda Murphy. Cambridge: Cambridge University Press, 1999. 134–51.

Williams, Dana A. *Contemporary African American Female Playwrights*. Westport, CT: Greenwood Press, 1998.

Williams, Ora, Thelma Williams, Dora Wilson, and Ramona Matthewson. "American Black Women Composers: A Selected Bibliography." *All the Women Are White, All the Blacks Are Men, But Some of Us Are Brave*, ed. Gloria T. Hull, Patricia Bell Scott, and Barbara Smith. New York: Feminist Press, 1982. 297–306.

Williams, Sherley Anne. *Dessa Rose*. New York: Berkley Books, 1986.

Foreword to Zora Neale Hurston, *Their Eyes were Watching God*. Urbana: University of Illinois Press, 1978. v–xv.

"Meditations on History." *Black-Eyed Susans: Midnight Birds: Stories by and about Black Women*, ed. Mary Helen Washington. New York: Doubleday, 1977.

"Some Implications of Womanist Theory." *Within the Circle: an Anthology of African American Criticism from the Harlem Renaissance to the Present*, ed. Angelyn Mitchell. Durham, NC: Duke University Press, 1994. 515–21.

Willis, Susan. *Specifying: Black Women Writing the American Experience*. Madison: University of Wisconsin Press, 1987.

Wilson, Fancille Rusan. "All the Glory...Faded...Quickly: Sadie T. M. Alexander Black Professional Women, 1920–1950." *Sister Circle: Black Women and Work*, ed. Sharon Harley and The Black Woman and Work Collective. New Brunswick, NJ: Rutgers University Press, 2002.

Wilson, Harriet E. *Our Nig: Or Sketches from the Life of a Free Black*. 1859; New York: Vintage, 1983.

Wolff, Janet. "Dance Criticism: Feminism, Theory and Choreography." *The Routledge Reader in Gender and Performance*, ed. Lizbeth Goodman and Jane de Gay. New York: Routledge, 1998. 241–46.

Woll, Allen. *Black Musical Theater*. Baton Rouge: Louisiana University Press, 1989.

Wright, Richard. "Between Laughter and Tears." *New Masses*. October 5, 1937.

Ya Salaam, Kalamu. "Historical Overviews of the Black Arts Movement." *The Oxford Companion to African American Literature*, ed. William Andrews, Frances Smith Foster, and Trudier Harris. New York: Oxford University Press, 1997. 70–74.

Yellin, Jean Fagan. *Harriet Jacobs, a Life*. New York: Basic Civitas, 2004.

Yellin, Jean Fagan and Cynthia Bond. *The Pen Is Ours*. New York: Oxford University Press, 1991.

Young, Hershini Bhana. *Haunting Capital: Memory, Text, and the Black Diasporic Body*. Lebanon, NH: University Press of New England, 2006.

Zafar, Rafia. *We Wear the Mask: African Americans Write American Literature, 1760–1870*. New York: Columbia University Press, 1997.

INDEX

Cambridge Companions To ...

AUTHORS

Edward Albee edited by Stephen J. Bottoms

Margaret Atwood edited by Coral Ann Howells

W. H. Auden edited by Stan Smith

Jane Austen edited by Edward Copeland and Juliet McMaster

Beckett edited by John Pilling

Aphra Behn edited by Derek Hughes and Janet Todd

Walter Benjamin edited by David S. Ferris

William Blake edited by Morris Eaves

Brecht edited by Peter Thomson and Glendyr Sacks (second edition)

The Brontës edited by Heather Glen

Frances Burney edited by Peter Sabor

Byron edited by Drummond Bone

Albert Camus edited by Edward J. Hughes

Willa Cather edited by Marilee Lindemann

Cervantes edited by Anthony J. Cascardi

Chaucer edited by Piero Boitani and Jill Mann (second edition)

Chekhov edited by Vera Gottlieb and Paul Allain

Kate Chopin edited by Janet Beer

Coleridge edited by Lucy Newlyn

Wilkie Collins edited by Jenny Bourne Taylor

Joseph Conrad edited by J. H. Stape

Dante edited by Rachel Jacoff (second edition)

Daniel Defoe edited by John Richetti

Don DeLillo edited by John N. Duvall

Charles Dickens edited by John O. Jordan

Emily Dickinson edited by Wendy Martin

John Donne edited by Achsah Guibbory

Dostoevskii edited by W. J. Leatherbarrow

Theodore Dreiser edited by Leonard Cassuto and Claire Virginia Eby

John Dryden edited by Steven N. Zwicker

W. E. B. Du Bois edited by Shamoon Zamir

George Eliot edited by George Levine

T. S. Eliot edited by A. David Moody

Ralph Ellison edited by Ross Posnock

Ralph Waldo Emerson edited by Joel Porte and Saundra Morris

William Faulkner edited by Philip M. Weinstein

Henry Fielding edited by Claude Rawson

F. Scott Fitzgerald edited by Ruth Prigozy

Flaubert edited by Timothy Unwin

E. M. Forster edited by David Bradshaw

Benjamin Franklin edited by Carla Mulford

Brian Friel edited by Anthony Roche

Robert Frost edited by Robert Faggen

Elizabeth Gaskell edited by Jill L. Matus

Goethe edited by Lesley Sharpe

Thomas Hardy edited by Dale Kramer

David Hare edited by Richard Boon

Nathaniel Hawthorne edited by Richard Millington

Seamus Heaney edited by Bernard O'Donoghue

Ernest Hemingway edited by Scott Donaldson

Homer edited by Robert Fowler

Ibsen edited by James McFarlane

Henry James edited by Jonathan Freedman

Samuel Johnson edited by Greg Clingham

Ben Jonson edited by Richard Harp and Stanley Stewart

James Joyce edited by Derek Attridge (second edition)

Kafka edited by Julian Preece

Keats edited by Susan J. Wolfson

Lacan edited by Jean-Michel Rabaté

D. H. Lawrence edited by Anne Fernihough

Primo Levi edited by Robert Gordon

Lucretius edited by Stuart Gillespie and Philip Hardie

David Mamet edited by Christopher Bigsby

Thomas Mann edited by Ritchie Robertson

Christopher Marlowe edited by Patrick Cheney

Herman Melville edited by Robert S. Levine

Arthur Miller edited by Christopher Bigsby

Milton edited by Dennis Danielson (second edition)

Molière edited by David Bradby and Andrew Calder

Toni Morrison edited by Justine Tally

Nabokov edited by Julian W. Connolly

Eugene O'Neill edited by Michael Manheim

George Orwell edited by John Rodden

Ovid edited by Philip Hardie

Harold Pinter edited by Peter Raby

TOPICS